T H E

BURIED MIRROR

Reflections on Spain and the New World

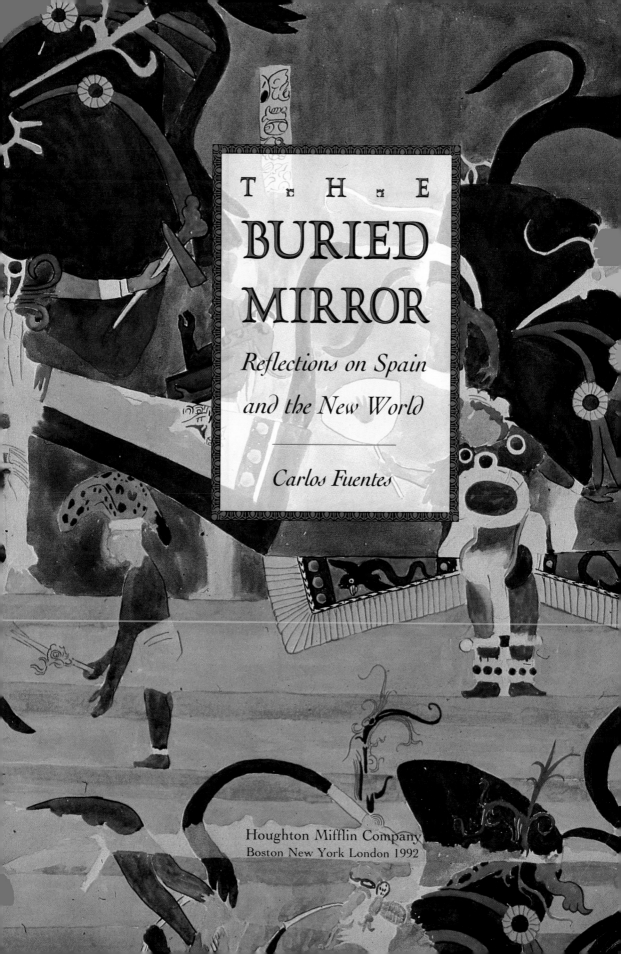

THE
BURIED
MIRROR

Reflections on Spain

and the New World

Carlos Fuentes

Houghton Mifflin Company
Boston New York London 1992

For information about permission to reproduce selections
from this book, write to Permissions, Houghton Mifflin Company,
215 Park Avenue South, New York, New York 10003.

Library of Congress Cataloging-in-Publication Data

Fuentes, Carlos.
  The buried mirror : reflections on Spain and the New World /
Carlos Fuentes.
      p.   cm.
  Includes bibliographical references and index.
  ISBN 0-395-47978-9
  1. Spain — Civilization — 711–1516.   2. Spain — Colonies —
America.   3. Spain — Civilization — 1516–1700.   4. Latin America —
Civilization.   I. Title.
DP96.F84   1992   91-34312
946'.02 — dc20   CIP

Printed in the United States of America

Book design by Renée Khatami

HOR 10 9 8 7 6 5 4 3

For Silvia, always

BOOKS BY CARLOS FUENTES

Where the Air Is Clear

The Good Conscience

Aura

The Death of Artemio Cruz

A Change of Skin

Terra Nostra

The Hydra Head

Burnt Water

Distant Relations

The Old Gringo

Myself with Others

Christopher Unborn

Constancia and Other Stories for Virgins

The Campaign

The Buried Mirror

CONTENTS

INTRODUCTION   8

❧ PART I   THE VIRGIN AND THE BULL ❧

ONE: SUN AND SHADOW   15

TWO: THE CONQUEST OF SPAIN   33

THREE: THE RECONQUEST OF SPAIN   51

FOUR: 1492: THE CRUCIAL YEAR   79

❧ PART II   THE CONFLICT OF THE GODS ❧

FIVE: THE RISE AND FALL OF THE INDIAN WORLD   93

SIX: THE CONQUEST AND RECONQUEST OF THE NEW WORLD   119

❧ PART III   CHILDREN OF LA MANCHA ❧

SEVEN: THE AGE OF EMPIRE   151

EIGHT: THE CENTURY OF GOLD   171

NINE: THE BAROQUE CULTURE OF THE NEW WORLD   195

TEN: THE AGE OF GOYA   215

ELEVEN: TOWARD INDEPENDENCE   233

❧ PART IV   THE PRICE OF FREEDOM ❧

TWELVE: SIMÓN BOLÍVAR AND JOSÉ DE SAN MARTÍN   249

THIRTEEN: THE TIME OF TYRANTS   261

FOURTEEN: THE CULTURE OF INDEPENDENCE   277

FIFTEEN: LAND AND LIBERTY   299

❧ PART V   UNFINISHED BUSINESS ❧

SIXTEEN: LATIN AMERICA   313

SEVENTEEN: CONTEMPORARY SPAIN   331

EIGHTEEN: HISPANIC U.S.A.   341

THE MONARCHS OF SPAIN   356

SOURCES AND READINGS   366

ILLUSTRATION CREDITS   385

ACKNOWLEDGMENTS   388

INDEX   389

Introduction

On October 12, 1492, Christopher Columbus landed on a small island in the Western Hemisphere. Against all evidence, he had put his wager on a scientific hypothesis and won: since the earth is round, one can reach the East by sailing west. But he was wrong in his geography. He thought that he had arrived in Asia. His desire was to reach the fabled lands of Cipango (Japan) and Cathay (China), cutting short the route along the coast of Africa, south to the Cape of Good Hope and then east to the Indian Ocean and the Spice Islands.

It was not the first or the last Occidental dis-Orientation. In these islands, which he called the Indies, Columbus established the first European settlements in the New World. He built the first churches, and the first Christian masses were celebrated there. Finding a domain empty of the Asian wealth that he had hoped for, he invented and reported back to Spain the discovery of great richness in forests, pearls, and gold. Otherwise, his patroness, Queen Isabella, might have thought that her investment (and her faith) in the highly inventive Genoese sailor had been misplaced.

More than offering gold, Columbus offered a vision of the Golden Age: these lands were Utopia, the happy place of the natural man. He had come upon the earthly paradise and the noble savage. Why, then, was he immediately forced to deny his own discovery, attack the people he had so recently described as "naked, unarmed and friendly," hunt them down, enslave them, and even send them back to Spain in irons? In fact, young women who were taken prisoner in Cuba all died before they even reached Spain.

At first Columbus did step into the Golden Age. But very soon, through his own doing, the earthly paradise was destroyed and the formerly good savage was seen as "fit to be ordered about and made to work, to sow and to do aught else that may be needed." Ever since, the American continent has existed between dream and reality, in a divorce between the good society that we desire and the imperfect society in which we really live. We have clung to Utopia because we were founded as a Utopia, because the memory of the good society lies in our origins, and also at the end of the road, as the fulfillment of our hopes.

Five hundred years after Columbus, we are being asked to celebrate the quincentennial of his voyage — undoubtedly one of the great events of human history, a turn in events that heralded the arrival of the modern age. But many of us in the Spanish-speaking parts of the Americas wonder whether there is anything to celebrate.

A glance at the Latin American republics would lead us to reply in the negative. Whether in Caracas or in Mexico City, in Lima or in Buenos Aires, the fifth centennial of the "discovery of America" finds us in a state of deep, deep crisis. Inflation, unemployment, the excessive burden of foreign debt. Increasing poverty and illiteracy; an abrupt decline of purchasing power and standards of living. A sense of frustration, of dashed hopes and lost illusions. Fragile democracies menaced by social explosion.

Yet I believe that in spite of all our economic and political troubles, we do have something to celebrate. The present crisis throughout Latin America demonstrates the vulnerability of our political and economic systems, which have come crashing down around our heads. But it has also revealed something that has remained standing, something that we were not acutely aware of during the decades of economic boom and political fervor following World War II. Something that, in the midst of our misfortunes, has remained on its own two feet. And that is our cultural heritage — what we have created with the greatest joy, the greatest gravity, and the greatest risk. This is the culture that we have been able to create during the past five hundred years, as descendants of Indians, blacks, and Europeans in the New World.

The crisis that has impoverished us has also put the wealth of our culture back in our own hands and forced us to realize that there is not a single Latin American, from the Rio Grande to Cape Horn, who is not an heir to each and every aspect of our cultural heritage. This is what I wish to explore in this book. It ranges from the stone of Chichén Itzá and Machu Picchu to modern Indian influences in painting and architecture. From the baroque art of the colonial era to the contemporary literature of Jorge Luis Borges and Gabriel García Márquez. From the multifaceted European presence in Latin America — Iberian, and through Iberia Mediterranean, Roman, Greek, and also Arab and Jewish — to the singular and suffering black African presence. From the caves of Altamira to the graffiti in East Los Angeles. And from the earliest immigrants across the Bering Strait to the latest undocumented workers crossing the U.S. border at Tijuana–San Diego.

Few cultures in the world possess a comparable richness and continuity. In it, we Spanish Americans can identify ourselves and our brothers and sisters on this continent. That is why we find it so striking that we have been unable to establish a comparable economic and political identity. I suspect that this has been so because all too often we have sought or imposed on ourselves models of development that are scarcely related to our cultural reality. For this reason, a rediscovery of cultural values can give us, with luck and effort, the necessary vision of cultural, economic, and political convergences. Perhaps this is our mission in the coming century.

This book is therefore dedicated to a search for the cultural continuity that can inform and transcend the economic and political disunity and fragmentation of the Hispanic world. The subject is both complex and polemical, and I will try to be evenhanded in dealing with it. But I shall also be passionate about it, because it concerns me intimately as a man, as a writer, and as a citizen, from Mexico, in Latin America, who writes in the Spanish language.

Searching for a guide through this divided night of the soul of the Hispanic world, I found it near the site of the ancient Totonac ruins at El Tajín, in Veracruz, Mexico. Veracruz is the native state of my family. Its capital has been the port of entry for change, and at the same time the abiding hearth of Mexican identity. Veracruz is a city that holds many mysteries. The Spanish, French, and North American conquerors have entered Mexico through it. But the oldest cultures — the Olmecs to the south of the port city, dating from 3,500 years ago, and the Totonacs to the north, 1,500 years old — are also rooted here.

In tombs surrounding the religious sites of these native peoples, mirrors have been found, buried, ostensibly, to guide the dead through the underworld. Concave, opaque, polished, they contain the spark of light in the midst of darkness. But the buried mirror is not only an Amerindian occurrence. The Catalonian poet Ramón Xirau has titled a book of his *L'espil soterrat*, the buried mirror, recovering an ancient Mediterranean tradition not far removed from that of the ancient Amerindians. A mirror: looking from the Americas to the Mediterranean, and back. This is the very sense and rhythm of this book.

On this shore are the slate-black pyrite mirrors found at the pyramid of El Tajín, an astounding site whose name means "lightning." In its Pyramid of the Niches, rising 82 feet on a base of 115 square feet, 365 square windows open out, symbolizing, of course, the days of the solar year. Created in stone, El Tajín is a mirror of time.

On the other shore, Cervantes' Knight of the Mirrors does battle with Don Quixote, attempting to cure him of his madness. The old *hidalgo* has a mirror in his mind, reflecting everything that he has ever read, which, poor fool, he considers to be the truth.

Nearby, in the Prado Museum of Madrid hangs a painting by Velázquez in which he pictures himself painting what he is actually painting, as if he had created a mirror. But in the very depth of his canvas, yet another mirror reflects the true witnesses of the work of art: you and I.

Perhaps the mirror of Velázquez also reflects, on the Spanish shore, the smoking mirror of the Toltec god of night, Tezcatlipoca, as he visits the god of peace and creativity, Quetzalcoatl, the Plumed Serpent, to offer him the gift of the mirror. On seeing himself reflected, Quetzalcoatl identifies himself with humanity, and falls, terrified.

Does he find his true nature, both human and divine, in the House of Mirrors, the circular temple of the Toltec pyramid at Teotihuacán, or in the cruel social mirror of Goya's *Caprichos*, where vanity is debunked and human society cannot deceive itself as it gazes into the mirror of truth? You thought you were a dandy? Look, you are truly a monkey.

Mirrors symbolize reality, the sun, the earth, and its four corners, its surface, its depths, and all of its peoples. Buried in caches throughout the Americas, they also cling to the bodies of the humblest celebrators in the Peruvian highlands or in the Mexican Indian carnivals. As the people dance, with scissors hanging from their legs and arms and bits and pieces of mirrors embedded in their headdresses, they now reflect the world, salvaging this reflection of their identity, which is more precious than the gold they gave Europe in exchange.

Are they not right? Is not the mirror both a reflection of reality and a projection of the imagination?

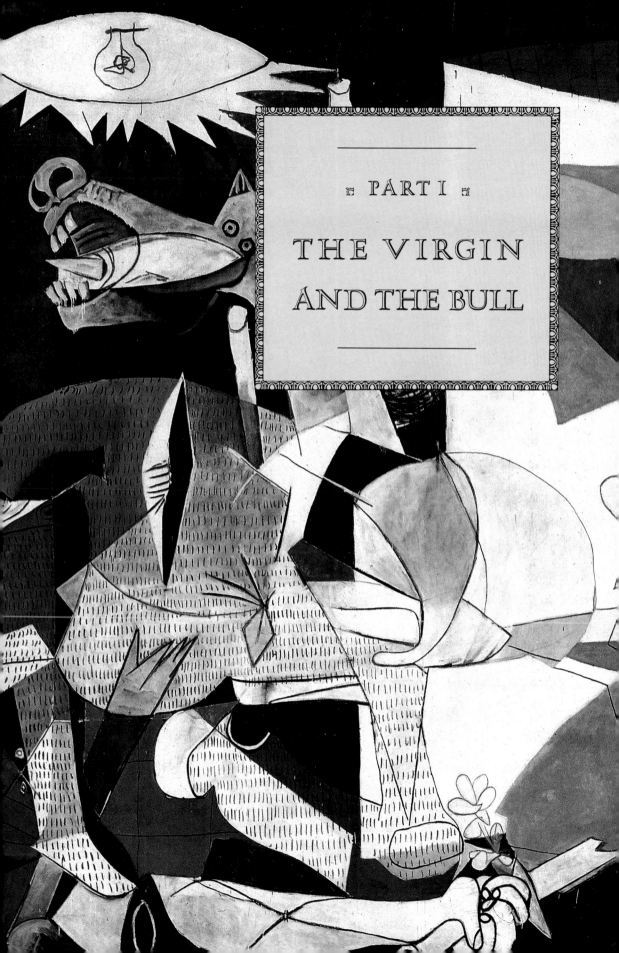

PART I

THE VIRGIN AND THE BULL

ONE

Sun and Shadow

I t was through Spain that the Americas first received the full sweep of the Mediterranean tradition, for if Spain is not only Christian but Arab and Jewish, she is also Greek, Carthaginian, Roman, and both Gothic and Gypsy. We might have a more powerful Indian tradition in Mexico, Guatemala, Ecuador, Peru, and Bolivia; or a stronger European presence in Argentina or Chile; or a stronger black tradition in the Caribbean, Venezuela, and Colombia than in Mexico or Paraguay. But Spain embraces all of us: she is, in a way, our commonplace, our common ground. La Madre Patria, the Mother Fatherland, Spain is a double-gendered proposition, mother and father rolled into one, warmly hugging us, suffocatingly familiar, the cradle through which we come into the inheritance of the Mediterranean world, the Spanish language, the Catholic religion, the authoritarian political tradition — but also the possibilities of identifying a democratic tradition that can be genuinely ours and not simply a derivation of Anglo-American or French models.

The Spain that arrived in the New World on the ships of the discoverers and conquerors gave us at least half our being. So it is not surprising that our debate with Spain should have been, and continues to be, so intense. For it is a debate with ourselves. And if out of our arguments with others we make politics, advised W. B. Yeats, out of our arguments with ourselves we make poetry. It is not always a well-rhymed or edifying poetry, but rather, at times, a harshly dramatic, self-critical, even negative lyricism, as dark as a Goya engraving or as compassionately cruel as a Buñuel image. Positions for or against Spain, her culture and her tradition, have colored the debates of our political and intellectual life. She is seen by some as a pure virgin, by others as a dirty whore. It has taken

Detail from The Bullfight. *Eugenio Lucas Villamil*

Overleaf: *Detail from* Guernica. *Pablo Picasso*

some time for us to realize that our relationship with Spain is like our relationship with ourselves. It is as conflictive as Spain's relationship to herself: unresolved, at times masked, at times resolutely intolerant, Manichaean, divided between absolute good and absolute evil. Sun and shadow, as in the bullring. Spain has often addressed herself in the same way that we have addressed Spain: the measure of our hate is identical to the measure of our love. Is this but a way of naming passion?

There are several traumas that brand the relationship between Spain and Spanish America. First of all, of course, the conquest of the New World. We have a terrible knowledge, that of being present at the instant of our own creation, the observers of our own rape but also of the contradictory cruelties and tenderness that went with our conception. Spanish Americans cannot be understood without acknowledgment of this intense consciousness of the moment in which we were conceived, children of a nameless mother, we ourselves anonymous, but fully aware of our fathers' names. A sort of magnificent pain welds together Iberia and the New World; a birth occurs along with the knowledge of all that had to die so that we should be born: the splendor of the ancient Indian civilizations.

There are many Spains in our minds. There is the Spain of the Black Legend — Inquisition, intolerance, Counter-Reformation — a vision promoted by the alliance of Protestantism and modernism in a centuries-old opposition to Spain and things Spanish. Then there is the Spain of English travelers and French romantics: bullfights, flamenco, and *Carmen*. And there is Mother Spain as seen by her colonial offspring in the Americas: the ambiguous Spain of the cruel conquistador and the saintly friar, as rendered in the murals of the Mexican painter Diego Rivera.

The problem with national stereotypes is, of course, that they contain a grain of truth, but by now the constant repetition has blurred it. The text is there, loud and clear, but the context has disappeared. To restore that context can be both surprising and dangerous. Do you merely reinforce the cliché? Not if you reveal, both to yourself as a member of a nationality or a culture and to a foreign audience, the deeper meanings of cultural iconography, of intolerance and cruelty, and what they disguise. Where do they come from? Why are they real and persevering?

The Spanish context seems to have two constants. First, that each commonplace is denied by its opposite. There is, for instance, the colorful, romantic Spain of Byron and Bizet adjacent to the somberly clad, aristocratic figures of El Greco or Velázquez; and these in their turn are adjacent to the deeply uncompromising, extreme figures of a Goya or a Buñuel. The second constant of Spanish culture, as revealed in the artistic sensibility, is the capacity to make the invisible visible by embracing the marginal, the perverse, the excluded.

This rhythm and richness of opposites is the result of an even more basic Spanish reality, which is that no other country in Europe, except perhaps Russia, has been invaded and settled by so many people.

THE SPANISH ARENA

Look at the map of Iberia. It is like a taut bull's skin, crisscrossed by the paths left by men and women whose voices and faces we in Spanish America dimly perceive. The message is clear: the identity of Spain is multiple. The face of Spain has been fashioned by many hands: Iberians and Celts, Greeks and Phoenicians, Carthaginians, Romans, and Goths, Arabs and Jews.

The heart of Spanish identity began to beat even before history was recorded, 25,000 to 30,000 years ago, in the caves at Altamira, Buxo, and Tito Bustillo in the northern region of Asturias. The ribs of Spain, the philosopher Miguel de Unamuno called them. Even if their shapes today seem as strikingly modern as a sculpture by Giacometti, the first Spaniards once huddled here, near the entrances, protected from the cold and the wild beasts. They reserved a broad subterranean space for their ceremonies in these underground cathedrals. Propitiatory rites? Events of initiation? The taming of nature?

Whatever their purpose, the images they created here were artistic marvels, the first icons. Among them the people left a signature — prints of their hands — and a potent image of animal strength and fertility. If the hand of the first Spaniard is a bold signature on the blank walls of creation, the animal image became the basis of ancient Mediterranean cults and transformed the bull into a symbol of power and life. It is, of course, a bison that is represented in the Spanish caves. He maintains, after all the centuries, his eye-catching ochre coloring and the black contours that single out his shape. And he is not alone. There are also depictions of horses, boars, and deer.

Two curious facts cannot escape notice at Altamira. One is that the ceiling where the bison are painted was already sealed in darkness during the Upper Paleolithic period. The other is that this cave should have been discovered only in 1879, by a five-year-old girl, María de Santuola, who was playing near it. It is the Spanish bull that emerges, symbolically, from the ageless darkness of Altamira and then takes possession of the land to this day, all the way from the Iberian representations of the jacent bulls at Osuna, dating from the fourth to the third century B.C., to the splendid

Celtic representations of the guardian bulls of Guisando, which could be signed by Brancusi, to the black billboard bull one can see today on all the roads of Spain announcing Osborne brandy, and to the tragic bull's head presiding over the man-made night of Picasso's *Guernica*.

But maybe little María de Santuola, like Dorothy in the Land of Oz or Alice in Wonderland, really saw a mythological figure, that "beast of Balazote" which today watches us from the stately halls of the National Archaeological Museum of Madrid. A bull with a human head, the Balazote beast directly links the taurophile culture of Spain to its larger cultural arena, the Mediterranean basin, for in Crete, the island where bullfighting is said to have originated, man and bull were seen as one: the Minotaur. Perhaps all further derivations of the bull symbol are, when all is said and done, just a longing for that original tauromorphosis — to have the strength and virility of the bull along with the intelligence and the imagination of the human being.

Mediterranean humanity regarded the bull as a playful companion, as in the Cretan depictions of bull leaping and bull riding; or as a brutal symbol of rape, as in the abduction of Europa by Zeus disguised as a bull; or as a sublimation of the rape into cosmogony, as when the symbol becomes a constellation in the heavens, Taurus; or as a participant in a love affair, as when Europa consents adoringly to her bull's passionate request.

The first matador was the Athenian national hero, Theseus, who slew the Minotaur. His contemporary, Hercules, brought the mythology of the bull to Spain. Like Theseus, Hercules killed a fire-breathing bull in Crete. But he also traveled to Spain, there to steal the herd of red bulls belonging to the three-bodied giant, Geryon, and drive them back to Greece. Hercules had to cross the narrow strait between Africa and southern Spain to do this; therefore the name of that passage, the Pillars of Hercules. Yet the strait is more than a geographic recognition. It symbolizes both the bond and the separation inherent in one of humankind's oldest ceremonies: a ritual slaying of the sacred animal. Hercules proved his nobility by returning some of the cattle to Spain, in recognition of the hospitality he received there. The ruling king, Chrysaor, then established the ritual of sacrificing a bull to Hercules every year.

Hercules is but the symbol of the cavalcade of peoples that came to Spanish shores, beginning in the remotest antiquity. All of them shaped the body and soul not only of Spain but of her descendants in the New World. The first Iberians arrived over three thousand years ago and gave the peninsula its lasting name. They also left their own image of the bull, guarding their cattle trails, protecting a route that takes us all the way to

the first great commonplace of Spain, the bullring. But a "common place" means exactly that, a meeting ground, a place of recognition, a place that we share with others. What exactly is it that meets and recognizes itself in the bullring? Well, first of all, the people themselves. Impoverished, agrarian, isolated in a rough and remote geography, in the bullring they come together for what was once a weekly ritual, the Sunday afternoon sacrifice, the pagan incline of the Christian mass. Two ceremonies united by the sense of sacrifice but differing in their time of day: mass at noon, corridas at vespers. The mass, a corrida illuminated by an unambiguous sun at its zenith; the corrida, a mass of light and shadows, tinged by impending dusk.

In the *plaza de toros*, the people meet themselves and meet the symbol of nature, the bull, rushing out toward the center of the space, dangerously scared, fleeing forward, menaced but menacing, crossing the boundary between sun and shade that divides the ring like day and night, like life and death. The bull rushes out to meet the human antagonist, the matador in his suit of lights.

Who is the matador? Again, a man of the people. Bullfighting has existed since the time of Hercules and Theseus, but in its present form it was only organized around the middle of the eighteenth century. It then ceased to be a sport of heroes and aristocrats and became a popular profession. In the age of Goya, which was an age of slumming, the aristocracy delighted in aping the common people by imitating bullfighters and actresses. This gave the entertainment professions an emblematic power comparable to the one they enjoy today. Spanish bullfighters have

Bulls at Guisando, Spain, 1989

Osborne brandy advertisement

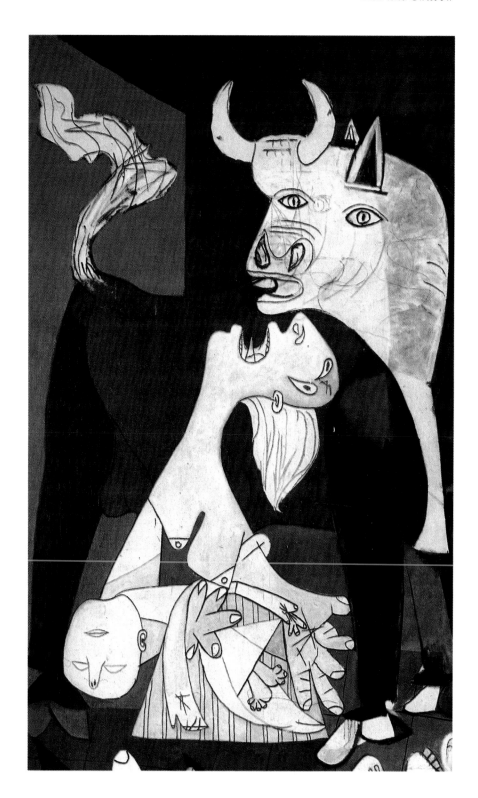

Detail from
Guernica.
Pablo Picasso,
1937

been every bit as idolized as Elvis Presley or Frank Sinatra in our own time. Like these singers, they represent a triumph of the people.

But bullfighting is also, lest we forget it, an erotic event. Where else can the male strike such provocative sexual poses except in the bullring? The effrontery of the suit of lights, its tight-hugging breeches, the flaunting of the male sexual organ, the importance given to the buttocks, the obviously seductive and self-appraising stride, the lust for blood and sensation — the bullfight authorizes this incredible arrogance and sexual exhibitionism. Its roots are deep and dark. When the young villagers learn to fight the bulls, they can do so only by night and by stealth, perhaps crossing a river naked, or a thorny field ragged, to get into the rich man's cattle ranch, there to fight the forbidden bulls, secretly, illegally, in the darkest hour. Traditionally, the young *torerillos* have been tempted toward this sort of encounter because they must fight the bull at extremely close quarters, guessing the shape of the beast, feeling its warmly aggressive body, since they cannot see it. In this way the novitiates learn to distinguish the form, the movements, and the quirks of their opponent, the bull.

So the young matador is a prince of the people, a deadly prince who

The Bullfight. *Eugenio Lucas Villamil (formerly attributed to Goya), c. 1890–1900* can kill only because he exposes himself to death. The bullfight is an opening to the possibility of death, and it is subject to a precise set of rules. The bull is deemed to have been born fully armed, with all the gifts that nature endowed him with, like the mythological Minotaur. It is up to the matador to discover what sort of animal he has to contend with, in order to transform his meeting with him from a fact of nature into a ceremony, a ritual, a taming of the natural force. The bullfighter must first of all measure himself against the horns of the bull, see which way the bull charges, and then cross himself *against* the bull's horns. That is, he must fight the bull on the opposite horn to that with which the animal charges. This is done by the stratagem of "breaking the bull's charge," *cargar la suerte,* which is at the heart of bullfighting. It consists, simply put, in using the cape artfully to control the bull instead of letting him follow his instincts. By capework and footwork, the matador makes the bull change direction and go toward the field of battle chosen by the bullfighter; leg forward, hip bent, the matador summons the bull with the cape, bull and bullfighter moving together, achieving the perfect *pase,* the astonishing instant of a statuesque coupling, bull and fighter enlaced, entwined, giving each other the qualities of force, beauty, and risk, in an image that seems at the same time immobile and dynamic. The mythic moment is restored: man and bull are once more, as in the labyrinth of Minos, the same.

The matador is a tragic representation of man's relation to nature, the actor in a ceremony of remembrance of our violent survival at the

Matador, plaza de toros, *Seville, 1989*

expense of nature. We cannot refuse the exploitation of nature, because it is the condition of our survival. The men and women who painted the animals in the cave of Altamira already knew this.

Spain rips off the mask of our puritanical hypocrisy in relation to nature and transforms the memory of our origins and our survival at the expense of the natural into a ritual of bravery and artistry, perhaps even of redemption. On the Sunday of Resurrection, the bullfighting season begins at the great plaza of La Maestranza in Seville. As the cuadrilla comes out to the music of the *paso doble* honoring the Virgen de la Macarena, the circle that goes from the bullfight to the flamenco to the cult of the Virgin and back to her protected son, the bullfighter — the Iberian ring, as the modern playwright Valle Inclán would call it — closes in upon itself.

Whatever the face of the matador on this particular afternoon, one always remembers the quintessential bullfighter, Pedro Romero, as painted by Goya. The portrait depicts Romero with noble features, firm jaw, taut cheeks, a small, pressed mouth, a perfectly straight nose, fine, separated eyebrows, a clear forehead, and the hint of a widow's peak. On his temples the first silvery strands have appeared. But the center of attention is the eyes, full of competence and tenderness. He has long, delicate, strong hands, and is wearing a dark pink velvet cape, a dark blue jacket, and a colorless waistcoat, which gives the linen of the front and neck of the shirt an exceptional whiteness. The whole painting offers an extraordinary impression of serenity and masculine beauty, which one feels, and fears, the painter himself envied.

Pedro Romero was painted by Goya when the matador was forty years old. Romero started modern bullfighting in the arena at Ronda. In his lifetime, he killed 5,558 brave bulls, and he died at eighty without a single scar on his body.

It could be argued that the virgin body of this perfect bullfighter, who never shed his blood in the ring, is not deserving of the black tears of a single one of Spain's virgin mothers. But Jesus Christ, the God who died lacerated on the cross, his body wounded on hands, brow, feet, knees, the side, does deserve this motherly pity — and Spain gives it to him in abundance.

MOTHER FIGURES

The original mother figures of Spain are near each other in Madrid's Archaeological Museum. La Dama de Baza was excavated from a tomb near Granada in 1971. Sitting on her armchair, holding a dove, her ringed hands a symbol of maternal authority, she is dressed in flowing robes and

The Matador
Pedro Romero.
Francisco de Goya,
c. 1795–1798

forever presides over the birth and the death of her people. Interpreted as a funerary goddess, she is also entitled, by the fact that she remained buried for twenty-four centuries, to the name of earth goddess.

But next to the mother figure, always, we find the temptress, in this case la Dama de Elche. The dates are controversial (she could have been created anytime between the fifth and the second century B.C.), and she possesses equally confusing physical and symbolic traits. Although she has come down as the prototypical work of art of Iberian Spain, almost

*La Dama de
Baza*

its Gioconda, Greek influence is absolutely apparent in the execution of the face: the symmetry, the realism, the sense of proportion, and the finesse of the lines. Yet if this is a classical lady, she is also a classy barbarian act. The Greek balance is broken by the sumptuous Oriental ornaments she is decked out with — headdress, earrings, necklaces. Wearing, perhaps, the first mantilla, she sports enormous disks that cover her ears like some kind of primitive headset, which communicates to her the music of a region that only she understands. Heaven? Earth? Hell? She seems deaf to moral platitudes. Erotically perverse maiden, voluptuous lover, priestess: one could cast her in any of these roles.

Her most disturbing feature, nevertheless, is that she is slightly cross-eyed, an ageless sign of erotic secrecy. The woman stares at you with the eyes of a basilisk. A forbidding vamp, la Dama de Elche, by breaking her classical purity with strabismus and barbarian fashions, sends us back to the elemental truth that all original earth goddesses are mysterious, two-faced, tender and demanding, mother and lover, virgin and temptress. And they are figures of fecund impurity, like the terribly ambiguous goddesses of the Aztec pantheon. The supreme earth mother, Coatlicue, gave birth to a brood of gods through signs of extreme pain and cruelty. And the Venus figure of ancient Mexico, the goddess Tlazolteotl (the Devourer of Filth), represents both purity and impurity: she devours filth in order to cleanse the earth.

La Dama de Elche

The virginal figure that has presided over the life of Spain and Spanish America with such power and for so long is not a stranger to these ancient maternal symbols of both Europe and the New World. In Spain during the great Easter celebrations, and in Spanish America through a reimposed link with the pagan religions, this figure of veneration becomes a troubling, ambiguous mother too, directly linked to the original earth goddesses.

Christianity intensely enriched the previous imagery of Spain with God the father, creator of the world, and his son, Christ the redeemer, who suffered and died for us and for our salvation. But along with them came the Madonna, who gives birth and protection. Mother and son are united by compassion and mystery. The supreme mystery, of course, is that of the Immaculate Conception. Christ is born of a virgin and is therefore the object of faith. The early Christian writer Tertullian said of the faith, "It is true because it is absurd." Which means that you must believe, even if you don't understand.

All of these religious and erotic mutations of the Spanish psyche reach the heights of passion and compassion in the bond between the Virgin and her son. It is at the center of the most ravishing and troubling, sensuous and mystical of all Spanish spectacles — Holy Week in Seville. Over fifty images of the Virgin Mary are displayed in processions that move through the city from Thursday night to Saturday morning. In every neighborhood, men from the lowest to the highest rank march in brotherhoods honoring their own Virgin and doing penance for the love of Christ and his mother. Each *penitente* wears the solemn robes of his brotherhood and carries a cross or, according to the size of his sins, a short or a long candle.

During the whole year, but also from generation to generation, guilds of dyers and textile merchants, weavers of linen, and dealers in gold thread labor to make cloaks and mantles, the veils and tunics of the divine seraglio: Virgen del Rocío, Señora de los Reyes, Virgen de la Macarena, Virgen de Triana. Now, in their shirtsleeves, these men carry the floating temple of their Virgin along the streets of Seville on their shoulders. They are barefoot, invisible beneath the skirts of the Virgin, protected by her billowing drapery, bearing the throne of the Mother of God.

She is, of course, the center of attention. Her face, wrapped in a cowl, is moon-colored and streaked with heavy black tears. She is crowned by a sunlike tiara with razor-sharp rays and hugs dead roses to her bosom. A great triangular cape contrived with the most elaborate ornamentations of ivory and precious stones, medallions shaped like flowers and coiled like metal snakes, drapes her.

What is the meaning of this "multicolored feast," as the philosopher José Ortega y Gasset called it? Is it an exercise in collective narcissism, by which Seville mounts its own spectacle and then becomes its own spectator? Or is it the way in which Andalusia deals with the cultural shock of repeated invasions — Greeks, Romans, Arabs — absorbing them all in the melting pot of religious sensuality and sacred paganism?

It is also a playful ceremony. How else to understand the cries that follow the Virgin everywhere, "Guapa, guapa," meaning beautiful, gorgeous? This playfulness is best expressed by the Gypsy song that says, "The Child Jesus is lost, his Mother is looking for him. She finds him by the side of the river, having fun with the Gypsies."

> El Niño Dios se ha perdido.
> Su Madre lo anda buscando.
> Lo encuentra a orillas del río,
> De juerga con los gitanos.

A RIVER OF VOICES

The second commonplace of Spain is the *tablado flamenco,* the almost
sacred stage where the Spanish temptress, Carmen, the goddess in movement, can perform.

On the *tablado,* the male singers and guitarists strum, prepare, hum,
intone, while the women sit and clap. They are as nubile and thin as
broomsticks, or old and paunchy yet full of fire, animating the proceed-
ings with their clapping hands and stumping twirls. But mostly they are
the beautiful *bailaoras,* dark, tall, and full-figured, their hair sometimes
teased but usually combed straight back and held together by the *peineta,*
the tall Spanish comb. Their bodies are swathed in frills, satins, silks, lace,
complicated girdles, unimaginable underwear, stockings, shawls, knots,
carnations, combs. They will never undress, but their hair is certain to
come apart and spring forth like Medusa's during the dance. They raise
their arms, wrote Rainer Maria Rilke, who went to see them in Ronda,
"like startled serpents."

The dancing woman comes from afar. She can be found on the floors
of Pompeii. The dancing girls of Cádiz were the rage of imperial Rome.
Martial wrote of their "practiced writhings," while Juvenal described
them as "fired by applause, sinking to the ground with quivering buttocks." Lord Byron might have seen them as "black-eyed maids of
heaven," but another, less flamboyant but more moralistic English traveler of the nineteenth century said that while the dances of Spain might
have been indecent, the dancers themselves were inviolably chaste. Federico García Lorca, as always, had the final word in matters Andalusian.
The dancing Gypsies, he wrote, were half bronze, half dream. He saw
them as women paralyzed by the moonlight, as if under a lunar spell.

And so it is, for the flamenco *dance* is but the satellite of the Gypsy
song, cante jondo, the deep song, "the river of voices," to quote García
Lorca again. The dance is the moon, revolving around the song, which is
the center of the solar system of the *cante jondo*; the sun-song goes right to
the solar plexus with its ancient, atavistic magnetism. It is a hybrid form,
and it attracts into its system over five hundred different musical types,
from the Arab call to prayer to the latest tropical rumba, transforming
them all so that our deepest urge will be fulfilled: to sing the most extreme
and intimate human situations. Love, jealousy, vengeance, nostalgia, desperation, death, God, the Mother — here tragic destiny takes over completely, and words start to lose their everyday shape, becoming in effect a
river of song, a mere verbal fountainhead of the most inexpressible emotions. The flamenco sometimes can translate its form of improvised song

Flamenco dancer   into something that resembles a cry — a cry, it has been said, not beneath words but above them, when words are not enough. For the soul speaks out in the *cante*, uttering its darkest, most uncontrollable emotions.

The center of the flamenco dance and the *cante jondo* is the erotic event, and at the center of the center is, of course, the woman once more, the temptress, fully decked out in the swashing draperies of the Gypsy costume, shawled, high-heeled, beribboned, swimming in frills. She provides a sharp contrast to yet another Spanish and Spanish American trait: sexual turbulence clad in saintly longings, as exhibited by the Virgin figures carried through the streets of Seville. That is sensuality repressed by faith but sublimated in mystical dreams. The *cante jondo* is translated to a religious setting, the processions, which come to a halt when a man on a street corner or a woman on a balcony sings out the *saeta*, literally the dart, addressed to the Virgin in a lovingly familiar way. The Virgin gazes on, offering both power and protection. Her power comes from love. She is intimately known. She is like a member of the family. She is the Virgen de la Macarena, the patroness of bullfighters, crying for the death and destiny of her sons.

S.LVCIA.

TWO

The Conquest of Spain

The destiny of Spain is inextricably linked to the Mediterranean, which begins and ends in Spain. You enter through Andalusia if you are coming from the Atlantic. But who came from the Atlantic before Columbus returned from his first trip to the New World? For several centuries, Spain was the only way *out* of the Mediterranean. Was there anything beyond it? The Mare Nostrum — "our sea," as the Romans called it — was entered from the Atlantic through the Pillars of Hercules. There was no other way of leaving it by sea prior to the Suez Canal. Today we call the exit point Gibraltar, in memory of the Moorish chieftain who invaded Spain from Africa in 711. This is for us a name associated with the rock and with insurance policies, but above all with the British assurance that the Mediterranean would remain open to trade and naval movements. It is now, as are many things British, an anachronism. But it does point out that for centuries the term *Mare Nostrum* referred to the geographical center where Europe, Asia, and Africa met and where their civilizations fertilized one another. Philosophy, literature, politics, commerce, war, religion, and art: none of these is comprehensible without the shaping contour of the Mare Nostrum. You could timidly explore the coasts of Africa to the south, but going west there was nothing except fear, the unknown, not "our sea" but the Sea of Mystery, Mare Ignotum.

So Spain became something like the cul-de-sac of the Mediterranean. You went westward to Spain and there you stopped. There was nothing beyond it; one of the western tips of the peninsula was appropriately called Cape Finisterre, the End of the World. Spanish culture was fashioned to the highest degree by this finality, this eccentricity, of the country's geographic position. If you went to Spain, you stayed there, because there was nothing after it. Or you went back east, where you came from.

This double movement shaped the two cultures of Spain. One, the interior, agrarian culture, turned its back to the sea. It was basically the

Saint Lucy.
*Francisco de
Zurbarán,
c. 1625–1630*

culture of the Iberians (the Ebro, or Iberian, River was their habitat, *iber* meaning river and the origin of Spain being, to prolong a Joycean pun, a Riber-run). The Iberians came to the peninsula more than two thousand years before Christ, from the south. Around 900 B.C. they met the Celts, coming from the north, and these groups fused into the Celtiberians, who formed the core of interior Spain, extant to this very day. This was a culture of shepherds and village life, peasantry and tribal instincts, surviving on meat, cheese, and bread. Its isolation from the Mediterranean grew as the Spanish littoral, from Catalonia to Andalusia, became a necklace of foreign settlements, emporiums, and entrepôts. This Mediterranean presence, certainly more commercial than political, was spearheaded by the Phoenicians one thousand years before Christ. Their "ships of Tarshish" created the great myths of Spain's second, outgoing culture. It is the culture of Hercules and the bulls. It is the culture of commerce and communication, headed by Ezekiel's "worthy merchants," but it is also land's end, the fear of disaster, the omen of a dark void, a nothingness, where only a scream can be heard: "Howl, ye ships of Tarshish . . . for your strength is laid waste." It is, finally, once more, the culture of the eccentric, the cul-de-sac, the place you escape to, as Jonah flees "from the presence of the Lord."

In the Biblical flight of Jonah may be found a perverse symbol for both Spain's withdrawal into herself, her own mountainous, rural, tribal hinterland, and her temptation to come out and face the sea, the tall ships, the challenge of a world beyond the Pillars of Hercules, where the sun sinks. This history of conquest and invasion, which draws foreign forces to Spain, was repeated by Spain in the New World. Her response to the challenge of the Other — Arawaks in the Caribbean, Aztecs in Mexico, Quechuas in Peru — was to be shaped by the experience of many centuries, when Spain was on the receiving end of the conquest.

The conquest was benign as long as the Phoenicians, and then the Greeks, simply created commercial enclaves on the shores, with limited zones of influence around the ports of Gades (Cádiz) and Malaca (Málaga), further isolating the primal Celtiberian culture and establishing their own Mediterranean civilization of wine, olive oil, seafood, cereals, monetary circulation, and cities. It was the lack of urban development in the interior that most contrasted with the flourishing coastal communities of the Phoenicians and Greeks.

A CITY BESIEGED

The conquest of Spain ceased to be purely mercantile when the Mediterranean became the theater for great military conflict, pitting two powerful states, Carthage and Rome (Africa and Europe, land and sea, elephant and sailing ship), against each other. As Greece abandoned Spain, Carthage and Rome stepped in to conquer, to create alliances, and above all to set up bases on Spanish territory from which to launch attacks against each other. As the Carthagineans prepared their final assault on Rome, Hannibal, the young commander-in-chief of their army, made Spain the base from which to begin his epic march over southern France and the Alps into Italy. After defeating the Romans at Lake Trasimeno, Hannibal, badly supplied, repaired back to his Spanish shelter, confirming Roman suspicions that if they did not conquer Spain, they would never conquer Carthage. So, curiously, it was Hannibal's victory in Italy that brought Rome to Spain in hot pursuit. And with Rome came the most lasting influences on Spanish culture. Language, law, philosophy, a view of universal history, communications: all of this, associated eternally with Rome's prolonged Spanish presence, is based on the one paramount reality of the city.

Rome was the culminating experience of conquest in Spain for a long time, until the Muslim invasion of 711 and Spain's own overseas conquest of the Indo-American world after 1492. It was a singular experience, for if in the Americas Spain deliberately crushed a previous civilization, cutting it at the bud, destroying the good along with the bad, and violently substituting one form of government for another, her own experience with Rome was exactly the opposite. Italy created in Spain a government and public institutions where there were none; it instilled an idea of unity and wider human allegiances where none existed. And it did so through the instrument of city life. Along the way, a number of traditions were established that shaped not only Spain's culture, institutions, psychology, and responses to life, but those of her descendants in the Americas.

Beyond the national stereotypes, then, a number of significant factors created a Spanish and Spanish American tradition from the time of Roman domination. Nothing reveals the form of the tradition better than the clash with the Other, he or she who is not like you or me. In that encounter, all foreign chronicles agree that the people of Hispania were, in the words of Trogus in his *Historiae Philippicae*, strong, sober, and hard-working: *"Dura omnibus et stricta abstinentia,"* "tough and sober." Strong people, yes, but also extremely individualistic, as the Romans learned when they invaded the peninsula in 200 B.C. They quickly realized that the Iberian armies were brave indeed but ineffectual, because every man fought for himself and resisted integration into a larger unit and obedience to absent commanders or abstract rules. The regional particularism that, for good and evil, has haunted the Spanish nation throughout the centuries was immediately perceived by the Romans. "Local pride," Strabo called it, drawing the conclusion that the Iberians could not join together to repel a foreign threat.

Two important facts derived from this deeply felt attachment to the locality, the village, the hereditary landscape. One was that the Iberians were not very good at offensive operations, which required precisely the kind of unified command they would not bring themselves to create, and at which the Romans excelled. But they proved extremely good at *defending* themselves, in an atomized, disaggregated manner that complicated life enormously for the invaders. Instead of vanquishing a representative army whose defeat would permit them to claim victory, the foreign commanders had to fight one village after another, each offering prolonged and rooted resistance.

In its turn, this bred yet another tradition. Discovering that their strength lay in defense, the Spanish refused to offer a visible front line and instead invented guerrilla warfare. Surprise attacks by very small bands, preferably at nighttime; armies that became invisible by day, blending into the whitewashed villages and the gray mountainsides; dispersion, counterattack — these made up *la guerrilla*, literally, the little war, a local micro-war, as against the invading macro-war, that is, the big war waged by the Roman legions.

Particularism, guerrilla warfare, individualism. Plutarch writes that the Spanish chieftains had a group of loyal henchmen called solidarians, who devoted their lives to their chief and died when he did. By finding out that the Spanish refused to federate, that they felt allegiance only to their land and their chieftains, the Romans were able to defeat them very much in the same way that the Spanish were able to defeat the Aztecs and the Incas: by superior weaponry, certainly, but also by superior information. Realizing that the Mexican peoples were a mosaic of tribes without any allegiance wider than fidelity to locality and chief, Cortés defeated them as Rome had defeated the Iberians.

The cost was high, and it revealed yet another trait: honor. The extraordinary cult of honor in Spain is buttressed by the fidelity to hearth and chieftain. In the war with Rome, the hearth was a city called Numantia. The chief was called Viriatus.

Holding out against the Roman invaders for six years, Numantia was a sort of Vietnam for Rome. Its lack of success demoralized the Roman army, the Roman public protested furiously at the prolongation of war, which devoured draft after draft of young men, and the Senate refused to send any more troops. When the youngest member of the Scipian dynasty of military men, Publius Cornelius Scipio, was given charge against the proud, individualistic township, he was accorded no troops beyond those already in Spain. Scipio put his prestige on the line, receiving money, troops, and a personal guard from his clientele of Asian and African monarchs, among them the Numidian prince Jugurtha, who was to attempt the liberation of North Africa from Rome a few years later and who came to the campaign against Numantia with twelve elephants. Ostensibly, it was there he picked up a few guerrilla tactics that he later applied in his own rebellion against Rome. Scipio was certainly not alone, because quite a regiment of distinguished friends came along to record the events: the great historian Polybius, the poet Lucilius, and a bevy of chroniclers and younger politicians.

Scipio then cleansed the standing army of prostitutes, effeminates, pimps, and soothsayers and ordered the soldiers to sell all excessive paraphernalia, stick to a copper kettle and one plate, and eat nothing except boiled meat. Scipio slept in hay; the soldiers were denied beds and masseurs. Lucilius recounts that twenty thousand razors and instruments of depilation were taken from the troops, who were sent on forced marches, made to do strenuous exercises, and finally, in the summer and fall of 134 B.C., set to dig trenches and erect obstacles. They built six miles of ramparts around the city, doubling its perimeter. The walls were eight feet wide and ten feet high, and a tower was built every one hundred feet. The army was renovated to include 50,000 Romans. All around them, the Numantians were forced to face a mirror image of themselves. And although Scipio refused to attack, he forced the Numantians, with forces only 6,000 strong, to do so or perish from hunger.

As the grand Latin warlord watched the signals of flags by day and fires by night, dressed in a long black woolen cloak to signify that he mourned for the previous incompetence of the Roman army, his own thoroughly disciplined forces, also dressed in black, obliged the Numantian populace to eat hides, then human bodies: the dead, the sick, at last the weaker. But Numantia would not surrender, until, in the year 133, according to Appianos' *Iberian Wars*, "the majority of the inhabitants having killed themselves, the rest . . . came out . . . offering a strange and horrible sight, their bodies dirty, squalid, and stinking, their nails long, their hair unkempt and their dress repugnant. If they seemed worthy of pity because of their misery, they also inflicted horror because on their faces were written rage, and pain, and exhaustion."

If Numantia is not exactly the Iberian equivalent to the Jewish Masada, as it is sometimes made out to be, it does symbolize the tradition of resistance, which is not particular to Spain but peculiarly colored, concentrated, and heightened by the events of her history and culture, as well as by the experience of the Hispanic world in the Americas.

The incarnation of honor was the chief, specifically the military chief — the *caudillo*, as he later became known, an adaptation of an Arab word meaning leader. The traditions of honor, individualism, guerrilla warfare, and attachment to place and chieftain all come together in the figure of Viriatus, who appeared in the wake of the Roman praetor Galba, whose scandalous corruption in administering Spain gave the guerrilla forces a respite in the year 147 B.C. Preparing for a prolonged war, Viriatus practiced a strategy of deception, pretending to flee, attracting the Roman forces, defeating them by surprising them, disappearing into mountains only he knew about, exhausting Rome — but also being exhausted by it. Eight years later, he sued for peace and got it on honorable terms. Rome declared him a friend, but then corrupted three of his emissaries and sent them to kill the unsuspecting leader. Viriatus could be felled only by treason. Burned on a funeral pyre, he became a symbol. He was his own man, described by the historian Justin as the "most important military personality of the Spanish tribes" but as a man also of great simplicity, humane and close to his soldiers.

The death of Viriatus and the fall of Numantia assured the Romanization of Iberia. By saying "Numantia" and "Viriatus," we evoke traditions that were to prove persistent. Nevertheless, Rome was extremely intelligent in not touching the deeper traditions of Iberia but filling in the voids it found. By establishing the great cities of the interior — Augusta Emerita (Mérida), Hispalis (Seville), Corduba (Córdoba), Toletum (Toledo), Caesaraugusta (Zaragoza), and Salmantica (Salamanca) — and connecting them with splendid systems of highways, Rome linked the open cities of the sea to the closed villages of the mountains. It thus created the first and firmest basis for Spanish unity. But an independent, unified Spain did not appear until 1492. In the meantime, the yeast of the Celtiberian soul was put into the furnace of Roman law, language, and philosophy.

ROMAN SPAIN

The external signs of Romanization are still to be seen everywhere in Spain: the theater at Mérida, dating from 18 B.C.; the bridge at Alcántara, finished in A.D. 105; the famed Segovia aqueduct, probably erected in the first century. But the internal signs appear, in the first place, in the language — precise, at times oratorical, at times epigrammatic, as ringing as a phrase by Cicero, as businesslike as a dispatch by Julius Caesar, as

intimate as a love lyric by Catullus, as epic as a poem by Virgil. Very soon, Roman Spain was producing her own batch of writers, including Quintilian, the educator; Martial, the epigrammist, who so sensually evoked the dancing girls of Cádiz; Lucan, the epic poet; and, most important, Lucan's uncle, the preceptor of the emperor Nero and Stoic philosopher from Córdoba, Seneca.

Stoicism was the response of antiquity to the end of tragedy and the loss of divinity. Liberated from the tragic inheritance of fate and subjection to the whims of the gods, man became the measure of all things, but found out that his freedom was inseparable from his loneliness. To become a true man, the individual had to have a clear notion of himself, his strengths and also his limits. He had to understand that he was part of nature, constantly becoming, forever changing. Could man find unity within change? He knew that he was subject to passions, but he had to learn to control them. Finally, he had to know that death awaited him. He had to have a response, an attitude, a style, worthy of his death.

Seneca explained that in times of stress, when everything around us seems to fail, we have no resource left but our interior life. And interiority must bring together all of the values of the Stoic soul — freedom and passion, nature and death — as consciously accepted realities, not as tragically suffered fates. In response to the aggressions of the world, Seneca advised, "Do not let yourself be conquered by anything except your soul."

The effect of Seneca's philosophy on Spain was strong and lasting. To this day, in Spain, "Seneca" means wisdom, and wisdom means understanding that life is not happy — for in a happy world, who would need philosophers? In response to death, Seneca himself adopted a stoical manner. Having fallen from Nero's grace, he anticipated the emperor's wrath by committing suicide. But he also provided Spain with an abiding philosophy, which is at the heart of the Spanish soul, tempering its excesses and bringing it back into itself after the grand adventures of war and discovery, conquest, violence, and death. Spain, a land of saints, painters, poets, and warriors, has endlessly repeated the truths of Stoicism — notably, let me say it at once, in Cervantes' *Don Quixote,* where the protagonist must finally moderate his mad adventures by returning home, to himself and to his death.

Perhaps the most interesting facet of Spanish Stoicism, however, is the individualized portrait of the man who dominates his passions, his natural being, indeed his destiny, through self-knowledge. The extreme individualism of Iberian Spain, the exalted force of its guerrilla leaders, the deranged sacrifices of its besieged cities, and the incapacity to organize collectively are corrected by the philosophy of the Stoic.

Iberian individualism and Roman Stoicism bred the essential Spanish figure of the *hidalgo,* literally, the "son of something," that is, the inheritor, the man of honor, the man of his word, the man of noble exterior and equally noble interior. El Greco gave us the definitive version of this ideal in his painting *Gentleman with His Hand on His Breast*; Cervantes, its literary counterpart in the figure of the Gentleman with the Green Cloak in *Don Quixote.*

The fusion of individualism and Stoicism deeply affected the Spanish manner of accepting Roman law. There is a clear tradition of statutory law, that is, the written law, which is of Roman origin and through Spain became one of the most important traditions of Spanish America. For Rome, the fact that the law was written down, instead of being purely customary or orally transmitted, as in previous times, meant that everyone was bound by it and no one could pretend ignorance of it to impose force or personal whim on others. We shall see that this respect for the written law as a source of legitimacy went right down the backbone of Spain and into her relationship with the New World, through the chronicles of the discovery and the conquest and, more important, through protective legislation, such as the Laws of the Indies, which, more than the naked fact of conquest, truly legitimized the Spanish Crown in the Americas. In independent Spanish America, the importance of the written constitution (whether or not it is respected) is offset by the piece of written paper, even if only a scrap, by which the dispossessed peasant claims his right to the land. Roman law is at the source of these attitudes.

It is also at the source of yet another Hispanic tradition: the idea, formed through language and the law, of the state as the cocreator of development and justice. All of those theaters, aqueducts, roads, and bridges were but the exterior signs of Rome's decision to impose progress and economic development through the benevolent authority of the state. The census, the tax system, politics, and administration — Rome was extremely able in associating all the virtues and duties of civilized life with the state while respecting the local cultures and Hispanic traditions. Under these flexible circumstances, it was easier for Iberia to accept the Roman gift, the state connecting the country, developing the economy, giving Spain a sense of participating in universal history, but respecting the people's sense of local pride.

The danger of having the state represent development and justice was, of course, that somehow the state would be seen or see itself as superior and beyond the reach of its votaries, the citizens. From the beginning, Spain created, in this sense, yet another constant. We could call it the poetic dramatization of injustice and the right to rebel. Plays

Gentleman with
His Hand on
His Breast.
El Greco, 1578–
1585

such as Lope de Vega's famous *Fuenteovejuna*, in the seventeenth century, explicitly dramatized the confrontation between political power and the citizen. *Fuenteovejuna* describes a whole township's revolt against injustice. The township takes on responsibility for each and every one of its inhabitants, and when asked who is responsible for killing the feudal *comendador*, it answers as one man: "All of us, the town of Fuenteovejuna." At last, through the fusion and development of Roman government and Stoicism, Spaniards were able to find a means of acting collectively.

It has been explained that the genius of Rome in Spain was that it never imposed any absolute, totalitarian scheme but that it fostered change, openness, mixture, and circulation. The aqueducts took water from the river valleys to the dry upper *mesetas* in the same way that law and language conveyed a growing sense of community. Whatever the case, early attempts at forced Italo-Hispanic integration failed, and by the first century of our era, Ibero-Romans were participating fully in the life of Rome itself. It is therefore not surprising that three Roman emperors — Trajan, Hadrian, and Theodosius — should have been Spanish-born.

The constant movement in the cities and on the highways, a movement of artisans, muleteers, merchants (*mercatores*), public officials, soldiers, and immigrants, finally gave the whole process of Romanization a popular cast, permitting everyone to speak Latin, more and more with a native inflection, inventing words, adapting them to sounds, vulgarizing the language, even militarizing it. The Latin language broke up into three Romance variations, the speech of the clerics (*sermo clericalis*), of the army (*sermo militaris*), and of the people (*sermo vulgaris*). From this heady mixture came the language of Spain and of 300 million people in Spanish America and the United States.

CROWN AND CROSS

Although the wisdom of Roman law, language, and philosophy remained in Spain, the empire withered and died. Two new forces appeared on the already scarred Spanish landscape. The first Christians arrived from the east during the first century A.D. Then a wave of Germanic invasions overcame the declining Roman power, culminating in the rule of the Visigoths — Christian in name but barbaric in deed.

Spain was certainly not the cause of the collapse of Roman power in Spain. The peninsula was the granary of Rome, probably the wealthiest province in the empire, and so thoroughly Romanized and loyalist that only one legion was stationed there, for purely symbolic reasons. Roman Spain was a far cry from the irreducible Iberian Spain that had sacrificed herself in Numantia. But the disappearance of the Roman order, which for a thousand years had dominated the ancient world, left a void, which Spain could not protect by herself. It was filled by the barbarians and the Christians.

In the fifth century, Rome was in such an advanced state of decomposition that all of its armies could not defend Spain from the waves of incoming tribes — Suevi, Alans, Vandals — pouring down from Gaul and Germany toward Europe's "sun belt." They besieged and then sacked the Hispano-Roman cities and then turned against one another. The Alans were defeated by the Suevi, who then attacked the Vandals and defeated them with the help of some new arrivals, the Goths, which led to the confrontation of Goths and Suevi. Things grew complicated as the Romans sent in legions to recover Spain. The Goths made pacts with Rome until the last Roman emperor, Romulus Augustulus, fled from the scene. Then the Visigoths became masters of Spain.

Their votive crowns are sumptuously barbarian, a male counterpart to the headdress of la Dama de Elche. But the crowns rested uneasily on the heads of the Visigoth kings, whose monarchy was elective and constantly disputed. A nobility of warriors, barbarians in love with lavish jewelry and heavy crowns, they squabbled endlessly on religious matters. They had embraced the Arian heresy, which held that Christ was not a part of the Holy Trinity at all, and therefore not a part of the nature of God the Father, but merely a prophet. And they squabbled endlessly on political matters, resolving the problems of dynastic succession with one bloodbath after another.

The arrival of the first Christians in Spain continues to be shrouded in mystery and legend. Some of the earliest Spanish saints came from Africa, as did Saint Felix, who took the word of Christ to Barcelona, and Saint Cugat, who also preached in the Catalonian port city. Many martyrs were female. The Spanish heresiarch Priscillianus, who proposed the doctrine that our bodies are the Devil's creation and must be exhausted in earthly pleasures and free love, prompted (with success) mixed gatherings of men and women for the reading of Scripture. Numerous women adhered to this heresy. But others found the consolation of martyrdom only because they refused to submit to male demands. Lacking all contemporary illustrations of these martyred Spanish women, we can imagine them as depicted by the painter Francisco de Zurbarán in the seventeenth century, dressed in handsome gowns and bearing the symbols of their torture. His young women are some of Zurbarán's most noteworthy martyrs. Legend has it that the Mediterranean Saint Lucy, who was sacrificed in Syracuse, was denounced by her rejected suitor as a Christian, where-upon a Roman soldier killed her by thrusting his sword into her throat. She is represented as carrying her eyes on a platter. Saint Agatha, also of Sicily, carries her breasts on yet another platter; she too was courted by a rejected suitor who denounced her as a Christian. Her breasts were cut off and she became the patroness of bell-founders and of bakers. So much for the powers of metamorphosis. The most famous Spanish martyr, Saint Eulalia, a thirteen-year-old virgin, rebuked the Roman persecutors and was then tortured and burned to death. As she cried, "God is all," a white dove flew out of her mouth and snow suddenly fell on her dead body.

True or legendary, these stories reveal that the Christian faith grew and planted strong roots in many Spanish communities between its cloudy origin and the appearance of Priscillianus in the fourth century. And from the beginning Spanish Catholicism bore an erotic uneasiness, a sexual turbulence clad in saintly longings.

Yet there was certainly far more than this, including the political significance of Catholicism in Spain. Between the passions of politics and the malaise of martyrdom, the Catholic church tried to create a semblance of order. And between the martyred Christian virgins and the mauled Gothic princesses there appears a figure who has been hailed as the savior of civilization in Spain, the first medieval philosopher, the first Spaniard. There is a bit of truth in each affirmation, but only one is indisputable, that the bishop of Seville, Isidore, was the most important Spaniard of the whole era between the fall of Rome and the Muslim invasion of the peninsula.

THE SAINT OF SEVILLE

"Spain," wrote Isidore, "is the most beautiful of all the lands extending from the West to India. . . . She is the Mother of many peoples and right-fully the Queen of all the provinces, for through her East and West receive light." This Spanish mission, to receive diverse peoples and disseminate knowledge, was to be tested and found at times hopefully true, at times dismally false, over the centuries. But the glorification of Spain, "the most illustrious part of the globe," was also to serve as a foundation for empire, when that time came and Spain became, in its turn, the greatest world power since Rome. Saint Isidore was one of the founders of the Spanish Empire.

He was born in exile and persecution. His family, Catholics from the city of Cartagena, fled from Arian persecution and settled in Seville, where the young Isidore lost both parents at an early age. His mother left

Visigothic crown

a note that many Spaniards — Jews, Arabs, or Christians, liberals or republicans — repeated in coming centuries: "I shall die in exile and in exile I shall find my grave."

Isidore was raised among the calamities of the violent disputes between King Leovigild, the first Gothic monarch to put his head on a Spanish coin, and his children, Hermenegild and Recared, which ended in Hermenegild's renunciation of the Arian heresy. He did so in Seville, in front of that city's bishop, Leander, who happened to be the elder brother of Isidore. But King Leovigild advanced against Seville, captured his son, and condemned him to prison, where he died, clinging to his Catholic faith. Leander was, like his parents before him, exiled. The old King Leovigild repented on his deathbed, called Leander back from exile, and asked to be pardoned. The heir to the throne, Recared, became a

Saint Agatha.
Francisco de
Zurbarán, c.
1630–1633

Catholic, and in 598 Isidore, now a priest, witnessed the Catholic Council's meeting at Toledo, where the king affirmed the Catholic religion as the basis of unity for his people.

But a declaration was not enough. Around him, Isidore saw a formal adherence to Catholicism but not the language or the law with which to structure the church in Spain. He saw a rampant, abusive, lawless, stuttering royal power — again, law and language were missing in public affairs. To restore these to both the ecclesiastical and the public domain became Isidore's political and intellectual mission. Everything was against him. The culture of Rome was lost. In the words of the Spanish historian Marcelino Menéndez y Pelayo, Isidore was placed between an old, agonized society and a childish, savage one. He set out to educate the barbarians. Through his book *Origins*, also known as *Etymologies*, he restored the sense of language. Through his recompilations of Roman law, he gave Spain a sense of legal continuity. A saint in a political and cultural desert, he had to rescue a whole culture from near oblivion and propel Spain, once again fallen into an isolationist torpor, into a rising medieval world, where Celtic and Merovingian monks traveled, preached, and organized.

He started by putting his own house in order. When his brother Leander became bishop of Seville, Isidore became abbot of the cloister. He enforced traditions of austerity and harsh discipline. In opposition to a society in which false monks roamed and false hermits lived capriciously, Isidore created an ideal of monastic perfection, whose rule was poverty — but not so much that it "induce[d] sadness of the heart, or pride of spirit." After the final prayers, the monks were obliged to pardon each other for their daily trespasses, embrace in peace, and go singing to their beds in a communal dormitory, where the abbot slept at the very center of the congregation.

At age forty-three, on his brother's death, Isidore inherited the bishopric of Seville. He was now able to campaign for a new agreement between church and state. He had strengthened the church through discipline while the monarchy floundered in undiscipline. He had swept away the confusion of Gothic and Byzantine laws in favor of a precise continuity of Roman law and its clear, logical, and architectural sense of procedure. Now he put all of this at the service of the great question that dominated European politics until the late Middle Ages: the relationship between church and state. After the disappearance of the Roman bureaucrats, the bishops of Spain had become the real administrators of the country, which gave him a political advantage. The chaos and incompetence of the Gothic kings only compounded this situation. Isidore, a man of balance, did not propose the supremacy of either church or state, but advanced the idea that the state should be subordinate to the church in spiritual matters and the church to the state in secular ones. When necessary, each could step into the other's orbit. There should be no vacancy of power. Of course, in Isidore's Spain, given the great power that the bishops already wielded, it was disingenuous to defend the elective monarchy on the grounds that it was one of the fundamental laws of the kingdom. Isidore must have known how disruptive the system was, and how much the church stood to profit from his triumphal campaign to put all of the power to name bishops in the hands of the bishops themselves. The king would have no say in this matter.

The culture of Spain has been saved again and again from imminent disaster, decay, and oblivion. Isidore of Seville, in his barbarian wilderness, saved the Roman culture of the country. But his ideal of a new Hispanic unity based on the fusion of Romans and Goths fell to pieces. The constant abuse of power, the family rivalries, and the partisan squabbles made it well nigh impossible for Gothic Spain to organize effectively and with united purpose.

The nobility of Gothic warriors was by nature centrifugal; it started to create independent fiefdoms as thirty kings succeeded one another in two centuries of Visigothic rule. The continuing coups and massacres that permitted the church to gain decisive power established yet another constant of Spanish and Spanish American politics: the almost continuous presence of the church in public affairs. But while the church learned to govern itself and administer the country, it failed to check the persistent atrocities of the barbarian monarchs; it proved incapable of establishing an order of succession or of impeding the more outrageous atrocities launched by the Visigothic monarchs, such as King Sisebut's persecution of the Jews in the time of Isidore.

When Isidore went from his monastery to the basilica of Saint Vincent in Seville, in March of 636, he did so in public penitence, in spite of the fact that he was dying. He put on the sinner's sack and had ashes poured on him. A multitude was there to see him for the last time. His sins, he publicly proclaimed, were more abundant than the sands of the sea. He asked all to forgive him; if he had sinned, he said, he had also worked. On April 4, he died. Less than a century later, the strong, Christian, lawful, articulate Spain he had longed for faced its greatest peril, as a new power rose to challenge her across the strait of Hercules. This newcomer was to give the ancient Mediterranean passage a new name: Gibraltar.

THREE

The Reconquest of Spain

The Roman nucleus, which dominated not only Europe but the whole Mediterranean basin, including the Near East and northern Africa, was successively shattered by the barbarian invasions and by the spread of Islam. But while the several Germanic tribes were finally absorbed into a Christianity that had established its capital in Rome and attempted to continue Roman legitimacy, Islam proved unamenable to such assimilation. Riding the crest of religious and political expansion, eight years after the death of the Prophet Muhammad the Muslims conquered Egypt, then went on to Tunis, and by 698 they had expelled the Byzantines from the former imperial center of North Africa, Carthage. And in 711, exactly a century after the Prophet had begun his teachings, Islam reached the southern shores of Europe, invading Gothic Spain.

That year, Count Julian, governor of Ceuta, joined in a rebellion against the Visigothic monarch, Roderick, and called in what he thought to be a mercenary troop of thousands of Berbers from North Africa, under the command of Tarik. In the gossip-mongering world of the Visigoths, it was said that Count Julian was avenging himself against King Roderick, who had raped his daughter one day as she bathed in the waters of the River Tagus near Toledo. The truth was that the successful Muslim invasion was the final proof of the extreme debility of the Gothic realms. Tarik's army, which set sail from Morocco, landed at Gibraltar, named Jebel-al-Tarik after the Berber invader. Weighed down by a golden crown, a heavy robe, archaic jewelry, and an ivory carriage drawn by two white mules, the last king of the Visigoths, Roderick, could not stop the Moors at Guadalete. They swept north toward Toledo and the Pyrenees, and Gothic Spain ceased to be.

Islam would remain on the Iberian peninsula for eight hundred

Detail of the Gate of Glory, Santiago de Compostela

years. With little initial resistance from the divided Christian realm, its armies swept north across Spain. Overextended, they were stopped by Charles Martel near Poitiers in 732, and Europe did not become Muslim. But within Spain herself, tradition says that they were first stopped in 718, at the battle of Covadonga, by the Gothic chieftain and guerrilla leader Pelayo.

In the mists of the mountains of Asturias, the Christian remnant survived and began pushing southward over the centuries. Between 711 and 1492, Christians and Arabs gazed at each other across twilight frontiers, doing battle but also mingling, trading culture, blood and passion, knowledge and language.

Sometimes the Christian armies pushed southward from the front line of Castile, so called because it became dotted with castles; sometimes they were pushed back north, when the Moors organized themselves into a strong state. But when the Moors faltered and broke up into puny fiefdoms, the Christians once more marched south, taking Toledo and decisively defeating the Moors at the battle of Las Navas de Tolosa in 1212. From then on, the arrow of Christian victories only pointed south, toward the final, isolated Moorish kingdom of Granada.

Although the Arabs were finally defeated and expelled, their presence during eight centuries created a bicultural experience unique in Western Europe. The same twilight quality of the shifting war frontiers applied to race and allegiance. The division between the Christian faithful and the Muslim infidel was less than clear. *Mozárabes,* for example, were Christians who had adopted the Muslim culture. *Mudéjares* were Moors who lived as vassals of the Christians. *Muladíes* were Christians who had adopted the Islamic faith. And *tornadizos* (a pejorative word, this, comparable to *turncoat*) were Moors who had converted to Christianity. Finally, the *enaciados* sat on the fence between both religions and were used as spies by both Moors and Christians. Their bilingual talents were much in demand as a source of intelligence. To this day, fully one quarter of all Spanish words are of Arab origin. Even in the bullfight, we use an Arab word to salute the matador, for *ole!* comes from the Arab word *wallah.*

ARAB SPAIN

The Moors quickly passed from being a highly mobile tribal militia to becoming a landed class, and from there they moved to the cities. That is, once the military and agricultural base had been acquired, it was from the urban centers that Islam best governed its military, agricultural, and commercial interests. The cities — Córdoba first, then Seville, then Granada — were built on the rapid growth of a monetary economy, the commercial value of produce, the strength of the bureaucracy, and the development of the service sector. Muslim Córdoba was, and will remain in memory as, the supreme Muslim city, dominating Spain between 711 and 1010.

The three successive Abd ar-Rahman monarchs of the Umayyad dynasty chose Córdoba to seal the Muslim presence in Spain. It was a presence based, in spite of the exceptions, on openness and inclusion, not on exclusion. Córdoba became the gateway through which the culture of Islam was sent to northern Europe, but it was also the gateway through which the Europe of the barbarians came to renew its links with its lost Mediterranean past. From the Spanish caliphate of Córdoba, Greek philosophy and classical literature marched back over the Pyrenees to Gothic Europe. The classical texts had been translated into Arabic during the caliphate of Baghdad; the School of Translators at Toledo then disseminated them anew throughout the West. Science, medicine, astronomy, went from the Muslim south to the Christian north, as did the compilations of the Hindustani tales.

Muslim Spain invented algebra, along with the concept of zero. Arabic numerals replaced the Roman system. Paper was introduced to Europe, as were cotton, rice, sugar cane, and the palm tree. As Córdoba assimilated Greek philosophy, Roman law, and the art of Byzantium and Persia, it also demanded respect for the theologies of Judaism and Christianity, as well as for their bearers, who were considered, along with Muslims, "the peoples of the Book." Extermination and forced conversion were reserved for idolaters and pagans. In principle, the "peoples of the Book" deserved another moral and intellectual treatment — even as they were being implacably fought on the battlefield.

During the years of the Córdoban supremacy, the idea gained ground that a pluralism of cultures is not at war with the concept of an only God. It was in this new region of southern Spain, which was called Al-Andalus by the Muslims — today's Andalusia — that the three great monotheisms of the Mediterranean world, the religions of Moses, Jesus Christ, and Muhammad, began their long, often fruitful, and more often conflictive interrelationship.

The Great Mosque at Córdoba is the beautiful embodiment of this attitude. Its original 1,200 pillars, of which only 80 remain, reproduced every Mediterranean style that passed through Spain: Greek, Carthaginian, Roman, Byzantine. The mosque offers the sensation of walking through a centerless vision of the infinite, where God and man can be imagined ceaselessly searching for each other in a cool labyrinth, each depending on the other to continue the unfinished task of creation. The

forest of stone pillars seems to be changing constantly, thanks to the physical gaze but also to the eyes of the imagination, into a million mirrors. Indeed, all things have to be reimagined at this, one of the most marvelous and stimulating buildings in the world.

The Great Mosque at Córdoba

The Muslim abundance of beauty and luxury was sustained by taxes, war booty, the subjection of Christian states, and levies imposed on Jews and Christians, in addition to a flourishing trade in all directions of the compass. From the Orient came books and jewelry, dancers and musicians; from North Africa came slaves, gold, and cereals; and from Europe, financially strapped in comparison with Islam at that time, came wood for naval construction and arms (in spite of the pope's interdiction of such commerce with the infidel). The West has a long history of selling arms to Islam and then repenting.

The three great Umayyad rulers of Córdoba progressively freed Muslim Spain from Oriental power, culminating with the third Abd ar-Rahman's decision to proclaim Córdoba an independent caliphate, separate from Baghdad. This action united both political and religious power in what became, in effect, an independent Andalusia. Controlling both the unruly North African tribes and the peninsular Arabs, Abd ar-Rahman III took Al-Andalus to its supreme splendor. But this splendor was menaced by the uninterrupted Christian war, and when Arab Toledo fell to the Christians in 1085, Córdoba had to call in the fanatical Almoravids from North Africa. As they crossed through Gibraltar, the glory that was Córdoba came to an end.

Abd ar-Rahman III had left as a parting gift the great palace at Medina Azahara, built to honor his wife. Resting on 4,300 columns, the palace was served by 13,750 male servants along with 3,500 pages, slaves, and eunuchs. Only to feed the fish ponds, 1,200 loaves of bread were used each day. Nevertheless, wise to the fleetingness of all glory, Abd ar-Rahman dressed in rags and covered himself with sand when he received foreign ambassadors. He died an old man, but at the end he sighed, "I have known only fourteen happy days in my life."

Between 1010 and 1248, Seville became the new center of Muslim culture in Spain. The Almohads presided over a century of artistic and intellectual splendor in this city. The foundations of the great Alcázar were set, and the minaret of the Giralda was built. The transept vault was

*The palace at
Medina Azahara*

introduced into Europe, where it was to become one of the characteristics of Gothic architecture, and choral music as well as lyrical poetry was also transmitted to Europe during this time.

This was the period of the two greatest thinkers of medieval Spain. One, Maimonides the Jew, was a doctor, writer in Arabic, conciliator between Judaism and Greek philosophy, and abridger of the Talmud. The other, Averroës the Arab, was the philosopher who reintroduced Aristotle to Europe and who dared to think of "a double truth," that is, one religiously revealed, the other scientifically found. This distinction became one of the hallmarks of modern thought.

As Arab power in Spain began to wane after the defeat at the battle of Las Navas de Tolosa, and after the fall of Seville to Ferdinand III of Castile (Saint Ferdinand) in 1248, only a third great city was left to preserve the Muslim heritage: Granada. This was the final kingdom, presiding over the dusk of Arab Spain, between 1248 and 1492.

As one approaches it today, one must imagine that once there was nothing here except the valley, the river, and the mountains, the Sierra Nevada. Here the wandering people of the desert came to their rest, and here they decided to build a garden whose beauty could not be compared to anything in this world. It was as if they had heard the voice of God commanding them: "Build here, by the light of the torches, a palace, and call it Alhambra," which means "the red citadel."

Perhaps only a people who had known the thirst of the desert could have invented this extraordinary oasis of water and shade: a succession of gates and towers, rooms and courtyards, give the Alhambra a sense of both containment and contentment, as if all the pleasures of the world could be had here, at the reach of the hand and the eye. Surrounded by a belt of walls — Wall of Justice, Wall of Wine — and watched over by the towers of the Captive Woman and the Homage, the towers of Comares and the Alcazaba, the Alhambra is a labyrinth of noble rooms in which even the shadows are golden. The audience room of the Mexuar, with its tile patterns following the breathtaking regularity, harmony, and surprise of a Bach fugue; the intimate sense of luxury achieved in the stuccoed grace of the Room of the Two Sisters; the carved perspective of the Ambassadors' Hall; the sensation of being caught in a sweet, honey-combed prison from which no one would wish to escape — there are both a seraglio and a harem room here — are suddenly brought face to face with their own essence in one of the poems written on the arches of the mirador, the balcony overlooking the gardens of the palace: "I believe that the full moon has its home here."

Finally, one realizes that this network of filigree, stucco, blue tiles, and unbelievable perspectives has but one purpose, and that is to protect the water, to allow one to hold a mouthful of liquid in the cup of one's hand, to surround the life-giving element with a caressing, sheltering, yet open defense. The patios, the unique courtyards of the Alhambra, are like temples of water: the slender columns of the myrtle trees are just as protective as the twelve lions circling their patio. But during the daytime, or even at night, one comes to understand that it is the constant fusion and coexistence of all the graduations of time and nature — light, shadow, air, earth, sun, moon — that truly protect the heart of the Alhambra: its pools, its fountains, its outlets.

It's not only water that ripples in the gardens here. Since the Koran frowns on the representation of the human body, the Alhambra became a written building, its body covered with script, telling its tales and singing its poems from its inscribed walls. It is filled with a kind of celestial graffiti, where the voice of God becomes liquid and where the joys of art, the intellect, and love can be experienced. No wonder that a poem by a Mexican writer, Francisco de Icaza, has entered the anonymous world of the proverbs describing this city: "There is no greater sorrow than to be blind in Granada."

La Reconquista

While this sensually magnificent and intellectually exciting civilization was flourishing in southern Spain, in the north the harsh realities of war and of militant faith excluded such pleasures. The Moors transformed southern Spain into an oasis of irrigated lands, pleasure gardens, splendid architecture, and superb cities. In the tenth century, Córdoba was the most populated city in the West. But Christian Spain had, after Isidore of Seville, no Averroës and no Maimonides. It built nothing comparable to the Alhambra or the Great Mosque at Córdoba.

It is astonishing, however, that given a perception of the superior power and culture of Islam, Christian Spain did not succumb to it, as Syria and Egypt did, in spite of their long-lasting Hellenistic culture. Perhaps this fact is related to the equally long Hispanic tradition of fighting back through guerrilla warfare; individualism and the cult of honor had certainly become ingrained in the Spanish soul. The added ingredients of Stoicism, Roman law, the Romance language, and certainly the still fresh and militant spirit of Christianity contributed, no doubt, to Hispanic fortitude. But perhaps even stronger than all of these factors was the root element: the attachment to hearth and village, family and

*The Alhambra:
filigree work, the
Court of the Lions,
and a fountain*

图 59

family history, kinship, lore, and graveyard, song and harvest, of what had been, since Celtiberian times, basically an agrarian, small-town society of craftsmen, artisans, cattle raisers, shepherds, field laborers, and petty merchants.

Christian Spain was to define herself in the struggle against the Islamic invader. Spain, conquered by waves of assailants since the earliest times, was now about to stage her most prolonged war, not of conquest but of reconquest, which lasted until the fall of the last Moorish kingdom in 1492. Spain had been lost. Spain had to be recovered. Such was the sense, and the name, of the great enterprise that was to concentrate the attention and the efforts of Christian Spain for the next eight hundred years: *la reconquista*.

La reconquista was above all a military event. Against the fulcrum of war, many things either survived or were created, fashioning the profile of Spain, and eventually of Spanish America. A central fact, both military and, as it turned out, cultural, is prominent: of all the major European countries, Spain was the only one that did not go on the crusades to the Holy Land. All of her energy had to be devoted to fighting the infidel at home.

Islam had an initial advantage over Christianity: it admitted, even exalted, the concept of *jihad*, holy war. From the very beginning, religious asceticism and the war against the infidel were inseparable in Islamic politics. The institution of the *ribats* in Al-Andalus was in this sense typical. Created by the Almoravids, these fortress monasteries sheltered brotherhoods of religious hermits who alternated sacred devotion with the armed defense of the Moorish frontiers.

In principle, Christianity did not authorize its clergy to engage in war. Still in its youth, the church found the idea of clergymen killing human beings repugnant. This was something better left to the "secular arm," that is, the state. But on the one hand, the Visigothic state had lost its authority, and on the other hand, Saint Isidore had exerted enormous influence with his ideas of Christian perfection and of separation of religious and political spheres. The net result was that before the Moorish invasion in the eighth century, so many men were entering the monasteries and avoiding military service that the Gothic kings were asked by the nobility to forbid further ordinations, or there would be no one left for the army. The Islamic invasion in 711, though, triggered the militarization of the church, and by the eleventh century the northern armies of *la reconquista* were filled with monks who had become soldiers. Yet another facet of the identification between war and religion, between sword and cross, to be so determining in the conquest of the New World, had been established. The militant religious orders were founded to conciliate a warring clergy with holy aims.

The three great military orders created during the crusade against the Moors were called Calatrava, Santiago, and Alcántara. They welded together an army of the land, which the kings financed, thus establishing the base for the future standing army of unified Spain under the Catholic Monarchs, Ferdinand and Isabella. The armies of *la reconquista* were also the seed of the future Latin American armies.

Nothing illustrates this connection better than the figure of the most famous Christian warrior of them all, El Cid, born Rodrigo Díaz de Vivar near Burgos in 1043 and dead in 1099, in the Valencia he reconquered. "We win our bread fighting against the Moors," he declared. El Cid continued the tradition of Viriatus and Pelayo — that of the Spanish, and later the Spanish American, *caudillo*, or military leader. Sporting an Arab nickname, "El Cid" meaning "My Lord," he symbolizes the tradition of the army leader as an arbiter of power — and of an army that is wealthy and strong thanks to the generosity of its commander. "They asked for land, and he gave it to them in Valencia, with houses and plots, thus did he pay them," the *Song of El Cid* informs us. The conquistadors in the New World, and after them the liberators in South America, were to do the same in their own time; Cortés in Mexico, Bolívar in Venezuela, proceeded as El Cid did in medieval Spain, repaying their soldiers with land. Military chieftains, and particularly the great military orders, thus came into possession of great territorial tracts.

El Cid is the embodiment of the politics that was at times secularly opportunistic, at times fervently religious, spurred by the rise of the army and of army leaders in the long war of reconquest. The chronicle of his deeds is the great epic poem of medieval Spain. Yet at times it is a strange epic indeed, recounting as it does numerous dishonorable actions on the hero's part. If the *Song of El Cid* is the Spanish *Iliad*, it portrays some realistic, even picaresque traits that would hardly suit Hector or Achilles. The poem begins with the hero, El Cid, swindling two Jewish merchants, in itself a surprising introit to heroism. It goes on (like many epic poems) to become a tale of family vengeance, as El Cid fights to repair the dishonor inflicted upon his daughters by the villainous princes of Carrión, and it ends on an almost slapstick note of revenge against another villain, Count García Ordóñez, who gets his beard pulled.

In between, the poem is also a striking demonstration of a particularly Spanish and Spanish American vice: envy. Everyone envied El Cid, including his relatives, the nobles, the court, and the king himself, Alfonso VI of Castile, who instead of using him wisely, exiled the battling com-

El Cid.
Spanish woodcut,
artist unknown,
1525

mander. El Cid riposted with an attitude that seems amazing to us today: he served the Muslim king of Zaragoza. But his chief lieutenant, Alvar Fáñez, went on to fight with the Moorish king of Murcia against another Muslim monarch, the king of Granada. This was simply a part of the shifting realities, political and otherwise, of the protracted struggle of Islam and Christianity in Spain, which was also an embrace. The twilight borders, the inevitable fusions of blood, customs, and language, bred all sorts of alliances during the wars. If *la reconquista* was a war against Islam, it was also a war of the Christian kingdoms among themselves, all of them fighting to achieve hegemony once Islam had been defeated.

El Cid lives today through his poem. Written in a direct and realistic popular style, its air of bravura and military grandeur gives it its most characteristic moments: "Thou shalt see . . . so many white banners turn red with blood and so many good horses, riderless, roam, while the Moors call 'Mahomet!' and the Christians 'Santiago!' respond."

THE ROAD TO SANTIAGO

There was a leader greater than El Cid in the Spanish crusade — none other than Santiago, Saint James, one of the twelve apostles, the companion of Christ. But the people willingly confused Saint James the Greater, son of Zebedee, with Saint James the Lesser, called in the Gospels "the brother of the Lord." In popular iconography, the lesser James is even presented as Christ's twin.

This "twin" of Christ was transformed in Spain from a peaceful apostle into a fierce warrior, capable of panicking the Moors when he appeared fully armed on a white steed, descending from a cloud. He became Santiago Matamoros, Santiago the Moor-slayer, the figure that inspired popular resistance against the Muslims and fortified the soul of the reconquest. In the battling Santiago, the spiritual and the armed components of Christian Spain came together; no doubts, no suspicions, were now possible. If Santiago was on our side, then so was God, and our war was every bit as holy as the other side's. The army and the church were united in the cult of Santiago. Santiago was drafted to fight the Moors, and he in turn drafted all of Christian Spain into his crusade.

The grave of the saint in Compostela became the great goal of European pilgrimage in the Middle Ages, and this offered Christian Spain a chance to organize its culture and continue the work of Saint Isidore, even if now under a bellicose banner. The monks of Cluny in France had worked mightily since the tenth century to re-create a civilization around the isolated, reckless, Christian barbaric kingdoms. A whole necklace of monasteries, abbeys, libraries, and roads to and from them began to appear in France and then in Spain, leading pilgrims to the final outpost of heaven on earth: Santiago's tomb at Compostela. Compostela — *campus stellae,* the field of stars — was a magnificent shrine, erected between 1075 and 1150 to house the remains of the apostle and the growing multitude of his worshippers.

The Spanish clergy provided an infrastructure for both the crusade against the Moors and the pilgrimage to Santiago. It created a network of monasteries in northern Spain; it provided roads, books, cultural community, and the shelter of architecture in the splendid Romanesque style, which peppered the road from Paris to Compostela. Germans, Burgundians, Normans, Englishmen (and Englishwomen, highly favored on the road to Santiago), princes and abbots, merchants, thieves, bandits, lepers, all mingled in the great pilgrimage and functioned as a kind of original Common Market, bringing commerce, culture, activity, and violence to Spain.

Indeed, the crush to reach the apostle's corpse was such that pilgrims sometimes murdered one another next to the tomb. The cathedral at Santiago had to be reconsecrated over and over again. And this medieval humanity brought with it not only faith and violence but stench. The greatest attraction in Santiago Cathedral these days is the great silver *botafumeiro,* a gigantic censer that at certain hours of the day swings in a wide arc, dispensing incense to woo the supernatural and fumigate the unwashed bodies. *Olor de santidad,* a smell of holiness, was the euphemism used to describe the people who came to Santiago.

There is a grouping at Santiago Cathedral, nevertheless, that is supremely unaffected by violence, commerce, or stench. The pilgrims were received by the angels, prophets, and apostles of the Christian church at the aptly named Gate of Glory. This is undoubtedly one of the greatest pieces of architectural sculpture in Christian Europe, and it testifies to the self-assurance, the spiritual and material rebirth, of the West in the twelfth century, after the long night of barbarism. On each side of the "gate," four prophets and four apostles seem to be talking to one another. A particularly humane and sympathetic figure stands out: the prophet Daniel. He is the Mona Lisa of the Middle Ages, and his enigmatic smile tells us that the world is well ordered, secure, and truthful under God's architecture. In conversation, the saints and the prophets seem to be in the midst of some heavenly cocktail party. What is their small talk about? Surely, about the admirable symmetry of the medieval Christian order, where everything and everyone knew their rightful place and where collective wisdom had vanquished individual pride. The political philosophy of the Middle Ages, which was to shape the public life of Spain and Spanish America, was already evident in the certainty, here expressed, that the common good superseded all other goals, and authorized that unity be imposed in order to obtain it. If individuality should suffer in consequence, so be it.

But if one looks closely enough, one will find, in a tiny corner of the heavenly conclave, a squinting little man ironically peering at the holy figures. This is the artisan of this medieval marvel, Master Mateo himself, head of the masons' guild at Santiago in 1183, humbly asserting his presence in the otherwise anonymous spirit of its creation. The Gothic cathedrals (and the Aztec sculptures) survive beyond that anonymity; the medieval spirit would even say that *because* of the anonymity, they live on.

LORDS, CITIES, KINGS

During the eight centuries of *la reconquista,* Spain responded not only to Islam but to the West, and to herself. Closely bound to the Islamic enemy she both fought and embraced, Spain was also a part of the general European pattern: the barbarian invasions had left in their wake weak kingdoms and a legal vacuum that was filled by a powerful church and strong, locally based feudal lords.

The cathedral
at Santiago de
Compostela

The smiling
prophet Daniel,
second from left

Feudalism gained an early foothold in Spain, with all of the characteristics that we associate with this form of society. The Roman Empire gave way to local warlords and chieftains, who imposed their own law, and more often their own whims, on the land and its workers. As the concept of the Roman state faded, so did the authority of the rickety Gothic kingdoms; Roman law was superseded by the use of brute force. Once again, Saint Isidore's interest in reviving Roman legal traditions was important as a corrective against feudal caprice and atomized authority. To revive the former and discredit the latter was a constant, if difficult, goal of the kingdoms and the cities of Spain as they withstood the double pressure of Islamic war and feudal power. It meant substituting for the private links of feudalism the public links of the state and even of an incipient nationhood. Between both, the society tried to create a third pole of cultural identification, private and public, attempting to render both Caesar and God their due.

In Spain, as elsewhere in Europe, the landed aristocracy dominated society and imposed on it a social scale that placed the nobility and the clergy at the top and freemen in descending order leading to the serf. But although Spanish feudalism was naturally based on possession of the land, *la reconquista* gave to the land itself a peculiar shape. Spain is again singular in Europe, because of the many exceptions she brought to the feudal regime as practiced in France, England, and the Germanic regions. The reconquest accentuated feudalism's strengths as well as its weaknesses. Both were united in a single concept: the frontier. During the long centuries between Charlemagne and the discovery of America, feudalism was as strong in Spain as anywhere else, but it was also questioned more than anywhere else, for the simple reason that its very rationale — stable power over the land and the population — was constantly disturbed by the shifting frontiers between Islam and Christianity.

The extreme division of the peninsula and the fluctuating frontiers strengthened the feudal nobility. The state was discredited. The lord could thrive on both a war and a peace economy. In wartime, he lived on booty and the tributes of the Moorish kings. In peace, he dominated the two sources of landed wealth, farming and cattle. And as the war pushed south, he was rewarded with new lands. But at the same time, the war strengthened the urban physiognomy of Spain. If a battling Christian lord wanted to claim land from the Moors, he had to build a city where a city did not exist or had ceased to exist.

A whole policy of repopulation changed the face of the no-man's-land constantly emerging between the Christian and Moorish lines. As the Christian armies moved south over the centuries, they built and settled new townships. Who built them, who settled them, who could be counted on to defend them? Certainly not serfs, but more surely freemen. Who would want to travel all the way to the dead land of the Duero Valley or the inhospitable and lonely plains of Castile? Only frontiersmen and frontierswomen, hardy people willing to go where no one else would go, but also exacting a price for their hardships.

So while feudalism gained important footholds in Catalonia and the northern, more secure regions of León and Aragon, where the field hand labored on the lord's lands and could not leave them without his permission, in Castile, on the frontier with the Moors, the need to repopulate and defend the land gave rise to a class of peasants who were guaranteed freedom of movement, personal liberties, and possession of their own lands in exchange for living in the reconquered region. Even in such a stronghold of feudalism as Catalonia, the development of commercial and artisanal cities with ports open to Mediterranean trade soon created a mercantile class with a mind of its own. As the church built its fleet of monasteries to further the faith in the reconquered lands, an army of merchants followed in its wake, profiting especially from the movement along the road to Santiago, and attracted by the many favors and privileges that the ruling princes accorded to them.

For centuries Spain was frontier country; and the frontier of Spain was within Spain herself. The towns of the frontier were the front line of the reconquest. Cradles of Spanish power, they were also cradles of Spanish liberties, for the very fact that the dividing lines with Islam shifted gave them an edge over the powers of the diverse Christian kingdoms that were forming themselves along with the cities. This was the advantage of offering or denying support to the king of Castile, the king of Aragon, or the king of León. The towns could barter their support in war for their freedom in peace.

Trade and war thus gave rise to independent cities, settled by horsemen and foot soldiers, by nobles and peasants, by the church as well as by settlers armed with royal charters. They believed in and practiced self-rule. They created town halls, municipal assemblies, and independent judiciaries, and gave themselves local constitutions. The growth of the townships transformed the popular cavalries of *la reconquista* into burghers, knights (*caballeros*), and lesser nobility (hidalgos). The concept of honor that had existed since Iberian times became even stronger, writes the historian José Antonio Maravall, as *la reconquista* gave all who fought in it — the people, the nobility, the king, and all the king's men — the sense of participating in a common cause, honorable to all. The feudal mentality, adds Maravall, was transcended by *la reconquista*. More and more, allegiance was due not to the feudal lord but to Spain. But where was Spain? In the king? In the city?

Along with the movement of the Christian armies, villages became towns, and some towns became cities. One can distinguish, though, the city conceived for military defense and the city that, even if originally a fortress town, soon developed on commercial impulses. Ávila is the supreme example of a city built for military defense: impregnable, turreted, moated. Not for nothing is it the highest city in Spain, a citadel made by man and nature to watch over the wide spaces of Castile, the land of the castle, the *castellum*, which means "high place." Equally wide are the walls of Ávila: ten feet thick, protected by eighty-eight round towers and nine

The walled city of Ávila

fortified gates. Its town fathers were renowned warriors who went to fight and came back with cattle, treasure, and slaves.

This means that cities conceived for war soon became cities that lived on trade. A rapid screen montage would show us the isolated high *castellum*, the redoubt of the warrior and nobleman, being covered with a creeping vine coming from the lowlands: peasants, then merchants, establishing their own quarters near the castle, finally absorbing it into a larger urban concept, the *burgo* or *bourg*, the place of the bourgeois, the tradesman, the artisan, the lawyer, and the pharmacist, but also of the field laborers. Not only arms were needed to defend a reconquered piece of real estate. Trade, work, craftsmanship, and professional activity became equally important. But the people needed freedom to move, to trade, to marry, to inherit — freedom from feudal obligations.

This concept of repopulating gave Spain a distinguishing characteristic in Europe, soon to be tested in the New World, where perhaps Spain's greatest legacy was the capacity to create cities. In the Spain of *la reconquista,* León was founded in 856, Zamora in 893, and Burgos in 884. The latter is a typical township that, created for military defense (remember that El Cid was born near here), soon developed into a powerful commercial center. The story of Burgos confirms Marc Bloch's description of renewed economic life in eleventh-century Europe, bringing with it "a powerful and differentiated mass of urban classes."

The magnificent cathedral at Burgos, begun in 1221, is the crown of this new urban reality. It sheltered a social mobility that elevated the fortress town to city, or *civitas,* conceded it to a *fuero,* or local statute, and gave privileges to its inhabitants, raising them all the way from the condition of villains to that of citizens. *"Citizens,"* said the laws of King Alfonso the Wise, were people whom the monarch "should love and honor . . . since they are the wealth and the root of kingdoms."

The cathedral at Burgos

"The air of the city makes you free" became a proverbial saying of the European Middle Ages. The city was the means of escaping feudal servitude. Spain was no exception. Yet another factor was to have a decisive voice in the opposition between feudalism and urban culture in Spain: the royal factor, the emerging monarchies, who profited from the urban enclaves to wrest powers from the feudal lords, whom the weak kings originally had had to respect if they were to counteract the Moorish presence effectively. After the battle of Las Navas, the peninsula appeared clearly divided into five kingdoms: Portugal to the west, facing the Atlantic; León-Castile, from the north to the center: Navarre, in its mountainous northern enclave; Catalonia to the east, facing the Mediterranean; and Granada, the last Arab monarchy, deep in southern Spain.

So *la reconquista* truly formed a triangle, whose three vertices were the feudal lords, the free cities, and the emerging kingdoms. They were united in the fight against Islam but far from coordinated in their struggle among themselves. Indeed, the frontier situation so characteristic of this era of Hispanic life was not limited to the land between Islam and Christianity. As I have said, Spain was a frontier within herself, lying between strong feudal organizations based on the land, rising mercantile and artisanal activities based on the townships, and princes struggling to recapture the Roman sense of authority and statehood over lands and cities.

As the frontiers ceased to shift, all three of these groups quickly realized that without the excuse of *la reconquista,* possession of the land more than ever meant economic wealth and political power. More than ever the feudal lords fought for the survival of their privileges and the kings for political superiority over the lords, while the cities were caught in the middle, naturally opposed to feudalism but wary of ever-encroaching royal powers.

Nowhere was this more evident than in the very kernel of medieval democracy, the parliamentary institution. In fact, the first European parliaments that took hold and incorporated the third estate, the commons, all appeared in Spain. Called to this day the Cortes, these assemblies were the result of a prolonged democratic development. Based on their *fueros* (won, as we have seen, by resisting the Moors on the frontier and repopulating it), citizens of the cities developed rights of self-government under elected magistrates (*alcaldes*) and met in municipal assemblies (*ayuntamientos*) to decide on public affairs. The kings were certainly interested in attracting people with no feudal obligations, and were willing to confirm them as free citizens, thus creating a power base against the nobility. As the townships gave a king financial and military help, so the king gave them political rights.

In 1188, the first Spanish parliament was convoked by King Alfonso IX of León, preceding all other European parliaments by at least half a century, while the first Catalonian Cortes, in 1217, and those of Castile, early in the thirteenth century, preceded the first English parliament, in 1265. In all cases, the parliaments signified that the privileged orders, clergy and nobility, were now joined by what in Spain was called "good men of the cities," in England "the commons," and in France *"le tiers état."* Their functions varied in the Spanish kingdoms. While in Castile the parliament basically debated matters of taxation, in Aragon it was authorized to receive complaints against the king (and the king's men). Alongside the parliament, the cities had their own local councils, which were originally open assemblies, town hall meetings practicing direct democracy (permitted by the small number of inhabitants). As the population grew, the city dwellers had to delegate representation to a few "good men." At the end of the day, these "good men" would all be *corregidores*, royal functionaries appointed by the king and permanent representatives of royal power. Democratic decision-making was to suffer accordingly.

The cities mostly went along with the kings as a better option (or a lesser evil) than feudal whim and violence. How much did they finally barter away? This is the story of democracy in Spain and Spanish America. The development of society and of local institutions through statutes of self-government, freedoms chartered in numerous urban communities, and a continuous revolution of rising expectations, headed by the bourgeois cultural and commercial centers of medieval Spain, were incipient, and needed more time to take root and more care to be properly nurtured. In all of Europe, the rationales of royal authority and national unity would soon pit civil freedoms fashioned during the Middle Ages against royal powers consolidated after the Renaissance. Freedom eventually fared better in England than in Spain. France experienced a dramatic tension between centralized absolutism and the *tiers état* that only the French Revolution could resolve. And both Germany and Italy had to postpone until the nineteenth century the national unity achieved by Spain, England, and France in the fifteenth century.

Of all these histories, probably Spain's is the saddest, for nowhere else in Europe had fundamental civil rights been obtained so soon. Yet the same thing that made them possible — a war against another religious and military force in Spain's national territory — prevented their flourishing. Once the war with Islam was over, the monarchy won a prestige it did not have in England or France: the aura of victory over the infidel at home. The drive toward imperial conquest, the nature of Spanish colonization in the New World, and Spain's continuing role as defender of the Catholic faith against the heresy of Protestant Europe all derived from the experience of the reconquest.

This was also the origin of Spanish and Spanish American democracy, so many times defeated, never destroyed. Our present-day democratic life, fragile as it is, has its deepest roots in these medieval townships. We have often deceived ourselves by ignoring the true Hispanic tradition of democracy, founded on the free municipality. This has served as an excuse for two aberrant forms of self-denial: imitation of the democratic institutions of the French and Anglo-American worlds, which *have* functioned; and adaptation of authoritarianism in a modern, progressive guise, since only such a course, as imitative as the first one, will eventually give us the material conditions for democracy. Capitalism and socialism have both failed in Latin America because of our inability to distinguish and strengthen our own tradition, which is authentically Iberian and not derivatively Anglo-American or Marxist.

In other words, medieval Spain was just as prepared as England and France, if not more so, to become a modern European democracy. That this did not happen when it should have — between the sixteenth and the nineteenth centuries — is deeply troubling, with dramatic implications both for Europe and for Spanish America. Yet even stronger than the democratic tradition was the cultural tradition fostered by the coexistence of Christian, Muslim, and Jew in Spain.

THE THREE CULTURES

Ferdinand III, king, warrior, and saint, took Seville from the Moors in 1248. Twice a year, his tomb in the Cathedral of Seville is opened, and Fernando is shown to us in his royal robes, crowned and sporting a long white beard. He is said to be incorruptible. But more important than his corpse are the striking contradictions of his life.

Here lies the Christian warrior who besieged Seville for sixteen months, until the night of war enveloped the city even in daylight. Storming, sacking, slaying everything in sight, he expelled 100,000 Muslims from the fallen city. And he did have a sense of vengeful humor, as the story of the bells proves. The Arab conqueror Al-Mansur had brought the bells of the cathedral of Santiago all the way south to Córdoba in 997. Then the Christian king Ferdinand III of Castile recovered them when he conquered the former capital of the caliphate. Whereupon he ordered them returned to Santiago, this time on the shoulders of the conquered Moors. For whom the bells toil.

Here lies also the saint who, as he was dying, received the host while kneeling upon the earth with a rope around his neck, to signify his humility before God and the deep consciousness of his sins. And here lies the humanist who appealed to the pope to protect the Spanish Jews from wearing distinguishing stigmata on their clothes.

His tomb bears inscriptions in all four languages of the cultural continuity of Spain: Latin, Spanish, Arabic, and Hebrew, that is, the languages of the three monotheisms, Christianity, Islam, and Judaism. Ferdinand liked to be known as the sovereign of the three religions, equally respectful of all the "peoples of the Book," the Testament, the Koran, and the Talmud. Thus, if practical politics led him to combat the Moors, his spiritual mission was to recognize Spain's European singularity as the only nation where Jews, Christians, and Moors intermingled.

But cultural coexistence as an explicit policy by a Spanish monarch truly reached its apogee under Saint Ferdinand's son, Alfonso X of Castile, who organized the greatest university of Spain, in Salamanca, and in 1254 granted this university its charter and created the library, which became the first state library in Spain, with the first paid librarian. It is a fitting symbol for a king who in his own time was dubbed "the Wise."

Alfonso brought to his court Jewish intellectuals as well as Arab translators and French troubadours. He asked his Jewish and Arab brain trust to translate into Spanish the Bible, the Koran, the Cabala, the Talmud, and the Panchatantra. With the Jewish intellectuals, he wrote the monumental *summa* of the Spanish Middle Ages, which includes a legislative compilation (*Las siete partidas*), a judicial treatise (*El fuero real*), treatises on astronomy, and two great histories, of Spain and of the world. Alfonso's tricultural court even had time to write the first Western book on an Arab game, chess (whose most definitive move, checkmate, or *jaque mate* in Spanish, is yet another translation from the Arab: *shah'akh maat*, "kill the shah").

The purpose of this extraordinary feat of medieval intelligence was to put down all the knowledge of the times. In this sense, it was a continuation of the work done in Seville by Saint Isidore. The result was a sort of encyclopedia, before encyclopedias came into vogue in the eighteenth century. The most striking point is that the king of Castile had to call on Jewish and Moorish intelligence to do the job. And it is no less significant that the Jewish writers insisted that the works be written in Spanish and not, as was then the academic custom, in Latin. Latin was the language of Christianity, and the Jews of Spain wanted knowledge to be spread in the tongue common to all Spaniards, whether Christians, Jews, or converts. From their work in the court of Alfonso was to come the future prose of Spain, which was in essence the language of the three cultures.

Inscriptions on the tomb of Ferdinand III: Latin, Spanish, Arabic, and Hebrew

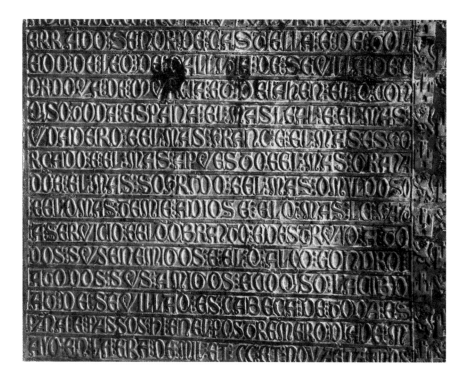

Two centuries after Alfonso, it was still the Jews who employed the vulgar tongue to read the Scriptures, comment on them, write philosophy, and study astronomy. One can say that the Jews fixed and circulated the use of the Spanish language in Spain.

Nevertheless, in the tricultural sweepstakes, with their bonuses of tolerance and intolerance, none suffered more than the Spanish Jews, the Sephardim. The first Jews arrived in Spain during the emperor Hadrian's reign, in the second century, and they became not only intellectuals but artisans, farmers, traders, and physicians. But under the Visigoths they were fiercely persecuted. They were accused of creating economic depressions as a means for expropriating property. Saint Isidore of Seville was not above a stale and repugnant reason for rejection of the Jews: they were condemned by their father's sins to dispersion and oppression.

It is not surprising that, rejected (but not expelled) by the Gothic kingdoms, the Jews should have welcomed the Arab invasions of Spain, preparing for them with great anticipation and remaining in Andalusia as part of the Muslim society, where they were recognized as children of Abraham. But the successive invasions of the Almoravids and the Almohads, after the death of Al-Mansur, brought to Muslim Spain a wave of strict orthodoxy directed against all non-Muslims, including Mozarabs and Jews. These then fled north, to the Christian territories, swiftly migrating from city to city. They lived in their separate ghettos (*aljamas, juderías*) and enjoyed royal support because of their special talents (commerce and medicine), but they were constantly harassed by popular hatred. Had they not killed Christ? Had they not "lost Spain" to the Muslims? Were they not richer than most, and also oppressively usurious?

Indeed, the Catholic church forbade usury, and Saint Thomas Aquinas himself wrote that lending money with interest was a crime against the Holy Ghost. Capitalism could hardly prosper under these circumstances; it kills the Holy Ghost every morning as soon as Wall Street opens. But anti-Semitism could and did. And along with it, the criterion that purity of race and religious orthodoxy were somehow basic to the very notion of Spain came into being. First Jews were forbidden to occupy the same houses as Christians; then Jews could not judge or bear witness against Christians; and finally the pogrom exploded, fanned by envy (Hispanic envy — the most virulent), by the Black Death, which brought extreme paranoia in its wake, and by extremist preachers who, lacking television to inflame their bigoted audience, developed verbal fanaticism into a fine art. Not only was the plague attributed to the Jews;

if a battle against the Moors was lost and converted Jews had participated in it, they were blamed for the defeat.

In 1391, pogrom followed pogrom. It was a year of poverty and plague. Four thousand Jews were killed in Seville. In Córdoba, two thousand dead men, women, and children lay in heaps among the burned synagogues. Hundreds of Jews committed suicide in Barcelona to escape persecution, and also in response to the pain of seeing their families butchered.

The *conversos:* where else could a Spanish Jew trying to save his or her neck go but into the arms of the Catholic church, always ready to receive the repentant? Yet mass conversions, often against the will of the converted, permitted anti-Semitic preachers to blame the *conversos* for all the sins that before they had placed on the Jews. Converted, the Jews soon found that they were suspected of heresy and malignant practices. Called "new Christians," they began to intermarry with "old Christians." And they gained access to the Spanish Catholic church, there becoming, as is common with the converted, the most zealous persecutors of their former community, their Torquemadas.

Events now rushed forward to a new world situation in which Spain had to face the challenge of becoming a modern, unified nation-state. Would she become modern and unified with or without her tricultural heritage? This question previews Spain's role in the New World. Both were decided in the events of the watershed year of Spanish history: 1492.

FOUR

1492: The Crucial Year

Throughout the West, the Middle Ages waned and were followed by a sense of renewal, of expansion, and of discovery, forcing each European polity to take stock of itself and imagine what its place would be in a new world order defined by a single word: renaissance. For Spain, the national agenda comprised ending *la reconquista* by defeating the last Moorish kingdom remaining in the peninsula, Granada. This would assure territorial unity and the possibility of establishing a national state.

The legal map of medieval Spain was that of a true archipelago of laws and habits, going from the private pacts imposed by the feudal lords, to customs shared by many on a local basis, to judicial decisions, to royal decisions. But given the tricultural nature of Iberia, this pattern also had to include the statutes privy to Jews, Mozarabs, *mudéjares*, and others. Out of the jumble nevertheless emerged a constellation of local rights and rights of the kingdom, which opposed each other as long as the local rights were identified with the private, feudal link. The transformation of local rights into public laws gave the kingdoms added force, as they championed a return to Roman law and legal allegiance to one traditional ruler and to public institutions. Once more, it was Alfonso the Wise who, through his compilation of Spanish laws, gave the most important thrust since Saint Isidore's to a restored Roman tradition. The reception of Roman law and of Aristotelian political theory through King Alfonso, the gradual replacement of feudal jurisdictions in matters of justice, taxes, and armies by the kings of Castile, Aragon, and Navarre, and their policy of renewing the nobility by ennobling their own allies prepared the stage, in spite of the turmoils of succession and dynastic rivalry, for the unified Spain of the fifteenth century.

Detail of Columbus, from a map by Theodor de Bry

ACHIEVING UNITY

When the frontiers ceased to budge, between 1280 and 1480, the boundaries between each kingdom became clearly established. The fight against feudalism had signified two things: first, that the power of the king should be imposed over all the territory, and second, that the inhabitants of each territory should owe allegiance to the king. To this end, the kings, as we have seen, attempted to protect the freedoms of the cities and the citizens. But in truth they were interested in changing the status of each person from that of a *vassal* of a lord to that of a *subject* to themselves. Each princely court established itself in one capital city, instead of roaming all over the territories of *la reconquista*. A royal bureaucracy came into existence. And the *corregidores* milked the towns for taxes.

Nevertheless, the Roman "full powers," *potestatis plenitudo*, were severely undermined by political instability and dynastic warfare, which plagued Spain as much as the Black Death did. The plague appeared around 1350, along with the reign of Peter the Cruel, who inherited the throne of Castile at age fifteen, went on to fight five bastard brothers, and was dominated by his mistress, María Padilla, who encouraged him to fratricide. Finally, on a wintry day in a tent outside Montiel, Peter fought his brother Henry in hand-to-hand combat, then perished when Henry thrust a dagger into his heart.

Henry's triumph established the Trastámara family on the Castilian throne. The effects were far-reaching, for through their lineage came the final dynastic struggle, which, significantly, was also a battle between nobility and monarchy for the succession in Castile.

The handsome but weak King John II of Castile permitted the government to be run by the authoritarian and unscrupulous Alvaro de Luna, who was executed on orders of the king's wife, who then secured the throne for her son. This was the impotent Henry IV, whose daughter was allegedly sired by a nobleman called Beltrán de la Cueva. Known as La Beltraneja, she was proclaimed heiress by her putative father, only to meet the opposing will of the nobles, who chose and imposed the king's sister, Isabella of Castile, as queen.

Bright, energetic, intolerant, driven by dreams of faith and unity, but quite alien to the dream of cultural unity, Isabella married the king of Aragon, Ferdinand, in 1469, thus sealing the union of Castile and Aragon. After her triumph over La Beltraneja and her marriage to Ferdinand, Isabella was sure of one thing: her wedding enabled Spain to unify the medieval kingdoms and bring forward, now without great impediments, all the forces furthering order, legality, and unity, at the expense of both feudal power in the countryside and civil power in the cities. Isabella and Ferdinand had learned the lessons of Spain's long fight for national integration. Their actions promptly showed it; their motto was "Tanto monta, monta tanto, Isabel como Fernando," Isabella was as worthy as Ferdinand, and Castile the equal of Aragon. They created a bureaucracy of merit, not of favoritism, and established all the trappings of Roman law, beginning with the identification of monarchy, sovereignty, national jurisdiction, and a centralized administration. The subjects' new allegiance was to the monarchy and no longer to the feudal lord — not even to his city, and certainly not to another culture or another religion.

The unity of Spain formally achieved by the royal couple now required a particular sanction: Islam had to be expelled for good from the peninsula. As they prepared the assault on Granada, the Catholic rulers were unaware that they were embarking on the watershed year of Spanish history.

Ferdinand and Isabella were certainly clear about the importance of capturing Granada, but they could not have truly calculated the harm that they would bring down on Spain by expelling the Jews, also in 1492. And when they sent an obscure sailor named Christopher Columbus on a wild goose chase over the horizon, the monarchs' hopes that they would outflank the Portuguese on the quickest route to the Indies certainly did not include coming upon a whole new continent, the third great event of 1492.

The fourth act of that crucial year is hardly mentioned in the history books. Antonio de Nebrija published the first grammar of the Spanish language, an instrument of artistic achievement, moral strength, political alternative, and multiracial union that was to outlive many of the virtues and most of the follies of the Catholic Monarchs, Isabel de Castilla and Fernando de Aragón.

THE EXPULSION OF THE JEWS

Perhaps the worst blunder of the unified kingdom and its rulers, the expulsion of the Jews, was determined by both ideological and material forces. Ideologically, Ferdinand and Isabella wanted to consolidate unity on the basis of religious orthodoxy and racial purity. The ideal scapegoats were, as usual, the Jews. The Catholic Monarchs decided to sacrifice Spain's greatest cultural asset, its mutually enriching tripartite civilization. Statutes calling for purity and orthodoxy were the basis for expelling the Jews and then for persecuting, supervising, and if need be exterminating the converts, who remained in Spain and who were suspected of being closet Jews or even outright heretics. To this end, the weak medieval Inquisition, dependent on the pope and the bishops, was transformed into a potent tribunal under the direct orders of the Spanish kings. In exchange for this power, the church had to change its practical allegiance from Rome to Spain.

Ferdinand and Isabella in 1492. Spanish manuscript illumination, n.d.

As Gabriel Jackson explains in his *Medieval Spain,* the Inquisition fattened as it spread its persecution not only against the infidels but against converts as well. It stalled conversion and forced what was left of the Jewish community to become more intolerant than the Inquisitors themselves in order to prove their orthodox trustworthiness. The supreme paradox of this dead-end situation was that converted Jews at times became the persecutors of their own people and the most interested defenders of monolithic order. The first inquisitor-general of Castile and Aragon, Torquemada, belonged to a family of converted Jews: the zeal of the converted.

Religious considerations alone did not guide the policy of Ferdinand and Isabella. They were also interested in filling the royal coffers with the expropriated wealth of the most industrious castes in Spain. It is truly ironic that the immediate benefits that the unified Crown received were but a pittance compared with what it mediately and immediately lost. In 1492, out of a total population of seven million, there were in Spain only half a million Jews and *conversos.* Yet about one third of the *urban* population was of Jewish stock. The result was that one year after the edict that expelled the Jews, rents in Seville dropped by one half and Barcelona saw its municipal bank go bankrupt.

Above all, the expulsion of the Jews meant that Spain in effect deprived itself of many of the talents and services it would later sorely need to maintain its imperial stature. The Jews were the doctors and surgeons of Spain, to a degree that Charles V, in the 1530s, congratulated a student of the University of Alcalá on being "the first hidalgo of Castile to become a medical man." The Jews were the only tax collectors and the principal taxpayers of the realm. They were the bankers, the merchants, the moneylenders, and the spearhead of the nascent capitalist class in Spain. Throughout the Middle Ages, they had been the intermediaries between the Christian and Moorish kingdoms, the *almojarifes,* or finance administrators, for the sundry kings who incessantly repeated that without their Jewish bureaucracy the royal finances would disappear, as they indeed did when the Jews left. The Jews served as ambassadors, public servants, and administrators of the royal patrimony. In fact, they took upon themselves what the Spanish nobility would not deign to accomplish, considering it beneath their dignity as hidalgos. This meant that after the edict of 1492, the converted Jews had to disguise or abandon their traditional occupations, since these openly branded them as people of "impure blood."

Who would take their place?

"ALL IS POSSIBLE"

In the fifteenth century, new ideas influenced physical reality as much as physical reality influenced the intellectual climate. The so-called discovery of America, whatever one might ideologically think about it, was a great triumph of scientific hypothesis over physical perception. Improve-

The Catholic Monarchs receiving a Jewish deputation before the expulsion of the Jews. 19th-century engraving, artist unknown

ments in navigation increased trade and communication among peoples, while the invention of the printing press aroused great curiosity and a growing thirst for knowledge about the world. Scientists wondered whether this planet of ours could really be the center of the universe. And they also wondered about the shape of the earth, while artists pondered the sense of the human presence on earth, including the shape of the human body, male and female, by celebrating the here and now rather than life eternal. "All is possible," wrote the Italian humanist Marsilio Ficino. "Nothing should be disdained. Nothing is incredible. Nothing is impossible. The possibilities that we deny are but the possibilities that we ignore."

Spain was as prepared as any other European culture to join in the élan of the Renaissance. The tricultural experience produced two great books that nourished the Renaissance spirit in Spain. The first is *The Book of Good Love, El libro de buen amor*, published in 1330 by a jovial itinerant priest, Juan Ruiz, the archpriest of Hita. His book is a song to the pleasures of the body, a celebration of the female form, and a refusal of sin. Deeply influenced by Arab poetry, Juan Ruiz is the Spanish Chaucer, and his conciliatory message is that faith and pleasure should not be at odds.

Even more significant, perhaps, is the tragicomedy *La Celestina*, written by Fernando de Rojas sometime after the expulsion of the Jews. It is the story of an old go-between, her female pupils, two young lovers, and their servants. A rambling, episodic, not to say itinerant play, it is set in the unprotected modern city, seen by Rojas as a sieve of historical reality, where the exemplary voices and virtues of medieval morality are defeated by money, passion, sex, interest. Everything and everyone moves in the modern city imagined by Rojas. But this energy leads only to death.

Rojas, the descendant of converted Jews, wrote his masterpiece as a student at the University of Salamanca, which saw itself as a humanistic alternative to the growing orthodoxy and intolerance of the Crown. When Rojas finally decided to publish his book in 1499, after much hesitation, he was supremely aware of the hard fate of his Jewish brethren. There was in this world, as *La Celestina* proclaimed, nothing but change and blind fate, leading everyone to a "bitter and disastrous end." It is a book that taught the Spanish people, says Ramiro de Maeztu, to live without ideals. The archpriest and Rojas were humanists who both dreamed and warned, clearly seeing the pitfalls of human action.

The expansion of Europe, toward the east first and then westward, was in a sense a feat of Renaissance imagination. It was also a triumph of hypothesis over perception, of imagination over tradition. Simple observation told us that the world was flat. Scientific hypothesis held that it was round. Science won out. In itself, this was quite a revolution.

The facts remained that the Mare Nostrum, the Mediterranean, had been to all effects and purposes an Islamic lake for nearly eight hundred years, and that European expansion was severely hindered by such mastery. To find a way out, a way around, a way toward the Orient became a European obsession. It began in the Venetian republic, with Marco Polo's opening of overland trade routes to China. But soon the rise of a new Muslim power, the Ottoman Empire, once more threatened the Mediterranean; the Ottomans captured Greece and the Balkans and forced Europe and its rising merchant class to look elsewhere.

From his castle in Sagres, on the Atlantic coast of Portugal, Prince Henry (1394–1460), the son of King John I, gathered together all of the nautical wisdom of his times, perfected cartography and navigational instruments, developed new, swift, easily maneuverable seafaring vessels such as the caravel, and trained crews to man them. Henry the Navigator, as he came to be known, had a grand design: to outflank the Turks by sailing south to Africa and then east to the Orient. With the help of Flemish bankers, Portugal hopped from Madeira to the Azores to Senegal, and finally, with Bartholomeu Dias, to the very extreme of the African continent, the Good Hope, in 1488. From there the Portuguese proceeded quickly to India (Vasco da Gama, 1498). Along the way, sugar was planted and slaves were recruited. In 1444, a slave-trading company was established in Lagos, under the patronage of Prince Henry.

But while Portugal looked east and south, it hesitated to look west over the Mare Ignotum — the Unknown Sea, the Ocean of Mystery — even when a headstrong sailor said to be of Genoese origin, cast ashore by a shipwreck near Prince Henry's castle, argued that the best way to reach the East was to sail west. The man was personally far less impressive than his work on many counts — feverish, at times uncontrolled, suspected of being a mythomaniac. But he certainly had courage and determination. His name was Cristoforo Colombo — Christopher Columbus — Cristóbal Colón. Portugal did not listen to him. He then headed for Spain, the isolated, inward-looking country fighting its protracted war of *reconquista,* and there, in a propitious moment, offered his plan to the Catholic Monarchs. Flushed with victory after the defeat of the Moors in Granada, Ferdinand and Isabella gave Columbus the means to achieve the third great event of that crucial year of Spanish history, 1492: the discovery of America.

A tiny fleet made up of three caravels, the *Pinta,* the *Niña,* and the *Santa María,* set off from the port of Palos on August 3, 1492. Sailing

El Almirante Christoval Colon Descubre la Isla Española,
ij haze poner una Cruz, etc.

Christopher Columbus landing on Hispaniola. Spanish engraving, artist unknown, 1728

westward, after sixty-six days of false hopes, shifting stars, phantom islands made of clouds, grumbling, and open mutiny, Columbus reached land: the tiny island of Guanahani, in the Bahamas, which he christened with the Savior's name, San Salvador. It was October 12, 1492, and Columbus thought that he was in Asia. Driven by courage, the desire for fame, the thrill of discovery, lust for gold, and the duty to evangelize, he made Europe see itself in the mirror of the Golden Age and the Good Savage. For the men and women of these islands were peaceful, innocent, and dazzled by glass beads and red bonnets. "They are very unskilled in arms," Columbus wrote in his journal. "With fifty men they could all be subjected." And so they were — kidnapped, murdered, and enslaved.

How are. we to understand the discovery of America? Aren't all discoveries basically mutual? The Europeans discovered the American continent, but the indigenous peoples of the Americas also discovered the Europeans, wondering whether these white and bearded men were gods or mortals. And whether they were as merciful as their crosses proclaimed or as merciless as their swords demonstrated.

For these men, coming out of the townships of medieval Spain — soldiers and clergymen, lawyers and chroniclers, sailors and artisans —

The meeting of Portuguese sailors and Brazilian natives, as drawn by Theodor de Bry

the conquest of the New World went to the heart of existence. They were the bearers of the energy of *la reconquista,* of hundreds of years of fighting against the infidel. They were the bearers of a militant faith and a militant politics.

After 1492, the Jews went to northern Europe, where their talents served Spain's Protestant enemies. The Arabs went back to Africa, mourning their exile from the gardens of the Alhambra, recalling the words of the mother of the last Moorish king of Granada, Boabdil: "Do not weep like a woman for what you did not defend like a man." But where would the rushing energy of Christian Spain channel itself? The energy, the movement, the sheer dynamics of army, church, royalty, city life, the burghers and the masses who walked to Santiago, fought at Las Navas de Tolosa, built Avila, traded in Burgos, defended the city rights of Toledo, elected the Cortes, and united the kingdoms — where would all of this rushing force go now?

The answer came from the townships and villages of Castile, Extremadura, and Andalusia. These were the hometowns of the conquistadors: Hernán Cortés, Francisco Pizarro, Pedro de Valdivia. These men sprang from the dry, parched hide of Spain and brought to the Americas church, army, a militant spirit, and a wrenching choice between the democratic traditions nurtured by the medieval townships and the authoritarian use and abuse of power soon to be confirmed by the united monarchy. They brought to the New World the dilemmas of the Spanish character, its image of sun and shadow dividing the soul as they divide the bullring. Tolerance or intolerance? Respect for the point of view of the other, the right to criticize and inquire, or the Inquisition? Ethnic mixture or racial purity? Central or local authority? Power from above or power from below? And, perhaps the question that contains them all, tradition or change? These alternatives would divide the Hispanic world, in Europe and in the Americas, for many centuries.

CONQUEST AND THE SOUL

In 1492, Ferdinand and Isabella were driven by a single-minded vision of Christian unity, reconquest, and expansion. Undoubtedly, their captains and soldiers overseas shared this vision. But they were also the heirs to a multicultural experience of coexistence, of commingling in tension with Jews and with Moors. All of the exceptions to tolerance cannot detract from the fact that the tendencies toward coexistence with and respect for others did structure a tricultural reality, which stood in stark contrast to the official policy of expulsion and denial of Jews and Moors.

The conquerors of the New World were a part of this reality, but they could not squirm away from the choice of Spain. The friars, writers, chroniclers, and polemicists who followed the conquistadors saw to it that Spain faced its humanistic and multicultural alternative. The country's cultural singularity was the recognition of the Other: battling him, embracing him, mixing with him. Hell, Jean-Paul Sartre once wrote, is other people. But is there any paradise other than the one we can fashion with our brothers and sisters? History begs the question, How to live with the Other? How to understand that I am what I am only because another person sees me or completes me?

This question, which rises every time that white and black, East and West, predecessor and immigrant, meet in our own times, was a central reality of medieval Spain and then became the central question of conquest and colonization in the Americas. It is a question forecast, however contradictorily, by the Spanish historical experience, from the Iberian conquest by Rome to the expulsion of the Jews in 1492. At that point it became the central question of the Americas, as Spain came into contact with the radically "other" — people of another race, another religion, another culture. Who were these people? What was the shape of their souls? Did they even have souls?

These questions divided Spain. And if one part of her heart said "Conquer!" the other part, remembering Seneca the Stoic, said, "Do not let yourself be conquered by anything except your soul." The stage was thus set for a tremendous clash of civilizations, a great epic, compassionate at times, bloody and ruthless at others, but always conflictive, as it both destroyed and created the culture of the New World.

PART II

THE CONFLICT
OF THE GODS

FIVE

The Rise and Fall
of the Indian World

Amerca was once an empty continent. Everyone who has ever set foot on our shores or crossed our borders, physical or imaginary, has come from somewhere else. Imagine, then, that some 130,000 years ago, vast masses of ice began shifting in the Arctic regions, with the result that the level of the Bering Sea descended and a great continental causeway was opened between Asia and America.

Over this bridge, on foot, small numbers of nomads entered the Western Hemisphere, 48,000 years ago. Carvers, hunters, cave dwellers, they chased the mammoth, before it became extinct. There were vast spaces to traverse, from mountain ranges to deserts to valleys and jungles. And there were rabbits and venison, boar and wild ducks — the game that Bernal Díaz was to describe in 1520.

Between 7500 and 2500 B.C., the development of agriculture turned the nomads into sedentary farmers, living in villages. It was Quetzalcoatl, the Plumed Serpent, the creator of humankind, who discovered the first grain of maize, with the help of an ant, succeeding where all the other gods had failed. No wonder that he was so honored in the Mesoamerican world: creator of man, of agriculture, of village society. For there was nothing at the beginning, say the most ancient chants of the empty continent. "When it was still night, in the dark, the gods assembled." And they created humankind. "Let there be light," exclaims the Mayan Bible, the *Popol Vuh.* "Let the dawn rise on heaven and earth. There shall be no glory until the human creature exists."

Humanity was born in sacrifice. When the gods met in the dawn of creation, they assembled around a vast fire. They decided that one of them should sacrifice himself by jumping into the conflagration. A beautiful god, arrogant and covered with jewels, hesitated in fear. A dwarfish god, naked and covered with ulcers, did not. He threw himself into the flames

Quetzalcoatl, the Plumed Serpent

Overleaf: *Detail from the Bonampak murals*

and promptly resurrected as the sun itself. On seeing this, the handsome god plunged into the fire as well, but he was rewarded by reappearing as the moon, the satellite. So was the universe created.

Because the gods had sacrificed themselves so that the world and humanity might exist, humanity was obligated to plunge, if needed, into the great, permanent bonfire of life and death. The need for sacrifice was an undoubted thing in Indian society, not subject to discussion or skepticism of any sort. For the ancient Americans, the forces of the universe were a constant source of danger as well as a constant source of the very survival that they menaced. This ambiguity was resolved in sacrifice, which was no more in doubt for them than the formula $E = mc^2$ is for us today. Not only the continuity of life, but the very order of the universe depended on it. We, women and men, are puny things indeed when set on the stage of the cosmos. But the universe itself is a fragile matter, being subjected as it is to life and death, to creation and destruction, to death and resurrection.

As it evolved from village to ceremonial center to city to empire, the aboriginal culture of Mesoamerica — the region stretching from central Mexico to Nicaragua — carried a set of beliefs in which the idea that the world had been created not once but several times was absolutely essential. Developed by the Aztecs as the legend of the five suns, it is told in their famous stone calendar, where the center of the disk is held by an image of the sun sticking its tongue out (which means that it is shining). The four cardinal points frame this image, indicating the previous four creations of the world and the catastrophes that wiped them out. The first sun was destroyed by a jaguar or tiger; the second sun, by the fierce winds; the third, by incessant rain; the fourth, by the waters of the great flood. The people were now living under the fifth sun, which was born of the sacrifice of the gods and which could continue only through the sacrifice of their creatures, men and women.

Only sacrifice would uphold the world, the sun, and thus life itself: continuity, the village, the family, work, agriculture, maize. Such a conception of reality naturally led to the fear that a catastrophe so recent, so well remembered by all aboriginal peoples, could repeat itself at any minute: the death of the fifth sun. Nature had to be both loved and feared. Time had to be both known and forecast. And power had to be given to those who knew, remembered, and forecast the future while holding at bay the destructive forces of nature.

Myth was the interpretation that explained this reality. The natural and supernatural forces so close to the skin of all living creatures were called gods, the cause of all things. Time and death thus became the axes

*An Aztec stone
calendar*

of the Indian world, the gods the cause of everything good and bad. The Indians elected as their leaders those who could listen to the gods, forecast time, and administer death in peace and in war. In this way, kings, priests, and warriors came to dominate the empty spaces of the Americas. They ordered the building of the ceremonial centers that served as shrines to the sometimes frightening duality of the gods and to the self-evident truths they embodied.

Like giant shadows cast by the fires of creation, these truths cover the succession of Indian civilizations of Mesoamerica from the early hunters, 6,000 years before Christ, to the beginnings of agricultural life, to village life around 1500 B.C., to the appearance of the "mother culture" of the Olmecs in the basin of the Papaloapan River (the River of Butterflies) on the Gulf Coast of Mexico around 900 B.C. The village culture then crept upward from the sea to the mountains of the Zapotec peoples in Oaxaca, the valleys of central Mexico, and became the first signs of the civilization of the Mayas, between the third century before Christ and the first century after.

Migrations and exoduses continued, the people bearing the fear of cosmic catastrophe. The need to respond creatively and sacrificially to it persisted throughout the six hundred years of the early classic periods of Teotihuacán in central Mexico and Monte Albán in Oaxaca, and through the preparation of the great period of Maya civilization, which grew and then collapsed between 600 and 900. It also persisted through the years of the early Middle Ages and the empire of Charlemagne in Europe. The final gasp of the Mayas at Chichén Itzá, the life and death of the Toltecs in central Mexico, followed by the rise of the Aztecs around 1325 and their downfall in 1521 at the hands of the Spanish, ended the historical cycle of the Mesoamerican civilizations but by no means, as we shall see, their cultural cycle.

Each of the great themes and certainties that fed and structured this world is evident in the Indians' magnificent constructions, comparable to those of Mesopotamia and ancient Egypt. They are, first of all, as their architecture reveals, a response to the question of nature: a human landscape of soaring temples dedicated to the gods. In Europe, the Romantic mind gave this question its modern shape. Goethe said of nature, "We live within her and we are foreign to her." Even more dramatically, Hölderlin imagined the anguish of the first man who became conscious of being part of nature, issued from nature, yet at the same time separate, distinct from nature, so that he could survive and identify himself. Built long before the Freudian fear of being captured or expelled became a cultural given, the great temples of Mesoamerican antiquity reveal this same uneasiness over being swallowed by a menacing nature or being left, shelterless, outside its embrace.

Palenque is the supreme example of this ambiguous response to nature. Sunk deep in the arms of the jungle of Chiapas, each building seems carved out of the primeval forest. Actually achieving this apogee in the seventh century and abandoned once more to nature's appetites in the eleventh century, Palenque's magnificent series of structures — the palace, the House of the Jaguar, and the Temples of the Sun, of the Cross, and of the Inscriptions — today seem forever tugged between the claims of the jungle and the claims of humanity, whereas up on the great plateau above the valley of Oaxaca, the ruins of Monte Albán are superbly, even abstractly, separate from nature. They seem to be suspended between heaven and earth, truly closer to the clouds and the sky than to any earthly bonds — until we take a second look and realize that Monte Albán is the eloquent visual evidence of its own equivalence with the landscape. It is almost as if the architecture were a replica of the surrounding mountains.

Palenque

Monte Albán

This second look permits us to answer the immediate question that arises on reaching this rarefied height. What was the function of a place such as this? Was it conceived as a ceremonial center, as a fortress, as a sanctuary, as a monument to the fallen in the civil wars that raged through Oaxaca? Or was it a memorial of the great epic of exodus and war at the root of life and movement in the empty continent? Whatever the case, the constant questions of the Indian mind are implicitly stated in Monte Albán: How long will we last? How can we build something that will protect us from destruction?

The response to nature led to the preoccupation with time, but this worry was quickly displaced by the power of man, who would see to it that time lasted, that natural chaos did not overtake the people once more. The murals of Bonampak, discovered as recently as 1946 in the jungles of southern Mexico, offer us a multicolored vision of a ritualistic world. Dominated by images of a princely child who is being offered as the ruler of future generations, they form an awesome panorama of power in the ancient Americas. Processions of priests and servants among the rulers and ruled permit us to see, as in a moving picture, human labor organized by an emerging caste of princes and clergymen. As agrarian villages became city-states and the cities expanded over a wider territory through warfare and conquest, demanding tribute — harvests and women — civilization began to organize itself to uphold the bureaucracy, the priesthood, and the army. Indeed, the Bonampak murals end in a cruel and overpowering vision of war: battle, death, enslavement. But they also hark back to the once and future king, the child prince who is being sanctified in the first mural. He will rule over this world, so strikingly depicted. He will rule in the manner described and for the stated purpose of maintaining human life, through the paradox of shedding blood in war and sacrifice.

The need to understand time was of paramount importance in such a world, for it meant the difference between survival and destruction. To dominate time was to assure the continuity of life. "Those who have the power to count the days," one of the Mayan poets said, "have the right to speak to the gods." At Chichén Itzá in Yucatán, Mayan astronomers established a precise solar calendar symbolized by the structure of the great pyramid. Nine terraces and four staircases represent the nine heavens and the four cardinal points. Each staircase has 91 steps, for a total of 364, plus the summit platform: 365, the number of days in the solar year. The greatest pyramid in Mesoamerica, the Temple of the Sun at Teotihuacán, is built in such a way that on the summer solstice the sun sets precisely in front of the main facade, so that nature and civilization can mirror themselves in celebration.

The Toltecs, builders of Teotihuacán, attempted to join this set of preoccupations — time and nature, power and survival — to a moral principle and found it once more in the figure of Quetzalcoatl. The Plumed Serpent was the creator of the human world, which was slowly and painfully born from chaos and fear. He gave human beings their tools and their crafts, and he taught them to polish jade, knit feathers, and plant corn. The myth further attributes to Quetzalcoatl the invention of architecture, agriculture, song and sculpture, mining, and jewelry. The body of his teachings came to be identified with the very name of the Toltecs, the Toltecayatl, or "totality of creation."

And so Quetzalcoatl became the moral hero of ancient Mesoamerica, in the same way that Prometheus was the hero of the ancient time of the Mediterranean — its liberator, even if liberation cost him his freedom. In the case of Quetzalcoatl, the freedom he brought to the world was the light of education — a light so powerful that it became the basis for legitimation of any potential successor state to the Toltec legacy.

THE EAGLE AND THE SERPENT

This successor state, and the final nation of the ancient Mesoamerican world, was that of the Aztecs. The long march of these people from the deserts of North America through Arizona and Chihuahua down into central Mexico was fixed by the vision of an eagle devouring a serpent on a cactus on an island in a lake. They were driven to this place by their ferocious god of war, Huitzilopochtli, whose name means "the Hummingbird Wizard," and by the priest Tenoch. When they arrived, around A.D. 1325, the Aztecs founded their city, Tenochtitlán, on the swamplands and islands of Lake Texcoco. They added the prefix "Mexico" to it, which means "the navel of the moon." (Today, Mexico City is the oldest continuously inhabited city in the Americas.) According to the chronicles, the Aztecs were despised by the established settlers in the central valley, descendants of the Toltecs, who called them "the last people to come" and said that "everyone persecuted them," "no one wished to receive them," "they had no face."

This facelessness contrasted with the highly visible cultural profile of the Toltecs, the tribe that had mysteriously disappeared around the time that construction of Canterbury Cathedral began, windmills were introduced to Britain, and Chrétien de Troyes wrote *Parsifal*: the second half of the twelfth century. The Toltecs too left behind an ensemble of

One of the
Bonampak murals
in the jungle of
Chiapas

The great pyramid
at Chichén Itzá

creations deemed to be the most valuable of the Indian world. In fact, the very designation "Toltec" was synonymous with "artist." It was the culture of the exiled god, Quetzalcoatl; it was the highest and most desirable inheritance in the Indian world; and the Aztecs, as they spread their power throughout the central valley of Mexico with the instruments of war, exaction, and human sacrifice, were prompt to seize on the Toltec heritage.

They needed power. They also needed legitimation of their power, moral legitimacy in addition to military might. This equation, which bound the politics of the Aztecs, also pitted the two gods, Quetzalcoatl, god of creation and brotherhood, and Huitzilopochtli, god of war and conquest, against each other.

Huitzilopochtli, the
Aztec god of war

Toltec art and morality gave the Aztecs the face they had been seek-ing. But if memory and identity demanded this, power and legitimacy combated it. In the fifteenth century, Tlacaelel, son and brother of kings, who never accepted the crown himself, organized what came to be known as the Aztec Empire through traditional means. He distributed lands and titles, set up the administration (including the exacting system of tributes and taxes), and initiated conquests that took the Aztecs as far south as Guatemala, Honduras, and Nicaragua. He also built the great temple to Huitzilopochtli in Mexico-Tenochtitlán, devoting the might of the Aztec nation to the principles of war and sacrifice. He ordered the burning of the ancient writings of the peoples defeated by the Aztecs, because in them the latter were described as barbarians. History was burned, but this Orwellian travesty was coupled with an anxiety to be seen as the heir of Quetzalcoatl.

Coatlicue, the earth goddess

The pantheon of Aztec divinities brings back, with a terrifying sense of actuality, the chaos, the force, and the terror bound to assault any human being who comes face to face with the time of the origins. The central figure in this pantheon is the mother goddess, Coatlicue, "the Lady of the Skirt of Snakes." Square, decapitated, with no anthropomorphic features, Coatlicue was created in the image of the unknown. The ele-ments of her decoration can be called, separately, skulls, snakes, lacerated hands. But they fuse into a composition of the unknown. She admits no cracks in her body. She is the perfect monolith, a totality of intensity, self-contained.

As the myth goes, Coatlicue, the earth mother, was first impregnated by an obsidian knife and gave birth to Coyolxauhqui, goddess of the moon, and to a brood of male siblings, which became the stars. Then one day Coatlicue found a ball of feathers, which she tucked carefully into her bosom. When she looked for it later, it was gone, and she discovered that she was once again with child. Her children, the moon and the stars, did not believe her story. Ashamed of their mother, whom they believed to be guilty of promiscuity, they resolved to kill her. A goddess could only give birth once, to the original litter of divinity and no more. A second litter of gods was a monstrosity. But while they were plotting, Coatlicue gave birth to the fiery god of war, Huitzilopochtli. With the help of a fire serpent, he destroyed his brothers and sister, murdering them in a rage. He decapitated Coyolxauhqui and plunged her body down a deep gorge in a mountain, where it lies dismembered forever.

This myth illustrates the certainty that the natural cosmos of the Indians was born of catastrophe. The heavens literally crumbled to pieces;

the earth mother fell and was fertilized while her children were torn apart by fratricide and then scattered, disjointed, throughout the universe. But the sculpture of Coatlicue is an artistic form which, even if born from a myth, no longer fulfills a religious function. It has become a part of the artistic imagination, so that beyond its sacred origins, what we now see is a modern, ambivalent composition. Reality is sundered but claims reintegration at the same time, much as in cubist paintings. Imagining the gods, the anonymous sculptor of such a piece, like his equally anonymous and religiously inspired counterparts in Europe during the Gothic period, created a timeless work of art, which is fully appreciated beyond its religious context only in our own time. The condition for this is that of all great art. True artists not only reflect reality; they add something new to it.

Between the stones and the hands that fashioned them, the Indian artists established a form of communication that finally became universal. Not only did André Breton see in the ancient art of Mexico an expression of surrealism; far more concretely, the British sculptor Henry Moore found inspiration in the Chac Mool figures of ancient Mexico and based his splendid series of recumbent statues on them. Because of their connection with an ancient tradition, these became some of the most representative and unforgettable works of the modern tradition. What Moore said of his own art can be said of the great sculptures of ancient Mexico: if a sculptor understands the material he has to work with, he can transform a closed block of matter into an animated composition of masses that expand and contract, push and overlap.

Caught between sheer air and the dynamism of stone, these sculptures are products of a plurality of realisms, a multiplicity of visions that are deemed equally real as they manifest themselves in art. The great colossal heads of the Olmecs (the heads of La Venta, Tabasco) are strikingly negroid, to the extent that they make us wonder if the Caribbean was originally settled by black emigrants. Yet we must wonder what is more important, the probable religious or ethnic background of the art or its contemporary presence among us? Ultimately, no facet of this art excludes the other: reality is multiple.

Albrecht Dürer, the German painter, was the first European artist to see the work of the Aztecs when it arrived in Brussels in 1520, on the way to the Flemish court of Charles V. "I also saw the things that were sent to the king from the golden lands. . . . It is a marvel to behold," he noted in his *Travel Diary to the Netherlands*, concluding, "Never in my life have I seen anything which has made my heart happier." More than three

Reclining Figure. *Henry Moore*

Chac Mool at Chichén Itzá

*A colossal Olmec
head at Tabasco*

centuries later, again in Brussels, Charles Baudelaire saw pictures of the Aztec sculptures and concluded that they belonged to a "barbaric art," barbaric in the sense of being totally alien to the concept of human personality.

Looking at these great monuments of the Indian past and trying to understand both their beauty and their political function, one is tempted to ask, in the words of the Chilean poet Pablo Neruda, "Stone in the stone, but where was man?" Beyond and below the gods, priests, and warriors, swarming all around, was a whole society, alive and sentient, surrounding the pyramids and creating the continuity of popular culture in the Americas. This tradition was to become one of the strongest realities with which these societies countered the clash with Europe.

Perhaps the answer to Neruda's question lies in the myriad artifacts of popular art created by the Mesoamerican peoples, at the village level and over thousands of years. Humanity is in the smiling, perhaps mocking "little faces" of the Olmecs, in the fun and games of figures that look to us like wrestlers, acrobats, and even baseball players, in the emphasis on the symbolic continuity of life in the figures of old men, fertile women, and young children. Perhaps it is to be found in the infinite elegance and finesse of the figures of Jaina, an island off the coast of Yucatán: ladies, orators, salesmen, farmers, beggars and boasters. All the characters of daily life were crafted, given a place and a presence over the centuries. Perhaps eternal beauty is best preserved in the most fragile objects, the ceramics, vases, and pottery, and the stylized representations of animals and birds. The splendid menagerie of the early Olmecs lives on in their figurines of ducks, crocodiles, monkeys, tapirs, armadillos, and jaguars. Indeed, the jaguar figure, which strides over the whole span of Indian Mexico, is a counterpoint to the delightful little Olmec dogs, the parrots and turtles of the Occidental cultures, the frightening Zapotec bats, the carnelian Aztec grasshoppers, or the utterly stylized, almost abstract, Brancusi-like fish-vessels from Tlatilco.

We can still see this undying culture in the bearing, the dignity, of the Indians' contemporary descendants and in the unceasing production of their artisans. This is the people's response to the power of the gods and potentates: the values of community, the love of the earth and nature, work, and respect for one another. Even when their cities withered and died, the people survived. And so, perhaps more mysteriously, did their art, even when it was not a humanistic or popular art at all, but rather an awesome, unearthly celebration of the divine, of death, and of time.

Indeed, in the name of Quetzalcoatl, Aztec society kept alive the cult

*Jaina figures: a
lady, an orator, a
bird, and a jaguar*

of life through its educational system, which was universal and obligatory, and through the exhortations said at weddings, births, deaths, and elections. Aztec poets, but also fathers and mothers addressing their children, loved ones addressing their spouses or their dead, and elders selecting their kings, spoke of this earth as a place of sad happiness, a happiness that hurts, a hostile and mysterious place, where life is but a dream, all is passing, and only death is sure. But this should not be a reason for despair, they said, for we have laughter, dreams, food, our health, and finally the sexual act, celebrated as "the seed of peoples."

The great festivals of the Aztec world were but the external, ceremonial expression of the interlocking relationship between fate and nature, life lived as a myth, a myth that was not only represented but vitally believed in and acted out. For example, consider the story of what happened when Quetzalcoatl provoked the envy of the lesser gods of the Indian pantheon. As the myth goes, one of these, a dark, eternally young puck named Tezcatlipoca, whose name means "smoking mirror," said to the other devils, "Let us visit Quetzalcoatl, bearing a gift for him." So they went to the god's palace in the city of Tula and handed him the gift, wrapped in cotton.

"What is it?" wondered Quetzalcoatl as he unwrapped it.

It was a mirror. The god saw his reflection and screamed. He thought that being a god, he had no face. Now, reflected in the mirror, he saw his own face. It was, after all, a man's face, the face of his own creature. Since he had a human face, he realized, he must also have a human destiny.

The nocturnal demons vanished, shrieking gleefully, and that night Quetzalcoatl drank himself into a stupor and fornicated with his sister. The next day, full of shame, he embarked on a raft of serpents, sailing to the east and promising to return on a fixed day — Ce Acatl, the Day of the Reed in the Indian calendar. When fate and nature coincided under the sign of fear, the Indian universe would be shaken to its very roots, and the whole world would be afraid of losing its soul.

This is precisely what happened when, following a frightful series of auguries, the Spanish captain Hernán Cortés landed on the coast of the Gulf of Mexico, on Maundy Thursday, 1519.

THE RETURN OF QUETZALCOATL

The time was right. As Ce Acatl, the Day of the Reed, approached, the Aztec world was filled with portents. The waters of the lake on which Tenochtitlán was built churned up gigantic waves, toppling houses and towers. Comets streaked for long hours across the sky. Mirrors reflected a starry sky at noon. Strange women roamed the streets at midnight, crying over the death of their children and the loss of the world. Even the closest allies of the Aztec emperor, Moctezuma, after observing the skies night after night, knew that the prophecies were coming true, that the sea, the mountains, and the air were trembling with premonition. Quetzalcoatl was about to return.

So certain was the king of Texcoco that the prophecy of the blond, blue-eyed god was about to become reality that he abandoned his reign, dismissed his armies, and told everyone to enjoy what little time was left. And the emperor, who rarely wore the same clothes twice and was waited upon by a multitude of servants and maidens, went into penance, sweeping his palace with a broom and dressed only in a loincloth, as omens of disaster accumulated over the terrified city. Was the time of the fifth sun about to end?

Moctezuma's anguish was temporarily assuaged when a messenger arrived from the coast and told him that floating houses had approached from the east, bearing men dressed in gold and silver and riding four-legged beasts. These men were white, bearded, some of them even blond and blue-eyed. Moctezuma sighed. No more anguish. The gods had returned. The prophecy had been fulfilled.

But Hernán Cortés did not see himself as a god. He was a man, and his will to action propelled him to act on human terms, employing to the hilt his sagacity and his information. He had set sail from Cuba in the spring of 1519, with an expedition of eleven ships. On board were 508 soldiers, 16 horses, and several pieces of artillery. On Holy Thursday, he moored his ships off the Gulf coast and founded the city of Veracruz, in the name of Emperor Charles V. In a matter of days, another emperor, Moctezuma, received the news. Who was this Spanish captain, who suddenly found himself treated as a god?

When Cortés arrived in Mexico, he was just thirty-four years old.

He was born in the town of Medellín, in the province of Extremadura, where his father had fought the Moors during the final stages of *la recon-quista*. Now the elder Cortés was the modest owner of a mill, a vine, and a beehive. Along with his wife, who is described as an honest and religious woman, he scrimped and saved and sent his son to the University of Salamanca, where he failed as a student but read the novels of chivalry and heard the fabulous accounts of the discovery of America. His head became forever filled with the dream of the New World.

At nineteen he sailed to the Indies and there became a modestly successful landowner. But Cortés had not come to the New World to repeat the destiny of his father in the Old World. He had come to fashion his own destiny, a destiny of power, wealth, and glory, achieved not through inheritance but through personal determination, aided by a bit of good luck. The perfect Machiavellian blend of willpower and fortune, Hernán Cortés was to become one of the greatest figures of the European Renaissance as he embarked on one of the epic adventures of all time: the conquest of the Aztec Empire.

To begin with, there were constant skirmishes with the local tribes along the coast. Their chieftains came to realize that the intruders, whoever they were, were not to be defeated in battle. *They are armed with lightning,* the Indian informers sent word, *and they belch smoke.* So the chieftains brought gifts of gold and other precious objects. Then one day Cortés was presented with a tribute of a different kind. A gift of twenty slave girls arrived at the Spanish encampment, and out of these Cortés chose one.

Described by the chronicler of the expedition, Bernal Díaz del Castillo, as outgoing, meddlesome, and beautiful, this woman's Indian name was Malintzin, a word that indicated that she had been born under the signs of strife and misfortune, whereupon her parents had sold her off as a slave. The Spanish named her Marina, "she who came from the sea." But her people called her La Malinche, the conquistador's woman, the traitress. Whatever name she was given, she was faced with an extraordinary destiny. She became *"mi lengua,"* my tongue, for Cortés, who took her as his interpreter and lover.

Through La Malinche, Cortés found out that a great king called Moctezuma lived in a magnificent city up in the mountains. His armies, lined up in a field, would cover it like the waves of the sea. He had thirty vassal kings. But they hated Moctezuma, La Malinche claimed, and could quickly be persuaded to change their allegiance to someone who proved more powerful than the Aztecs. The Aztecs had conquered most of the other tribes of Central America, but their domination was based on terror,

Cortés and
Malinche.
*José Clemente
Orozco, 1926*

not on the support of the people, and some of the kingdoms, such as Tlaxcala, had even managed to retain their independence, doing constant battle with the power of Mexico and preparing themselves for the time of vengeance.

Cortés quickly made up his mind. He would march up toward Tenochtitlán to see Moctezuma, and then he would turn the discontent of the people in his favor. However, though the captain was ready to march, his troops were not. Skirmishes were taking their toll. Bread was becoming scarce, as were salt and bacon. Some feared the cold of the mountains; others complained of the weight of the armor. But Cortés refused to turn around and return with empty hands. He knew that the Spanish soldiers were divided between desire for fame and wealth and fear of defeat and death.

"We're only five hundred," they beseeched Cortés.

His response: "Then our hearts must be doubly courageous."

"We are dying of fevers and Indian attacks," others complained.

"Then let us bury our dead at night, so our enemies will think we are immortal."

"Let us go back to Cuba. Let us sail back," some said, in open mutiny.

"But there are no ships," Cortés answered. "I have sunk them. There is no way but up; there is no retreat. We must go forward to Mexico and see if this Moctezuma is as great as he proclaims himself to be."

So the soldiers cheered and acclaimed Hernán Cortés as their leader, and they began the march toward the city of Moctezuma. Along the way, Cortés had to prove that he was not only a military conqueror but a Christian who would spread the faith and destroy the abominable idolatry of the heathen Indians. In Cholula, the greatest pantheon of the Aztec Empire, he destroyed the statues and massacred the people, invoking reasons both religious and political. (La Malinche had informed him that the heathen priests of Cholula were conspiring to murder the Spaniards.)

Between his Spanish duties as a Christian soldier and the Indian illusion of him as a god, Cortés had to choose, finally, the former. But if his image as a god was beginning to tarnish, his military prowess was reaffirmed in the battles between the Spaniards and the forces of Tlaxcala at the gates of Tenochtitlán. The brave Tlaxcallans, fiercely independent of the Aztecs, did not wish to exchange one domination for another. They defied Cortés and were crushed, in spite of their superior numbers, by the superior European weaponry.

The real reward for Cortés and the Spaniards lay in the awesome sight of the city on the lake. "We stood in wonderment," wrote Bernal Díaz, "and told each other that this resembled the enchantments told in the book of Amadís . . . and some of our soldiers even said that perhaps they were seeing all of this as through a dream."

Then Moctezuma came forth to receive them on the causeway that led into the city, clinging to the belief that Cortés was the god Quetzalcoatl. "Welcome. We have been waiting for you. This is your home."

LA NOCHE TRISTE

Rarely has there been a meeting of such contrasting personalities in history. It was an encounter between a man who had everything and a man who had nothing — an emperor likened to the sun, upon whose face his subjects could not gaze, and with the title of Tlatoani, He of the Great Voice, and a soldier with no greater treasure than his wits and his will. Moctezuma was ruled by fate: the gods had returned. Cortés was ruled by will: he would achieve his goals against all odds.

Cortés soon found out that Moctezuma had chambers in his palace where even the walls were made of gold. He promptly repaid the Indian monarch's hospitality by taking him prisoner and melting down the gold. Everywhere, he destroyed the idols and erected Christian altars. And his henchman, Pedro de Alvarado, after cheating Moctezuma at dice, massacred the unarmed populace at a religious festival.

Were these really gods? No, the people finally realized. They were greedy, cruel foreign invaders, and they could be defeated. During the battle of La Noche Triste, the Sad Night, the Indians, led by Moctezuma's nephew Cuauhtémoc, drove the Spaniards out of Tenochtitlán. Many were drowned in the canals, trying to flee with knapsacks bulging with gold. Cortés himself sat at the foot of a tree and wept. But he returned, having built ships on the lake to attack the city, and with the full confidence that information plus superior technology would eventually guarantee European triumph.

While the Aztecs, under Cuauhtémoc, fought bravely, theirs was still a sacred world whose fall had been forecast by the ancient books of memory. "Prepare yourselves, oh my little brothers, for the white twin of heaven has come, and he will castrate the sun, bringing the night, and sadness, and the weight of pain." Such was the prophecy to be found in the Mayan *Chilam Balam*, a codex formed of mystical texts, chronologies, and prophecies attributed to the priest Chilam Balam.

Cortés finally vanquished the Aztec capital, after a bloody siege, in 1521. It was, in the words of the historian Hugh Thomas, one of the world's great battles. Not only did the conquest of Mexico destroy the greatest center of Indian power and religion in North America at the time,

*The meeting
between Cortés and
Moctezuma at
Tenochtitlán,
November 8, 1519.
Artist unknown*

it also staged, in the figures of Cortés and Moctezuma, one of the greatest clashes between opposing civilizations that the world has ever known.

The conquest was more than an astonishing success for a band of fewer than six hundred European soldiers confronting a theocratic empire. It was the victory of the *other Indians* over the Aztec overlord. It was the victory of the Indian world against itself, since the results of the conquest meant genocide and slavery. But it was also, as we shall see, a defeat of the victor.

Even when the Spaniards proved beyond all doubt that they were not gods but quite rapacious and vicious human beings, Moctezuma did not falter in his fatalistic acceptance of their divinity. If he was a prisoner, his jailers were gods. If he and his people were despoiled, the gods were only taking back what was theirs. When he was finally stoned to death by his own people, in June of 1520, he had already accepted this as his fate. He knew that power was not to be shared with gods. Moctezuma and his predecessors had sat alone on top of the pyramid of Mexico for almost two hundred years. They ignored many things, but they knew that Mexico's power was exercised vertically, and it was exercised by one man. There was no place for more than one ruler on the pinnacle of the pyramid. This is as true today as it was in 1519.

All of the Indian societies of the Americas, whatever their political failings, were young, creative civilizations. The Spanish conquest arrested them, stunted their growth, and left them with a legacy of sadness, which one hears in the "visions of the defeated," as the compiler of their writings, Miguel León-Portilla, calls them. This sadness was sung by the ragged poets of the defeated Indian world:

> Where shall we go now, oh my friends?
> The smoke is rising, the fog is spreading.
> Cry, my friends.
> The waters are red.
> Cry, oh cry, for we have lost the Aztec nation.

The time of the fifth sun was at an end.

As for the conquerors, they could echo these words, for what they had at first admired, they had now destroyed. But when it was all over, when the emperor Moctezuma had been silenced, when the conquistador himself, Hernán Cortés, had been silenced by the Crown of Spain, which denied him political power as a reward for his military exploits, perhaps only the voice of La Malinche remained. She was the interpreter, but also the lover, the woman, of Cortés, and in these roles she established the basis of our multiracial civilization. She bore the child of the conqueror, the first mestizo, the first American of mixed blood. She was symbolically the mother of the first Mexican, the first child of Indian and Spanish blood. And she spoke the new language that she learned from Cortés, the Spanish language, a language of rebellion and hope, of life and death, which was to become the strongest link between the descendants of Indians, Europeans, and Africans in the American hemisphere.

topa ynga yupanqui   mama bello coya

lleuan al ynga los yndis callaua
ya - españo
apasearse

pascase el ynga   como

SIX

The Conquest and Reconquest of the New World

Eight years before the conquest of Mexico, on September 25, 1513, Vasco Núñez de Balboa had discovered the Pacific Ocean, opening the way for new conquests and discoveries to the south.

In 1530 Francisco Pizarro sailed from Panama with his half-brothers Hernando, Juan, and Gonzalo and two hundred men, landed on the coast of Ecuador, and after an extremely long and meandering expedition plagued by skirmishes, epidemics, and hesitations, entered Peru in September of 1532. The Europeans quickly discovered that the country was ravaged by civil war. The legitimate ruler, Huáscar, had been defeated by his half-brother, the usurper Atahualpa, who had murdered Huáscar and all of his family in cold blood. Atahualpa was camped outside the city of Cajamarca, so Pizarro swiftly went into the town, sending an invitation to the Peruvian lord, known as the Inca, to meet with him.

Trusting the Spaniards and believing, perhaps, in his own immortality, Atahualpa approached the town unarmed. Besides, it was said, he could not resist the beauty and novelty of the horses. Francisco de Xerez, acting as secretary to Pizarro (who was illiterate), left us this striking portrait of the Indian emperor: "Atahualpa was a man of thirty years, good-looking and poised, somewhat stout, with a wide, handsome and ferocious face, and the eyes flaming with blood. He discussed vividly . . . and although crude, he was gay."

As Atahualpa approached Pizarro, the Spaniards came rushing out of the houses where they were hidden. The astonished Indian retinue tried to protect the Inca, but the Spaniards cut off their hands as they held Atahualpa's litter. Not one of the Spanish soldiers was killed or even wounded. As with the conquest of Mexico, two factors came together to defeat the Indian nation: myth and weaponry. On his deathbed, Atahualpa's father, the Inca Huayna Capac, had prophesied that bearded men

Guamán Poma de Ayala line drawing of 16th-century Peru

would soon come over the sea and destroy the world of the Incas. These men would be messengers of the main Incan god, Viracocha, who, like Quetzalcoatl, created humanity and then sailed off to the west, promising to return. The lack of efficient weapons further determined the Indians' fate. In the words of John Hemming, the armies of Peru "could never produce a weapon that could kill a mounted, armored Spanish horseman."

As a ransom for his freedom, the captured emperor offered Pizarro enough gold to fill a large hall, "as high as he could reach." When the gold arrived — more than two hundred loads of it — the conquerors melted it down into bars. As for Atahualpa, Pizarro's promise to release him was never kept. He was simply given the choice between being burned alive as a pagan and becoming a Christian before being strangled. He chose to be baptized. It is said that his last words were "My name is Juan. That is my name to die with."

AN ORGANIZED MAGIC

The conquest of Peru was something of a paradox. As fulminating as a blitzkrieg, it seemed to be over the minute it began, with Pizarro's capture and execution of Atahualpa and then with the Spaniards' rapid advance over a country that was crisscrossed by a magnificent network of highways. But the fact is that in spite of the Spaniards' early successes (although they did seal the fate of the empire of the Incas), the conquest was a protracted affair, far longer than the conquest of Mexico. It was long, in the first place, because of Indian resistance. Slowly organizing themselves after the death of Atahualpa, the Indians blossomed forth between 1536 and 1544, constantly harassing the Spaniards until the death of the Incan leader, Manco Inca Yupanqui. The resistance was then taken up by his children, until one of them, Tupac Amarú, was beheaded by the Spanish in 1572, forty years after Pizarro's ambush of Atahualpa at Cajamarca.

The Spanish conquest was also besieged from within, by the constant civil wars between the conquistadors, savagely disputing over gold and political power, and between the conquistadors and the Crown, as the viceroys tried to establish royal authority and respect for the humanitarian Laws of the Indies. In both instances, the conquistadors saw a menace against their right of conquest, which of course included the right to plunder and to usurp land and labor. The destinies of the Pizarros speak for themselves. Francisco, the leader, the brutal former swineherd from Extremadura, was murdered by supporters of his rival, Diego de Almagro. His half-brother Hernando, returning to Spain, was imprisoned for twenty years, while another half-brother, Gonzalo, rebelled against the viceroy and was executed in 1578. Román y Zamora, in his *Republics of the Indies,* calls the Pizarros "the worst men who ever set out from any nation and who, with their comrades, brought the greatest dishonor to the kings of Spain."

This nervous contraction of Peruvian history between the precipitate and the protracted, the hare and the turtle, is like a spasm hiding the true rhythm of the country and the culture that the Spaniards conquered. And it is around the greatest city of the Incas, Cuzco, that many of the conflicts between Indian and Indian, Spaniard and Indian, Spaniard and Spaniard, took place. A city of perhaps 200,000 people on the eve of the conquest, Cuzco, along with the hidden fortress city higher up in the Andes, Machu Picchu, was the final witness to the glory of the Incas. We still marvel at the precision with which these cities' walls, made of polygonal stones, were fit tightly together without benefit of mortar. When the stones were too heavy, they were left by the wayside and called "tired stones" — not wearier, surely, than those who carried them.

From Cuzco, a system of communications unparalleled in the ancient world and perhaps comparable only to the Romans' spread over nearly 25,000 miles, all the way from Quito in Ecuador south to Chile and Argentina. This was the largest of all political states in pre-Columbian America. But the extension of the empire was complicated by the variety of its climates and terrains. Called by the historian Jean Descola "a three-faced land," Peru is part coastal (desert and fire), part mountainous (air and heaven), and part jungle (forest and river). Both fertile oases and sterile deserts existed between the coast and the highlands. Some welcomed the cultivation of cotton and corn; others produced the potato, Peru's gift to Europe. And in the highlands, Peru developed the only livestock culture of the Americas, the world of the llama, the guanaco, and the alpaca, the constant companions of the highland Indians — almost as constant as the music of the *quena,* the melancholy flute of the Andes.

To unite and govern this immense, variegated land required enormous gifts of statesmanship and a most energetic organization. Ancient Peru had both. The bureaucracy was vast and closely watched; the emperor himself traveled widely over his roads, preceded or followed by secret agents, checking matters and ordering displacements of population to inhabit newly conquered territories or army campaigns to subdue rebellions. But as in ancient Mexico, the bureaucracy and the army were in

Machu Picchu

Stones at Cuzco

the end the arms of a theocratic rule, in which religion gave true legitimacy to the empire. This religion, in acute contrast to the plodding, austere, workmanlike organization of society, was one of myth, magic, and metamorphosis.

Perhaps the greatest enigma of the Indian cultures of Peru was not perceived until our own time, thanks to the airplane, for only from the air can the human eye see the lines of the Nazca, a colossal geometrical design with a mysterious message from the depths of time. The Nazca lines, inscribed in the valleys of southern Peru, are a mysterious telegram about the life and death of ancient Peru, and like the lines of fate in a human palm, they continue to veil the truths about those who made them. Yet the Nazca's enigma defies us to find the logic behind a culture that was based on magic and cosmological vision but could at the same time propose a new structure for human beings in society with such exactitude and success.

The question of the land was of paramount importance. The basic division set apart the lands of the Sun, which were those cultivated by all and for all, and the lands of the Inca, which were meant to sustain the

The Nazca lines

king and the state. But in theory all land belonged to the state, which yielded use of it to the communities. These were based on a unit called the *ayllu,* a clan related by blood ties and organized as a cell stronger than the family (or the individual) to exploit collectively a vast, bountiful, but hostile environment. Talk about Incan socialism is interesting but perhaps irrelevant for an economy devoid of money but élitist in structure. The Inca at the summit, the superior castes of earringed aristocrats (the *ore-jones,* or big-ears, as the Spanish called them), and the *curacas,* or provincial chieftains, were certainly at the top of the successive family organizations, which ranged from ten-family groupings at the very bottom, ruled by a family chieftain, to forty-thousand-family organizations near the top, ruled by a governor. But an individual who distinguished himself could be co-opted into a superior rank, and private property existed as a reward for merit, while individual fortunes tended to be erased as generations succeeded each other and the land became subdivided among descendants.

The death of the infant Indian civilizations of the Americas was a loss to the West, especially in Peru, since they were not barbarous, heathen nations but nascent human societies with many lessons for Renaissance Europe. The Old World was also grappling with new forms of social coexistence, and even projected many of its most idealistic notions onto the New World. In the tension between the illusions of Utopia and the realities of conquest, another tension arose, from the beginning of our post-Indian existence in the Americas. The naked facts of conquest were answered by the more secret and insinuating facts of counterconquest. Both the defeated Indian peoples and the mestizos, eventually joined by the African arrivals in the New World, began a process of conquering the conquerors, thus fostering the rise of a properly American, multiracial, polycultural society.

UNDER THE SIGN OF UTOPIA

The Renaissance had reopened for all Europeans the political possibilities of the Christian community. It reopened the theme of the City of Man, which had been overshadowed during the Middle Ages by the importance given to the City of God. The Renaissance man now asked, How should human society be organized? Is there a place where the divine project and the human project meet in harmony? Thomas More, the author of *Utopia* (1516), answered in the very title of his work that there is no such place; *ou topos* is *nowhere.* But the European imagination promptly responded, Now there is such a place. It is America.

America was not discovered, it was invented, according to the Mex-

ican historian Edmundo O'Gorman. It was invented by European imagination and desire because it was needed. There *must* be a happy place, a
restored Golden Age, where man lives in accordance with the laws of
nature. Columbus described an earthly paradise in his letters to Queen
Isabella. But he believed, after all, that he had merely found the ancient
world of Cathay and Cipango, the empires of China and Japan. Amerigo
Vespucci, the Florentine explorer, was the first European to say that our
continent was in actuality a New World. We deserve his name. It was he
who firmly rooted Utopia in America. Utopia is not nowhere, it is a
society, and its inhabitants live communally and scorn gold.

"The people live in agreement with nature," Vespucci wrote in his
Novus Mundus of 1503. "They have no property; instead, all things are
held in community." And if they have no property, they have no need for
government. "They live without king and without any form of authority,
and each one is his own master," he concluded, confirming the perfect
anarchist Utopia of the New World for its Renaissance audience.

From that moment on, the Utopian visions of Renaissance Europe
would be confirmed by the discoveries in the Americas. "O brave new
world, that hast such people in 't!" exclaimed Shakespeare in *The Tempest*.
Montaigne, in France, shared this sentiment. The people of the New
World, he wrote, "are said to live under the sweet liberty of nature's first
and uncorrupted laws." The first chronicler of Columbus's expedition,
Pedro Mártir d'Anghera, echoed that "they go naked . . . and live in a
golden age, simple and innocent, without laws, quarrels, or money, con-
tent to satisfy nature." And the first chronicler of Brazil, Pedro Vaz de
Caminha, wrote to the king of Portugal in 1500, "Sire, the innocence of
Adam himself was no greater than that of these people."

But on the Sunday before Christmas in 1511, the Dominican friar
Antonio de Montesinos mounted the pulpit of a church on the island of
Hispaniola and lashed out at his scandalized Spanish parishioners: "Tell
me, by what right do you keep these Indians in cruel servitude? . . . You
are in mortal sin for the cruelty and tyranny you deal out to these innocent
people. . . . Are these not men? Have they not rational souls?"

Indeed, many colonizers, and their anti-Utopian defenders in Europe, denied that the aboriginal men and women of the Americas had any
souls or were human beings at all. Foremost among them was the Spanish
humanist and translator of Aristotle, Juan Ginés de Sepúlveda, who in
1547 (that is, after the peoples of Mexico and Peru had been conquered
by the Europeans) quite simply denied the Indians any true humanity and
gave the Spaniards every right in the world to conquer them: "It is with
perfect right that the Spanish dominate these barbarians of the New

World . . . who are so inferior to the Spanish in prudence, intelligence, virtue, and humanity, as children are to adults, or women to men, that I am tempted to say that there is between us both as much difference as between . . . monkeys and men." He concluded that "nothing more healthy could have occurred to these barbarians than to be subjected to the empire of those [the Spaniards] whose prudence, virtue, and religion shall convert the barbarians, who hardly deserve the name of human beings, into civilized men, as far as they can become so." Thanks to the Spanish conquest, the Indians would go from being "impious" and "serfs of the Devil" to "Christian adorers of the true God."

Throughout the history of Spanish America, the dream of paradise and the noble savage has coexisted with the history of colonization and forced labor. The illusion of the Renaissance has persisted in spite of everything that has denied it, becoming a constant of Spanish American thinking and desire. We were founded as a Utopia; Utopia is our destiny.

However, the newfound lands were not precisely the source of ideal societies but the source of inexhaustible wealth. Columbus insisted on the abundance of woods, pearls, and gold. The conclusion was that the New World was *only* nature. It was an ahistorical Utopia; civilization and humanity were absent from it. This conclusion begs the question of whether Faith and Civilization had to be given to the American Indians by the Europeans. It also begs the question of whether the American Indians had to transform the New World into a literal City of Gold by laboring in the mines and fields of these lands, which the Spaniards, under the rights of conquest, now considered lawfully theirs. Hard labor, European diseases, and sheer culture shock wiped out the Indian population of the Caribbean. Some estimates establish the Indian population in central Mexico as high as 25 million on the eve of the conquest; barely half that number existed fifty years later, "and it was down to something over one million in 1605," according to Barbara and Stanley Stein in *The Colonial Heritage of Latin America.*

From the earthly paradise, America had quickly become the hostile continent. This hostility developed on several concomitant levels. It had to do with the conquerors' treatment of the conquered; it had to do with their pretensions to power in the New World; and it had to do with the contrary claims of the Crown.

THE PRINCE WHO NEVER WAS

The relationship between the Spanish Crown and the explorers and conquerors was one of the great conflicts of the Brave New World. This conflict had to do with the appropriation of land and labor, and thus of political power. It continues to be relevant, if only to the question of rightful ownership of the wealth of Spanish America. How and to whom should this wealth be distributed? Are the property and the distribution justified? This battle is still being fought, from Mexico and Nicaragua to Peru and Argentina.

But in the sixteenth century, the Spanish monarchy faced a difficult dilemma. At home, unified central government had overcome the opposition of petty feudal lords but now met the challenge of rising independent townships and their democratic demands. Having established the momentum toward centralization in Spain, the Crown now saw this dilemma reflected in the New World. Perhaps the conquistadors wished to create private feudalities; perhaps they even felt, as middle-class individuals, an urge for democratic self-government. The monarchy was not about to permit the development of either factor — feudalism or democracy — in the Americas.

The conquistadors had few qualms about distributive justice as, quite simply, they took over the New World. They had conquered. They were the only power. They could usurp land and labor at will. Who was to stop them? The system of domination that they set up was exercised through the *encomienda*, a system whereby land was given to the conquistadors and the services and tribute of the Indians were required, in exchange for protection and the salvation of their souls through religious indoctrination. In reality, it was a disguised form of slavery.

Hernán Cortés, who had a small *encomienda* in Cuba, saw at close quarters the demographic and even the economic disaster of the colonizers' practices. At first he wanted to avoid the same experience in Mexico, but he was accused of being too lax in his attitude toward the defeated, and his men felt that their courage should be rewarded with land and Indians. Acting as the advocate of his soldiers, Cortés even made the mistake of pleading in favor of the *encomienda* system to Charles V. It was an untimely move, and it proved to be the conqueror's undoing. Charles wrote back, forbidding *encomiendas*. He must have formed an undesirable image of Cortés as a separatist satrap of the New World.

Cortés compounded his folly by abandoning Tenochtitlán, now known as Mexico City, in 1525 in order to undertake an expedition to Honduras, which proved to be a costly, protracted, and useless adventure. Honduras means "deep waters" in Spanish; therefore the common phrase *"No te metas en Honduras,"* "Do not go into Honduras." Another phrase in constant use in Spanish is *"Entre abogados te veas,"* "May you be surrounded by lawyers." This sounds almost like a Gypsy curse, and Cortés certainly must have felt cursed when he returned from Honduras and found that Mexico City had been reconquered by the men in black — the Spanish royal bureaucrats, bristling with parchments and quill pens. Two treasury officials, Chirinos and Salazar, took over the government and instituted a trial against the conquistador. The charges against him ran the gamut from stealing Moctezuma's treasure to defending the nobility of the Indians and protecting them from servile labor. Cortés was accused of strangling his wife, Catalina Juárez, whom he had brought over from Cuba after he discarded La Malinche and gave her to one of his soldiers, and of financing and leading the disastrous expedition into Honduras, and of murdering his rivals for the governorship with poisoned cheese.

Hernán Cortés, the victor and then the victim of the conquest of Mexico, was condemned, humiliated, and shipped back to Spain. Although he was given the consolation prize of a title, the governorship of Mexico went to a mediocre official, and Cortés, one of the great figures of Renaissance Europe, was reduced to shabbiness. His repeated petitions for recognition and money finally bored the court and the bureaucracy. The novelty of Indian dwarfs and rubber balls, which he brought with him to amaze the Spanish aristocrats and the royal councillors, soon wore off. Furthermore, his appeals to "His Most Sacred, Caesarean and Catholic Majesty," Charles V, were pathetic. Cortés pled his case. He spent his youth bearing arms in remote lands, sleeping badly and eating worse. He conquered for Charles a nation nine times the size of Spain, won it with no help from the Crown, but rather was hindered "by leeches best left unnamed." He saw himself old and poor, his properties pawned, his servants suing him for salaries due, and his tailors presenting ancient bills. At sixty-three, he would not want to prowl around the Spanish inns anymore, but "to receive the fruit of my labors and return to Mexico as soon as justice is done to me."

Cortés did not do worse than others. He was not sent back to Spain in irons, as Christopher Columbus was. And he was not publicly executed for insubordination to the Crown, as Gonzalo Pizarro was in Peru. And while he was not poisoned by his Spanish companions, as Diego de Ordás, one of Cortés' former captains, was during the exploration of the Orinoco, neither did he simply adapt to a comfortable situation and accept a second-rate status, like Gonzalo Jiménez de Quesada, a true Cincinnatus of the conquest, who, after conquering the Chibcha Indians in what is today Colombia, ended up wandering off to search for El Dorado and eventually settled down to retirement on his country estate. And of course Cortés never took the road of sheer folly (nor did any other conquistador), as did

Lope de Aguirre, who joined an expedition to El Dorado in 1560, murdered the leaders, rebelled against the king of Spain, and attempted to carve out a kingdom for himself at the source of the Amazon River. Aguirre killed everyone who seemed to oppose his madness, from the priests accompanying him to his own daughter.

Cortés' last great humiliation, the grief that broke him, was that the expedition against the Moors in Algiers in 1541 was not entrusted to him. Perversely, once his spirit had been subdued, he was given a vast but spotty fiefdom sprinkled over long distances between Cuernavaca and Oaxaca, but deprived of the capital city of his domain, Antequera, in southern Mexico. He had wealth, finally; he was the marquis of the valley of Oaxaca. But he was shorn of the glory that he thought was rightfully his. The dreams of fame of the five hundred rugged and ambitious warriors who marched with him from Veracruz to the golden throne of Moctezuma must have seemed very distant indeed.

Nonetheless, it is for more than his military feats that Hernán Cortés is regarded as a singular figure of the Renaissance. He was a Machiavellian character without knowing it. Machiavelli indeed was the elder brother of the conquistadors, for what is *The Prince* but a manual for the new men of the Renaissance, the *hominis novi* who set out to create their own destiny, through will and in spite of providence, free from excessive obligations to inherited privilege or nobility or birth? The prince conquers the kingdom of this world, the reign of that which *is*, the negation of Utopia. But Cortés was the prince who never was.

In truth, neither fate (Moctezuma) nor will (Cortés) really won. The institutions of Crown and church, of royal absolutism and the Catholic faith, defeated both the vanquished and the victor, and established in place of the vertical power structure of the Aztecs the equally vertical power structure of the Spanish Hapsburgs. Today's Spanish Americans are descendants of both verticalities, and our stubborn struggles for democracy are all the more difficult and perhaps even all the more admirable for it. Yet we must understand that the conquest of the New World was part of the momentum of the reconquest of Spain from the Moors. The conquistadors were products of that drive, but also of a modern individualism of a Machiavellian stripe, common throughout Renaissance Europe. They were *arrivistes*, climbers, men on the make. They came from all walks of life. Some were laborers; others were petty nobleman. But mostly they came from the growing middle class.

Yet they did not further in the New World the ideal of democratic communities that many of their forefathers had defended during the Middle Ages. They could have chosen, as the *hominis novi* of England and France did, to stake their claims of personal ambition and social ascension on a constitutional order. Having conquered the Indians, they would then perhaps have conquered the Crown. They might have been the fathers of their own political democracy, as the settlers of New England were to become. But the conquistadors did not (perhaps they could not) choose this avenue. Between individualism as democracy and individualism as feudal might, they chose the latter. They thus sacrificed their individualistic virtue, their civilian dimension, to a spectral vision of the power that their ancestors in Spain had never had. They wanted to be hidalgos, gentlemen of property. Being a hidalgo means not having to work, having others work for you. It means winning glory in war and then receiving a reward in lives and land.

This claim to land as a reward for war was one of the bases of economic power in Spanish America, as it had been in medieval Spain. The conquistadors wanted feudal power for themselves, but the Crown, wanting to establish a far-reaching, absolute authority, thwarted them. The very vast distances and the local demands of governance gave the conquerors and their descendants a fair share of immediate control, but whatever compromise the Crown and the settlers eventually reached, there was first a tremendous debate on the nature of the Indians and the limits of authority in the New World.

"THE INDIES ARE BEING DESTROYED!"

This was the cry of Father Bartolomé de Las Casas, who picked up Father Montesinos' Christmas sermon of 1511 and his question about the Indians: "Are these not men? Have they not rational souls?" — "the first cry for justice in the Americas," wrote the modern Dominican writer Pedro Henríquez Ureña.

Bartolomé de Las Casas was a slave owner in Cuba who renounced his holdings and joined the Dominicans in 1524, accusing the conquistadors of "endless crimes and offenses against the Indians who were the king's subjects." Over a period of fifty years, from the moment he forsook his *encomienda* in 1515 to his death in 1566, Father Las Casas denounced the "destruction of the Indies" by the conquistadors, accusing them of "the torts and offenses that they do to the kings of Castile, destroying their kingdoms . . . in the Indies." He went so far as to praise the Indians for the religiosity that they displayed, even if they were pagans. Had not the Greeks, the Romans, and the Hebrews been idolaters too? And had this pagan religiosity excluded them from the human race, or rather, nicely predisposed them for conversion?

Statue of Father Bartolomé de Las Casas overlooking the Zócalo in Mexico City

Las Casas denied the rights of conquest, especially the institution of the *encomienda*, which he considered "more unjust and cruel than Pharaoh's oppression of the Jews," and which deprived "both masters and subjects of their freedom and of their lives." These modern ideas on the master-slave relationship, along with Las Casas' principal demands, were incorporated into the Laws of the Indies in 1542. The *encomienda* was legally abolished, although it remained, disguised as *repartimientos,* or provisional allotments of Indian laborers, as a self-perpetuating fact within the real economic system in the New World. The Crown went on combatting it, substituting administrative systems and royalist controls for it, refusing the conquistadors and their descendants property rights to their lands, and endlessly postponing decisions that would grant them feudal domination, titles of nobility, or hereditary rights.

In this sense, it can be said, with all due respect to Father Bartolomé de Las Casas, that he was the Crown's most useful tool in attacking feudal pretensions while defending humanitarian values. But in the final analysis, this struggle left a wide margin for the de facto powers of the conquistadors while preserving the eminent domain of Spanish royalty. The conquistadors and their descendants were purposely left by the Crown in the legal light of usurpers. But the Laws of the Indies, it was said, were like a spider's web, which caught only the smaller criminals and let the big ones get off scot free.

Many sixteenth-century testimonies depict the actual brutality of the *encomienda* and its even more severe form, work in the mine (*la mita*). In his marvelous line drawings of the life of Peru before and after the conquest, Guamán Poma de Ayala, a descendant of the Inca nobility, depicted the absolute impunity of the *encomendero* and his henchmen. The drawings of Theodor de Bry, which accompanied the best-selling volume by Father Las Casas, *The Destruction of the Indies*, fathered the so-called Black Legend of a brutal, sanguinary, and sadistic Spain, torturing and killing wherever she went — in tacit contrast, no doubt, to the lily-white colonialists from France, England, and the Netherlands. Yet while the latter piously disguised their own cruelties and inhumanities, they never

Three illustrations by Theodor de Bry: Indians Mining Silver, Indians Defending Their Hill, *and* Indians Retaliating

R.Holata Outina.

14

did what Spain permitted. A debate on the nature of the conquered peoples and the rights of conquest raged through the Hispanic world for a full century, becoming the first full-fledged modern debate on human rights. This was hardly anything that the other colonial powers worried about.

There were even notes of humor in the debate, from both the Indian and the Spanish sides. During the conquest of Chile, the Araucanian chieftain Caupolicán was impaled by the conquistadors, yet as he was dying, he said, "I wish I had invaded and conquered Spain." The same idea, from the other side of the water, was expressed by a defender of human rights just as important as Las Casas, Father Francisco de Vitoria. A Jesuit teaching at Salamanca in 1539, he asked his students if they would like to see Spaniards treated by Indians in Spain the way Spaniards treated Indians in America. Discovery and conquest, he said, gave Spain no more right to American territory than the Indians would have if they discovered and conquered Spain. No doubt the same thing could have been said of the English colonization of North America. But what Father Vitoria did in his books and teachings was to internationalize the problem of power over the colonies and of the human rights of the conquered peoples. He attempted to set down rules limiting colonial power through international law, then called *jus gentium,* or the rights of people. His nemesis was the aforementioned Juan Ginés de Sepúlveda, who accused the Indians of cannibalism and human sacrifice in a society not very different from a colony of ants. As the Indians were presocial, they could legitimately be conquered by "civil men" from Europe, and all their goods could be put to civilized use, argued Sepúlveda. But were not the Spaniards, Vitoria argued right back, also guilty of crimes against nature? Were not all European nations culpable of acts of destruction and war? If this was so, no one had the moral right to conquer the Indians.

As this intense debate was going on in Spain, many friars in the Americas tried to apply rules of compassion and humanity to the Indian peoples. Most eminent among these was Vasco de Quiroga, a Franciscan bishop of Michaocán in western Mexico, who in the 1530s arrived with Thomas More's *Utopia* under his arm and promptly set about applying its rules to the communities of Tarascan Indians: communal property, a six-hour work day, the proscription of luxury, elective family magistrates, and equitable distribution of the fruits of labor. Quiroga, lovingly called Tata Vasco, Our Father Vasco, by the Tarascans to this very day, was fired by the vision of the New World as Utopia, "since it was not in vain but in good cause and with good reason," he wrote, "that this world here

Detail from The Epic of American Civilization: The Departure of Quetzalcoatl. *José Clemente Orozco, 1932–1934*

actually deep in cahoots with the local plantation owners and political bosses.

No wonder, then, that when new humanitarian laws arrived from Spain, local officials in the New World simply placed them on top of their heads and solemnly stated, *"La ley se obedece pero no se cumple,"* that is, "The law is formally obeyed, but actually it is disregarded." A deep divorce between the *legal* country, enshrined in royal laws and later in republican constitutions, and the *real* country, festering behind the legal facade, thus demoralized and disrupted Spanish America from the very start.

The legal facade indeed could not have been more majestic, more attuned to our symmetrically ordained Roman tradition, and more vertically ordained as well. The structure of government during the colonial days was topped, of course, by the king, ruling from Spain. Dependent on him, in descending degrees, were the Council of the Indies, the chamber of commerce, and the local authorities. The Council of the Indies was directly concerned with governing the colonies as part of the royal patrimony, not the patrimony of the Spanish people, for Mexico, Peru, and Chile were added to the possessions of the *king,* not to those of the people. The next step down, the Casa de Contratación in Seville, the chamber of commerce of the Indies, centralized and monopolized trade and was, all-importantly, authorized to receive the gold and silver of the Americas. Finally, dependent on these higher institutions in Spain were the local authorities in the distant colonies, with viceroys and captains general, all named in Spain, at the top, and governors, provincial district leaders, and mayors beneath them. Crushed under the whole heavy structure was the municipality, the town hall, struggling — hardly to any avail — to maintain a minimum of local justice.

The original system of power in Spanish America was thus a vertical autocracy, governed from afar through paternalistic laws which were rarely implemented, while at the local level practical arrangements between landowners and political bosses assured the harsh and often inefficient exploitation of land and labor. Significantly, there was a strong sense of continuity between these vertical structures from Hapsburg Spain and those of the Aztec and Inca worlds. Even the concept of eminent domain, whereby the state was and remained the original owner of land and simply yielded to private interests, represented a common tradition of the Indian empires and the Spanish monarchy. Yet these legal facts were in daily contradiction with political practices. Although the Crown deprived many disobedient colonizers of long-standing rights and constantly attempted to atomize their power, diminishing them as *segundones,* second-class citizens, the colonizers organized themselves in spheres where the Crown could not touch them and created an isolated rural politics of oppression and exploitation, which persists to this day.

A NETWORK OF CITIES

Behind the majestic facade of the law and the shabby practices of real politics, other factors energized the life of colonial Spanish America. The first, of course, was the people. Spanish conquerors and their descendants. European immigrants in the Americas. Mestizos, the children of Spanish men and Indian women. Creoles, whites born in the Americas. Later on, Africans and their mixed descendants. And certainly the Indians themselves, the vanquished ones.

The first conquistadors, Cortés wrote to Charles V, were rough, uneducated people of lowly origin. Perhaps Cortés was doing some one-upmanship by flashing his university credentials at the king; the truth is that not only field laborers and city workers but petty noblemen and middle-class individuals participated in the conquest. The historian Céspedes del Castillo referred to a broader cast of migrants during the sixteenth century. Numerous friars, priests, and many lesser hidalgos "gave the general tone of the immigration," wrote Céspedes, "warriors who were more numerous at the beginning than at the end; almost no aristocrats; many merchants, farmers, and artisans, and lawyers of greater influence than numbers."

Nevertheless, the colonizing process was highly selective. Jews, Moors, and heretics were expressly forbidden to cross the Atlantic. Although it is true that the conquistadors generally traveled as bachelors and mixed freely first with Indian women and later with black women, there was no express prohibition on women's emigration to America, and in fact many of them played notable roles in the initial phases of colonization. The wife of Pedro de los Ríos, a governor in Panama, refused to return to Spain when her husband's period in office ran out; she preferred to stay in Panama, with her cattle and her high expectations that Peruvian gold, then flowing from the Pacific to the Atlantic, would also come her way. A woman called Inés Suárez, like so many of the conquerors a native of Extremadura, followed in her husband's footsteps to Venezuela, where she did not find him, and then on to Peru, where she discovered that he had died. There she met Pedro de Valdivia, and she accompanied him during the conquest of Chile and the founding of the southernmost capital of the Spanish New World, Santiago del Nuevo Extremo, whose name recalled both the battling apostle of *la reconquista* and the province com-

mon to Inés and Pedro, Extremadura. She nursed the wounded and
served Valdivia faithfully as lieutenant and lover, yet bowed to a priest's
demands that she abandon him when the conquistador's wife was brought
from Spain. As a moral lesson, perhaps, Valdivia was killed by the Araucanians before Señora Valdivia arrived. I don't know whether the two
widows ever met.

Women were also crucial in the most dramatic foundation of a Spanish American city during this period, the foundation of Buenos Aires. But
Buenos Aires is a city of two tales. It was founded twice on the banks of
the River Plate, first in 1536 by Pedro de Mendoza, a vain courtier who
had already made a fortune during the sack of Rome by Spanish troops in
1527. He came looking for more gold. Instead he found fever, hunger,
and death. The Indians in these southern regions were poor and unafraid
of horses and muskets, and they attacked the Spanish palisades night after
night. Perhaps the only consolation the Spanish had was that many
women had come on this expedition, some of them disguised as men. They
were sentinels. They kept the fires going. And, as one of them wrote, "we
eat less than men." But soon there was nothing left to eat, and as in every
bona fide gold rush, the Spanish ate the soles of their boots. It was
rumored that they even cannibalized their dead. Mendoza died of syphilis
and was thrown into the river. Perhaps the only gold ever seen at that
spot was the rings on the fingers of the explorer as he went down.

Buenos Aires was burned and abandoned. The first foundation
turned out to be a disaster, the greatest of any Spanish city of the Americas. But forty-four years later, in 1580, a no-nonsense administrator called
Juan de Garay came down from Asunción on the Paraná River and
founded Buenos Aires for a second time. This time it was laid out on a
checkerboard pattern and conceived not as a city of gold-seekers and
adventurers but as a city of order, hard work, and eventual prosperity,
which is what it became. A port city, an outlet for trade in hides and cattle,
on the misnamed River Plate, Rio de la Plata, River of Silver — a muddy
river the color of a lion's hide, as the poet Leopoldo Lugones wrote. A city
built on swamplands. The great drain of the silver mine of Potosí into the
Atlantic.

The two foundations of Buenos Aires clearly dramatize two impulses
of Spanish colonization in the New World. One was based on fantasy,
illusion, imagination. The conquistadors were driven not only by the lust
for gold — "the fever of Peru," as it came to be known — but by fantasy
and imagination, which at times were an even stronger elixir. As they
entered the willful world of the Renaissance, these men still carried with

them the fantasies of the Middle Ages. They were convinced that they saw whales with breasts and sharks with two penises, flying fish and beaches with more pearls than sand in them. When they caught sight of sirens, they wryly commented that the mermaids "were not as beautiful as they were said to be." But their search for the fiery women warriors of myth led them all the way from California, named after the Amazon queen Calafia (or perhaps after a mythical island), to the source of the greatest river in South America. Were they wrong to search for the Fountain of Youth in Florida — La Florida, the land of flowers — explored by Ponce de Léon? Their search for El Dorado, the Indian chieftain who was painted in gold twice a day, led them to Potosí, the largest silver mine in the world. And the search for the fabled Seven Cities of Cibola took Francisco Vásquez de Coronado on his dramatic pilgrimage to what later became Arizona, Texas, and New Mexico.

These dreamers never found the magic cities. But, as the second establishment of Buenos Aires showed, they were capable of founding the real cities, not of gold but of men. Never since the times of the Romans has any nation displayed such amazing energy as Spain did in building the cities of the New World. The distances were enormous and the wealth was vast, as the men of Spain pushed north to what are now California and Oregon and south toward the very tip of the continent, Tierra del Fuego. But to dominate both distance and wealth, they had to found cities. Literally hundreds of cities, all the way from San Francisco and Los Angeles to Buenos Aires and Santiago de Chile, sprang up. These were not mere settlements but urban centers of great nobility and permanence, reflecting Spain's decision to be here "for all eternity."

Taking only the extremes of Spanish America, Mexico and Argentina, the list is truly impressive. In Mexico, city followed upon city: Veracruz in 1519; Antequera (now Oaxaca) in 1521; Colima in 1522; Taxco in 1529; Culiacán, on the Pacific Ocean, in 1531; Puebla in 1535; Guadalajara in 1542; Querétaro, in the central valley, in 1550; and San Cristóbal (Las Casas) in 1561. In Argentina the pace was comparable: Santiago del Estero in 1553, Mendoza in 1561, and San Juan a year later; Tucumán in 1565; Salta and Corrientes in the 1580s; La Rioja and San Luis in the 1590s; Santa Fe in 1609; and Córdoba in 1617.

Sometimes the cities were ports built like fortresses, on both the Caribbean and the Pacific: Acapulco, Havana, Cartagena. Others were capital cities on the grand scale of Mexico City and Lima. Most were solid provincial townships built according to the grid pattern of the Renaissance, each with its central square, church, and city hall, establishing the enduring rhythm of life — the plaza where lovers court and old men pass the time of day playing dominoes or discussing the news, where the laws are proclaimed and the revolutions launched. Some were mining towns that simply followed the capricious windings of the hills where gold and silver were exploited. In all cases, once a town was founded, the settlers each received an urban lot, or *solar*, and a plot of agricultural land outside the city, as well as rights to the lands reserved for communal use.

The Spanish Empire, says Francisco Romero, the Argentine historian of the Latin American cities, became a network of cities, which dominated the rural areas as much as they could. But both the cities and the rural areas created their own centers of power, developed their own peculiarities, and broke down the homogenous vision of empire dreamed up in Madrid. The cities were Hispanic, adds Romero, in a very formal and legalistic sense. They were founded as a political act, to occupy land and establish the right of conquest. But no city could be legitimate if it was not preceded by law. The city had to be imagined, fixed in law, before being fixed in fact. The legal form of the Roman tradition had to precede reality and remain above it. The law produced the fact of the city, and the city then proceeded to radiate Spanish power, as it was meant to, and subdue the Indian population.

The cities became the centers, as well, of a new culture. The first university in the New World was founded in Santo Domingo in 1538, and the universities of Lima and Mexico City in 1551, well before the first university in Anglo America, Harvard College, founded in 1636. The first printing press in the Americas was set up by the Italian typographer Giovanni Paoli (Juan Pablos) in Mexico City in 1535, whereas the first Anglo-American press was inaugurated by Stephen Daye in Cambridge, Massachusetts, in 1640.

The universities basically taught the traditional medieval studies — the trivium (grammar, rhetoric, and logic) and the quadrivium (geometry, arithmetic, music, and astronomy), along with theology, law, and the central political philosophy of scholasticism, that is, the ideas of Saint Thomas Aquinas. His ideas were determinant for the political culture of Latin America, since for three hundred years everyone from Mexico to Argentina studied them. It was in the universities that people learned once and for all that the purpose of politics, its supreme value, superior to any individual value, was the common good. In order to attain it, unity was required; pluralism was a hindrance. And unity could best be achieved by the rule of a single individual, not by the whim of multiple voters.

In one of the eleven chapels of the Church of Santo Domingo in

*A silver mine at
Potosí, c. 1584*

*The fortress at
Cartagena*

Oaxaca, Saint Thomas Aquinas sits in heaven, as if presiding over the basic political truths bred into the bones of Spanish America. He sits in front of Saint Augustine, the doctor of the church, who laid down another cornerstone of our political and spiritual life, preaching that the grace of God is not attainable by any individual without the assistance of the church. To reach God, you must pass through the church hierarchy. This was a hermetic system of teaching the revealed truth, denying the participation of individual research or criticism while stressing the paramount need for tradition and the church's role as the rightful depository of that tradition, propagandist of truth, and unfailing denouncer of error.

But by insisting that the common good was granted from above through authoritarian concession, this political philosophy assured that it could be wrested from below only through violent revolution. Once more the principles and practices of democracy were postponed. Spanish America was to grope blindly through authoritarianism and imitation of foreign models of progress and democracy before it found in its own interrupted traditions — the medieval townships of Spain, the humanistic side of Aztec society, the social value of Incan culture — its own democratic roots.

Colonial education was a system of learning best defined as guided intelligence. Furthermore, the system of publication that went with it was also sometimes highly restrictive. Only six years after the conquest of Mexico, the Crown ordered no further publications of Cortés' letters to Charles V relating the events of that conquest. Spanish royalty did not wish to foster the cult of personality of the conquistadors. In effect, we were forbidden to know ourselves. In 1553, a royal decree prohibited the exportation to the Americas of all histories dealing with the conquest. This is not to mention any histories praising the defeated Indian cultures.

The Crown was capable of taking very enlightened initiatives, such as the early creation of schools for gifted Indians who were members of the aristocracy of the defeated nations. In one such college, at Tlatelolco in Mexico, the young Indians learned Spanish, Latin, and Greek and proved to be excellent students. But in the end the experiment came to naught, first because it embarrassed the conquerors to have Indian subjects who knew more than they did, and second because they did not want Indians who could translate Virgil, but Indians who could work for them as cheap labor in the mines and haciendas. And Indians who would build the temples of the new religion, Christianity, while razing those of the old religion, those "temples of the Devil," as one Christian missionary named them.

FATHER AND MOTHER

Whether the conquest was right or wrong, the church knew that its primary mission was to evangelize. Its missionaries met a population torn between the desire to revolt and the desire to find protection. The church offered the latter as abundantly as it could. Many Indian groups, including the Coras in Mexico, the Quechuas in Peru, and the Araucanians in Chile, resisted the Spanish for a long time. Others thronged to the church, asking for baptism in the streets and roads. The Franciscan priest Toribio de Benavente, who arrived in Mexico in 1524, was called Motolinia by the Indians, which means "the poor and humble one." He wrote, "Many come to be baptized, not only on Sundays or feast days, but even on weekdays, children and adults, healthy and sick, and from all the regions; and when the friars travel, the Indians come out to the roads with their children in their arms, and with their sick on their backs, and even decrepit old people come out, demanding to be baptized. . . . And as they go to baptism, some pray, others complain, others implore on their knees, others lift their arms, moaning and twisting, and others receive it crying and sighing."

Motolinia affirmed that in this way, fifteen years after the fall of the Aztecs in 1521, "more than four million souls had been baptized." Even if this is church propaganda, the fact remains that the formal events of Catholicism, from baptism to death rites, became a permanent fixture of popular life throughout Spanish America, and that church architecture displayed a practical imagination in uniting two vital factors of the new societies of the Americas: the need for a sense of parenthood, a father and mother, and the need for a protective physical space where the old gods might be admitted in disguise, behind the altars of the new gods.

Most mestizos did not know their fathers. They knew only their Indian mothers, the common-law wives of the Spanish. Miscegenation was certainly the rule in the Iberian colonies, as opposed to racial purity and puritanical hypocrisy in the English colonies. But this did not soften the sensation of orphanhood that many offspring of Spaniards and Indian women must have felt. La Malinche had a child by Cortés, who recognized him and had him baptized Martín. Cortés had another son, also named Martín, by his not yet strangled wife, Catalina Juárez. In time the brothers met, and in 1565 staged the first rebellion of Mexican Creole and mestizo nationalism against Spanish rule. The legitimation of the bastard, the identification of the orphan, became one of the central, if at times unspoken, problems of Latin American culture. It was dealt with by the Spaniards through religious and legal means.

The flight of the gods, who had abandoned their people; the destruction of the temples; the razing of the cities; the wholesale pillage and destruction of Indian culture; the devastation of the Indian economy by the mine and the *encomienda*; plus the almost paralyzing sense of amazement, of sheer wonder at what had happened — where was hope to be found? The subjugated Indians could hardly see a glimmer anywhere. How were despair and insurrection to be avoided? This was the question raised by the humanists of the colonies, but also by their wiser (and wilier) politicians. One answer had been Las Casas' denunciation; another, Quiroga's Utopian communities and the Crown's Indian colleges. But it was truly the second viceroy and first archbishop of Mexico City, Juan de Zumárraga, who found the lasting solution: give a mother to the orphaned children of the New World.

In early December 1531, on Tepeyac Hill near Mexico City, a site previously dedicated to the worship of the Aztec goddess Tonantzin, the Virgin of Guadalupe appeared, bearing roses in winter and choosing a lowly

The Virgin of Guadalupe

tameme, or Indian bearer, Juan Diego, as the object of her love and recognition. In one fabulous stroke, the Spanish authorities transformed the Indian people from children of violated women to children of the pure Virgin. From Babylon to Bethlehem, in one flash of political genius, whore became virgin and Malinche became Guadalupe. Nothing has proved as consoling, unifying, and worthy of fierce respect since then as the figure of the Virgin of Guadalupe in Mexico, the Virgin of La Caridad del Cobre in Cuba, and the Virgin of Coromoto in Venezuela. The conquered people now had a mother.

They also found a father. Mexico imposed on Cortés the mask of Quetzalcoatl. Cortés refused it and instead imposed on Mexico the mask of Christ. Ever since, it has been impossible to know who is worshipped at the baroque altars of Puebla, Oaxaca, and Tlaxcala: Christ or Quetzalcoatl? In a universe accustomed to seeing men sacrificed to the gods, nothing amazed the Indians more than the sight of a god who had sacrificed himself to men. It was the redemption of humankind by Christ that fascinated and really defeated the Indians of the New World. The true return of the gods was the arrival of Christ. Christ was the recovered memory that in the beginning it *was* the gods who sacrificed themselves for the benefit of humankind. This misty memory, engulfed by the somber human sacrifices ordained by Aztec power, was now rescued by the Christian church. The result was flagrant syncretism, the blending of Christian and aboriginal faiths, one of the cultural foundations of the Spanish American world.

Yet a striking fact remains: all the Mexican Christs are dead, or at the very least in agony. Whether in Calvary, on the cross, or laid out in a glass bier, the Christ that one sees in Mexico's village churches is bleeding, prostrate, and lonely. By contrast, the Virgin, as in Spain, is surrounded by perpetual glory, celebration, flowers, and processions. And the decor itself, the great baroque architecture of Latin America, is both a celebration of the new religion and a risky celebration of the survival of the old one.

The marvelous chapel at Tonantzintla near Cholula is one of the most startling confirmations of syncretism as the dynamic basis of postconquest culture. What happened here happened throughout Latin America. The Indian artisans were given engravings of the saints and other religious motifs by the Christian evangelizers and asked to reproduce them inside the churches. But the artisans and masons of the temples had something more than a copy in mind. They wished to celebrate their old gods as well as the new ones, but they had to mask this intention by blending a praise

of nature with a praise of heaven and making them indistinguishable. Tonantzintla is in effect a re-creation of the Indian paradise. White and gold, it overflows with plenty as all the fruits and the flowers of the tropics climb up to its dome, a dream of infinite abundance. Religious syncretism triumphed as, somehow, the conquerors were conquered.

In Tonantzintla, the Indians depicted themselves as innocent angels on the way to heaven, while the Spanish conquistadors were shown as ferocious, fork-tongued, bearded devils. Paradise can be regained after all.

SEVEN

The Age of Empire

Charles V was the creator of the Spanish Empire. He was the grandson of the Catholic Monarchs, Ferdinand and Isabella, through their daughter, Queen Joanna, who lost her reason over the death of her husband, Philip the Fair. On Philip's death, after strenuously playing ball and then drinking cold water, the queen refused to bury him, and for a long time she took his corpse from monastery to monastery, avoiding convents, where the gallant Prince Philip, even in death, might seduce the nuns. Finally persuaded to give up her mad love, Joanna was shut up in Tordesillas Castle, while her son became king of Spain at age sixteen and Philip the Fair was given Christian burial.

Already, at age six, Charles had inherited the Netherlands. Now, beardless and youthful, he showed the world the stigmata of the Hapsburg dynasty: a prognathous chin that made it impossible for him to chew properly or even close his mouth. A fly, it was said, could penetrate the Hapsburg lips with no difficulty at any time. Charles grew a beard. He put on armor. He mounted his horse. He was painted in a superb equestrian pose by the Italian artist Titian. Charles I of Spain, better known in history under his title as Holy Roman Emperor Charles V, could shrug off the blights of inheritance to which we are all prey. He was the heir to the Hapsburg dynasty, the greatest ruling house in Europe. There was no limit to what he held in his power. Wherever he looked from on top of his (or Titian's) horse, he could see a possession of his Crown. To the north, Germany and the Netherlands. To the east, Naples, Sicily, and Sardinia. To the south, his African dominions. To the west, the Americas, and beyond, after Balboa's dramatic discovery of 1513, the Pacific. He ruled the first and the greatest of all modern empires. No one before him, not even the Caesars, had controlled so much territory, such a variety of peoples, and such potential wealth.

Detail of allegorical figures representing Spain, the papacy, and Venice, from a painting by Giorgio Vasari

Overleaf:
Detail from
Las Meninas.
Diego Velázquez.

The Emperor
Charles V at
the Battle of
Mühlberg.
Titian, 1548

But Charles, throughout his career, was determined to join his earthly power to the spiritual power of Christendom. He wanted to be the political head of Christianity, in the same way that the pope was its religious head. This self-imposed goal was to wear him out prematurely. Charles had come into his vast inheritance not through feats of conquest but thanks to matrimonial alliances and other secular arrangements, at which the Hapsburgs were extremely good. In these matters, they were abundantly helped by the powerful banking house of the Fugger family of Germany, which raised an enormous sum of money to buy the electors and raise Charles V to the position of Holy Roman Emperor in 1519. But now the possessions stemming from the position had to be defended, not by marriage, briberies, and seductions but by acts of war.

His troubles began at home, in Spain itself, and were associated, first of all, with his Flemish allegiances. He did not speak Spanish. Unpolitically, he surrounded himself with Flemish courtiers and even named them to sensitive Spanish posts, such as the bishopric of Toledo. But his political problems in Spain went deeper than this; they concerned nothing less than the continuing battle between centralized, absolutist royal powers and the lingering potential democratic powers of the towns.

THE REVOLUTION OF THE TOWNSHIPS

In the cities of Castile, the concept of citizenship was in the process of gestation. More and more people had been incorporated into the political assemblies. Citizens were aware of the rights granted them by their constitutional charters, but when Charles acceded to power as king of Spain in 1516, they saw their freedoms menaced in various ways. Apart from the xenophobia that turned them against the young king, the city-dwellers rightly suspected that Charles' policy was to centralize Spain further in order to have a strong base from which to pursue his twin external goals, assuring the power of the Spanish Empire and the unity of the Christian church. The growing presence of the royal representatives, the *corregidores*, in the townships moved them to act against absolutism before it was too late. In 1519, they rose in revolt against King Charles.

Perhaps it is far-fetched to see the ensuing civil war as a forerunner of the English and French revolutions. But it certainly has been one of the strongest, and most permanent, references for Spanish and Spanish American democracy. "The consent of all" and "the will of the people" were common and recurrent concepts in the letters, speeches, and proclamations of the *comuneros*. The social composition of the revolt speaks for itself. A few urban noblemen; a great number of mayors, aldermen, and judges; quite a few lesser clergymen, including canons, abbots, archdeacons, and deans; a sprinkling of university teachers; a great number of doctors, physicians, lawyers, and bachelors of arts; an even greater number of merchants, money-changers, public notaries, and pharmacists; and an overwhelming majority of store owners, innkeepers, silversmiths, jewelers, ironmongers, butchers, hatmakers, cobblers, tailors, barbers, and carpenters acted politically through the Junta General, an executive assembly based on the majority vote and expressly said to represent the general will of all. Their clearly stated aim was a constitutional, democratic monarchy based on popular representation.

As such, the revolt could not be countenanced by the young king, whose double policy of power — both internal and international, Spanish and imperial — was threatened. The townships may have been rebelling in Castile (and in Aragon, through a movement parallel to Castile's, the *Germania*), but the sons and brothers of the lawyers, artisans, mill owners, field laborers, and petty noblemen who were rebelling were fighting for Charles V in Mexico and the Caribbean, and on the Spanish Main. So it became one of the great ironies of our history that as Charles met and defeated the *comunero* forces at Villalar in 1521, Cortés met and defeated the Aztec forces in Tenochtitlán.

What kind of order was going to be created in the aftermath of the coincidental victories? The response, unfortunately, was that in Spain an authoritarian order imposed itself on the movement toward a democratic order. And in the New World, the vertical structures of the Aztec and Inca empires were simply superseded by the vertical, authoritarian structure of the Hapsburgs.

The further irony of it all is that the conquistadors were not very different from the men defeated at Villalar. Believing that they had triumphed in the New World, they had in reality been defeated in the Old World. Having missed the opportunity to create seminally democratic communities in the New World, only to sacrifice their standing and the potential extension of their power, the conquistadors were unable to govern the lands that they had conquered. The king promptly and definitively structured the new forms of government in the Americas in his favor. What the conquistadors and their descendants won were de facto, *in situ*, and finally illegitimate advantages over the king. It was a great deal, but not enough, either from the point of view of potentially democratic communities or from that of potentially autonomous feudalities.

Could it have been otherwise? Could we have had a democratic system after the reconquest in Spain and after the conquest in the New World? This question still hangs over Spain and Spanish America.

After the defeat of the townships of Castile at Villalar and the defeat of the Aztecs in Tenochtitlán, Charles not only consolidated the central state, he transformed Spain from a purely peninsular community, waging its own crusade against Islam and attempting to find a compromise among its tricultural strains, into a continental empire that, in the words of Ángel Ganivet, "embraced it all" in Holland, Italy, Tunisia, and the Americas. This headache of overextension was compounded by Charles' dual nature: secure and insecure, harsh and gentle, divided by his national allegiances. Of his fifty-eight years on this earth, he preferred to spend most in Flanders (twenty-eight years), far more than in the Germanic lands of his inheritance as emperor (nine years) and even in his Spanish estate, which he visited seven times in his life, spending in all eighteen years there. But Charles was divided above all by his uncertainty over whether to respond to the challenges of governance through conciliation (his Erasmian, Renaissance inclination) or by outright battle (his Hispanic, imperial inclination).

He was fighting the Indian nations of the Americas through his uncompromisingly violent captains Cortés and Pizarro, yet he wished to wrest feudal control of the New World from them through legislation that protected the Indian communities and restricted, de jure, the conquistadors' de facto powers. He was fighting the new Islamic power, the Ottoman Empire, as it dared to spread from the Mediterranean to the Danube and the gates of Vienna, and he was fighting his French rival, Francis I, over an exhausting quarter of a century. He suffered the mutiny of his unpaid troops, who then sacked the pope's city, Rome, as Charles battled the Protestants in Germany. In the end he failed to overcome them, and accepted his defeat at Augsburg in 1555.

It was too much for any man. Prematurely drained, Charles V retired to the Spanish monastery of Yuste, in the isolated ranges of Extremadura, there tinkering with his clocks and at times rehearsing his own funeral. Death finally came to him in 1558. Titian, who had painted the powerful equestrian figure in armor, now portrayed a plain, slightly hunched, defeated old gentleman completely clad in black and seated on a simple Roman chair, looking wistfully, perhaps absentmindedly, at a world with which he never came fully to terms.

A SHOWER OF GOLD

Charles V abdicated in favor of his son, Philip II, leaving him the unwieldy Spanish Empire. The Protestants flourished, thanks to their sanctification of princely ambitions. The Turks prowled the Mediterranean.

The Netherlands were in revolt against Spain; the Moriscos, the Moors remaining in Spain, rose against Philip's decrees depriving them of their language and customs; and even the Aragonese nobility revolted against his restrictions on the traditional *fueros*, or constitutional charters. Yet Philip not only kept his empire going but truly affirmed it, for several decades, as the world's leading power.

To do this, he needed revenues. And he got them, mostly by overtaxing his now defenseless subjects through the church, in both Spain and the Americas, and from the gold and silver of the New World. In the sixteenth century, American mines multiplied Europe's silver reserves by seven. The mining center at Potosí, in the Peruvian highlands (present-day Bolivia), became the largest city of the New World in the seventeenth century: fifty thousand Europeans and forty-five thousand Indians lived there, nearly a third of the Indians working in the shafts under the system of forced labor that bound them to the mine during their whole lifetime, and even bound their descendants. It was the Indians, starved and decimated by disease, who supplied Spain, and through Spain the rest of Europe, with riches. Yet even at the height of production, the mines of Mexico and Peru produced only one quarter of the wealth provided by agriculture and cattle ranching. And even at their worst, the foremen on the landed estates treated their laborers better than the overseers at the mines did. Many miners fled to the haciendas, the lesser evil.

Private entrepreneurs scouted and exploited the veins of ore. Potosí was a virgin mountain, untouched by the Incas, but the Spanish soon discovered four great veins running "like the poles" from north to south, as Father Joseph de Acosta, the Jesuit chronicler of the flora and fauna of the New World, put it. In each one they opened multiple shafts. But all of the veins, recalled Acosta, looked toward the east, toward the rising sun, toward Spain, where the king received the shipments and took one fifth for himself.

The Spanish Crown licensed only two ports of entry, Cádiz and Seville, to receive the gold and silver of the New World, and even as it forbade the exportation of bullion from Spain, the monarchy became, in the words of the North American economist Rondo Cameron, "its own worst offender." Bullion had to pay for Spain's costly wars in Europe, its ostentatious monuments, a luxurious aristocracy, the fight against the Protestant Reformation, the administration of empire, and the importation of manufactured goods.

The enormous injection of Spanish metals revolutionized the European economy, bringing inflation, high prices, growing demand, and flourishing banks throughout the continent. Many of those banks were creditors to the Spanish monarchy, willing to extend generous loans to Philip on the promise of an unending stream of bullion from Potosí and Zacatecas. Who would repay these loans? Naturally, Philip's successors.

Smuggling contraband from Spain became a lucrative and popular occupation. One of the characters in *Don Quixote*, Roque Guinart, was based on a true-life individual who won his bread by smuggling the metals of the Indies out of Spain. From Italy, Germany, and the Netherlands, where Spain had possessions, gold and silver quickly spread all over Europe, provoking the sixteenth-century "price revolution," which, although common to all the continent, affected Spain first and worst. Prices rose more and more rapidly in the country containing the ports of entry.

During the reigns of Charles V and Philip II, northern Europe began its spectacular stage of capital accumulation. Spain, a mere intermediary, was deprived of modern capital and modern capitalists and was forced to buy manufactures from abroad at high prices and to sell raw materials cheap; consequently, it entered a prolonged phase of economic decline. A simple statistic tells the tale. In 1629, according to a Spanish economist of that time, Alonso de Carranza, 75 percent of the gold and silver from the American mines had ended up in only four European cities: London, Rouen, Antwerp, and Amsterdam.

Imperial Spain abounded in ironies. The staunchly Catholic monarchy ended by unwittingly financing its Protestant enemies. Spain capitalized Europe while decapitalizing itself. Louis XIV of France put it most succinctly: "Let us now sell manufactured goods to the Spaniards and receive from them gold and silver." Spain was poor because Spain was rich.

What did this mean for us in the New World? Partly, that Spain became the colony of capitalist Europe, and we in Spanish America in a sense became the colony of a colony. From the very start, we were two very different entities, what we seemed to be and what we really were. So was Spain, our colonial mistress.

FIGHTING THE ELEMENTS

The legitimacy of the Spanish American empire was based not only on the "rights of conquest" but on nothing less than a series of papal bulls dividing the colonial world between Spain and Portugal. Protected by Ferdinand and Isabella, the Spanish pope Alexander VI, born Rodrigo Borgia, had more or less bought his way into the papacy, and there he devoted many hours to furthering the fortunes of his bastards, Lucrezia and Cesare Borgia. But he had time left over to favor his royal patrons. Through the Treaty of Tordesillas (1494), Alexander VI issued a bull that drew a line from the North to the South Pole, 370 leagues west of the Azores, giving Portugal all lands to the east (from Brazil to India) and Spain all lands to the west (from the Caribbean to the Pacific).

The other European powers were not pleased. Francis I of France, Charles V's greatest rival, protested. "Show me the clause in Adam's will," he said, "which gives the king of Spain dominion over half the world." The Dutch were equally unhappy, as was their imminent ally, Elizabeth I of England, who proclaimed the general principle that the sea and the air were common to all nations but added a corollary that would determine the future power of both England and Spain: "Since the sea belongs to everyone, it belongs to me." She encouraged her most adventurous captains to confront the Spanish at sea and in the New World. England, after all, must have its share. Throughout the Caribbean — Spain's Mare Nostrum in the Americas — veritable fortress-cities were built to defend against pirate attacks, but also against attacks from foreign powers. From Veracruz to Havana, from San Juan de Puerto Rico to Maracaibo, from Portobelo to Cartagena de Indias, the Spanish were forced to defend their riches in every corner of their possessions.

The English captain John Hawkins raided Veracruz and other ports, all the time carrying on, with England's support, the slave trade between Africa and the Caribbean. But the quintessential corsair acting on behalf of his sovereign was Francis Drake. When his fleet sailed into San Juan Bay in Puerto Rico, chains were slung across the entry to stop him. The trick succeeded in sinking two of his ships. But from Veracruz in Mexico to Valparaíso in Chile, Drake attacked, briefly occupied, sacked, and left.

He was not the first or the last pirate to be knighted by the English monarchy. But then, in 1587, Drake raided Cádiz, the port of entry for Spanish gold, sinking over twenty ships and "singeing His Catholic Majesty's beard." The raid on Cádiz effectively postponed preparations for the supreme enterprise of Philip II's reign: the creation of an Invincible Armada to attack Protestant England, not so much because it was Protestant but because it had assisted Philip's rebellious Dutch subjects. Philip had defended Elizabeth I from the pope's threats of excommunication, as he feared the ascension to the English throne of the Scottish pretender, the Catholic Mary I, whom he saw as a puppet of his greatest rival, France. But when Elizabeth sent the earl of Leicester to aid the Dutch against Spain, Philip drew the line.

Philip was flush with victory after defeating the Turks in the eastern

Mediterranean at the great Battle of Lepanto, where, on October 7, 1571, his bastard half-brother, Don Juan of Asturia, not only vanquished but killed the Turkish commander, Ali Pasha. Painted and praised to the heavens, the victory at Lepanto was notable for another occurrence: a sailor named Miguel de Cervantes lost the use of a hand in combat there.

After Lepanto, irritated by Elizabeth, Philip set about the adventure of the Armada. On its success hinged Spain's ambitions to become not only the world's greatest empire but Europe's leading power. Philip delegated authority to organize the vast fleet, which was conceived to crush Protestantism once and for all and make Spain's hegemony in Europe and the world concomitant.

For twenty years Philip meditated on these matters, as he meditated on the ultimate riposte to Elizabeth, the Grand Armada. Would it suffice to safeguard the routes from the American treasure-lands? Could it bring England back to Catholicism? Whatever Philip's thoughts, there was never an adequate relationship among them, his goals, and the means he used to further those goals.

A tuna-fish magnate, the duke of Medina-Sidonia, was given overall direction of the enterprise, in spite of his repeated complaints that he was not fit for the job and was furthermore prone to seasickness. Philip named him for political, not technical, reasons. Only a grandee such as the duke could impose authority on the ants, from admirals to biscuit makers, scurrying to service and outfit the Armada with provisions, passing yet again through an obscure bureaucrat named Miguel de Cervantes, who had been sent out to collect fees from the church to finance the enterprise — and who ended in prison when the ecclesiastical authorities revenged themselves against his zeal.

Medina-Sidonia proved to be a prophet of disaster. In spite of the money invested to equip 20 galleons, 130 other vessels, and 30,000 men, there never was an overall plan for the operation. The Armada was to triumph through sheer numbers and acts of devotion (180 monks and friars were on board, singing daily masses and Ave Marias). Sent off as tightly packed as Medina-Sidonia's tunas, the Spanish ships were often useless in the stormy northern waters and far slower than the English craft. They were also leaking, along with their water casks, and indeed with news of the whole adventure.

Philip's old enemy, Drake, attacked the Armada off Calais, and the ships were dispersed and tossed by violent storms as far out as Ireland. Only half the Armada and a quarter of the men came back. "I did not send my ships to fight the elements," exclaimed Philip II.

*The Christian
fleets at Messina
before the Battle of
Lepanto in 1571.
Giorgio Vasari,
n.ð.*

*The "Armada
Portrait" of Queen
Elizabeth I,
attributed to
George Gower, n.d.*

*The retreat of the
Spanish Armada,
1588*

VIOLENCE IN HEAVEN

The defeat of the Armada was in effect the defeat of Spain's pretensions to be the paramount power in Europe. From then on, Spain's traditional enemy, the other superpower, France, defied it. The rapidly emerging Protestant world, led by the English and the Dutch, allied to produce a military power that challenged Spain's and a naval power that had been proven superior. Besides, the merging of Protestantism and capitalism throughout northern Europe was creating a modern success story that compared very favorably to Spain's continuing reliance on American treasure, heavy taxation, and agricultural industry. The Protestants had found an ironclad political and religious formula for power: *Cuis regio, eius religio.* The ruling prince decided what the religion of the realm would be, and this choice sanctified his political and economic sovereignty. In Spain, the possibilities that had existed at the beginning of the sixteenth century — the modern revolutions in science and free inquiry, parliamentary government, and the traditional rights of the townships — had practically flickered out. The Council of Trent (1545–1563) established the rigid demands of the Counter-Reformation. Dogma was defined and strengthened, the church had the exclusive right to interpret the Bible, and reconciliation with Protestantism was doomed.

The Council of Trent also gave the pope the exclusive right to name bishops. But this was something that, for all his devotion, Philip could not countenance. He went on appointing his own bishops and only agreed to publish the decrees of Trent on the condition that his powers over the Spanish clergy were explicitly respected. Under Philip, the Inquisition, which was accountable only to him, grew in power as his favorite arm of religious authority, and further strengthened his hand against Rome. Bishops loyal to the pope were imprisoned and accused of Lutheranism, and the Inquisition extended its vigilance and persecution not only against Protestants, Jews, and Moors but especially against the converted, suspecting them of bad faith and secret practices.

Complex and full of conflict, at odds with the Protestant Reformation but also with papal power, perhaps Philip was even more at odds with himself. Like his father before him, he retired into a living tomb. El Escorial, the citadel of this man, his faith, and perhaps also his secret doubts, was conceived as a sepulcher for Charles V and Philip's other ancestors, but it also served as a symbol of the orthodox faith and as a memorial to Philip's military victory over the French at Saint-Quentin in 1557. The first and greatest architectural monument of the Counter-Reformation, it became the Vatican of Spain's temporal powers.

El Escorial.
Pier Maria Baldi,
late 17th century

"Build with the greatest haste!" Philip ordered his architects. But although it was begun in 1563, the sober (and somber) building — vast, forbidding, deprived on the king's orders of any frivolous adornments — was not finished until twenty-one years later, in 1584. The quarries and the woodlands of Castile were plundered to build it; an army of masons, carpenters, carriers, blacksmiths, painters, and plumbers worked and died there, and sometimes mutinied. A thousand oxen carried the materials, and a hundred omens, in the form of storms, bloody accidents, and a howling, haunted dog, hung over the building as it was erected. Finally, on the great day, the corpses of all of Philip's ancestors rumbled into El Escorial from everywhere in Spain. He was there to receive them and bury them in the *pudridero*, the rotting pit. His first orders were that a perpetual death mass should be sung there, for himself and his predecessors and descendants. And immediately after, he ordered that thirty thousand additional masses be celebrated for "the repose of my soul."

Devoted to death, this fortress, necropolis, and monastery was designed to "give violence to Heaven," wrote the French author Louis Bertrand. But alas, Philip had to continue ruling the affairs of the earth. His love of hard work was proverbial. He did not like to grant interviews. Preferring to drown in paperwork, he was said to write faster than any secretary, know everything in his files, and supervise it all. A contemporary observed, "The king is the sort of person who does not move or betray himself by any movement, even if he has a cat in his pants."

He was called "the Prudent" — a euphemism, everyone agrees, for his extreme difficulty in making decisions. But he held on to the ideal of restoring the unity of Christendom while maintaining the power of Spain, its empire, and his dynasty. He also gave himself a role model: his father, Charles V, whom he idealized to the extent that he could never measure up to him.

Described as small, incredibly soft-spoken, with eyes that were red from reading so many state papers, he smiled only rarely and then with a frozen rictus; his stare, half dreamy, half cruel, as much absent as foxy, makes us wonder whether he was prudent or insecure, mighty or over-burdened. Perhaps Philip could only answer in the solitude of his bed-chamber. Imagine his anguish as he pondered whether his human will was sufficient to make him God's lieutenant on earth. Would he fail in his attempt to restore the unity of the Catholic faith and be rendered account-able in the next life? Thoughts of death must always have been near him, given the deaths of his three wives, of most of his children, and especially of his son Don Carlos, imprisoned by the king himself, "for the service of our Lord and for the public welfare."

The Dream of Philip II. *El Greco, c. 1576–1577*

Federico García Lorca called El Escorial "the sad place from which all the cold rains in the earth come." El Greco, in his stunning *Dream of Philip II*, put the king on his knees, suspended between heaven and earth. But an even greater wonder is that this omnipotent monarch devoted so much of his time and income not only to gathering his family's corpses around him but to surrounding himself with such an avalanche of saintly relics. His agents searched far and wide to bring him the skulls, shinbones, and withered hands of saints and martyrs, the relics of Christ's thorns and the True Cross, which he worshipped more than gold and silver. In fact, Philip managed to amass all 290 holy teeth from the mouth of Saint Apollonia, the patroness of toothache. The relic deposit at El Escorial must have looked like Citizen Kane's warehouse at Xanadu.

THE DECADENCE OF SPAIN

On the death of Philip II (an atrocious, excremental death at El Escorial), all of his debts and failures fell on the head of his less than able son Philip III. Lazy (he worked only six months of the year), Philip III delegated power to his favorites, who committed the colossal blunder of expelling the remaining Moors from Spain, all 275,000 of them, shipping them off to Africa. This counterproductive act practically ruined the middle classes of Valencia and Aragon, who had lent money to the Moors, and the nobility, who had leased land to them; it even threatened to diminish the Inquisition, now bereft of more than a quarter of a million heretics to persecute. All of these groups lost money or power; many defaulted. Much as the homeless have suddenly filled the modern cities of the pros-perous West, so imperial Spain under Philip III came to resemble a nation of bankrupts, beggars, and bandits. Inflation, devaluation, and the sub-stitution of copper for gold and silver followed, and this in the nation that had conquered Mexico and Peru.

Spain also became the first example of an anomaly that the United States runs the risk of repeating as our own century ends: that of being a poor empire, debt-ridden, incapable of solving its internal problems while insistent on playing an imperial role overseas, but begging alms from other, surplus-wealthy nations in order to finance its expensive role as a world policeman. Spain had no Germany or Japan to finance its military operations, however. Instead, it had the bankers, most prominently the Fuggers, who had played the all-important role in elevating the Hapsburgs to head the Holy Roman Empire in 1519. Having bought the votes of the German electors, the bankers then chose Charles V over Francis I of France — exclusively, they admitted, on the strength of the news of the Mexican mines. Jacob Fugger, a shark whose canniness was comparable only to his pride, reminded Charles V that "without my help, Your Imperial Majesty would never have been crowned." Dare any financier speak with such imperiousness today, to any far less impressive head of state?

The Fuggers' and other loans, as we have seen, both financed and milked the Spanish Empire for all it was worth. Spain continued to be dazzled by the accumulation of gold and silver as the essential goal of economics. This mercantilist delusion survived, becoming more and more chimerical as the European, and thus the world, economy became more and more a network of commercial, financial, industrial, and technological relationships. In his splendid essay *Spanish Imperialism and the Political Imagination*, Anthony Pagden notes the Spanish tendency to value *otium*, leisure, over *negotium*, the negation of leisure: business. And though Pagden properly sees this distinction as part of a larger one based on honor (the seed of leisure) and public faith (the bulwark of business), it is not inconsistent with Spain's general attitude toward economic matters. For Spain, everything that shone *was* gold, and as long as it kept coming from the seemingly inexhaustible mines of the New World, Spain would maintain the paraphernalia of empire, both its leisure and its business. Never has credit gone on for so long and such a long way.

Nevertheless, for years the Spanish escudo continued to be the strongest international currency, much like the dollar in our century, the pound sterling in the nineteenth century, and the deutsche mark, perhaps, in the twenty-first century. The juggernaut of empire can go on for a long time. Inertia is a powerful force, and appearances are important, even as the internal organs decay.

Part of that decay was due to corruption, which began on an intensive, virulent scale during Philip III's reign. His favorites, the duke of

Lerma and his son, the duke of Uceda (who ousted his father), were engaged in high-style graft, for themselves and for their associates. Public posts were up for sale, and even the place where the court would reside could be bought. The city fathers of Valladolid suborned the duke of Lerma to have the capital transferred from Madrid to their own city, but it returned to Madrid when, a few years later, the latter city's burghers bribed the prime minister, who thus made a neat double deal.

But again, Spain neither invented administrative corruption nor took it to greater lengths than were to be found elsewhere. Closely allied to the reason for decadence is again a generalized vision of the Spanish character as being partial to laziness and unpunctuality. In one of his playlets, Cervantes let it be known that in military matters, help from Spain was bound to come too late. A proverb much in vogue throughout Europe at the time expressed the desire that one's death should come from Spain, for then it would surely be late for the appointment.

The great paradox of this situation is that unpunctuality, sloth, aristocratic self-indulgence, and innate corruption were attributed to perhaps the most energetic nation of the post-Renaissance world. Though Spain was less organized than the France of the cardinals, Richelieu and Mazarin, which finally defeated the Spanish army once and for all at Rocroi in 1643, and less astute than the English, who deprived Spain of any hope of retaining naval mastery after the disaster of the Armada, it was energetic beyond all that had been conceived since the times of Rome. Evidence lay in the discovery and conquest of half the globe, including the New World, in the founding of hundreds of cities in the Americas, and in the battles on every front — against the Turks, the Protestants, the other European powers.

Spain at her height could do anything. She could exhaust her treasury and forget her poor, her bankrupts, her devalued currency, her incompetent economy, her overvalued currency, her recessions and depressions, her debts both internal and foreign, her deficit spending, her negative trade balance, as long as she could keep herself at the head of the mission against the infidel, the Islamic threat and the Protestant threat. But eventually reality caught up and imposed the limits that imperial folly had so easily hurdled over.

The Spanish writer Fernando Díaz Plaja finds a provocative parallel in this situation between Spain and the United States. Both, at the height of their influence, joined military and economic force to an obsessive belief in their own moral justification. Whether against Protestantism, in the case of Spain, or against communism, in the case of the United States, the nation overextended its power, postponed solving internal problems, and sacrificed generations. And even when the enemy ceased to be menacing, the desire to use power persisted, inebriating, addictive.

The analogy can be stretched if one considers that in the middle of its protracted economic decline, Spain remained an extremely powerful military force and indeed the great innovator and wielder of armed technology. The famous Spanish *tercios*, regiments of three thousand men, were admittedly the best fighting units in Europe. They were part of the best infantry in Europe, which again belonged to Spain, a nation that organized modern military command structures. Both "general" and "admiral" are Spanish military concepts; *admiral* is a derivation, once again, of an Arab word.

It was France, Spain's nemesis, that finally stripped the Spanish Hapsburgs of their pretensions to a universal monarchy, a unified Christianity, and a monolithic Europe on Spanish terms. Through compromise and political flexibility, good administration, Machiavellian perversities, and sheer determination, France established the final truth that this was a war of national interests, bereft of religious or imperial considerations, between France and Spain. The Battle of Rocroi exploded forever the prestige of the Spanish army.

No crueler, or even more perverse, manner of driving home this fact can be found than the story of Louis XIV's humiliation of Spain in a simple matter of protocol. In 1661, at the Court of St. James's in London, the French envoy announced that if the Spanish envoy was admitted first, his servants would cut off the Spaniard's horse's reins. Whereupon the Spanish envoy joined his horses to his carriage with chains. Whereupon Louis XIV sent an ultimatum to Philip IV: French ambassadors were to be granted precedence over Spain's envoys at all European courts, or else. The decline of Spanish power can be judged by the fact that Philip IV, rather than risking war, apologized to Louis XIV and admitted French precedence from then on.

That this war was a matter of etiquette is also significant. During two centuries, Spain not only pretended to European political hegemony; it also imposed — this was no pretension, but a reality — cultural fashions throughout Europe. This went from the manner of dress to the manner of war, and back to the formalities of court etiquette, diplomatic style, and conduct in polite society, which, according to Oswald Spengler, "gave [European life] a stamp that lasted till the Congress of Vienna and in essential points till beyond Bismarck." From Charles V to Philip IV, adds the author of *The Decline of the West*, Europe lived "the Spanish century in religion, intellect, art, politics, and manners." Again, this was not the first or the last time that a vast empire, overextended, unaware of its many flaws, went surely toward its doom but actually created out of the corruption of its deterioration the ferment necessary to achieve the heights of creativity.

In spite of intolerance, corruption, incompetence, and commitment beyond its abilities, the Spanish monarchy of the seventeenth century coexisted with the greatest flourishing of culture that Spain would ever know: *el siglo de oro*, the Age of Gold, the greatest century of Spanish literature and painting — the age of the painters El Greco, Velázquez, Zurbarán, and Murillo, of the dramatists Lope de Vega and Calderón de la Barca, of the poets Quevedo and Góngora, and of the novelist Cervantes.

EIGHT

The Century of Gold

During the seventeenth century, the Spanish monarchs kept taking for themselves whole shipments of American bullion in order to pay for their wars and especially to repay their debts. The quick passage of gold and silver through Spain led to the devaluation of the local currency; no one would accept the copper vellum. The Spanish Empire had about 35 million inhabitants, including some 17 million Europeans outside Iberia, which had a mere 8 million, and the division between the haves and the have-nots had grown with the uneven distribution of wealth.

The cities were full of beggars, some of whom were authentic mendicants, with a certificate that gave them the right to beg. The blind were especially privileged, being authorized to sing songs and sell almanacs. But of the 150,000 Spanish beggars at the time of Cervantes and Velázquez, the majority were fakers with a talent for simulating bleeding ulcers and sudden fevers. Thieves could be cat burglars, who burglarized homes; "devouts," who stole from churches; "apostles," who were specialists in breaking down doors; or artful dodgers, who could leave you naked in the middle of the street. Countryside bandits were sometimes old soldiers left without an occupation, sometimes men fleeing from the Inquisition, or even ruined field hands.

Who fled the Inquisition? Again and again, these were the converted Jews, disparagingly called *marranos,* or pigs, who had not gone into exile in 1492 and who were constantly harassed, suspected, and persecuted when they did not show the ability to integrate, as did the Torquemadas and, perhaps, the ancestors of Saint Teresa of Ávila and even Cervantes. But who in Spain (or indeed ourselves, the Americans descended from Spain) was not integrated with the blood of Jews and Arabs after a thousand years of intimate coexistence?

Don Quixote.
From an engraving
by Gustave Doré

Beyond the world of the beggars, the ruffians, and the burglars, or *pícaros* as they were known, was a great chasm reaching out to the world of the nobility. This included the petty hidalgos, and higher up the gentlemen or knights, and on the top the grandees. They were exempted from taxation. They were judged by special courts. They could not be imprisoned for debts. They could carry a sword. They had the right to dress in a different way from the lower orders. Any individual was subject to the rules and the privileges, or the lack of them, of his social order.

Officially, this was an ordered world, a prolongation of the medieval sense of place, meaning, and harmony. But it existed in the new Europe, where religious unity had broken down, where social classes struggled out of their traditional straitjackets and ambitiously claimed a place in the sun, where financial risk and mercantile audacity could find ample reward, where everything was moving, breaking boundaries, inventing languages and images for a new historical era. Spain could not wholly escape the effects of this wide transformation. But it certainly resisted the disorders of the outside world, as best it could, through championship of Catholic unity — which was now a mirage. Spain espoused a dogmatic approach because it was desirable, at the very least, to have a unified, orthodox language sustaining a unified vision of the world.

Between official order and unofficial disorder, the responses were multiple, giving the Spanish Golden Century its sense of urgency and perhaps even its beauty. For there is a pictorial, verbal, and dramatic beauty to be found in this long tension between what was permitted and what was forbidden. Desire clashed with prohibitions, the visible with the invisible, and the said with the unsaid. More eloquent than any silence, this tension also held a sense of danger, stimulation, intelligence. Rarely has one nation in such a short time proven itself capable of offering so many responses to the single challenge of a dogmatic, unified, ordered vision of the world. These responses go all the way from the extreme of the picaresque to the mystical.

There is no other painting in which the human and the divine coexist so graphically, so precisely, and so realistically as in *The Burial of Count Orgaz*. Divided between these two spheres, El Greco's work would be incomplete without one or the other. Split the picture with your hand. Singled out, the upper part is certainly a great religious portrait of the Kingdom of Heaven, while the lower part is certainly a magnificent portrait of the funeral of the Spanish grandee and soldier. The faces bear all the traits of our tradition: individualism, honor, stoic resistance, pride. But only when a figure in the center of the painting looks upward and

The Burial of Count Orgaz. *El Greco, 1586*

perhaps meets the downward gaze of God does the painting achieve its full power to mediate between heaven and earth, making one dependent on the other, welding matter and spirit through a precise articulation of life and death, of earthly dignity and supernatural glory.

Between the two, and indeed encompassing both, is an art that will not exhaust itself in the day-to-day, meaningless struggle for survival, or sacrifice itself to the renunciation of all worldly pleasure. Perhaps only between such extremes, in such a society, could the great narrative and figurative art of Miguel de Cervantes and Diego Velázquez have come into being.

IN PRAISE OF FOLLY

Miguel de Cervantes, born in 1547 into a family, it is said, of "shabby gentility," followed his father, a failed surgeon, in his wanderings around the Spain of Charles V and Philip II. He was certainly a student of the renowned Spanish Erasmist Juan López de Hoyos, and possibly a student in Salamanca.

The influence of Erasmus on Cervantes is as certain as the enormous influence of Erasmus on Spanish life at the beginning of the sixteenth century. The sage of Rotterdam pleaded with the church: Reform yourself before it is too late. He also pleaded for the new culture of humanism: All things have several meanings. Neither reason nor faith exhausts reality. In praising folly, Erasmus argued that both faith and reason had to become relative, not absolute, terms. His influence in the Spain of Charles V is revealed by the fact that the king's secretary, Alfonso de Valdés, was

Miguel de Cervantes. 19th-century engraving, artist unknown

Desiderius Erasmus. 19th-century engraving, artist unknown

a self-proclaimed Erasmist. But after the schism in the church and Luther's Reformation, Erasmus ceased to be glorified; his books were banned, and his noble features, as painted by Holbein the Younger, became disfigured and fanged in an atrocious caricature drawn up by the Inquisition. No wonder that Cervantes could not even mention his foremost intellectual influence in any of his works.

In 1534, the humanist Juan Luis Vives had written to Erasmus, saying, "The times we live in are extremely difficult, and I cannot truly say which is more dangerous, to talk or to keep silent." A century later, the great baroque poet and satirical writer Francisco de Quevedo painfully exclaimed, "I shall not keep silent!" and questioned himself and his society:

> No ha de haber un espíritu valiente?
> Siempre se ha de sentir lo que se dice?
> Nunca se ha de decir lo que se siente?
>
> Is there ever to be a courageous will?
> Are we always to regret what we say?
> Are we never to say what we regret?

They knew what they were talking about. Vives, an Erasmist who was also a *converso*, was exiled from Spain, his possessions confiscated, and his family burned at the stake by the Holy Office. Quevedo was repeatedly jailed for his irreverent writings. The index of works forbidden by the Spanish Inquisition (including those of Erasmus and Machiavelli) was harsher than the pope's. Philip II forbade Spaniards to study abroad, except in Rome. This intellectual cloistering affected the importation of books and, naturally, the publication of books in Spain itself.

Cervantes, the minor hero at Lepanto, initially was able to sing the orthodox glories of empire, as when he justified Philip II's famous exclamation that the Armada was defeated by "the elements." "Our ships," wrote Cervantes, "are not returned to us by the adverse arms but by the unbeatable storm, by wind, and sea, and sky." But at the end of Philip's reign, when he published one of his exemplary novels, *El celoso extremeño*, he was forced to revise his viewpoint in conformity with that of the church. The book had originally ended with two lovers in bed, joined in the flesh. But when the archbishop of Seville, Cardinal Fernando Niño de Guevara, read the manuscript, "the angels of the Counter-Reformation," as Américo Castro calls them, fluttered over the unfortunate lovers, and in the published version, the couple sleeps in perfect chastity. Cervantes bowed to His Eminence's suggestions.

As reality caught up and imposed the limits that imperial overreaching had disregarded, and as Cervantes felt the arrows of censorship in his own flesh, he began to evolve a comic, indirect language that went against the grain of official conformity. He invented an odd couple, a lesser hidalgo who thinks himself a knight errant of old, and a *pícaro*, his squire Sancho Panza, to bridge the gap between the extremes of Spain. Through the meeting of genius between the tarnished armor of Don Quixote and the hungry belches of Sancho Panza, we find a link between the picaresque and the mystical, the realism of survival and the dream of empire, the language of the epic and the language of the folktale. The result certainly contained the ambiguity searched for by Erasmus — the reasonable folly, a relative reason, a work of art. Quixote speaks the language of absolute abstractions; Sancho, the language of concrete relatives. They cease to understand each other; and the modern novel was born when its protagonists no longer spoke the same language. Ancient heroes — Achilles, Ulysses, King Arthur, Roland — all spoke the same way. In a novel, all the characters speak differently. But this can be a dangerous folly indeed.

Cervantes, let us not forget, lived in the age when Giordano Bruno was burned at the stake by the Inquisition. This happened in Rome in 1600, five years before the publication of *Don Quixote*. And in 1616, the year of Cervantes' death, the Catholic church officially condemned the system of Copernicus. In 1633, Galileo was forced to give up his ideas before the Holy Office. Galileo died in 1642. In that same year, Isaac Newton was born. And Europe, the Europe of the high Renaissance hopes, had become the Europe of failed hopes and religious strife.

Is all possible? Or is all in doubt? In the same year, 1605, *Don Quixote*, *King Lear*, and *Macbeth* were published. Two mad old men and a young assassin came forth on the stage of the world to remind us of all of the glory and servitude that humankind is prey to. Shakespeare sings of a "brave new world." Cervantes laments the passing of the "Golden Age . . . when all things were held in common, [when] clear springs and running rivers offered men their sweet and limpid waters in glorious abundance." Now, says Don Quixote, we live "in this detestable age of ours." And Shakespeare asks us if the world is "a tale told by an idiot, full of sound and fury, signifying nothing." Cervantes shared this world with Shakespeare. Indeed, they died on the same day, April 23, 1616.

MAN OF LA MANCHA

And yet, with *Don Quixote de la Mancha*, Cervantes invented the modern novel, in the very nation that refused modernity. Whereas the Spain of

An illustration from Gustave Doré's Don Quixote, *1862*

the Inquisition imposed one single, dogmatic, and orthodox point of view on the world, Cervantes essentially imagined a world of multiple points of view, and he did it through an apparently innocent satire on the novels of chivalry. And if modernity is based on multiple points of view, these in their turn are based on a principle of uncertainty. The beauty of it all, of course, is that Don Quixote is a man of faith, not of doubt, not of uncertainty. And his certainty comes from his reading. His faith is in his books, his "words, words, words."

When Don Quixote goes out of his village into the fields of La Mancha, he leaves behind his books, his library — his shelter. Quixote is a reader of books of chivalry, and everything he reads, he believes. Therefore, everything he reads is true. His madness is his reading. His *lectura* (reading) is his *locura* (madness). For him, the windmills are giants, because his books said so. When he attacks the windmills, is thrown into the air, and lands on his head, it can be none other than the work of giants and magicians, because that is what he has read, and no one can convince him of the contrary. He picks himself up and mounts his nag once more, going forth to do battle against villains and to rescue orphans, widows, and damsels in distress, because this is the mission demanded of him by the code of honor contained in his books.

But when he leaves the village and his books to sally forth into La Mancha, Don Quixote also leaves the ordered world of the Middle Ages, solid as a castle, where everything has a recognizable place, and enters the brave new world of the Renaissance, where everything is in doubt, agitated by the winds of ambiguity and change. The genius of Cervantes is that having established the reality of faith in the books that Don Quixote carries around in his head, he then established the reality of doubt in the very book that Don Quixote sets out to live, the novel *Don Quixote de la Mancha*. For where is Don Quixote's home? "In a certain place of La Mancha whose name I do not wish to remember."

Having cast doubt on the very place where the novel occurs, Cervantes established his principle of uncertainty, and then, with a bold step, went on to propose uncertainty of authorship. Who is the author of *Don Quixote*? we are constantly asked. A certain Cervantes? An Arab author translated by another Arab? Or the multiple authors of the several false *Quixotes*, apocryphal versions, abridgments, continuations? Or is the true author the illiterate squire Sancho Panza, the only character who is present throughout all of Don Quixote's actions, except when he goes off to govern the illusory island of Barataria? By casting such doubt on authorship, Cervantes put authority itself in doubt.

Names are uncertain in *Don Quixote* as well. "Don Quixote" is simply the *nom de guerre* that a country gentleman called Alonso Quixano — or is it Quixada? — gives himself. But he also names himself "the Knight of the Sorrowful Countenance," while others further deform or caricature his name, according to the circumstances. Quixote's power of nomination is such that he transforms a run-down nag into the gallant steed Rocinante. And who is Don Quixote's ideal lady, a lowly peasant girl who bellows and smells of garlic, or the high princess Dulcinea?

Finally, the genre of the book is uncertain. Don Quixote includes in his novel-ty all of the genres then in vogue — the epic of chivalry, the picaresque narrative, the play-within-a-play, the pastoral poem, the tale of love — blending them into a new genre, the genre of genres, the novel, with a new-won capacity to embrace the whole world and include its multiplicity. What clinches this variety of points of view is the fact that in *Don Quixote*, for the first time in literature, the characters find out that they appear in a novel, that they are read and judged by the multiple points of view of a radically new, modern entity: readers of books that are published on that other novelty, the printing press.

Faith and doubt. Certainty and uncertainty. These are the themes of the modern world that Cervantes presented as he invented the modern European novel. Dostoevsky called it "the saddest book ever written," for it is "the story of a disillusionment." This matter of great expectations dimming into lost illusions became the aura of many modern novels.

At the end, Don Quixote goes back to his village and recovers his reason. But for him, that is madness, and he dies. But isn't it really the old hidalgo Alonso Quixada — or is it Quixano? — who dies, while Don Quixote goes on living forever in his book, madly, heroically, comically, gallantly? For are not the doubt overcome and the disillusionment vanquished, after all, by love? The truth of Don Quixote is that he *is* aware of who Dulcinea is: simply the peasant girl Aldonza. He knows this, he admits, and yet because he loves her, she is, he says, "the highest princess in the land." He adds, "Suffice it for me to think that the good woman Aldonza is beautiful and honest, for the matter of lineage is of small account. . . . I paint her in my imagination as I desire her. . . . And let each man say what he wishes."

LAS MENINAS

To the demand of the Counter-Reformation and the Inquisition for only one point of view, Cervantes would answer that we are being seen. We are not alone. We are surrounded by others. We read. We are being read. We have not finished our adventure. We will not finish it, Sancho, as long as there is a reader who will open our book and thus give us back our lives. We are the result of the points of view of many readers, past, present, and future — but always present when they read *Don Quixote* or see *Las Meninas*.

In spite of the multiplicity of illustrations drawn from *Don Quixote* — from Hogarth to Daumier, from Doré to Picasso, from George Cruikshank in the nineteenth century to Antonio Saura in the twentieth — a more compelling pictorial correspondence to Cervantes hangs in the center of a large but quiet room in Madrid's Prado Museum. As we enter the room, we surprise the painter, Diego Rodríguez de Silva y Velázquez, doing his job, which is painting. But whom is Velázquez painting? The infanta, her *dueñas*, her dwarf, or a gentleman clad in black who is coming across a brightly lit threshold? Or is he really painting two figures dimly reflected in a mirror buried in the deepest, most shadowy recesses of the artist's studio: the father and mother of the princess, the king and queen of Spain?

Las Meninas.
Diego Velázquez,
1656

We might think that in any case, Velázquez is there, brush in one hand, palette in the other, painting the canvas we are actually viewing, *Las Meninas* — until we realize that the majority of the figures, except of course the drowsy dog and an oversolicitous *dueña,* are looking at us, at you and me. Could it be possible that *we* are the true protagonists of *Las Meninas* — that is, the canvas that Velázquez is actually painting? For Velázquez and the whole court invite us to join the painting, to walk into it, but at the same time the painting takes a step forward and moves toward us. This is the true dynamic of this great masterpiece. We are free to move in and out of it. We are free to see the painting, and by extension the world, in multiple ways, not in one dogmatic, orthodox way. And we are aware that the painting and the painter are watching us.

Velázquez's actual painting, the canvas of the painter in the painting, has its back to us, and it is unfinished, whereas we are looking at what we consider to be the finished product. But between these two central evidences, two big, wide, and surprising spaces open. The first belongs to the original scene itself: Velázquez painting, infanta and *dueñas* surprised, gentleman in black coming through lighted door, king and queen reflected in mirror. Did this scene ever occur? Was it posed, or did Velázquez simply imagine some or all of its components? And second, was the painting ever finished? Velázquez was not a popular painter in his own day, the philosopher José Ortega y Gasset informs us, and he was faulted for showing unfinished paintings. Quevedo even accused him of indulging in painting "distant smudges."

Is this not yet another opening on the closed society of dogma and a single point of view? Does it not raise the possibility that everything in the world — this painting, but also this history, this narrative — is unfinished? And that, more specifically, we are unfinished ourselves, men and women who cannot be declared "complete," enclosed within boundaries of finitude and certainty — unfinished even when we die, because forgotten or remembered, we do contribute to a past that our descendants must keep alive if they are to have a future?

Cervantes teaches us to read anew. Velázquez teaches us to see anew. Certainly all great writers and artists do as much. But these two, working from within a closed society, were able to redefine reality in terms of the imagination. What we imagine is both possible and real.

DON JUAN AND SAN JUAN

When Velázquez was named court painter by King Philip IV in 1623, he made a clear distinction between the freedom of his art, which he considered a gift of nature, and his service to the king, which was simply the means to an end. Astutely, he never presented himself as a painter but as the king's servant. When the pope sent him a golden chain as a prize for his art, Velázquez sent it right back; he was not a painter but a court official. He thus freed himself from any obligation to the king except painting him and his family as they aged, as they became theatrical props that ceased to resemble anything except the art with which Velázquez represented them.

Distant, says Ortega y Gasset. Velázquez was an artist of distances — distant from the court, from his subjects, from his technique, which only becomes "realistic" from afar, since at close quarters it is minutely abstract, daring, well beyond its time. The painting existed for the sake of itself. The post was due to the king. Velázquez had to make this distinction if he was to prosper and survive, and if he was to keep his sense of humor.

The king, it was widely believed, was the model for Don Juan, the rake of Seville, as depicted in the seminal play published in 1634 by the friar Gabriel Téllez, whose *nom de plume* was Tirso de Molina (though the true model for Don Juan could also have been another libertine, Don Miguel de Mañara, known for his seductions of cloistered nuns). Philip IV was more tempted by actresses than by handmaidens to the Lord. He had thirty bastard children, only one of whom he officially recognized: Don Juan, his son by the actress María Calderón. Once he had cast off a mistress, however, Philip did send her to a nunnery, thus assuring that no one would have her after he had. A lady of the court, when refusing the king's enticement, once told him, "Sire, I do not have a vocation for the convent." His fame as a libertine was indeed stupendous, and only comparable to his bouts of religious repentance and his attachment to the abbess of Agreda, who was his most steadfast friend and counselor.

Out of this court of tenacious sexual intrigue, religious penitence, and family inbreeding came the dwarfs and jesters painted by Velázquez, as well as the king's legitimate son and heir, Charles II, called the Bewitched. The final monarch of the Hapsburg line in Spain, Charles II, as painted by Coello, was a double of Velázquez's deformed buffoons — impotent, ignorant, implausible. Above them all glided the figure of freedom, the libertine, but also, in a perverse way, the *liberal* Don Juan, breaking out of the walls of El Escorial, out of the convents and monasteries, always in displacement, finding the velocity of pleasure in the velocity of change, moving beyond borders. Don Juan has lovers in Italy, in France, and in Turkey, Mozart's "catalogue song" in *Don Giovanni* informs us, but in Spain he has chalked up one thousand and three. He is the founder of the European Common Market of Eroticism. He is the Machiavelli of sex, escaping vengeance but especially outwitting boredom and repetition. Perhaps he loves only himself. His life is movement, change, circulation; he is insatiable, unsatisfied, inconsolable. Only music, not painting, not even poetry, can pretend to catch up with him. Don Juan is a fugitive and his music is a fugue. His perpetual movement is best rendered by Mozart in the most famous *Don Giovanni* of them all.

But the first Spanish Don Juan, Tirso's *Rake of Seville*, was an inexperienced young man, with hardly a laundry list of lovers — only four women, to be exact — and access to no pleasure garden beyond Seville, its palaces, and its convents. The masculine Don Juan was indeed a seducer, but how was he to avoid the seduction of the other sex, the female species, as painted by yet another Spaniard of the reign of Philip IV, Francisco de Zurbarán? These virgins and martyrs are among the

Don Sebastián
de Morra.
Velázquez, c. 1644

Charles II.
Claudio Coello,
c. 1685

The Jester.
Velázquez, c. 1639

A scene from the English National Opera's 1985 production of Don Giovanni

most tempting and troubling women ever portrayed. Zurbarán's nudes are pale and feeble. But as soon as he starts dressing his models, they become irresistible — sin and pleasure entwined, as in the flamenco.

As I have mentioned, Zurbarán picked up the tradition of the Spanish virgin martyr, the early Christian women who preferred death to sex, refused marriage or seduction, especially if offered by a non-Christian or a Roman legionnaire, and died for it. He painted them as splendid figures full of sexual turbulence and passion for saintliness, persecuted by spurned lovers and dissatisfied fathers, willing to be mutilated and burned, willing to dress like men and even to be accused of siring the baby of an innkeeper's daughter, as in the case of Saint Marina, or forced to dress themselves as men and be accused — going full circle — of seducing nuns, as in the case of Saint Margaret.

Zurbarán dressed them all, whatever the circumstances, in silks and brocades, multicolored shawls and flowing capes; they are wrapped in rose and pale green, knitted orange and fainting yellows. Zurbarán gave them peasant straw hats, pilgrim's staffs, golden tiaras, false farthingales, baskets of fruit, garlands of flowers. He also offered them the emblems of their martyrdom. Saint Dorothea is given back her basket of flowers, sent by her from heaven to the Roman procurator who had her beheaded. Saint Apollonia carries her teeth (those left uncollected by Philip II), and Saint Lucy bears her eyes on a platter.

The ambiguity of Zurbarán's erotic holiness had two important consequences. The first was that his celestial courtesans were easily presented not only as symbols of salvation but equally as paradigms of perdition. Figures practically identical to the female saints reappeared as she-devils in Zurbarán's painting of the temptations of Saint Jerome. The saint shoos them away with a gesture of his arms, but they, luxuriously attired, play harps and guitars and sing, for all we know, the aria "Voi che sapete" from Mozart's *Marriage of Figaro*. What do we really know about Love? both Zurbarán and Mozart asked.

As did Spain's greatest mystical poet, San Juan de la Cruz, but within a tension far more difficult than anything imagined by Don Juan, Zurbarán, or Mozart. San Juan de la Cruz, whose life spanned the reign of Philip II, was a monk bent on applying Saint Teresa of Ávila's strict reforms to the Carmelite order, which had become lax during the later Middle Ages. For San Juan, the order's founding symbol, Mount Carmel, became the symbol of an ascension, a spiritual voyage from the flesh to the utter immateriality required to see God, who is absent and invisible to even the most faithful human eyes.

To reach God was the supreme command of the soul. And all the writings of San Juan de la Cruz are infused with this obligation. Mere approximation is refused as weak and unworthy. San Juan speaks of a total surrender of the soul to God. His four great works, *The Ascent of Mount Carmel, The Dark Night of the Soul, Spiritual Canticle,* and the final *Flame of Love,* are stages in the soul's search for God, shedding all earthly desires, reaching union with God, marrying him, and achieving the most sublime identification with him.

Yet the trouble with San Juan's mystical journey was that it was bound on all sides by hedges of thorns. The thorniest question was that for San Juan, God was Nothing, the supreme Nothing, and reaching him meant traveling toward this Nothingness, which cannot be touched, or seen, or even understood in physical, human terms. God is not sensible; he is distant, and there is no relationship between him and the human being. This totally harsh, demanding stance would defeat even the most faithful, but not San Juan, the supreme Spanish mystic, who gave it all up in one of those transcendental voyages so dear to the Spanish ethos. "All the being of creatures is nothing compared to God's infinite being," he wrote. "All the beauty of human creatures is nothing but sovereign ugliness compared to God's infinite beauty."

He believed this; but far from renouncing union with God, he found his appetite whetted by the difficulty. If all things sensitive existed in silence and night, he would plunge into silence and night. The problem, of course, was that in this absolute silence, in this deepest of nights, perhaps no communication was possible except death. God is invisible while we live. We may see him when we die. This is the sense of San Juan's beautiful, extreme, impatient poem (perhaps one of the two most beautiful poems in Spanish), "I die because I do not die."

The genius of San Juan was that by utterly denying attention to any worldly, sensory matter, he admitted that he was left with only two ways of reaching God. One was death, the other poetry. While asking questions about the impossibility of joining God, even through poetic means, the poet joins God through poetry. As he searches in doubt, he achieves what he desires: union with God.

The other greatest poem in the Spanish language, *The Dark Night of the Soul,* is without doubt an extraordinary mystical work, in which the soul is female and God is male. One cannot escape, in spite of San Juan de la Cruz's symbolic terms, the sensual, erotic immediacy of the story. Symbolize as we may, we are taken by the hand of the poet on a sexual adventure, which begins in the deepest night. "She" leaves her house, without being noticed. She mounts a staircase, disguised, trembling in anticipation. She finds no guide in the dark, secret, blissful night except the light of her heart. And this guides her to "He," whom she knows; he is waiting for her so that she can exclaim, "O night that joins lover with lover, the She lover into the He lover transformed!" And it does not end there, for she informs us that he fell asleep on her "flowery breasts" as she caressed him. Then the wind blew, scattering her hair, while he, with his "serene hand," wounded her throat and "suspended all of my senses." Finally, she says,

> I remained, and forgot myself
> Resting my face on my Lover's,
> While all things stood still
> And I abandoned Myself,
> Leaving my sorrow forgotten among the
> White lilies . . .

Perhaps *The Dark Night* is the greatest mystical poem written in Spanish *because* it is the most erotic.

LIFE IS A DREAM

Is art all the richer when it has to struggle against structures, dogmas, prohibitions? A lot of great art has been born in harmony with the governing beliefs and demands of society, notably in classical antiquity and the Middle Ages. But the modern world was born of a critical impulse, and was legitimized by it. The orthodoxy of the Spanish Counter-Reformation was, as we have seen, antimodern, but was outwitted by the imagination of Cervantes, Velázquez, Don Juan, and San Juan de la Cruz, who proposed a critical experience from within.

The response to the Counter-Reformation within its very core — the religious life of Spain — is best exemplified by the lives and work of two saints. The first, Saint Teresa of Ávila (1515–1582), was a mixture of strong, active will and insecure intellect. As she set out to restore the austerity of the Carmelite order, she drew strength from her local Castilian roots. Her will to survive came from her *converso* Jewish ancestors; her combativeness, from the *reconquista* tradition of warfare and conquest (all of Saint Teresa's brothers became soldiers and left for America). Her realism came from the depths of domestic life — the clan, the family, the kitchen. Only she could say, "You will find God among the soup kettles." Her abrasiveness, too, was a product of the Castilian position as a frontier land, the pioneer land of Spain. Of that land she said as she left her hometown, vigorously stamping her feet on the ground outside the walls, "I will not take with me even the dust of Ávila." "An errant, wandering woman," Philip II called her; a pest, a busybody. But it was thanks to the king's protection that she was able to found thirty-two reformed convents, first for women only, but after her meeting with San Juan de la Cruz in 1567, also for men.

But San Juan was a poet, even if beaten and imprisoned by the enemies of the religious reform that he espoused after his meeting with Saint Teresa of Ávila. Saint Teresa did not possess his kind of literary genius. Her writings are marred by a need to explain everything, yet saved by a humility that stands in contrast to her forceful public personality. Her books abound in doubts, admissions of ignorance, and lapses of memory, but they shine with a true inner light. What Saint Teresa was attempting was the complete abolition of her biography so that she could become a purely contemplative being. There was, she said, no other way of achieving grace. Her symbol of the inner life is in its essence Castilian: the castle. The high fortress of *la reconquista* and of the novels of chivalry was the shelter of the Christian soul. Inside the Castle of Perfection, the soul could contemplate God.

Saint Teresa's reforms were castigated as being cold and remote, imposing a rule of contemplation far too removed from Christian charity. She answered that she and her sisters prayed for those who did not, and that their austerity was but an expiation for the sins of others. Whereas Saint Teresa's reformed Carmelites aimed for the pinnacle of self-denial, another order, founded in 1540 by a former soldier, Ignatius of Loyola, stressed the worldly activities of its members. The Society of Jesus quickly went outside the monastery walls to make worldly commitments, especially in education. The Jesuits were not only teachers but also the confessors of Europe's Catholic monarchs. No penances, fasts, or common uniforms here; no female branch, but a highly centralized male authority with extreme flexibility in human contact.

The vast influence of the Jesuits in Spain and Spanish America provoked jealousy, disputes, and finally their expulsion, under the enlightened policies of the Bourbons in the eighteenth century. But in the Golden Age, Saint Teresa and Loyola illuminated the religious extremes of the Spanish Counter-Reformation, as well as its central cultural products. Both signified religious renovations. They lived on the earth, in the woman's severe Castle or in the man's boundless world of politics, persuasion, education, and intrigue. San Juan de la Cruz lived in heaven. But the most interesting, or at least the most understandable, aspect of the culture of the Counter-Reformation was the stage.

This middle ground was represented by the priest and dramatic author Pedro Calderón de la Barca (1600–1681). He was the author of the greatest of all Spanish plays, *La vida es sueño (Life Is a Dream)*, which tells the story of Prince Segismundo, who is locked in a tower. He believes this to be his natural state. The cell is for him "cradle and grave," and he remembers or foresees nothing except his prison. He was put there as a newborn by his father, the king of Poland, because before he was born, his mother, the queen, repeatedly dreamed that she would give birth to a monster in human form, who would tear at her guts and bathe her in blood. So it was. The queen died, and the king was convinced that if his son ever reached the throne, he would be the cruelest, most vicious prince who ever misruled Poland. The king gave credit to augury, announced that the boy had died along with his mother, and sent him to live in the tower.

Yet the king, such being his authority, has now decided to break the chain of fatality and give freedom a chance. He brings poor Segismundo from the jail where he has been trapped since birth and gives him a tacit choice. If the prince rules wisely, fatality will be defeated and the people will be happy. If, on the contrary, he lives up to the evil omen and proves himself to be cruel and arrogant, then the king, the father, will send him back to prison.

So from the natural fatality of the dungeon, Segismundo is taken to the summit of both freedom *and* fatality. The augury is fulfilled by Segismundo's own free actions: he is cruel and murderous. Having risen to the top, he is once more sent to the bottom, and made to believe that whatever he did or saw or felt or understood while acting out the princely role was but a dream. He is put back in his cell, dressed as an animal.

Calderón's life spanned the Golden Age, a century of Janus, facing backward, toward the rise of the Spanish Empire and the extraordinary feats of discovery and conquest in the New World, and forward, toward its decline. Calderón lived in the imperial twilight of the libertine king, Philip IV, and his imbecilic son, Charles the Bewitched. He too faced both ways. He was a great dramatist; he was also a Spaniard and a Catholic, a soldier and a priest. He was the greatest author of religious plays, the famous *autos sacramentales*, in which he defended the dogma of the presence of Christ in the Eucharist against Lutheran and Calvinist impiety. But *Life Is a Dream* is an astoundingly modern play, the source of a whole brood of dream plays, from Kleist to Strindberg to Pirandello (and even to some popular spin-offs in Buster Keaton and Woody Allen). In spite of its radical modernity, however, it must be understood as a Catholic play of the Spanish Counter-Reformation; what we see is an action moving from nature, where man is fallen, to history, where he has a choice and can therefore choose incorrectly, to a second fall, which is finally redeemed through suffering, faith, and virtue.

Segismundo says that his only sin is having been born, and he compares himself to nature, which, having less soul than he, is freer. This absence of freedom he feels as a radical diminution, a sense of not being totally born, filled with a need to finish the act of birth in history. Yet is it a greater crime not to have been born at all? He killed his mother when he was born. While Oedipus was condemned to act, Segismundo is condemned to dream. This is his reality. But what kind of reality is a dream? Is it the rule, so that being awake is the exception? Understood on its own terms, as its own reality, a dream is timeless. It can be eternal, or it can have begun five seconds ago. And in a dream nothing can be had, nothing can be touched.

Life Is a Dream was written in 1635, right in the middle of the dispute between the Jesuits, who stressed free will and human intelligence, and the Dominicans, who faulted the Jesuits for their liberalism and instead underlined the omnipotence of divine justice. While not unresponsive to this classic debate of Christianity, Calderón was also responsive to artistic demands. His time, post-Renaissance Europe, and its problems put forward the great theme of the nature of reality: what is it, where is it, how can we define it, how can we ever know, where do we come from, where are we going? But Calderón also lived in an age that demanded the defense of dogma. He used art to cast an immense shadow on the possibilities of truth, reality, freedom, and predestination. He made a problem out of any certainty. He was a dramatist; he understood that only out of doubt and conflict can any harmony ever rise. And what greater conflict is there than that between nature and civilization, dream and reality?

"THE STAIN"

Don Quixote, says Ramiro de Maeztu, is "the exemplary book" of Spain's decadence. The hidalgo is too old for his adventures. The epic era of Spain is finished. Cervantes invented a ghost to tell Spain that the time of great deeds was over: You are exhausted. Go back home. And if God is good to you, die peacefully. The dream of Utopia had failed in the New World, and the illusion of a universal Catholic monarchy had dissipated. After eight centuries of reconquest, discovery, and conquest; after El Cid and Isabella the Catholic, after Columbus and Cortés, after Saint Teresa and Loyola, after Lepanto and the Armada, the party was over.

Certainly, one is tempted to say that the disasters of history were compensated for by the triumphs of art. We have Philip II, the Inquisition, the Armada, the persecution of Jews, Moors, and *conversos,* the favorites of Philip III, the debauchery of Philip IV, and the imbecility of Charles the Bewitched on the one hand; on the other, *Don Quixote,* San Juan de la Cruz, Saint Teresa, *Las Meninas, Life Is a Dream,* Don Juan, El Greco. But does not this confrontation tell us that the story of Spain, and that of its American colonies, is actually the story, and the dilemma, of being two nations, two cultures, two realities, two dreams, trying desperately to see, to meet, to understand each other?

Two contrasting values, two spheres of reality, levitating, jumping over the vacuum, trying to reach out from the shore of desire to meet the object of desire: that is why the two figures of Cervantes' novel, Don Quixote and Sancho Panza, remain so valid in their contrast, so universal in their appeal. In them, the dilemma of Spain is recognizable for all people, at all times; we all grapple with the ideal and with the real. We all struggle between what is desirable and what is possible. We all face abstract demands and try to face them down with absurdity. We would like to live in a reasonable world where justice is concrete. We are all, at times, epic characters, like Don Quixote, but mostly we live picaresque lives, like Sancho Panza. We would all like to mean something more than we do, but we are tied down to the earthly bondage of eating, digesting, sleeping, moving. "I wish to transcend all silence," claimed San Juan. "God is in the soup kettles," said Saint Teresa.

We are all men and women of La Mancha. In Spanish, *la mancha* means "the stain." When we understand that none of us is pure, that we are all both real and ideal, heroic and absurd, made of desire and imagination as much as of blood and bone, and that each of us is part Christian, part Jew, part Moor, part Caucasian, part black, part Indian, without having to sacrifice any of our components — only then do we truly understand both the grandeur and the servitude of Spain, its empire, its Golden Age, and its inevitable decline.

The reality of our humanity was now to be put forth with even greater urgency and need by the Spanish communities of the New World. If Spanish culture was saved by imagination and desire, beyond the limitations of power, the nascent communities of the New World had to become even more demanding, for they — we — were caught between the destroyed Indian world and a new universe, both European and American. *La Mancha,* the Stain, truly had a meaning in the Americas.

NINE

The Baroque Culture
of the New World

Following the Renaissance, the response to the great divide between ideals and reality was a sensual one. The Protestant Reformation banned images from its churches, considering them to be proofs of papist idolatry. But this puritanism was overcome by a great form of sensual compensation in the glorious music of Johann Sebastian Bach. The rigid Catholic Counter-Reformation also had to make a concession to sensuality. This was the art of the baroque, the expanding, dynamic exception to a religious and political system that wanted to see itself as unified, immovable, eternal. The European baroque became the art of a changing society swirling behind the rigid mask of orthodoxy. But if this was true of Catholic Europe, how true was it of the nascent societies of the New World and the obstacles to change that *they* faced?

During the Renaissance, the discovery of America meant, as we have seen, that Europe had found a place for Utopia. Again and again, when the explorers set foot in the New World, they believed that they had regained paradise. And it was to these lands that the Europeans transferred their failed dreams, moving from paradise to despair. The New World became a nightmare as colonial power spread and its native peoples became the victims of colonialism, deprived of their ancient faith and their ancient lands and forced to accept a new civilization and a new religion. The Renaissance dream of a Christian Utopia in the New World was also destroyed by the harsh realities of colonialism: plunder, enslavement, genocide. Between the two was created the baroque of the New World, rushing to fill in the void between ideals and reality, as in Europe. But in America, the baroque also gave the conquered people a place, a place that not even Columbus or Copernicus could truly grant them, a place where they could mask and protect their faith. Above all, it gave us, the new

The baroque facade of the Church of San Lorenzo, Potosí, Bolivia. Attributed to José Kondori, c. 1728

population of the Americas, the mestizos, a manner in which to express our self-doubt, our ambiguity.

What was our place in the world? To whom did we owe allegiance? Our European fathers? Our Quechua, Maya, Aztec, or Chibcha mothers? To whom should we now pray, the ancient gods or the new ones? What language would we speak, the language of the conquered or that of the conquerors? The baroque of the New World addressed all of these questions. And nothing expressed this uncertainty better than the art of paradox, the art of abundance based on want and necessity, the art of proliferation based on insecurity, rapidly filling in the vacuums of our personal and social history after the conquest with anything that it found at hand. An art that practically drowned in its own burgeoning growth, it was also the art of those who had nothing else, the beggars at the steps of the church, the peasants who came to have their birds blessed or who invested the earnings of a whole year of hard work in the celebration of their saint's day. The baroque was a shifting art, akin to a mirror in which we see our constantly changing identity. It was an art dominated by the single, imposing fact that we were caught between the destroyed Indian world and a new universe that was both European and American.

In the Indian quarter of the great mining capital of Potosí, hearsay has it, there once lived an orphaned Indian from the tropical lowlands of the Chaco. According to myth, he went by the name of José Kondori, and in Potosí he learned to work wood and the crafts of inlaying and furniture building. By 1728, this self-taught Indian architect was constructing the magnificent churches of Potosí, surely the greatest illustration of the meaning of the baroque in Latin America. Among the angels and the vines of the facade of San Lorenzo, an Indian princess appears, and all the symbols of the defeated Incan culture are given a new lease on life. The Indian half-moon disturbs the traditional serenity of the Corinthian vine. American jungle leaves and Mediterranean clover intertwine. The sirens of Ulysses play the Peruvian guitar. And the flora, the fauna, the music, and even the sun of the ancient Indian world are forcefully asserted. There shall be no European culture in the New World unless all of these, our native symbols, are admitted on an equal footing.

Beyond the world of empire, of gold and power, of wars between religions and dynasties, a brave new world was indeed forming itself in the Americas, with American hands and voices. A new society, with its own language, its own customs, and its own needs, was coming into being. In the Americas, Spain had to renew its cultural mission, which had always consisted of incorporating, not excluding, cultures.

"FOR ALL TIME TO COME"

Yet another cultural strain soon put this inclusiveness to the test. The first blacks came to the Western Hemisphere as servants accompanying their Spanish masters. After lengthy stays in Spain, they were both Christianized and Hispanicized. But the decimation of the Indians of the Caribbean by hard labor and disease transformed the predominant black immigration from servants passing through Spain to slaves coming from West Africa, specifically from the area between Senegal and Angola.

The Spanish Crown regulated the slave trade to its own profit. In 1518, Charles V gave one of his Flemish favorites a concession to introduce four thousand African slaves into the Spanish colonies. From then on, the black population in Spanish America grew at a rate of eight thousand people a year, to thirty thousand in 1620. Over the next three centuries, three and a half million African slaves crossed the Atlantic. Portugal imported several times as many blacks into Brazil as there were Indians already living there. Today, the Western Hemisphere has the largest black population outside of Africa.

Wherever they went, the slaves were tied to the plantation economy, that is, to the intensive and extensive cultivation of tropical produce. This rigid equation — black slaves plus plantation economy — was complicated by great power struggles to control both the slave trade and the source of products from the New World. Crunched between the demands of international politics and trade, the black slaves could not even appeal to the conscience of their Christian enslavers. They were hunted down

African slaves working in a sugar mill in Brazil, as drawn by Frans Post, 1640

for profit by African rulers, then bought by European traders, who said that they were liberating them from tribal violence, while the Christian church said that they were being saved from paganism.

This grandiose exercise in hypocrisy and injustice did not manage to destroy the creative or the rebellious spirit of the black slaves in the Americas. Rebels, runaways, and saboteurs, they often failed to liberate themselves, but sometimes they did gain their freedom and become overseers, artisans, farmers, teamsters. Their labor was intense, not only in the fields but also as masons and jewelers, painters and carpenters, tailors, cobblers, cooks and bakers. There was hardly an aspect of labor and life in the New World that was not marked by the black culture. In Brazil, which began importing slaves in 1538, blacks helped to explore and conquer the interior. Black regiments under black leaders fought the Dutch and defended Rio de Janeiro against the French. They were essential to the conquest, settlement, and development of Brazil. They also rebelled.

One of the earliest slave revolts took place in the early seventeenth century in Mexico, where the black rebel leader Yanga managed to occupy a large portion of the Gulf Coast estates and force the viceroy to negotiate. The revolt was eventually defeated by force of arms, but the defeated slaves were permitted to found the township of San Lorenzo de los Negros, in Veracruz. Venezuela was the stage for several black rebellions during the eighteenth century, culminating in the Coro rebellion in 1795, which, coupled with the revolution of independence in Haiti and the creation of a black empire there, fed the extreme fear among the Venezuelan upper classes of *pardos*, or blacks and their descendants, during the later wars of independence. Besides, during the revolt of Manuel Espinosa in Caracas, the blacks demanded not only full rights but the employment of their former white mistresses as cooks and laundresses.

Many times the former slaves simply disappeared into the interior, founding settlements known as *quilombos*. One such, at Palmares in Alagoas, Brazil, lasted well into the seventeenth century. With twenty thousand people, it became an African state in the heart of South America, with its own African tradition. But as was the case with the native Indians, the blacks became denizens of the New World, members of a mixed culture, in their encounter with the Europeans.

A slave had to adapt his language with protean agility to the rapid mixing of cultures if he wanted to understand and be understood by the overseers or by his fellow workers, also black but from elsewhere in Africa, or, certainly, by his newfound wife. And what language would the children speak? Obviously, the Iberian colonies gave their black populations a stronger identification with the common language (Spanish or Portuguese) than did the French, English, and Dutch colonies (Creole or pidgin). This reflected the greater tolerance and flexibility of the Spanish and Portuguese colonial authorities. Religious exceptionalism was forbidden in the Protestant dominions of the Caribbean; it was certainly tolerated in the Catholic possessions. If there was one identifying heritage that the New World blacks took from Africa, it was religious, and especially in Cuba, it was perfectly clear in its origins: the Yoruba states of what is now Nigeria, particularly the city of Oyo in the kingdom of Ulkami. This heritage became the "lukumí" culture, which to this day identifies a continuity of religious, aesthetic, and physical traditions in Cuba.

Christian-Yoruba syncretism in Cuba became as strong as Christian-Indian syncretism in Mexico and Peru. But in Cuba the syncretic religion came to have its own name, *santería,* and at the time of the Cuban revolution it was practiced by three quarters of the population. Also, in the same way that Tonantzin, the Aztec goddess, became the brown-skinned Virgin of Guadalupe in Mexico, in Cuba the African goddess of the sea, Yemayá, became Our Lady of Regla, patroness of sailors and particularly of the port of Havana, while Ogún, the African deity of blacksmiths, became Saint Peter, to whom Ogún gave the iron keys to paradise. A most remarkable assimilation was that of Xangó, the god of war, into Saint Barbara, the mythical Christian martyr who was cloistered in a tower to separate her from her suitors. There, as in Calderón's play, Barbara dreamed. She became a Christian. The Roman authorities ordered her father to kill her, which he did, instantly being struck by lightning. Surely as beautiful as a Zurbarán painting, surely as dreamy as a Calderón character, Saint Barbara joined Xangó in Afro-Cuban religion because in Christian Europe, owing to her association with lightning, she had become the patron saint of gunners and miners.

Rebellion and language were part of the influential continuum of Afro-American culture, to which was added the splendidly persistent identity of African rhythmic behaviors, body movements, physical aesthetics, the grammar of music and dance. From the very start, black music authorized a private, autonomous, free, and even rebellious rhythm on the part of the listener or dancer, instead of subjecting him or her to a dominant, foreseeable, or prewritten pattern, as was traditionally the case with Western music. Afro-American music forecast and practiced the forms of modern music, in which a center of tonal reference is promptly broken into multiple centers, each generating its own responses from the listener. Polyphony in music was further enriched by inventiveness in dance through the black culture of the Americas; dance as performance and dance as celebration became indistinguishable. Through all of this continuity, the body achieved a sense of reality, beauty, and movement that was absent from the restrictive commandments of the Catholic Creole and mestizo culture.

The joyful celebration of physicality, the incessant creation of language, the beauty of movement, and the rebellious spirit all added up to the central political fact that black culture was in the Americas, as Frank Tannenbaum wrote, for all time. Nothing identifies the United States and Latin America more, perhaps, than the imagination, the speech, and the rhythms of our common black basin: the South and the Caribbean, the cultural community that managed to spread from the Mississippi to the Orinoco and the Amazon through the "islands in the stream."

The fate of black culture has also permitted us to measure the quality of justice in the Americas. White supremacy has not stamped out black culture. The realities of the latter are to be found, nevertheless, not in appearances but in depth, in the all-embracing qualities described by the black poet from Martinique, Aimé Césaire, who points out that black culture comes from a people who "give themselves in ecstasy to the essence of all things, are possessed by the movement of all things, and throb with the very throb of the world." But also, to defend these qualities through the exercise of justice, black culture has given us some of the finest legal, parliamentary, and political minds of the New World.

For none of the cultures of the New World were born amid such pain and suffering as that experienced by the men, women, and children who came here on slave ships. Even before they embarked, many tried to commit suicide. Once on board, they were stripped naked, branded on their chests, and chained in pairs. Sold by the yard, they traveled within the space of a grave, deep in the holds, tightly packed, with no sanitary precautions. Suffocation and madness were common; even strangulation of a few to create more breathing space was attempted, as were revolts, though they generally failed. Prosper Mérimée, the author of *Carmen*, wrote a novel, *Tamango*, telling the true story of a successful revolt on board a slave ship. The rebels could not, however, control the ship, and perished as it went adrift.

That out of this suffering a culture could be both continued and reborn in contact with the previous cultures of the New World is in itself a proof of these people's will to survive, not to be defeated by suffering or even by justified rancor. And like the culture of the Indians, the black culture of the New World found expression in the baroque. In the same way that a Spanish American baroque came into being, from Tonantzintla in Mexico to Potosí in upper Peru, through the encounter of Indian and European, so the fusion of black and Portuguese created one of the greatest monuments of the New World: the Afro-Portuguese baroque of Minas Gerais in Brazil, the most opulent gold-producing region of the world in the eighteenth century.

There, the mulatto Antônio Francisco Lisboa, known as Aleijadinho, wrought what many consider the culmination of the Latin American baroque. The son of a black slave woman and a white Portuguese architect, Aleijadinho was shunned by both his parents, and the world: the young man suffered from leprosy. So instead of seeking the society of men and women, he joined a baroque society of stone. The twelve statues of the prophets he carved in the staircase leading to the Church of the Good Child Jesus in Congonhas do Campo reject the symmetry of classical sculptures. Like Bernini's Italian figures (but how absolutely remote from them geographically!), these are three-dimensional, moving statues, rushing down toward the spectator; they are rebellious statues, twisted in mystical anguish and human anger.

The roundness of the baroque, its refusal to grant anyone or anything a privileged point of view, its assertion of perpetual change, its conflict between the ordered world of the few and the disordered world of the many, were rendered by this mulatto architect in the Church of Our Lady of the Pillar, in Ouro Preto (literally, "Black Gold"), Brazil. The exterior of the church is a perfect rectangle. But inside, everything is curved, polygonal, egg-shaped, like the orb of Columbus. For the world is circular, and it can be seen from many points of view. Aleijadinho's vision thus joins that of the artists of Iberia and of the Indo-American New World. In Congonhas and Ouro Preto, our vision is reunited, we see with both eyes, and our bodies are whole again. Paradoxically, we are made able to see by the vision of a shunned man, a young leper who, it was told, worked only by night, when he could not be seen. But of Brazil itself, has it not been said that the country grows by night, while the Brazilians sleep?

Working at night, surrounded by sleep, perhaps Aleijadinho gave a body to the dreams of his fellow men and women. He had no other way of speaking to them, except through the silence of stone. As it shaped itself, however, this new culture of the Americas, this Indo-Afro-Iberian culture, demanded a voice, and it found it in the greatest poet of colonial America.

"MY SOUL IS DIVIDED"

No one could have predicted that from a convent in the male-dominated world of colonial Mexico, a woman, a nun, would become one of the great

baroque poets of the seventeenth century — some would say one of the great poets of all time.

Born Juana de Asbaje in central Mexico in 1651, she was probably an illegitimate child. When she was seven years old, she pleaded with her mother to dress her as a boy so that she could study at the university. Her brilliant intelligence led her to the viceregal court as a teenager. There she amazed the university professors with her knowledge of everything under the sun, from Latin to mathematics. An intellectual, she seemed to be familiar with absolutely everything, in spite of (or perhaps thanks to) the distance, the isolation, and the restrictions of the political and religious world in which she lived. She won praise and fame, but promptly saw the difficulties of being a woman writer in colonial Mexico. Not only would she face male opposition and ecclesiastical oversight, but her time would be drained and her security challenged. So she went into the church, hoping, perhaps, to find protection in the very heart of the institution that might one day attack her. In her cell at the Convent of San Jerónimo she collected over four thousand volumes, papers, pens and ink, and musical instruments. In that place she could write about everything and display her imagination and knowledge in both contentment and discipline. There, in the world of religion and letters, united for one moment in time, she would be known as Sor Juana Inés de la Cruz — Sister Juana.

Since no one was more silent in colonial society than women, perhaps only a woman could give a voice to that society, while lucidly admitting the divisions of her heart and mind:

> In confusion, my soul
> is divided in two:
> One is passion's slave;
> the other, reason's to command.

Passion? Reason? Slavery? Where was certainty, faith, blind acceptance of religious commands, not those of reason or passion? Who, after all, was this presumptuous nun, admired in Europe, consorting (perhaps sexually) with the viceroy's wife, holding court in her cell, admitting that "I suffer in loving and being loved"?

In the end, her monastic cell was not protection enough from authority, male and rigidly orthodox, personified in her persecutor, the archbishop of Mexico, Aguiar y Seijas. At age forty she was deprived of her library, her musical instruments, her pens and ink. She was driven back into silence, and died at age forty-four, in 1695.

Yet she defeated her silencers. Her baroque poetry had the capacity to hold forever the shapes and words of the abundance of the New World — its new names, its new geography, its flora and its fauna. She herself wondered if her poetry was but a product of the land, "a magical infusion brewed from herbs of the Indians of my own country."

THINGS NOT MENTIONED IN THE BIBLE

Religious syncretism, the Afro-American baroque, the Euro-American poetry of Sor Juana, were the manifestations of what the historian Peggy Liss calls "the Atlantic exchange," the network of trade, culture, and politics that immediately bound Europe and the Americas after 1492. At the basis of these "Atlantic empires" was an exchange of novelties, of

things never seen before by Europeans or by Americans. After 1492, flora and fauna thus migrated in abundance from one continent to another, sometimes with the same sense of estrangement that first greeted the now commonplace products tomatoes and chocolate.

At first Europeans feared that the tomato was poisonous, but later, of course, they discovered it to be a great delicacy. The word comes from the Aztec *xitomatl,* but probably the Italians found the most beautiful name for it: *pomodoro,* the golden apple, with its hint of paradise, of both pleasure and sin, as though the two could be separated.

Chocolate, *xocolatl,* is another Aztec word and another Aztec product. It was both precious and abundant, serving as common currency throughout the Aztec Empire. Moctezuma loved drinking it in the form of cocoa. Though first considered too bitter for most European tastes, Spanish ladies went mad over cocoa, and finally Louis XIV, who was married to a Spanish infanta, introduced it to the court at Versailles.

Whereas chocolate was abundant in Mexico, sugar was scarce in Europe and priced accordingly, after being carefully measured on scales. In the New World, sugar flourished in the tropics, invaded former wastelands, and made the fortune of the first producer, Gonzalo de Víbora, on the island of Hispaniola. When the Indian laborers of the Caribbean died out, the black slaves were brought to work in their stead on just these sugar plantations.

Of course, it was Columbus who sighted the first men and women smoking tobacco, while crossing a village, on Tuesday, November 6, 1492, in (where else?) Cuba. But as with all the strange things arriving from the New World, it took the Old World some time to get accustomed to this exotic novelty. It took all the dashing gallantry of Sir Walter Raleigh to make the weed acceptable in England, and even then King James I said, "Tobacco maketh a kitchen out of a man's internal organs."

Although America was discovered because Europeans wanted more pepper on their tables, the only spice found in the New World was chili, the fiery pepper that, said Father Joseph de Acosta, was "the principal sauce" of all dishes. In his *Natural History of the Indies* of 1590, the sanguine, obese Father, who huffed and puffed his way up and down the great altitudes of the Andes, warned about chili that "they say that it burns, going in or out." And even worse, his warning goes on, taken immoderately it "provokes sensuality." (More tellingly, a man "can walk for two whole days without eating," wrote Acosta, if he chewed the coca leaf, which was grown throughout the Andes.)

In Offenburg, Germany, there is a monument to Sir Francis Drake, who holds a potato in his hand. The inscription reads, "To Sir Francis

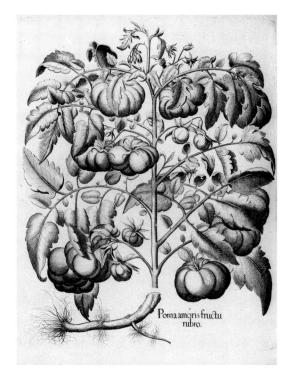

Drake, who introduced the potato to Europe, A.D. 1586." It adds, "In the name of millions of peasants who bless his eternal memory." But when the first potatoes arrived in Europe, they looked like dirty stuff indeed, resembling, it was said, either testicles or truffles — *truffles, kartoffel* — and a Russian religious sect, noticing that potatoes were not mentioned in the Bible, declared them to be a botanical monstrosity. Little did they know that vodka was to be made from fermented potatoes.

Colonial illustrations of tomato and chili crops

One thing Cortés found growing strong and abundantly everywhere was maize, the bread of the New World, the gift of Quetzalcoatl. America sent it to Europe in exchange for wheat. But for a long time Europeans used corn only to feed pigs, which they introduced to the New World, along with slaughterhouses.

Cattle and horses were perhaps the greatest novelty to the Indians. Bernal Díaz was able to say precisely how many horses arrived with Cortés in Mexico (sixteen in all), but a few years later, having escaped from the conquistadors, the horses reverted to a wild state and formed immense herds that roamed freely all the way from Colorado to Patagonia. Wheat and cattle, migrating southward like the ancient tribes from Asia, became the basis of the great agricultural wealth of Uruguay, Brazil, and Argentina. Wild cattle were captured by English, French, and Dutch buccaneers, so called because they dried and smoked the meat, a process called *boucan* by the Carib Indians.

But all was not peaceful. Mastiffs and bloodhounds also made their appearance, brought from Europe to track down runaway Indians and later black slaves. In Puerto Rico, Ponce de León considered his dogs to be so important that they shared the meals, the booty, and the wages of the Spanish soldiers. But the dogs, like those whom they pursued, fled from their masters and formed wild, wide-ranging packs.

European plants in the New World were more sedentary, and some of them were carefully monitored. Olives, grapes, oranges, and lemons were among the European novelties introduced to the Americas. Grapevines were considered so precious in colonial Chile that they were surrounded by armed men — an excellent precaution, as Chile still produces the best wine in Latin America. But forests of wild oranges soon spread over subtropical lands.

Sheep died in the tropics, but they bred wonderfully in the highlands and on the flat pampas, and the ass — the burro — was certainly here to stay. Or perhaps the Castilian donkey gazed mournfully at the native animals of the Americas — animals not included on Noah's Ark, Acosta wrote sagaciously, nor even mentioned by the Greeks or the Romans: the vicuñas and guanacos. Now they appeared perched on the Andean peaks, while over them soared birds never before seen by European eyes, such as the condor, light and strong, and the vulture, swift of wing and sharp-eyed, cleaning cities and streets, swooping down on carcasses of all kinds.

Parrots were talkative. The Aztec *guaxolotl* was delicious, whether called by the French, *dindon,* the bird of the Indies, or by the English, characteristically disoriented, "turkey." And the lovely quetzal bird, meant to fly freely, languished in a cage.

A turkey on a table, a parrot jabbering away on a patio, a quetzal dying in a cage, a vulture flying over the roofs. And under them, the new cities of the Americas.

THE BAROQUE CITY

New cities, as freshly minted as the silver of Potosí, extended Spanish dominion over the hinterland, so that even the agrarian and mining economies of the Americas had as their basis urban enclaves where Spanish power had become solidly entrenched. But within the cities themselves, extreme distinctions and tensions quickly developed. The port cities (Havana, San Juan de Puerto Rico, Cartagena de Indias, Maracaibo, Valparaíso) rapidly developed a modern, mercantile civilization, open to

The Introduction
of Horses to
Peru.
Artist unknown

influences from abroad and to conviviality in the streets. They were quite different from the mountain or highland cities (Mexico City, Bogotá, La Paz, Quito, Guatemala City) and even from the seaboard cities that evolved into viceregal capitals (Lima, Buenos Aires), for in these the mercantile impetus was slowed in favor of a courtly instinct.

To establish a court society was the unavowed dream of many in these capitals, and this gave them a parasitical veneer which was underlined by the great division between haves and have-nots. While a European capital, in spite of all its injustices, could develop a middle sector through commercial activities, in Spanish America the urban hidalgos were gentlemen only because they owned mines and haciendas outside the city. To be obeyed, served, admired, and respected was the average hidalgo's purpose in life. He was surrounded by those who were forced to offer him exactly this fealty. However, feudal obedience was hard to come by in the cities of the New World. Skits and broadsheets described and ridiculed the courtly ambitions of higher society, anchored in a sea of poverty. The privileged were few, the underprivileged many, and between them evolved a jocular cast of rogues, burglars, prostitutes, and mendicants, similar to the populations of the baroque cities of Spain's Century of Gold.

There were tensions between the haves and the have-nots, tensions between rich and poor hidalgos, tensions between all the hidalgos of Spanish origin and the bitter, ambitious, malicious, and mocking mestizos, gnawing away at the rigid differences between the upper and lower classes. And the Indians, blacks, and poor mestizos not only grew but menaced the upper strata. After the Indian uprisings of the earliest years, one great popular mutiny followed another. In 1624, the viceroy's palace in Mexico City was burned down by a mass of city laborers led by rebellious friars protesting against "bad government"; in 1692, in a famous *tumulto* inspired by food shortages and rising prices, workers again attacked the viceregal palace and other government buildings.

The most exuberant description of the life of a great seventeenth-century metropolis of the New World was given to us by Bernardo de Balbuena, a Spanish poet who arrived in the Americas as a child and who described the grandeur of Mexico City in 1604. Balbuena wrote of "a thousand gifts and pleasures," including conversations, games, receptions, hunting and garden parties, picnics and evening balls, concerts, visits, races, promenades, "a new comedy every day," fashions, the authority of litters and carriages, the fantasies and headdresses of women, the pains and worries of their husbands, and all of this swathed in jewels, gold and silver, pearls and silks, brocades and brooches, and attended to by liveried servants. Whatever whim may wish, said Balbuena, desire shall have.

These extraordinary pretensions were brought down to earth, notably, by the chroniclers of the other viceregal capital, Lima. Mateo Rosas de Oquendo ridiculed the Lima oligarchy, surrounded by "a thousand poets of scarce wit, courtesans of honor erased, and more crooked card-sharps than you dare to count." The viceroy, he said, was surrounded by "vagrants and duelists, gamblers and con men," while the police were "the most learned of thieves." Lima is a city, he ended by saying, "of murky suns, and darky births." Simón de Ayanque, in his description of colonial Lima, went further and more dangerously. This is a city, lest anyone forget it, of "Indians, zambos and mulatto women; of . . . mestizos and blacks." "In all occupations," wrote Ayanque, "you shall see Chinese, mulattoes and blacks, but very few Spaniards," as well as "many Indians come down from the sierra, so as not to pay tribute and pretend that they are gentlemen."

The pretense of being something or somebody else seems to have been one of the marks of the seventeenth-century urban societies, torn between rich and poor, disputing ecclesiastical orders, passionate love affairs, and equally passionate denials of sex and the body. A puritanical streak and an outbreak of debauchery coexisted during colonial times. Roland Barthes has written that sadism is most prevalent in underdeveloped regions. Sexual cruelty can be easily exercised in societies of strict social separation, where the sexual partner can be recruited from the legions of servants, the object of pleasure disposed of with ease, and impunity enjoyed while pleasure is practiced in hidden places. The cities of colonial Spanish America had all of the necessary attributes, with the added dimension (impunity, hideaway) of the religious world of the convent and the monastery.

The Mexican author Fernando Benítez, in a delightful book called *Demons in the Convent,* recounts many of the "hallucinating fictions" that gave Latin American societies, along with their libertine practices, the corresponding, repressive eroticism. The archbishop of Mexico City in Sor Juana's time, Aguiar y Seijas, so detested women that he would not permit them to be in his presence, and if by accident he ran into one, he would immediately cover his face with his hands. His hatred of water (another Catholic Spanish phobia) was equally fervent. His general fury was assisted by the fact that he walked on crutches, with which he would strike out when crossed — as the poet Carlos de Sigüenza y Góngora, a friend and protector of Sor Juana, discovered when the archbishop broke his glasses and cut his face in a theological dispute. Aguiar also managed to suppress cockfights, gambling, novels, and of course, when possible, women.

In a time presided over by such an uncompromising prelate, minor but crusading puritans were quick to act. A certain Father Barcia, toward the end of the seventeenth century, decided to gather up all the women in Mexico City and send them to the Convent of Belén, so they would never again go out or be seen by any man. Not surprisingly, Father Barcia only managed to round up a great number of prostitutes, actresses, and circus performers. But once he had jailed them in the convent, their lovers tried to free them and murder Barcia. The men besieged the convent, and when the women fled, telling the good Father that if this was heaven, they preferred hell, he went mad and tried to commit suicide by inserting suppositories containing holy water into his rectum.

This was also an age dominated by the triple tension of outlawed sex, the ideal of espousing an adult Christ, and the ideal of a virgin motherhood, which drove many Mexican nuns to blindfold themselves in an effort to convey their desire to be dumb and blind, to lick the paving stones of their cells until they formed a cross with saliva, to be flogged by their servant girls, and to smear themselves with their own menstrual blood. Monks and priests, too, says Benítez, liked to be whipped and kicked like San Juan de la Cruz, for in this they saw a compensation for Christ's suffering on Calvary.

THE LAST UTOPIA AND THE FIRST REBEL

The last outposts of Utopia in the New World were the Jesuit missions in Paraguay. The Jesuits had obtained a royal decree to free the Guaraní Indians, govern them, and educate them within the boundaries of a Christian republic resembling the City of God. Instead of dying from overwork or smallpox, the Guaranís of Paraguay abolished the use of money, established communal property, and lived a contented life due to the equal distribution of wealth.

But this Utopian commonwealth only lasted because of its isolation, and because the king of Spain gave the Jesuits the right to arm themselves and the Indians against Spanish and Portuguese colonists who were eager to take over. We may well ask whether an armed Utopia is a Utopia at all. Deprived of weapons and of the protection of the Jesuits, who were expelled from Spain and its dominions by the modernizing zeal of the Bourbons in 1767, the Guaranís were finally absorbed into the populations of desperate, enslaved Indians.

For one dramatic moment, however, they found a voice. In 1771, the

Indian leader of the province of Tuita in the Andes, José Gabriel Condor-canqui, took on the name of the last Inca emperor, Tupac Amarú. In 1780 he led a rebellion against Spanish rule. Followed by an army of Indian muleteers, Tupac Amarú extended the revolution throughout Peru. It was a rebellion steeped in violence, and in symbolism. Did the Spanish truly thirst for gold? Tupac Amarú captured the Spanish governor and executed him by forcing him to drink molten gold. Were the Indians only defeated by Spanish cavalry? Tupac Amarú was captured in 1781. An anonymous witness described his execution in the following manner:

> He was brought into the middle of the square and the executioner cut out his tongue. Then they unshackled his hands and feet and laid him on the ground. They tied four ropes to his hands and feet and fastened the ropes to the girths of four horses, which were then led . . . in four different directions, a sight this city had never before beheld. Either because the horses were not very strong, or because in all truth this Indian was made of iron, they did not manage to tear him apart, even though they tugged at him for a long time so that he was stretched out in the air and looked like a spider. Finally the commander, moved by compassion, decided to end the poor wretch's sufferings. He ordered the executioner to cut off the head of Tupac Amarú, and this was done. Then his body was laid under the gallows and his hands and feet were cut off. . . .
>
> A great many people had gathered that day, but no one uttered a cry or spoke a word. Many noticed, and I among them, that in all the assembly there were no Indians to be seen, or at least not in their customary garb; if there were any, they were disguised in capes or ponchos. Sometimes things happen in such a way that it seems the Devil must have had a hand in them to confirm these people in their abuses, beliefs, and superstitions. I say this because, although the weather had been fine and dry, that day dawned overcast, without a ray of sun, and threatening rain; and at twelve noon, when the horses were tugging at the Indian, a strong wind rose, followed by a sudden downpour. . . . So the Indians are now saying that the heavens and the elements are crying for the death of the Inca whom the cruel, impious Spaniards were killing in such an inhuman fashion.

The chronicle finishes by saying, "And this was the end of José Gabriel Tupac Amarú."

In our own time, Pablo Neruda wrote that even the seeds in the Andes silently repeat "Tupac." A tradition of endless revolt and endless betrayal, and another tradition of endless Utopian aspiration, had governed Spain and its territories in the New World. As the Bourbon monarchy succeeded the Hapsburgs in Spain, it clearly announced that this was to be a new age, the Age of Reason. It was also to be the age of the painter who imagined that the sleep of reason produced monsters.

TEN

The Age of Goya

On November 1, 1700, the Day of the Dead, Spain's last Hapsburg monarch, Charles II, died childless. He was the last descendant of Juana la Loca, Joanna the Mad, Queen Isabella's daughter. One of his biographers said that he had been poisoned one hundred years before his death.

All the seeds of madness and infirmity planted during the long Hapsburg reign crept into this poor imbecilic infant, who could never close his prognathous jaw and didn't learn to walk until he was seven. They called him El Hechizado, the Bewitched, and he was kept alive, it was said, for reasons of state, as a pretense that the Spanish Empire had a head and thus could keep the other European kingdoms at bay. A portent of sorts occurred when the Bewitched visited the country palace of the Hapsburgs, La Granja de San Ildefonso, near Segovia, and the place promptly burned down.

It was rebuilt as a sort of Spanish Versailles, in the French manner, by the next king of Spain, Philip V, who was the grandson of Louis XIV of France. Philip became king as a result of the War of the Spanish Succession, which once more pitted France against England in the fight to decide who should occupy the throne of Spain and rule over its extensive dominions.

The face of the last Hapsburg king of Spain symbolized all that the modernizing Bourbons were trying to reform and leave behind: tradition at the service of bigotry, intolerance, isolation from the winds of modernity. Yet another chapter of Spain's long struggle between the traditional and the modern was fought throughout the eighteenth century, again illustrating the almost constant cultural confrontation in Spanish and Spanish American history between the old and the new. The foremost historian of imperial Spain, John Elliot, puts it succinctly: "At a time

Gaspar Melchor de Jovellanos y Ramírez. *Francisco de Goya, 1798* when the face of Europe was altering more rapidly than ever before, the country that had once been its leading power proved to be lacking the essential ingredient for survival — the willingness to change."

The Enlightenment heralded a new age for mankind. The past was left behind as mostly irrational and barbarian. The future was acclaimed: man was perfectible, if only he applied his reason to the tasks of progress. Happiness on this earth was possible, thanks to science, education, and economic development. The Enlightenment put Europe on the threshold of the industrial revolution. Would Spain join these momentous events, or remain once more on the outside? Would Spain at long last come out of the night of El Escorial into the sunlight of the *Aufklärung, l'age des lumières, el siglo de las luces*?

Two men stood at the center of this cultural arena. One was a humanist, thinker, and statesman of patrician origin; the other was a painter of popular instincts and plebeian origin, lifted to the greatest heights of artistic genius. The humanist's name was Gaspar Melchor de Jovellanos; the painter's, Francisco José de Goya y Lucientes.

A "HAPPY REVOLUTION"

In 1798, Jovellanos sat for Goya. The result is the most radiant, yet saddest, portrait of an eighteenth-century man of lights, a *philosophe* embracing the ideals of the Enlightenment — reason, clarity, tolerance — without being properly skeptical about them. It is one of the great biographical portraits, condensing into the gaze, the attitude, the very air of one man and his surroundings the life of that man and of his times.

Born in the northern province of Asturias as the eleventh son in a system governed by primogeniture, Jovellanos was early on destined for the clergy, but after providentially flunking his canonical examinations, he went to Madrid, arriving just in time to catch the stagecoach of Bourbon reformism and the eye of Charles III's all-powerful prime minister, the count of Aranda. In fourteen years, between the ages of twenty-three and thirty-seven, Jovellanos rose from criminal judge in Seville to member of the Spanish Royal Academy in Madrid. He described himself as entering the world of the law armed only "with a barbarian's logic and a sterile and confused metaphysics," the result of his ecclesiastical studies; but one of his friends at the time described him as a man who "held his head high" and who "stepped firmly," because doing so was in his nature — although (this is the caveat) "many thought his demeanor to be wholly affected."

Jovellanos the judge set out to clean up the Andalusian jails and end the common practice of torture. He symbolized his reformist policies by throwing away the traditional wig of the magistrate and appearing bare-headed in court. But while others fought the battle for modernity on the purely formal issue of appearances, Jovellanos believed that enlightenment had to go beyond appearances.

The modernizing drive was temporarily stalled by the popular uprisings that followed in the wake of the riots on Palm Sunday in 1766, in Madrid, during which angry mobs attacked the residence of the marquis de Squillace, a minister in the court of Charles III. The marquis, who was Italian by birth, was judged guilty of promoting a decree forbidding the use of big hats and flowing dark capes, which the authorities argued helped criminals to strike and escape incognito. Instead, the citizens of Madrid were encouraged to wear the three-cornered hat and the short cape, which made them undisguisable. When they did not comply, special police squads proceeded to cut off their brims with shears in public until the modern hats properly fit the grumpy heads of those who favored the status quo. The rebellious populace took over the streets of Madrid and marched on the royal palace, forcing the king and his family to flee the city. Only the dismissal of Squillace calmed this traditionalist (and basically xenophobic) fury.

International events did not help the reformist Bourbon monarch, either. Spain had been defeated by England in the Seven Years War. Gibraltar was already in English hands, and now Havana and Manila were also captured by the perfidious Albion, and were only returned in exchange for Florida and all territories colonized by Spain east of the Mississippi.

The energetic count of Aranda was appointed prime minister to overcome these spells of bad luck and to further the reforms. He found a one-man brain trust, his individual think tank, in the young magistrate from Asturias, Jovellanos, in whose speeches, writings, and actions the "happy revolution" of the Enlightenment was given intellectual flight and practical purpose. "Let the light come into Spain's dominions!" exclaimed Jovellanos. What Spain needs is "useful science, economic principles, and a general spirit of enlightenment." Educators and writers such as Jovellanos and statesmen such as Aranda directed Spain toward development, pragmatism, improved communications, and public education. Under Charles III, a dozen societies for the diffusion of the liberal arts were founded, a thousand ideas for economic modernization were launched, and a hundred decrees tried to implement the spirit of the Enlightenment.

Unfortunately, another stroke of bad luck fell after the death of Charles III, when his son, crowned Charles IV, promptly undid as much of his father's work as he could. Sheer frivolity played an important role in this. Charles IV was more interested in the good life than in good education; there was very little under his powdered wig, and he was easily manipulated by his sexually voracious queen, María Luisa of Parma, known under the cheesy sobriquet La Parmesana. The queen had a scandalous affair with a twenty-seven-year-old officer named Manuel de Godoy, who was elevated to prime minister in 1792 and, after his defeats fighting France in 1795, named by the king "prince of peace." Such actions revealed that the worst vices of nepotism, favoritism, and corruption had succeeded Charles III's attempt at an enlightened despotism.

Jovellanos suffered accordingly. He kept his head high, but understood that the climate had changed. When Charles IV began persecuting the former ministers of Charles III, Jovellanos stood by them, even if they did not always stand by themselves. In a macabre forecast of the ideological persecutions of our own times, the accused often recognized, as a former prime minister put it in a letter to Jovellanos, that "I inspire fear. I shall be observed. I shall be in the list of the proscribed. I would like to be heroic. But I cannot." The message was clear: let others be heroes. McCarthyism is nothing new, with or without powdered wigs.

From then on, no one embodied the dilemma of remaining faithful to one's ideas while saving one's physical integrity better than Jovellanos. He returned home to Asturias, morally and intellectually content to give his ideas reality and root in his own soil. It was a soil rich in agriculture and a subsoil rich in coal, and Jovellanos seized on the need to make Spain conscious of its potential wealth. The industrial revolution was at hand; Spain must not be left behind once more. Jovellanos founded the Institute of Mineralogy in Asturias, promoted the use of coal in generating energy, and created new ports and new roads — roads leading into the heartland of a country sorely in need of agrarian reform. He denounced the practice of amassing fallow, unproductive land in the hands of a few absentee landlords, and he was outraged by the inhuman conditions of rural life, where sheep were better protected than men; he also fought for schools and archives, irrigation and more roads. He was called "the Traveler of the Enlightenment" as he penetrated the hard, isolated land of his forebears.

The dream of progress in the Spanish Century of Lights came to an end as French kings lost their heads and Spanish kings, deciding not to lose theirs, turned back to ultraconservative absolutism. The modernizing

Don Manuel de Godoy, Duke of Alcudia, Prince of the Peace. *Goya, 1801*

process was all but halted in the wake of the French Revolution. Were not education, science, and reform the arms of revolution? And had not Gaspar Melchor de Jovellanos proclaimed at the top of his lungs that social injustice permitted "the rich to establish their opulence on the misery of the poor and to build the happiness of the state on the oppression of the very members of the same state"?

In 1794 Jovellanos turned fifty, which was considered an old age at the time. Far from the court, he was content to wage a discreet rearguard action for his ideals of progress. He feared that like many of his friends, he would be openly accused, even punished. But as if his refinement stimulated the perversity of his opponents, he was presented with a poisoned gift from Godoy and Charles IV, when he was appointed Spain's ambassador to Russia in 1797. Along with the public office came the private pain. Should he accept and, as he wrote, "do the good I may and avoid the ills I can"? Or would he soil himself forever by collaborating with the corrupt, despotic, and frivolous government of Charles IV? In any case, he harbored few illusions: "Lucky me if I return innocent from this sally! Lucky, if I can retain the love and the good opinion of the public which I was able to garner in my obscure private life."

Public office, private pain. His dreams became "brief and turbulent" — "Even the stones make me cry." He had lunch with Godoy, for instance, in the presence of Godoy's wife and also of one of his lovers, the singer Pepita Tudó. "My soul could not suffer this spectacle," he confessed to his diary. "I neither ate nor spoke; much less could I calm my spirit. I fled from the place."

But Godoy seemed intent on catching the intellectual mouse, or perhaps he enjoyed playing with him, like a tomcat. When Jovellanos was suddenly offered the position of minister of justice, one of the five cabinet posts under Charles IV, a vista of enormous power was held before him. For eight months he labored in good faith. His foe was the Inquisition. But then, having had a taste of power, he was fired as suddenly as he had been appointed, and forced to look on as his friends were intrigued against, libeled, and sometimes jailed. The coldness was palpable; Jovellanos' *tertulia,* or intellectual circle, in Gijón got lonelier and lonelier. Would his intimidated friends return one day? "Maybe. I don't care," he wrote in the diary. And he braced himself for what was inevitably to come. He believed that his conduct had been honest and pure, and if this was held to be so, he would weather any disasters of fortune. If not, he would have to rely on the testimony of his own conscience — "and my conscience only accuses me of the weaknesses that are part of the human estate."

This, then, was Jovellanos, another example of the Spanish stoic, but this time as painted by Goya, sitting in a gilded chair, holding a piece of paper in one hand, which rests on the right knee; his head rests on the other hand, elbow planted on a working desk full of papers and books, a goose-quill pen and a statue of the goddess of wisdom, Minerva, fully armed, watching over the sage. But the gilt and the goddess are less impressive than the civilian quality of the portrait, which shows a wigless man in common breeches, common frock coat, simple stockings, and buckled shoes. If he were a North American, he would be Ben Franklin's cousin. But he is truly the enlightened version of El Greco's magnificent portrait of the gentleman with a hand on his chest. Goya's painting is an eighteenth-century version of the endless stoical profile offered by one part of Spain as a corrective against the picturesque or the cruel, the picaresque or the mighty; it reveals the exact equilibrium between the arrogance of the few and the humility of the many. It is the portrait of a man buoyed by his inner being, his values, his dignity, his private convictions, in a public sea of intrigue, adversity, and compromise.

Jovellanos, Seneca's last intellectual descendant in Spain, soon needed all of his fortitude to face his troubles. He was arrested in March of 1801 in his native Asturias. He had been secretly denounced by an informer for "reading forbidden books." "Send him far from his homeland," the informer insisted. "See that he does not communicate." Jovellanos, the letter of denunciation went on, had to be made an example of, for "the infinite libertines" who followed his ideas.

His house was surrounded at dawn; Jovellanos was dragged from bed, his papers were confiscated, and the next day he was sent off into exile with four armed guards. His trial was a secret one, and after a period of confinement at a charterhouse, the "traveler of the Enlightenment" became a prisoner in the castle of Bellver on the island of Majorca. He remained there for seven years.

Meanwhile, reaction against the incompetence and corruption of the unholy triangle of Charles IV, La Parmesana, and the prime minister, Godoy, led to support for the crown prince, Ferdinand. The mutiny of a mob at Aranjuez in 1808 forced the abdication of Charles IV in favor of his son (Godoy was almost killed in the fray). One of the first decrees of the new government was to free Jovellanos from the castle.

But Napoleon acted faster than any Bourbon ever dared. Before the new king, Ferdinand VII, could even set foot in Madrid, Bonaparte abducted father and son, Godoy, and his lover the queen and imposed a liberal constitution abolishing the Inquisition and internal customs barriers, depriving the nobility and the church of many privileges, and proclaiming the rights of man. He then installed his brother Joseph as king of Spain, and the Bonapartes invited Jovellanos to join in "the great work" of making Spain, at last, a modern nation.

Jovellanos looked toward Madrid. There, the people had risen against the French occupiers. When offered the freedoms brought by France, as opposed to the despotism of the Spanish kings, they cried

"Long live our chains!" and the French squads mowed them down. Goya painted this unforgettable scene; it was on the night of the third of May, 1808. Jovellanos made up his mind: he would fight for Spain, for its independence, but not for the stupid, corrupt, and venal Bourbons.

The Executions of the Third of May, 1808. Goya, 1814–1815

As Spain fought and died and was repeatedly crushed by the Napoleonic war machine, Jovellanos, feeling that "we have lost it all," returned home to Asturias. The people went wild. He was carried home in triumph by a throng; bonfires were lit to celebrate his return, people kept their homes lit up for him, and he was proclaimed "the father of the country." But he found his house, his books, and his paintings sacked by the French troops of Marshal Ney. The French were once more at the gates of Asturias. Jovellanos barely had time to embark. When navigation became impossible — it was a stormy night — he landed in a fishing village, and there he died of pneumonia, delirious, repeating incessantly "a headless nation, a headless nation."

THE SLEEP OF REASON

As if to establish a dramatic tension between the forces of reason and the warnings of the artistic imagination, Goya shared the stage of Enlightenment Spain with Jovellanos, his complement and antithesis. Both men arrived in Madrid at the height of the reformist regime of Charles III. But whereas Jovellanos was an aristocratic intellectual from the dignified province of Asturias, Goya was an instinctive, working-class son of the rough and tough province of Aragon. A son of artisans, he looked like one. He came from the Spanish boondocks, the Aragonese village of Fuendetodos, a town, it is said, "that makes your hair stand on end." Its people were indeed tough and stubborn, even rude at times, but they were also secret dreamers. (Aragon is also the homeland of the contemporary cinematic Goya, Luis Buñuel.)

Self-Portrait.
Goya, c. 1786

Goya was brawny, hairy; his eyes were dreamy, but they had a steely glint; his nose was common, upturned; his mouth was a mystery, sensuous, protuberant, like a kidney in the middle of his wide face. His shirts, too, were wide open, and his boots were caked with mud and excrement. He loved the people, was forthcoming, and joined in popular feasts. In fact, he lost his hearing in one ear by taking part in a strenuous cart-raising contest in Aragon. His capacity for hard work was stupendous.

When Goya was named court painter in 1786, he entered the world of corruption and deceit of the Bourbon decadence. Beautiful duchesses, brilliant philosophers, stupid princes, ugly and unfaithful queens, venal favorites, but also dashing bullfighters and actresses on fantastic ego trips surrounded him. Yes, he encountered corruption and deceit, but also elegance, sensuality, and a joy of living. The Century of Lights in Spain was also the century of footlights, of bullrings and aristocratic slumming. Goya was the painter of this world.

Certainly, when asked to give happiness and light, he complied. The great tapestry paintings at the Prado reproduce the brilliant skies and warm shadows of a festive Castilian summer. This extraordinary series of joyous, sun-drenched, and playful scenes is sometimes reminiscent of Cervantes in its popular raucousness, but ultimately it reflects the atmosphere of Bourbon Madrid as the city expanded and beautified itself under a progressive government. Some of Madrid's handsomest monuments and promenades were constructed under Charles III: the Prado Museum, the fountains of Neptune, Apollo, and Cibeles, the Puerta de Alcalá. No wonder that Jovellanos argued that it was better and less expensive to found two new cities in Spain than to conquer a foreign one.

Goya's intention, even when he painted the most delightful of pre-impressionist open-air party scenes, such as the festivities of San Isidro in Madrid, or the marvelous young woman under a parasol as her lover pays court, was not to illustrate but to introduce. He presented the people to the aristocracy. The noblewoman in her carriage crossed paths with the market vendors; aristocrats went about dressed as *toreros*, and actresses were the toast of Madrid. In Goya's work, the style of *majismo*, or showiness, both male and female, is enshrined; style over content, the cult of beauty and youth, the consecration of pose, attitude, and theatricality were all offshoots of popular energy. Society went slumming. And Goya topped it all off with the two great portraits of the duchess of Alba.

In one, *The Dressed Maja*, the great lady is seen disguised as a girl of the people. In the other, *The Naked Maja*, Goya has undressed her and shows us the pinkness of her nipples, the dark invitation of her sex, the

The fountain of Cibeles, Madrid

daring smoothness of her shaved armpits. This was not a model posing as a mythical goddess. This woman had an aristocratic title and a popular disguise, but even the body was a disguise for the soul, for the imagination, for its fears and yearnings.

Goya the social critic revealed the pretense of the vicarious show of proletarian vitality with the most acid of shadows, with the most cutting light. The *Caprichos* are an unsurpassed chronicle of human foibles, hyprocrisy, weakness, and cupidity. The beauty of the white-black-and-gray technique projects these scenes of moral misery beyond any possible hint of moralistic finger-wagging. The engravings finally resolve themselves, in the most famous of them, in a critique of reason — a critique of uncritical optimism and unbounded faith in progress.

It is useful to compare the dignified, almost republican likeness of Gaspar Melchor de Jovellanos as painted by Francisco de Goya with the most famous of the artist's *Caprichos, The Sleep of Reason Begets Monsters.* The quintessential portrait of the man of reason, sitting at his desk with a paper in one hand and his head resting on the other, becomes the *capricho,*

The Festival
of San Isidro.
Goya, 1788

Woman Under
a Parasol.
Goya, 1777

the caprice, of reason asleep, releasing the monsters of both the psyche
and the world. The custom and the setting are the same. But in the
engraving, it is as if Jovellanos has fallen asleep a minute after Goya
painted him in a state of total rationality. Now bats fly above the philosopher's head, gargoyles and owls plunder his dream of enlightened progress, reason is atrociously vampirized. But perhaps reason, when it forgets
its own limits and believes too uncritically in itself and its brainchild,

The Clothed
Maja. *Goya,*
1800–1803

The Naked
Maja. *Goya,*
1800–1803

progress, deserves this nightmare. Perhaps it is only the sleep of monsters that begets reason.

Through this startlingly dramatic comparison between vigil and dream, between the reality of the man awake and the fantasy of the man asleep, Goya throws an immense light (along with an immense shadow; they are rarely separated in his art) on his entire oeuvre. In these portraits he unites the sunny freedom of the tapestry paintings and the final, profoundly bitter "black works" that he painted in his seventies, when the party was over — when the court of Charles IV had dimmed the Century of Lights and Napoleon's armies had invaded Spain. "Tuesday 20," Jovellanos had written in the final entry of his diary. "Little sleep. Clouds. Cold."

Goya's grand design appeared little by little, revealing itself as both Spanish and universal, both past and contemporaneous, luminous as a Castilian summer sky and horrid as a cold, wintry bog. While history marshaled its demons — power, vanity, glory, courage, carnage — and damaged the dominions of nature with blood and death, Goya's final

Hunting for Teeth.
Goya; from Los Caprichos

All Will Fall.
Goya; from Los Caprichos, *1799*

The Sleep of Reason Begets Monsters.
Goya; from Los Caprichos

El sueño
de la razon
produce
monstruos

figure was that of the devouring, mad god Saturn. But between the de- mons of history and the dominions of nature, Goya was painfully, majes- tically capable of invoking the response of art.

What Courage! *Goya; from* Los Caprichos

Francisco de Goya y Lucientes died in Bordeaux in 1828, at age eighty-two, in exile. After Napoleon abandoned Spain and entered the final years of his defeats and exiles, the ultrareactionary Ferdinand VII regained the throne and behaved as if nothing had happened. "The Bour- bons," Talleyrand famously said, "forget nothing but learn nothing." Goya was forced to leave Spain, and when he died he was buried in France.

Only in 1899 did the Spanish government request that the great artist's remains be returned to Madrid. When the Spanish consul in Bor- deaux had the corpse exhumed, he discovered that the body did not have a head. He promptly sent a telegram to the ministry in Madrid: "Goya skeleton without a head. Please instruct me." The government wired back: "Send Goya, with or without head."

The Family of
Charles IV.
Goya, 1800

"LONG LIVE OUR CHAINS!"

Goya could get away with murder — figuratively, as he painted the court of Charles IV and the royal family without softening their asinine features. And his portrait of Godoy, reclining in a campaign chair and surrounded by the signs of military activity, only emphasizes the sloth of the character — his puffed-up anatomy, bland and unkempt, flabby and, one suspects, smelling of garlic.

And Goya could get away with murder literally, too, as he painted the Spanish resistance fighters being shot by the French troops — the murder of a paradox. For had not these French revolutionaries come to liberate the people of Spain from the likes of Charles IV and Godoy? If so, the Spaniards answered, long live our chains!

Little did they know that this same nationalism, these same guerrilla tactics, this same cry of independence, would soon be taken up by the insurgents of Spanish America against the Spanish king.

Jean-Jacques
Rousseau.
Allan Ramsay,
1766

ELEVEN

Toward Independence

Distances in the Americas have always been enormous. Even today, in the age of jet travel, it takes about sixteen hours of flying time to reach Buenos Aires from Mexico City; in 1800 it took several months to travel by ship from Acapulco down the Pacific Coast of South America, around Cape Horn, and up the Atlantic Coast to the River Plate. So it is all the more surprising that in a single year, 1810, movements for independence should have broken out with extreme velocity and amazing synchronicity all the way from Mexico, the viceroyalty of New Spain, to Buenos Aires, the viceroyalty of the River Plate. In April, revolutionaries in Caracas deposed the Spanish captain general. In May, citizens of Buenos Aires expelled the Spanish viceroy. On September 16, Father Miguel Hidalgo y Costilla rose against the Spanish regime in Mexico. And on the eighteenth, same month, same year, the independence movement was launched in faraway Santiago, Chile.

This simultaneity is amazing, not only because of the lack of communications and the vast physical distances, which were the negative factor. The positive side was the communality of language and purposes in the patriotic movements, again all the way from Mexico to Argentina, which revealed that a strong spiritual and intellectual bond had developed among the Spanish colonies. That this sense of common destiny should have broken down after independence, owing to national politics and regional tensions, is another matter. In 1810, independence was on intimate terms with itself.

The movement was even more amazing in that it happened at all, given the longevity of Spain's American empire and the customs, allegiances, and inertia that had been established between the peninsula and the New World since 1492. Independence was far from self-evident as the nineteenth century dawned. A Spanish American on the first day of the year in 1801 would have been gambling wildly if he had forecast that by 1821 Spain would have lost all of its possessions in the New World except two Caribbean islands, Cuba and Puerto Rico.

Yet as strong as the spiritual and blood ties were, they were in the end weaker than the new consciousness of self, the will toward nationalism, and the separation between Spanish and colonial interests that flowed into the great current of independence, giving birth to the Spanish American nations. Where did this new consciousness come from? How did it evolve? And who were its actors? The implicit question is, of course, who were the Spanish Americans?

In 1810, eighteen million people lived under Spanish rule between California and Cape Horn. Eight million were still considered Indians, aboriginal to the Western Hemisphere. Only one million were pure blacks, brought from Africa in the slave trade. And only four million were Caucasian, both peninsular Spaniards and Creoles, that is, descendants of Europeans born in the New World. Now, the Creoles (mostly of Spanish descent, but there were a few French, German, and Irish names here and there — O'Higgins, O'Reilly) outnumbered peninsular Spaniards nine to one. But in their turn, the white Spanish Americans were vastly outnumbered by Indians, blacks, and the new mixed-race individuals.

These, the mestizos, the fourth and perhaps the most original and dynamic of the racial groups, numbered some five million people in 1810. They were a mixture of all the rest, classified according to byzantine, and sometimes insulting, nomenclature. The *mestizo* was the child of white and Indian. The *mulato* (the offensive name was derived from *mule*) was the child of black and white. The *zambo* was the offspring of Indian and black. The *cuarterón*, or quadroon, of mulatto and white. The *tercerón*, or octoroon, of quadroon and white. *Tercerón* and *mulato* gave you *tentenelaire* — literally, "up in the air" — and the coupling of quadroon and black produced a *saltapatrás*, a "back-jumper," that is, a genetic throwback.

Two paramount facts to remember are that Creoles vastly outnumbered Spaniards, and Creoles were vastly outnumbered by the "colored" majority. Both facts determined the nature of Spanish American independence. The Creoles were acutely aware that they were on top of the pile but secondary to the peninsular Spaniards in matters of consideration, privileges, access to wealth, public posts, and political decision-making. Yet the lassitude of the Hapsburg administration in Spain (and the tremendous distances) fostered a sense of self-reliance and autonomous survival among them.

This is exactly what changed under the zealous reformist regime of the Bourbon monarch Charles III. After taking stock of the final Hapsburg years, the Bourbons realized that their colonies were financing Spain to a far lesser extent than Britain's and France's colonies were financing those countries. At the same time, Spanish America was producing more minerals, growing more agricultural produce, and raising more livestock as both its population and its cities expanded. Why, then, was Spain not *getting* more? Or, put in a slightly different way, why were the colonials *keeping* more?

While the Crown was undoubtedly motivated by a wish to see both itself and its American subjects prosper, it also wanted a communality of economic interests to develop; but these were cast in a new political philosophy that denied the experience of the previous three centuries. It was, not for the first or the last time in the Hispanic world, a revolution from above, imposed from within the government, not rising from the will and debate of the governed, and as such it failed because the Crown failed to understand that it was rubbing the élite of the colonies the wrong way. By forcing the Spanish American world into a tight organic unity with Spain, the Bourbon reforms menaced the multiple local interests that had developed during three centuries of colonialism, threatening the locals' sense of autonomy and even their sense of identity, not to mention the impunity with which they operated.

In 1801, a typical upper-class Creole in Buenos Aires or Mexico City might well wonder whether he and his kind could go on being considered simply a class. Were they not becoming a *nation*, a *Creole* nation? In any case, they felt irritated, perplexed, and even outraged as the Spanish monarchy lurched from its traditional detached paternalism to a frenzied interventionism.

THE EXPULSION OF THE JESUITS

The sensational event that triggered a growing sense of national identity throughout Spanish America was the momentous decision in 1767 to expel the Jesuits from Spain and its colonies. The Bourbon nation-state judged its own authority to be incompatible with the excessive powers of other corporations, including the church, and of privileged classes such as the old aristocracies of Castile and Andalusia. But rather than attacking them frontally, the Crown exemplified its modernizing statism by singling out a powerful but not all-embracing group that was closely linked to both the church and the aristocracy. The Jesuits were chosen to send a signal to their more powerful patrons. Charles III and his ministers decided to blame them for instigating the Squillace riots of Palm Sunday 1766. They believed that by doing so, the monarchy would gain greater independence from the papacy, to which it considered the Society of Jesus to be allied. But also it would wound the older, more conservative Spanish aristocracy, which was opposed to the Bourbon reforms. The Jesuits' quasi-monopoly on education would be shattered in favor of a more liberal program.

Whatever the reasons the monarchy had for expelling the Jesuits, the action definitely backfired in the New World. Yet another paradox ensued: the reforms unleashed a flood of scientific studies in Spain, but in the New World, the Jesuits had been promoting just such modern studies for some time. Far from being entrenched scholastics, they had wrested academic power from the Thomists, who had dominated political thought with the teachings of Saint Thomas Aquinas, and had served the Spanish American élites a big dose of Descartes and Leibniz. In fact, they had brought the reformist spirit of the Bourbons to Spanish America. The Crown's policy failed because the king's advisers did not realize that their modernizing efforts in education had been notably anticipated by the Jesuits, but, more important, because modernization of Spanish America meant identification of Spanish America. This the Jesuits understood and the Crown did not.

By the second half of the eighteenth century, Spanish America had embarked on this adventure of self-discovery, and it promptly outdistanced the reforms determined in distant Madrid. The Jesuits were identified with this renovation of self-knowledge. No wonder, then, that the edict of expulsion had the effect of a bombshell in the colonies, forecasting a collision between them and the monarchy. Whole communities throughout Hispanic America rose in mutiny, and the viceroy of Mexico, the marquis de Croix, who was charged with the operation of expelling the Jesuits, confessed in a letter to his brother that "they owned the hearts and minds of all the inhabitants of this vast empire." He could say this in private. In public, he showed the hard authoritarian face of the Spanish monarchy, condemning *to death* anyone who opposed the edict of expulsion and even warning, *urbi et orbi*, that "once and forever, the subjects of the Great Monarch who occupies the throne of Spain should understand that they were born to shut up and obey and not discuss or express opinions on the high affairs of the state."

This harsh position was not the whim of an eccentric viceroy throwing his weight around in an American colony. It was confirmed in the pragmatic sanction that the king himself, the enlightened Charles III, addressed to the Inquisition on the matter: "It is expressly forbidden for anyone to write, declare, or cause any commotion taking this decision as a pretext. You should, rather, impose silence in this matter on all my vassals and let those that contravene these orders be punished as guilty of *lèse-majesté.*"

Shipped out of Portugal, Spain, and their dominions, the Jesuits naturally flocked to the gates of Rome. But the pope, wary of offending the Iberian monarchies, closed those gates to the good brothers, who in one instance waited for weeks on their ships, anchored in the bay of the Roman port of Ostia, sick and vomiting, until the pope relented. If Spain and Portugal deprived themselves of the Jesuits' talents, why should the papacy?

But more than the pope, the true victor of this tragicomic incident was Spanish America, for from their refuge in Rome, the Spanish American Jesuits not only intrigued against the king of Spain; more important, they identified themselves with the cause of Americanism. They took revenge against the Crown by writing *national* histories of the colonies. The Chilean Jesuit Juan Ignacio Molina wrote (from Rome and in Italian) his *Natural and Civil History of Chile,* while the Mexican Jesuit Francisco Xavier Clavijero wrote (again from Rome and in Italian) his *Ancient History of Mexico.*

These books gave an enormous sense of identity to the nascent Spanish American nations, both to the Creole and white élite and to the rising mestizos, who had access to education and who more and more felt able to identify themselves with the places of their birth. They identified themselves through American reality, American history, American geography. Juan Pablo de Viscardo y Guzmán, a Jesuit born in Arequipa, Peru, wrote these extraordinary words from exile in London as the New World celebrated, in 1792, the third centennial of its discovery by Columbus: "The New World is our Fatherland. Its history is our history. . . . It is in it that we must become partisans in order to defend our own rights. . . . The history of the past three centuries . . . can be reduced to these four words: Ingratitude. Injustice. Slavery. And Desolation." And in Mexico, the editor and savant Antonio de Alzate began publishing a *gaceta* in 1788, in which, he promised, he would write of the men who had shed light on "our Hispanoamerican nation." The Mexican *nation,* he wrote, had its own culture, its own past, its own traditions, and these were both Indian and European.

This consciousness of place and time was given a tremendous boost by the presence of the German scientist Baron Alexander Von Humboldt, who, on a fact-finding junket through Spanish America that began in 1799, chronicled the rising wealth of the colonies but also lamented that they were benefiting Spain more than the local interests. Spanish America, he wrote, needed fewer taxes, more trade, a middle class, and better government. But none of these were available without greater freedom.

The Creole class in Spanish America faced a conundrum not very different from that of Spain itself. As economic wealth and labor diversity grew, so did social divisions and class animosity. As Mancur Olson has noted, rapid economic growth can be followed by growing discontent, as the pie gets bigger but its distribution does not. Olson, an impeccably conservative economic thinker, does credit Marx with understanding that the progress of a system can lead to its crisis — that the "advance of social systems, no less than their failure, can lead to their disappearance." This was true of both Spain and its rapidly growing American colonies.

A CREOLE NATION
On the first morning of the nineteenth century, Spain, the mother country, found herself saddled with increasing corruption in the state and embroiled in continental and transcontinental wars, which exhausted her domestic funds and forced her to turn more and more to the colonies through increasing taxation. Any granting of greater privileges to the colonies came only on a piecemeal basis, and only insofar as they were deemed profitable to Spain. Spanish American development was to be harnessed to the needs of Spain, the colonies modernized and liberalized only insofar as reform contributed to Spanish finances and international obligations better than the disorganized Hapsburg system had.

The harsh, authoritarian, and unnecessary rhetoric that at times punctuated the generally progressive discourse of the Spanish Crown can be summarized, at its best, in the words of the viceroy Revillagigedo, advising his successor in Mexico in 1794: "Let us not forget that this is a colony and that it must depend on Spain, its mother country, and must yield her some benefit because of the protection it receives from her." Revillagigedo did admit that "great skill is needed to cement this dependence." But "dependence" it had to continue to be, although making "the interest mutual." Were our interests truly reciprocal, though?

The Creoles in Mexico City and Buenos Aires were complaining about increasing taxation without a quicker advancement in representation and access to public posts. While the free-trade measures of the Bourbon monarchy whetted Creole appetite for more and more direct trade with other parts of the world, they also opened the Spanish American economies to international competition. Who would buy ponchos or spurs from the interior of Argentina if they could be had cheaper, better, and faster when imported from England? This fact posed a new problem, which was whether the mercantile interests in Spanish America should sacrifice their internal production to foreign competition or whether regional production should be protected from such competition.

Whatever the choice, the Creole classes now became aware that their own unity and survival were also menaced by the non-Creole majorities: Indians, blacks, and mestizos — the feared *pardocracia,* as they were called in Venezuela. The eighteenth century was punctuated with popular revolts. Some of them were led by blacks, others by Indians. But they tended to be short-lived until the great Indian rebellion of Tupac Amarú sent a shiver down the collective spine of the Creoles. It was the black and mulatto revolt of Coro in Venezuela that truly frightened the Creoles. In 1795, several thousand blacks and mulattos rose and killed the landowners of the haciendas where they worked, proclaiming "the republic and the freedom of the slaves" and basing themselves on "the law of the French," that is, the example of the French Revolution. They were brutally repressed, but others became fugitives and created autonomous communes deep in the jungles and plains, where Creole and viceregal authority could not touch them.

More and more alienated from both the Spanish government and from his own majority population, the Spanish American Creole had no recourse but to take the initiative before the monarchy or the people dragged him down. He had to become the leader of his own revolution. He was to guide it in his own interest, no longer sharing control with Spain but eliminating as well the danger of sharing it with Indians, blacks, and mulattos. This cold, naked calculation would be clothed in the warm cloak of budding national consciousness, in the sense of all-embracing unity provided by history and geography, to the exclusion of both Spanish imperialism and egalitarian politics.

This the Creole nation set out to do, hoping that the overarching moral, political, legal, nationalistic, and even sentimental justifications would embrace both the Spanish monarchy's continued need for its colonies and the colored majority's increasing clamor for freedom with equality.

NEWS OF THE WORLD

The fortress walls were ringing in the Spanish American world. The *morros* at Havana and San Juan de Puerto Rico, the imposing battlements in Cartagena de las Indias, and the fortress of San Juan de Ulúa in Veracruz had all been erected to isolate the colonies from foreign attacks and foreign influences. But now the walls showed visible cracks. News of the world started to pour in. The Spanish American societies, more and more conscious of their specific identity, less and less willing to be mere adjuncts of the Spanish corporate body, saw their hopes advanced by three international events, which came like tidal waves over the walls of the fortifications. These were the North American War of Independence, the French Revolution, and the Napoleonic invasion of Spain.

Humboldt's tour had given flight to the great expectations of the Spanish American Creoles. The German scientist had provided them with a recipe for success (fewer taxes, more trade, better government) that did not depend on allegiance to Spain or even partnership with Spain. In fact, by 1811, when Humboldt published his famous *Political Essay on New Spain,* a new nation had effectively appeared in the Western Hemisphere, and it followed the Humboldtian prescription to the letter. Starting with a tax revolt in Boston, the United States of America had rebelled successfully against Great Britain. It had given itself a constitution based on individual freedom and good government. Its middle class promoted the values (sorely lacking in the Hispanic world) of industry, education, and thrift. And to top it off, Spain had lent its support to the American Revolution as part of Madrid's anti-British strategy. Spanish American ports had been opened to rebel ships during the revolution, and now, in its aftermath, the United States promptly became Cuba's largest commercial partner, and its ships were trading up and down the Pacific and Caribbean coasts of the Spanish New World.

Admiration for the American Revolution was tremendous during the early years of the republic, which were also the final years of the Spanish Empire on the American continent. But the great ideological inspiration came from the French philosophers of the Enlightenment, whose grand ideas filled a deeply felt, if at time unconscious, need of the Spanish American intelligentsia. Lawyers, bureaucrats, parish priests, teachers, students, and budding scientists all needed a new secular alternative to the airtight explanations of the universe offered by Catholic scholasticism in the past. Instead of Thomas Aquinas, Thomas Paine and Thomas Jefferson. Instead of Saint Augustine, the civil saints Montesquieu, Voltaire, and Rousseau — especially Jean-Jacques Rousseau, the Citizen of Geneva, and his ringing cry "Man is born free, but everywhere he is in chains." Rousseau perhaps had the greatest influence that any single writer has ever had on the history, the sensibility, and the literature of Spanish America. He represented the writers of the Enlightenment, professing new principles of social and religious organization, against the monarchy and against the church, against the divine right of kings and in favor of popular sovereignty.

This was a heady blend, and it made the heads of curates in small villages, of lawyers in provincial townships, and of burgeoning writers in colonial capitals veritably swim as they hurriedly learned French in order to savor these great writers as one would savor an aged Burgundy. Imagine a young seminarian reading Voltaire for the first time in the colonial world, or a young lawyer fired up by the ringing prose and demanding sentences of Rousseau (since this was a writer who taxed the reader with the duty of action, of transforming words into realities).

Popular sovereignty, the rights of man, national independence — these were the ideas taken up by the enlightened Creoles and the leading mestizos, in spite of the hue and cry of the Inquisition, which denounced "the flood of seditious literature . . . full of general principles of equality and liberty for all men" and "contrary to the security of the state." The forbidden books were smuggled in original ways. Since churches and monasteries were exempt from customs inspection, enlightened clergymen in Europe filled up crates of holy objects, and often the objects themselves — sacred vases and eucharistic arks — with forbidden books, manuscripts, pamphlets. Voltaire might have modified his battle cry, "*Écrasez l'infâme,*" "Destroy the infamous," meaning the church, if he had known that *Candide* would travel from Europe to America inside a ciborium.

Their reading inflamed the young intellectuals of the Spanish American world, who developed their own credo above and beyond the lessons, good and bad, of the French Revolution itself. The iconography of the times, as usual more powerful than a careful analysis of events and ideas, fed on images of the guillotine, the Terror, regicide, and exile, and on the heroic thrill of mass enthusiasm and republican cockades. Less reflection was given to the fact that in a few months the French Revolution had caused the greatest extension of political rights and the most momentous turnover of property in the history of Europe. Four million new voters were enfranchised and one hundred thousand judges were elected, along with twelve thousand city magistrates, between 1789 and 1790. The feudal system was overthrown and hereditary nobility ended, as was hereditary guilt, passed from generation to generation. Special tribunals for the nobility were replaced with common tribunals for all. The church lost its wealth and France became unified, as internal barriers came crashing down and excise taxes were abolished.

It was as a result of all these factors that a personality such as Bonaparte's was able to appear from nowhere. He was proof that careers were certainly open to all. His rise was part of the grand revolutionary tide. He always saw himself as representing liberalism, progress, new ideas, in spite of the political despotism that he justified by war and the challenge of reactionary Europe. But even while waging war, he was capable of drafting laws. And what laws! The French civil code, the modern tax system, the Penal Code, the Legion of Honor, a balanced budget (in times of war), the modern educational and administrative systems. What could a man of the bourgeoisie, by force of will and intelligence, not accomplish? Napoleon ordered the first pavements and the first fire brigade in Paris; he even introduced the postal service to Egypt! The young Spanish American Creoles saw themselves in this model and dreamed that everything was indeed possible. Enlightened laws could change the face of Spanish America too.

The Napoleonic wars also made themselves felt in terms of new commercial relationships. As Spain became more and more embroiled in the conflict, Spanish America came to depend increasingly on trade with the neutral countries, particularly with the United States, which grew rapidly during this period. But as trade increased, so did competition, especially from Great Britain, which menaced native industries, notably around the River Plate. In fact, in 1806 a British invasion of Buenos Aires attempted to gain a commercial foothold in the region, but while the Spanish forces and the viceroy, the marquis of Sobremonte, fled from the attack, the local militias, led by Santiago Liniers, routed the British. This scenario was repeated a year later. One can imagine the sense of pride this sparked in the local militias, since Argentina had now defeated England, which had always defeated Spain. Could Argentina — the national idea was gaining extraordinary force — now defeat Spain itself?

The occasion to prove the validity of this enormous constellation of sentiments, hopes, ideas, and fears came as Napoleon, riding the crest of his European victories and confident that his eastern front was secured through alliance with Russia, embarked on the invasion of Bourbon Spain.

One might well wonder, at this stage, whether the cumbersome inertia of the Spanish Empire in the New World, which had now entered its fourth century, would have postponed the movements of independence if the situation in Spain had not drastically changed. For the first time since the Muslim invasion of 711, Spain was invaded by a foreign country. The Bourbons, in the splendidly idiotic figure of Ferdinand VII, lost their throne. In their stead, the Bonapartes now ruled, in the splendidly sloshed figure of Napoleon's brother Joseph, promptly dubbed for his intemper-

Napoleon in His Study. *Jacques-Louis David, 1812*

ate tastes Pepe Botella, or Pepe the Bottle, by the Spanish people. And even though the people bravely resisted the French invaders, the fact remained that the royal family was held prisoner by Napoleon in Bayonne and that Spain was no longer ruled by Spaniards.

What would the response of the colonies be?

After three centuries of colonial rule, suddenly a new, unforeseen, and dazzling reality blinded each and every inhabitant of Spanish America. The monarchy that had ruled us, ably or ineptly, paternalistically or tyrannically, aloofly or intrudingly, detachedly or zealously, was no more.

The questions were inevitable. If there was no king in Spain, did not sovereignty revert to us? If there was no legitimate imperial rule from Spain, were we not in fact independent? Or was it rather our duty to maintain the colonies in reserve for the restoration of the Spanish monarchy, acting in the name of the throne but against Napoleon? The effects of the North American and French examples piled on top of these immediate considerations. Could we oust a colonial power? Could we substitute a republic for a monarchy? Could we also become modern, independent nations, trading with everyone, publishing, reading, and speaking freely, free forever from the vigilance of the Inquisition?

In the wake of events in Spain, the *cabildos*, or town halls, throughout Spanish America came to life as the only place in which the more articulate social forces could act within a legal framework to ponder what had happened in Europe and the future of the colonies. For example, gathered together in the Buenos Aires *cabildo* in May 1810 were the leaders of the local militias, cocksure after their double victory over the British, and the intellectuals, the readers of Voltaire and Rousseau, hoping to bring their general ideas of freedom, popular sovereignty, and general happiness to fruition, if given half a chance. Among them was an intense young man, the young Mariano Moreno, a fervent Jacobin who gave voice not only to the liberal demands of the intelligentsia but to the demands of the Argentine business class for free trade, restrictions on exports, and an independent merchant marine.

Also galvanized were the members of the lower clergy, who bore their own grievances against Spanish rule. The reformist zeal of the Bourbons had hit them hardest with an ill-conceived law in 1805 that had deprived them of their threadbare privileges and called in all church mortgages on agricultural property. The purpose of this drastic act was to pay for the war and stave off Napoleon by giving him a subsidy of five million gold pesos. That very year, however, the Spanish navy was destroyed at Trafalgar, and the bulk of the money gained through the so-called Consolidation Bill remained in the pockets of the Bourbon courtiers. Meanwhile the clergymen of Spanish America were publishing incendiary newspapers, such as Father Camilo Henriquez' *La Aurora de Chile* in Santiago, or holding conspirational meetings under the guise of literary get-togethers, as did Father Miguel Hidalgo in provincial Mexico, or sitting in on *cabildo* meetings in Buenos Aires and elsewhere.

Clergymen, merchants, intellectuals, and army officers all signaled a decision in favor of united action in the face of extraordinary events. Their choice was between continued loyalty to Spain, provisional independence until Bonaparte was expelled and Ferdinand VII was restored, or outright, radical separation from Spain. As John Lynch puts it in his unsurpassed history of the Spanish American revolutions, "Americans now had to look to their own destiny."

PART IV

THE PRICE OF FREEDOM

*The meeting of
Bolívar and San
Martín*

TWELVE

Simón Bolívar and
José de San Martín

These radical questions and these events were not lost on a young Venezuelan aristocrat, nervous and impatient, with a mind as alert as his burning black eyes. His name was Simón Bolívar, and as he avidly read the forbidden philosophers, he too asked himself, *Can we not trade by ourselves, think by ourselves, and govern ourselves?*

Scion of an immensely rich family of landowners and army officers, Bolívar knew sorrow and loneliness at an early age. His father died when he was three, his mother when he was nine. From then on he considered his black nursemaid, Hipólita, his true father and mother. Bolívar's own racial makeup has been widely discussed. The Bolívars came to Venezuela from the Basque country in the sixteenth century. After two centuries, as the French writer Jean Descola noted, "among languorous Indians and black Venuses," Spanish families inevitably became mestizos and even mulattos. Bolívar's portraits underline, idealize, erase, or dissimulate the racial mixture. The relationship with Hipólita is far more revealing. As the Venezuelan novelist Arturo Uslar Pietri wrote, we Latin Americans are all tricultural, because of our black and Indian nannies. Even when pure white, we are black and Indian. But pure blacks and pure Indians also partake of the European world. Triculturalism is not a racial question. Rather, culture overcomes racism.

In 1799, at age sixteen, Simón Bolívar went on the grand tour of Europe prescribed for young men of his social standing. It was, as Descola wrote, a "discovery of the Old World." Small and wiry, Bolívar was an extraordinary waltzer, and he enjoyed the sunny world of Goya's Spain: the promenades in Madrid, the evenings at the theater, the outdoor feasts in the Bourbon summer palace, La Granja de San Idelfonso. He also fell in love with a young woman of Venezuelan origin, María Teresa Rodrí-

Simón Bolívar

guez, who was almost two years his senior. Eight months after their rapturous marriage began, it ended in tragedy. One of the unnamed "malignant fevers" of the age took María Teresa. Love in the time of cholera left Bolívar a widower at nineteen. He never married again, unless we consider Independence and Revolution his true brides.

The young Bolívar arrived in Paris on the eve of Napoleon's self-coronation at Notre Dame. He may have seen this action as a betrayal of the egalitarian and libertarian promise of the French Revolution; more important, it confirmed his republican fervor and led him to put aside any temptation to create a monarchy in the New World. In any case, Bolívar's interests were not in Napoleonic Europe but in the concrete situation of his native South America. Whatever the contradictions of the French Revolution, whatever the glory and flaws of Bonaparte the man and the emperor, Bolívar overrode them in favor of a dramatic, enthusiastic, rhetorical, and affirmative stance. At the top of the Sacromonte in Rome, in the company of his tutor and traveling companion, he made his own solemn pledge, his entry into history: "I swear by my honor and by the God of my fathers . . . that my soul and my arm shall not rest until I have broken the chains that bind us to Spanish power."

He was as good as his word. While others pretended to provisional independence while Spain remained in French hands, Bolívar tore off all masks and declared on his return to Venezuela that Spanish America should be radically independent of Spain and assert its own character:

"Let us lay the cornerstone of American freedom without fear. To hesitate is to perish."

Who was this man, this aristocrat fighting for equality? He was an immensely rich man who gave his life to the revolution; a humane visionary who waged war just as implacably as his enemies; a warrior and philosopher who went through history thinking his thoughts out loud; an impatient romantic who wanted to achieve so much in so little time — democracy, justice, even Latin American unity. Bolívar was above all a man of action, a military genius who covered a battleground as vast as Napoleon's Europe, ranging from the Caribbean to the Pacific to the Peruvian highlands. He bounced back from every defeat, even from temporary exile in Jamaica, fighting "the war to the death" against the vicious Spanish commanders, who left their prisoners to rot alive while tied to posts under the sun.

Bolívar judged the situation in Spain better than the doubters did. The absence of the kidnapped king did not mean that Napoleon effectively governed the Spanish colonies; these very much remained in the hands of a well-equipped Spanish army under the authority of viceroys and captains general, who had no intention of leaving their posts or renouncing their allegiance to a continuous, and eventually restored, Bourbon monarchy. Furthermore, the Napoleonic invasion not only left Spain without a ruling monarch, it provoked the liberal forces of the peninsula into action. While the French tried to subdue the Spanish guerrillas, the dormant Cortes, or parliament, organized itself to fill the void of power and present the monarchy with a *fait accompli*: a liberal constitution. Meeting at Cádiz, the rejuvenated Cortes prepared just such a document. Many representatives of the Spanish American colonies were present. The colonial authorities, from Mexico City to Caracas to Santiago, were frightened. The absence of a king in Spain, a liberal constitution, and independence in America spelled the end of their function.

As Napoleon disastrously turned east and embarked on his ill-fated Russian campaign, the local Spanish authorities in the colonies launched campaigns far more violent, perhaps, than a visible head in Madrid would have allowed. They were on their own. They were fighting for their survival. The return to the throne of the authoritarian and reactionary Ferdinand VII in 1814 only upped the ante. The restored king refused to acknowledge the Cádiz constitution and transformed Spain into a bulwark of the new conservative order in Europe, soon to be known as the Holy Alliance and blessed at the Congress of Vienna. Now the Spanish commanders really fought to kill the insurgent movement. Bolívar responded in kind. His declaration of war to the death was totally uncompromising: "Any Spaniard who does not work against tyranny in favor of the just cause . . . shall be considered an enemy and punished as a traitor to the country. . . . Depend upon it, you will die, even if you are simply neutral, unless you actively espouse the liberation of America."

Bolívar proclaimed the freedom of the slaves in exchange for their participation in his army. But although the Spaniards did not counter with a comparable declaration of freedom, they cannily exploited racial animosity in Venezuela, drafting whole regiments of blacks and mulattos to wield lances against white property and lives. The Creole property owners, who feared a "colored" revolution, supported Bolívar but condemned the blacks. As a result, the blacks felt that they were being used by the Spaniards, spurned by the Creoles, and offered candy-coated laws of emancipation by Bolívar. They refused allegiance to all.

Bolívar's army was strengthened, however, by *caudillos*, local military leaders who organized regiments of *llaneros*, lancers from the hot, humid plains of the Orinoco, who were willing to fight in exchange for land. Chief among the *caudillos* was José Antonio Páez, a plainsman who was Bolívar's exact opposite — a Sancho Panza to Bolívar's Quixote. Stocky, big-headed, practically illiterate, but close to the land and the people, he guaranteed Bolívar an incessant flow of soldiers.

"If Nature opposes our designs, we will fight her and make her obey us," proclaimed Bolívar in another of his famous rhetorical exclamations. He was true to its romantic resonance as he led his armies of "bad boys," *muchachos malvados*, over the numbing glaciers of the Andes and through the equatorial forest with its deadly spiders, liberating Colombia at Boyacá in 1819 and Venezuela at Carabobo in 1821. Everywhere he was received in a shower of glory, hailed as the Liberator, El Libertador. Dreaming not only of the independence of Spanish America but of its unity, Bolívar said, "We are a microcosm of the human race. We are a world apart, confined within two oceans. We are neither Indians nor Europeans, but a part of each."

A portion of Bolívar's intelligence lay in his self-deprecating humor, and next to his more grandiloquent statements, other remarks, addressed to himself, reveal not only his sense of proportion but his deeper sense of destiny and tragic failure: "I am the world's third largest fool. The other two were Christ and Don Quixote."

THE CAMPAIGN OF THE ANDES

After the *cabildo* meeting of May 25, 1810, Argentina quickly consolidated its independence by expelling the viceroy and establishing an alliance between the local militias and the intellectuals, which spread the revolution beyond the pampas, as far north as Potosí in the Peruvian mountains and into the villages of the ancient Inca Empire. The Argentine revolution was the most radical in Spanish America, and as it spread from its urban, Europeanized base in Buenos Aires, it unfurled the ideas of the Enlightenment on the Indian roof of South America, stopping the payment of tributes, distributing lands, and offering education and equality.

Few of these measures were fully understood by the illiterate, non–Spanish-speaking Indian peoples of the highlands. Alas, they could not even be implemented as long as Spain and its royalist army remained entrenched in the most powerful stronghold of the South American landmass, the viceroyalty of Peru, and its stately capital, Lima. Thus a stalemate developed in these regions, as the revolutionary armies of Buenos Aires were checked by the royalist armies of Peru. Between them, numerous guerrilla bands led by able and ambitious local chieftains fought incessant, haphazard rearguard actions, which sidetracked the Spaniards but did not give victory to the Argentineans. Perhaps they only gave power to the ubiquitous separatist leaders of these *republiquetas*, or little republics, as they came to be called. In these, the statesmen of the future national republics of Spanish America could well see the dangers of disunity, atomization, and incessant warfare between central and local political forces.

Then the second great leader of the South American wars emerged to break the deadlock. José de San Martín, a thirty-nine-year-old officer in the Argentine army, realized that the revolutions of independence would never be won as long as the Spanish remained entrenched in Peru. San Martín, who had fought with the Spanish army against the French in Spain, decided to attack the royalists by surprise on their southern flank in Chile. Chile, of course, was protected by the wall of the Andes. Not even Hannibal could have crossed this forbidding barrier.

By the end of 1816, San Martín had organized a war economy in the city of Mendoza, in the Argentine foothills of the mountains. In faraway Mendoza, he was isolated from the political intrigues of Buenos Aires and could concentrate on the job at hand. He was, as in all things, both meticulous and heroic. He wrung shirts and ponchos from the poor, jewelry from the rich, cornets from old soldiers, and horses from the landed estates. He made his own cannon and gunpowder, as well as the uniforms for his troops. He sent spies into Chile to spread false rumors, fooling the Spaniards into believing that he would attack through the Indian lands south of the Aconcagua peak. (The Indians themselves promptly informed the Spaniards, as San Martín expected.) The newly

named president of Argentina, Juan Martín de Pueyrredón, sent him two thousand sabers and two hundred tents. "I send you the world, the flesh and the devil," he wrote to San Martín, "and I send you no more, because, damn it, there is no more."

San Martín needed no more. He declared each soldier to be his own sentinel, he named the Virgin "general of the troops," and on January 18, 1817, he started to climb the Andes. He marched with 5,423 men, mules, horses, 18 pieces of artillery, and provisions, including a wagon full of wheat. Knowing it would be a long, hard haul, he took along masons and a baker, many lanterns, water wagons, and a carriage full of maps.

Up they went, thirteen thousand feet up, past the highest mountain in South America, Aconcagua, braving the winds, the ice, and the volcanic dust, fighting the royalists in gorges and capturing their garrisons but also combatting *soroche*, the dizzying, nauseating altitude sickness.

Finally, on February 12, San Martín reached the other side of the Andes, by moonlight. At dawn he swooped down on the Spanish forces for the decisive battle of Chacabuco. On the field after the encounter lay five hundred dead royalists and only twelve insurgents. San Martín embraced his ally, the Chilean commander Bernardo O'Higgins. They both knew that the southern portion of the Americas was now free from the Atlantic to the Pacific. The independence of Chile and Argentina was sealed at last. All that remained was to sail north and expel the Spaniards from their fortress in Peru.

Great physical and moral heights had been reached. San Martín's campaign demonstrated that we Spanish Americans were capable of organizing ourselves and of acting with excellent timing, courage, and fortitude against tremendous odds. The crossing of the Andes remains an example, a source of pride, and a reference point for the future of Spanish America.

SAN MARTÍN AND BOLÍVAR

From Valparaíso, San Martín sailed to liberate Peru with an armada commanded by the Irish admiral Lord Thomas Cochrane and a bevy of English captains dressed in white jackets and sporting red sideburns. In July 1821 he entered Lima and proclaimed the country's independence. But in Peru he also came to realize how deeply rooted the colonial realities were and gained a foretaste of the frustrations awaiting the newly independent republics. As protector of the new nation, San Martín abolished Indian tribute payments and forced labor in the mines. But the Peruvian upper classes, who had done very little to help win independence, argued that freedom would cause the Indians to desert the landed estates and thus cause an end to the colonial system of land tenure. San Martín's decree remained on paper, much like the humane laws of the Crown before it, but nothing changed. (As a matter of fact, independent Peru abolished slavery in 1855, seven years before Lincoln's Emancipation Proclamation.) As John Lynch succinctly states in his classic history, the Peruvian upper classes, while "jealous of their privileges and conscious of the underprivileged masses beneath them . . . were primarily concerned neither with the survival of Spanish rule nor with the winning of independence, but with the degree of power and control which they would have in any regime."

In 1822, Bolívar and San Martín, the two great emancipators, met for the first and only time, in the Ecuadorean port of Guayaquil. What transpired between them? Historical speculation has been rife on this subject. It would seem that the central problem was the future organization of the newly liberated states. The two men agreed on the substance of independence, but not on its form. San Martín was attracted to monarchical rule, but he may have been unable to persuade Bolívar, a staunch republican. While this is pure hypothesis, it is clear that the manner in which the republics should be organized was left unresolved.

There was also the question of collaboration between the two leaders. San Martín, the older man, offered to be Bolívar's second, but Bolívar would not accept this. San Martín feared a political fight among equals and wanted no rivalry with Bolívar. "I have done my job," he told the Venezuelan leader. "You can have the glory that follows. I am going home."

San Martín believed that the military should not govern. He wanted strong institutions, not strong men, and warned Argentina against giving itself over to a "fortunate soldier": "I will not be the executioner of my own countrymen." He had not soiled his hands in war and he would not soil them in peace. His was a deeply moral stand. Yet the question remains, was he right? Should he have run the risk of governing Argentina in order to undermine the very menace he was trying to exorcise — the rule of the military, which was to haunt Argentine history?

It is impossible to know. San Martín had made up his mind. "I want to go off to a corner and live like a man," he said, retreating to a hacienda in Mendoza. The government in Buenos Aires, suspecting him of that which he refused — dictatorial ambitions — hounded him, spied on him, and finally drove him off to exile in France. San Martín died at seventy-two, never having returned to the land that he had liberated.

Bolívar remained, grappling mightily with the question of how we should rule ourselves after independence. He racked his soul looking for solutions. At the Venezuelan Congress in Angostura, where the Constitution of 1819 was drafted, he tried to avoid the extremes that would eventually torment the existence of Spanish America throughout the nineteenth and well into the twentieth century. Tyranny or anarchy? Bolívar saw the people of Spanish America as living in "permanent childhood," although he qualified this paternalistic (and perhaps patronizing) attitude by saying that a people so lacking in political culture could not have instant democracy. In Angostura, he proposed instead "an able despotism," a strong executive capable of imposing legal equality where racial inequality predominated.

Perhaps he feared the power of local political chieftains, *caciques*, whose ambitions might disrupt and balkanize the nascent republics. Certainly he did not consider the alternative models of self-rule based on cultural loyalties that survived in many agrarian communities. Yet at the same time Bolívar promoted a magnificent vision of Latin American unity that was open to the promise of the future and to the shifting realities of world politics. The Conference of Panama in 1826 called on Latin America to seek instruments of conciliation, unity, and counsel. Significantly, Bolívar did not invite the United States. Perhaps he was aware of Thomas Jefferson's letter to James Monroe in 1823 predicting a rapid expansion of the United States beyond its borders and covering "the whole northern, if not the southern, continent." Perhaps he knew about Jefferson's letter to Lafayette in 1817, in which the Virginia democrat wrote that he considered "our southern brethren" unprepared for independence. "Ignorance and bigotry," he wrote, are "incapable of self-government."

Bolívar riposted by proposing a moral power that, in his words, could "regenerate the character and the mores that tyranny and war have left us with." His idea harked back to "remotest antiquity," when moral enlightenment was considered "our first necessity." In reality, Spanish Americans' first and continuous need was for an independent civil society, an autonomous pluralism of social, intellectual, political, and economic activity in which to breed democratic institutions. Since both "necessities" were absent, Bolívar conceived a "liberal nation" created by the state, which would in turn educate — create — a democratic citizenry. Could this be done without force? And if it had to be done with force, did the army have to rule the nation? Would the nation then be liberal and democratic?

The wars of independence did unleash new social forces. Heterogeneous and half-baked, they had no need for Bolívar's anguish. They included the Indian, black, and mulatto majorities, who were not even represented at the constitutional congress in Angostura. They included the Creole landowners, who had not supported independence only to lose their property or give power to the dark-skinned *pardos*. And, most important, they included the new military *caudillos* such as Páez, who now possessed the lands given to them by Bolívar himself as payment for their wartime services. If unity and force were needed, they would quickly supply it.

All these groups turned their backs on Bolívar, abandoning him to a long and lonely pilgrimage toward death. But that road passed through dictatorship and failure. Fearful that anarchy, factionalism, and eventually disintegration would befall the new republics, Bolívar made himself dictator of Greater Colombia in 1828, in the name of unity. The Liberator was now confronted with hatred, and even with the people's desire to have him killed. An assassination attempt that year was only foiled by his longtime mistress, Manuelita Sáenz, who distracted the would-be assassins while Bolívar escaped.

His sense of failure became all-consuming. He had fought for almost twenty years, drafting constitutions with one hand, wielding a saber with the other. "We have not had time to learn," he excused himself. "We have been too busy learning." Exhausted, he was now the prey of despair. "Venezuela is the victim of my own laws," he exclaimed. "Bolivia has had three presidents in five days, two of them assassinated," he moaned in 1829. As Bolívar left Bogotá in the middle of the night on May 8, 1830, people came out on their balconies and poured the contents of their chamberpots on his head. "Come, let us leave," he said to his military aide. "They don't like us here anymore."

Indeed, they didn't. Vilified, accused of dictatorial ambitions, and declared an outlaw in his native Venezuela, Bolívar followed the route of the Magdalena River to the sea, prolonging his journey as he would have liked to prolong his life. In Gabriel García Márquez' moving and imaginative re-creation of this final trip, the author visualizes the thousand memories, encounters, digressions, and pretexts that permitted the Liberator to extend his life for just a few more days. The lasting vision of the novel, *The General in His Labyrinth,* is that of a vibrant, creative mind carrying around a body that no longer responds to the will of its owner.

From his deathbed in Santa Marta, Bolívar pronounced his own epitaph: "America is ungovernable. Those who serve the revolution plow the seas." The young idealist, the brilliant military commander, the disillusioned statesman, was dead at age forty-seven.

THE MORNING AFTER

The morning after independence, we woke up to realize what an enormous distance existed between ideals and actions, and how often ideals were pummeled by lack of communications, isolation, absence of institutions, lack of democratic practices, and profound divisions between the capital city and the interior, between local initiatives and centralized government, between modernism and traditionalism, and between liberals and conservatives. A popular joke in Bogotá at the time held that the only difference between liberals and conservatives was that liberals went to mass at six A.M. and conservatives at seven A.M. The deepest, the cruelest, the most bitter division nevertheless continued to be that of social inequality.

All of this created a vacuum in the life of Spanish America. After fifteen years of continuous war, we now perceived the Spanish monarchy as the central political institution. Indeed, the monarchy was, along with the church, our oldest and strongest institution. Could it have acted in time to avoid the revolutions of independence? Such was the program of our old friend the enlightened count of Aranda, who advised Charles III of the explosion brewing in Spain's American colonies and also offered him the solution to the problem. He proposed the creation of a commonwealth of Spanish-speaking nations in America, linked to Spain and to one another in much the same way that Britain and its former colonies were in the next century.

Aranda went unheeded, and the political blindness of the succeeding monarchs, Charles IV and Ferdinand VII, made the commonwealth proposal a moot question. And perhaps we were not prepared to take on the burden of self-determination. Even San Martín, writing from Lima, deplored the "dangerous revolutionary disposition" of "the lower orders," whose "lack of education and general information is so strongly felt." Bolívar's bitter foe, General Francisco de Paula Santander, when president of Colombia, piously turned this fear into a hypocrisy worthy of Uriah Heep when he said, "A thousand times I bless the . . . rustic and ignorant people, [who are] endowed with great virtues and above all with an obedience worthy of the greatest praise."

These attitudes were part of a justification that would ring (hollowly) down the next century and a half. We were not ready for independence. We were not ready for democracy. We were not ready for equality. But is a nation ever ready? Was black Africa, was India? Indeed, were the United States?

No one learns how to swim unless he goes into the water, and what Spanish America had to learn, it could learn only through independence. We did learn that the Crown and the church were our oldest institutions. We had expelled the former; we would somehow have to cut the latter down to size. We learned that our weakest and newest reality was a civil society, formed by the incipient middle classes as well as the suppressed, if not crushed, rural communities. Entrepreneurial talents, intellectual circles, and political parties waited to manifest themselves. But between the absence of the monarchy and the weakness of the civil society, between the facade of the legal nation and the substance of the real nation, there was a vacuum, which would be filled by what San Martín feared most: the fortunate soldier, the strongman, the tyrant. He dominated the stage of Spanish America for a long, long time.

THIRTEEN

The Time of Tyrants

etween 1810 and 1815, the Argentine revolution of independence spread out from Buenos Aires with a radical message of freedom. The May revolution of 1810 saw the army and the intellectuals sharing a common purpose — the union of Arms and Letters, as Don Quixote would say. This alliance immediately faced a conundrum typical of revolutionary societies, the pursuit of democratic goals with undemocratic methods in order to stave off real or perceived dangers to the revolution. To this end, a Committee of Public Safety was created, with authority to identify the opposition, admit denunciations against suspected counter-revolutionaries, and summarily execute them, as happened to the royalist merchant Martín Alzaga and his co-conspirators in 1812. But such seeds of intolerance do not fully explain the emergence of tyrannical regimes in Spanish America.

The revolutions were fired by a libertarian fervor. Again, the Argentine case offers the best example. The fiery and fanatical Buenos Aires Jacobin Juan José Castelli spread the ideas of the French Enlightenment in upper Peru, preaching the gospel of Rousseau and Voltaire to the Quechua and Aymará Indians while forcibly suppressing tributes, distributing land, building schools, and promoting equality. "Rise," he told the Indian masses. "All this is over. We are now equals."

Writing from exile in Chile thirty years later, a thirty-four-year-old Argentine writer called Domingo F. Sarmiento wistfully evoked these revolutionary times. "Argentina started the revolution with unprecedented boldness, took the revolution everywhere, believed herself commissioned by the heavens to do so," he wrote. And Argentina had been rewarded, had been the one "who in fourteen years had taught England a lesson, galloped over half the continent, equipped ten armies, fought one hundred battles, won them everywhere, mixed herself up in all events,

Domingo F. Sarmiento

violated all traditions, essayed all the theories, risked it all and always came out on top." Sarmiento thought that all this vigorously new revolutionary republic had to do was "live, and enrich, and civilize herself." Instead, he was writing from exile in Chile, fleeing from the murderous tyranny of Juan Manuel de Rosas in Buenos Aires. What had happened to the promise of greatness and liberty? "With the revolutions came the armies and the glories," Sarmiento went on, "the triumphs and the defeats" — but also, he acknowledged, "the revolts and the coups."

A provincial from San Juan, Sarmiento had been a brilliant, self-educated child who had taught school to illiterate adults, and was now a vigorous young polemicist and writer. He could well wonder why the dream of independence had foundered so badly, from Mexico to Argentina, as the century neared its middle years. Had not the liberals proposed an ideal democratic republic, juridically and culturally based on European and North American models? "Rousseau's social contract flies from hand to hand," Sarmiento wrote in his classic book *Facundo: Civilization and Barbarism*. "Robespierre and the French Revolutionary Convention are the models. . . . Buenos Aires believes itself to be a continuation of Europe."

In this way he unconsciously answered his own question. The thinkers and liberal statesmen of the revolution, Simón Bolívar among them, had indeed imagined and proclaimed an ideal Spanish American democracy. But this democracy, stated in laws and proclaimed from above, disregarded the multiple realities that had to be changed if democracy was to be more than an intention, or freedom more than a declaration like Castelli's to the Indians.

The resistance of ancient traditions, both Indian and colonial, to sudden change, no matter how democratically inspired that change was, could not be underestimated. Like the Crown before them, the new republics seemed remote from the everyday concerns of the workers and peasants, and of the landowners and local political bosses, who wished to enhance their power and privileges, not hand them over to their laborers. The fervor of independent Argentina for solidarity with other revolutions, which Sarmiento so emotionally evoked, was in the end counterproductive. The Argentine campaign to impose radical revolution on Paraguay ended in the isolated dictatorship of José Gaspar Rodríguez de Francia, who sealed off his republic from the rest of the world. Castelli's Jacobin campaign in Peru frightened the local oligarchs, who became pro-Spanish, fought the revolutionary armies, and finally proclaimed independence for themselves, without making any concessions to the working classes.

As we have seen, the traditional oligarchs were joined and even strengthened by the new propertied class of army officers who had been compensated for their wartime services with lands. In 1817, Bolívar had signed a decree that gave public lands in Venezuela to republican soldiers. But then the congress decreed that the soldiers should be paid with vouchers, which they could redeem on a vague postwar date. When that date arrived, the bonds were claimed not by the illiterate soldiers but by the powerful victorious officers. José Antonio Páez, the republican *caudillo* of the Venezuelan plains, was a good example: he created an immense landed estate in the Apure Valley, and although he did not found a separatist republic, he became a law unto himself, far from the governance of Caracas.

Thus the wars of independence emboldened the decision of the conservative upper classes to hold on to power, churned up the ambitions of the *caudillos,* and set them all on a collision course with the newly established liberal national governments, from Vicente Guerrero's in Mexico to Bernardino Rivadavia's in Argentina. Both these presidents were succeeded by reactionary military dictators, Santa Anna in Mexico and Rosas in Argentina. The liberal central governments filled a political vacuum, but they proved to be incapable of replacing the provincial warlords, who counted on armed men, land, cattle, horses, and peasants to impose their will. The very existence of these men challenged the newly formed governments. The political idealism and naiveté of the ruling liberals did not help matters.

The liberals wanted to impose the rule of law on each country as a whole. These were the politics of Rivadavia, who during the 1820s extended education, limited the power of the church, and transferred vast amounts of land from the public to the private domain in the hope of establishing a modern system of private property. The grand irony of this design was that these lands were, naturally, bought up by a small group of ranchers, who concentrated power over vast landholdings, or *estancias.* By 1827, when Rivadavia was forced to resign, 21 million acres of public lands in Argentina had been transferred to only five hundred individuals, and the *estancia* system was established for a long time to come.

Rivadavia fell not because of his innocent, boomeranging property laws, but because he would not bend an inch from his centralist politics, which favored the rule of Buenos Aires over the autonomy of the regions. But it was in the regions that actual power, including the power to defy the national government, was being wielded. Of the myriad Argentine *caudillos* lording it over their provinces, Juan Facundo Quiroga in La

Rioja stands out. Quiroga, the subject of Sarmiento's celebrated study of Argentine politics, history, and mores, *Facundo,* was the very portrait of the barbarian in his physical aspect. A black beard rushed up his cheekbones, and long black curls spilled over his brow "like the serpents on the head of Medusa." According to Sarmiento, Facundo could kick a man to death, crashed his son's head open with a hatchet when the boy did not stop crying, and even set his own parents on fire when they refused to lend him money. Although he flew black flags with the motto RELIGION OR DEATH, Facundo never prayed, confessed, or heard mass. The good liberal Sarmiento wanted to educate, civilize, and modernize Quiroga's world of impunity and savage impulses, but the politics of civilization had to wait for the end of the time of the barbarians.

After Rivadavia unwittingly passed such great economic power to a limited group of landowners, they had other, more concrete matters to ponder. Who, for example, would protect their best interests, the local warlords or the national government in Buenos Aires? Yet another consideration crept into the picture. If the landowning system of the Argentine interior was to survive, and even to expand into the pampas, it demanded what was after all a central plank of the revolutionary platform: free trade. The landowners needed freedom to import manufactured goods from Europe and North America, and facilities in which to exchange them for exports of Argentine wheat, wool, hides, and beef.

This cumulus of demands, dangerously swirling around in the vacuum left by the defeated Spanish monarchy, explains the appearance of the supertypical Latin American tyrant, Juan Manuel de Rosas. This Machiavellian character, both lion and fox, quickly grasped the trenchant dualism of Argentina. There the centralists were called *unitarios.* They favored the hegemony of Buenos Aires and the coastal region surrounding it. The power of the capital was based on export-import operations, the *estancias,* and the importance of the *saladeros,* the meat-salting plants, which handled as many head of cattle as possible; these were the basis of Argentina's so-called cattle civilization. On the other side stood the *federales,* autonomists and regionalists who favored a loose association of provinces. Their power was based on mining activities and a population of nomadic, landless masses. Theirs was the trail of the ox cart; it took three months to travel from the northern frontier to Buenos Aires. Thus, the isolated provinces were the power base of the local *caudillos.*

Rosas, an extremely wealthy *estanciero* in Buenos Aires province, devised a deceitful ploy by which he would present himself as one more regional boss fighting for the local interests of his province while he

Juan Manuel de Rosas

actually won and consolidated centralized power. Claiming to be in favor of federalism, he swore to fight the unitarians to the death. But by confusing the issue, he managed first to seduce and then to defeat the local warlords. After Quiroga's death, he became the undisputed master of Argentina, in the name of the federalism to which he paid lip service.

The landowners and cattle barons had found their man in Rosas. Through sales and donations, he assured the continuing power of Buenos

Aires, the *estancia* and the *saladero*, as well as the concentration of land. Revenue for the government and its supporters was supplied through control of the Buenos Aires customs house. Rosas' wealthy allies were further enriched by outright confiscation of the property of their political enemies. And the landed interests were supremely gratified by Rosas' expansion of territory for grazing through wars against the Indians.

It took a nimble politician to pull off this balancing act, and Rosas was up to the task. Foreign observers commented often on his blond hair, his flinty eyes, and his physical prowess. In 1835 the French *Revue des Deux Mondes* stated that "no one could tame a colt, or break in a wild horse, or hunt a cougar better" than he. Indeed, Rosas made no bones about his populist demagoguery. "I have always considered it very important to acquire an influence over the poor," he explained, "in order to control and direct them; and at great cost and effort, I have made myself into a gaucho like them, to speak as they do, to protect them, to become their advocate."

There is an endearing sort of cynicism in such a declaration, which was absent from the sycophantic writings of some of his followers. "His talents, his vast knowledge, his political skill and wisdom, and his valor in military campaigns," gushed one, really piling it on, "[make him] a most consummate statesman with the intrepidity, agility, and bravery of a warrior." In a few words, Rosas was "the most perfect exemplar of the politician, the hero, the warrior, and the great citizen."

This distasteful homage, printed in a Rosas-dominated newspaper, *La Gaceta Mercantil,* was tempered by many foreign appraisals of the man. A French traveler recognized that Rosas had conquered the anarchy "which devoured the land," but qualified this triumph with a damning assessment: "Unfortunately, he went to the other extreme. . . . He substituted his personality for the existing institutions; he forced the entire population to adore his portrait; he had incense burned before that portrait in the churches; he had himself drawn by women in a carriage."

Posing as a friend of the people while actually furthering the interests of the landowning minority, Rosas, in Sarmiento's cutting phrase, "introduced the laws of the cattle ranch into the government of the republic." He did worse than that. The French diplomat Count Alexandre Walewski (Napoleon Bonaparte's child by the Polish aristocrat Marie Waleska) expertly discerned that Rosas did not know "how to maintain himself in power except by force." "Vindictive and imperious," he committed a host of bloody acts that surrounded him with "a halo of terror." He did not suffer opposition and created, as Walewski clearly saw, "a system of legal oppression by which he persecute[d] his enemies."

Rosas organized the *mazorca*, probably the first Latin American death squad, to silence his enemies. Sarmiento tells how, in the city of Córdoba, the local chief of the *mazorca*, one Bárcena, arrived at a ball and rolled out onto the dance floor the severed heads of three young men whose horrified families were present. Perhaps hyperbolically, Sarmiento writes that between 1835 and 1840, "almost all of the city of Buenos Aires passed through [Rosas'] jails." Rosas was systematically "disciplining the city," whether the person in question had committed a crime or not.

Anarchy or tyranny — this depressing pendulum swinging in our political life was Rosas' justification for using power as he did. He unified the country; even Sarmiento admitted that. By wresting power from the local warlords, he prevented the fragmentation of the Argentine republic. He promptly realized that whatever else was true in Argentina, Buenos Aires had to play a central role, as it was the only bridge between the nation and the outside world and also between the nation's commercial center and the products of the interior. Rosas masterfully played his political theater; nominally a federalist but actually a centralist, he used the conflict between the two groups to decimate his opposition and concentrate power in himself.

Rosas maintained himself in supreme authority for some twenty years between 1829 and 1852. His personality is still hotly debated among Argentineans. Did he not achieve unity, an end to anarchy, vigorous international trade expansion, patriotism, the resistance of foreign intervention, and an equally vigorous internal development of productive forces? But were lawlessness, cruelty, and terror disguised as order worth the price of freedom?

TYRANTS: VIRGINAL OR PROMISCUOUS

Across the river from Argentina, on the banks of the Paraná, another *caudillo* ruled Paraguay as a "perpetual dictator," between 1814 and 1840. Dr. José Gaspar Rodríguez de Francia exploited nationalism to the hilt. Caught between the ambitions of Brazil and Argentina, he did not resign himself, as the government of tiny Uruguay did, to ruling a buffer state between the two South American giants. Basing his action on the premise that Paraguay was not about to exchange the domination of Spain for that of Brazil or Argentina, Dr. Francia sealed off the nation to all foreign contact.

Isolated in the heart of South America, Paraguay had been a colonial preserve of the Jesuits. Now, surrounded by ambitious neighbors, the country was caught in a quandary as it commenced its national life. Dr. Francia decided to make virtue out of necessity and turned the fact of

Paraguayan isolation into a nationalistic virtue. Naming himself "El Supremo," he forbade commerce, travel, and even mail service between his fortress-nation and the outside world. Foreigners who happened to enter Paraguay remained there forever, like characters in an Evelyn Waugh novel.

Dr. Francia cloaked his iron chauvinism with a populist mantle. His introverted republic was by necessity autarkic; it created a subsistence economy; it favored demagogical mob rule under the tyrant's guidance; it attacked and weakened the church. Yet, as in Argentina, it finally protected and strengthened oligarchical interests, both traditional and new. Dr. Francia's prolonged reign demonstrated a commonly ignored fact in our history, that nationalism in Latin America has its origins on the right, while highlighting the commonly understood notion that despotic populism disguises the stasis the tyrant imposes on society. It gives the impression of movement, but nothing changes.

The "supreme dictatorship" of the virginal Dr. Francia ended in 1840, when he was seventy-four years old. He did not save his nation from unhappiness and continued strife. Paraguay later had to fight Argentina and Brazil quite literally to the last man: most of the country's male population was killed in the wars against them from 1865 to 1870. Paraguay was besieged by endless territorial strife with Bolivia over the Chaco jungles, and it suffered endless dictatorships, right up to the present time.

Mexico's contemporary to Rosas and Francia, General Antonio López de Santa Anna, was less fortunate than his colleagues. Unlike Francia, who is the subject of a powerful novel by Augusto Roa Bastos, he has never been done justice in literary terms. Indeed, Santa Anna seems to have escaped literary re-creation simply because his life was far more fictional than any novelist could imagine. In his biography, reality beats fiction. He was best depicted in the murals of Diego Rivera, which tend to look like glorified comic strips. But this suits Santa Anna, the prototype of the comic-opera Latin American dictator, perfectly. Wily and seductive, he managed to combine these traits with sheer gall, getting to be president of Mexico eleven times between 1833 and 1854. A grotesque figure, a cockfighter and ladies' man, he was not above succumbing to the temptation to stage coups against himself.

When he lost a leg in the War of the Pastries against France in 1838 — so called because French warships shelled Veracruz to defend the claims of a French baker whose shop had been sacked during a riot — Santa Anna buried his extremity in the cathedral at Mexico City with pomp, and with the archbishop's blessing. The leg was exhumed and dragged through the streets by angry mobs each time Santa Anna fell,

*General Antonio
López de
Santa Anna.
Lithograph, artist
unknown*

only to be reburied once more, with pomp and blessings, when he seized power again. Was it always the same leg, or finally only a useful prop?

If Francia was an ascetic, virginal tyrant, Santa Anna was a promiscuous, comical one. But no one laughed when, through bumbling ineptitude, he lost the northern province of Texas, then the whole northern tier of Mexican territories, including Arizona, New Mexico, Colorado, Nevada, California, and parts of Utah, to the expanding young giant, the United States of America, which was driven toward the Pacific Ocean by the imperial notion of manifest destiny. "Polk's war," as it was called by its critics, was opposed by a lone representative in the United States Congress, Abraham Lincoln. Henry David Thoreau, like Edmund Wilson during the Vietnam era, refused to pay taxes to finance the war. But in 1848 Mexico lost fully one half of its national territory, and the new frontier on the Rio Grande became for many Mexicans an open wound.

Santa Anna did not even have the consolation of being considered, like Rosas, a patriot. His only claim to influence abroad came as he waited to be received by President Andrew Jackson in the White House after the loss of Texas. A North American entrepreneur named Adams came in and saw Santa Anna chewing away but never swallowing. Mr. Adams was intrigued. What was His Excellency chewing? Santa Anna promptly demonstrated by stretching his piece of gum out of his mouth. "It is called *chicle.* I produce it in my tropical haciendas," he probably told Mr. Adams, who then proceeded to manufacture the product for the first time, under the trade name Chiclets.

A more generous claim to fame was that Santa Anna was an honest, if ridiculous, man. When he returned to Mexico from prolonged exile in his seventies, he was given a small government pension, which his wife used to pay beggars. The story holds that the beggars would wait patiently to be received by Santa Anna, who was by then a pitiful figure, peg-legged and dressed in rags himself. But he was sustained in his chimerical self-esteem by the mendicants, who addressed him as "Señor Presidente."

THE LIBERAL REACTION: BENITO JUÁREZ

In 1854, Santa Anna, who now called himself "His Most Serene Highness," began sporting an ermine cape and spent a big chunk of the national budget ordering yellow satin uniforms for his palace guards from Paris. He was overthrown by a reaction of disgust and national dignity, led by the Liberal Party, in whose ranks stood a figure diametrically opposed to the bemedaled strongman: Benito Juárez.

An austere lawyer of Zapotec Indian stock, Juárez lived as a shepherd, illiterate and ignorant of the Spanish language, until he was twelve years old, when he joined his sister in the home of a parish priest in the city of Oaxaca. It was there that he learned to read and write Spanish. His mind was acute and his ambition great. He always called his protector, the lay Franciscan priest Salanueva, "my godfather." But he did not study for the priesthood, as Father Salanueva hoped. In 1828, at age twenty-two, Benito Juárez left the house of Father Salanueva to embark on a legal career, which eventually transformed him into Mexico's great reformer and liberal president of the nineteenth century.

One can only imagine the forces that raged within the young man's soul as he left Oaxaca. His fatalistic Indian streak enabled him to withstand many defeats. He was formed in the environment of a poor Catholic clergyman, yet in the legal profession he acquired a ferocious will, which he used to help Mexico overcome the obstacles to becoming a modern, independent nation.

Juárez' first line of business, undertaken while he was minister of justice, was separating church and state. He confiscated the vast, unproductive wealth of the church and set it to circulate. He deprived the military and the aristocracy of their special courts of justice. He established civil laws and subjected all citizens to their rule. Known as the Reform Laws, these could not be countenanced by the Conservative Party. Juárez and the Liberals had opted for a clear solution: subject the church and the army to the control of the national state, and then subject everyone, including the state, to the control of the law.

For three years the Conservatives waged war against Juárez and his reforms. When they were finally defeated on the battlefield in 1860, they turned abroad and found support in the court of Napoleon III of France, who had just conquered Indochina and now dreamed of extending French imperial influence in the Americas. It was a dream instigated by his wife, the Spanish Empress Eugénie de Montijo, who imagined a Latin empire in the Americas that could stand up to the increasing influence and power of the United States. The outbreak of the War between the States gave Napoleon III a chance to emulate the greatness of his namesake and uncle.

Backed by Napoleon, the Mexican Conservatives trekked to the Castle of Miramar on the Adriatic, where Archduke Maximilian of Austria represented his brother, the Austrian emperor Francis Joseph, as governor of Trieste. There they offered him the crown of Mexico. Maximilian, an attractive, tall, blond, and bearded young man, was extremely irresolute, but his ambitious and politically alert wife, Charlotte, daughter of Belgium's King Leopold, urged him to accept.

Maximilian and his brother had different political ideals. In Vienna, Francis Joseph, after crushing the liberal, nationalist upsurges of 1848, ruled in the autocratic fashion native to the Hapsburgs. In Trieste, and before that in Lombardy, Maximilian sympathized with liberal reforms and an aggiornamento of the church and the empire. The Conservatives

Benito Juárez.
José Clemente Orozco, 1948

whom he received at Miramar in 1862, however, did not go into these political niceties. They claimed that Mexico needed Maximilian to restore order against barbaric, anarchical revolutionaries. The Mexican people begged him to come. The French army had occupied and now wanted to pacify Mexico. In a referendum gerrymandered by the French, the people had opted for the monarchy and Maximilian. And Maximilian and Charlotte had no chance of reigning in Vienna. In Mexico they could create the kind of enlightened modern monarchy that would put Francis Joseph to shame.

Sibling rivalry was the modus operandi, as revealed by the relevant correspondence that went back and forth between Trieste, Vienna, Brussels, and later Mexico. Charlotte convinced Maximilian that if they let the Mexican opportunity slip by, they would never head a monarchy, only serve one.

Maximilian, emperor of Mexico, and his wife, Carlota

If Charlotte was blinded by ambition and an honest need to prove herself worthy of Leopold's political education, even she must have winced as the *Novara* docked in Veracruz and she saw the steep, crooked ascent from the coast to the capital, beyond the triumphant arches and the flowers offered by the Indians. Cortés had followed the same route to Mexico City on foot, nearly three hundred and fifty years earlier. But Maximilian and Charlotte were not like Cortés, or even Maximilian's forebear, Charles V, who had conquered at a distance. Traveling in a heavy, gilded royal coach with enormous wheels, they suffered calamity after calamity — breakdowns, mud slides, even overturnings.

There were comical aspects to this saga. Arriving in Mexico City, the imperial couple occupied Santa Anna's former suite in the National Palace. The bedbugs chased them out and they were forced to sleep on billiard tables. Soon, however, they moved to more comfortable quarters in Chapultepec Castle. Perhaps they did not know that until recently, this had been a military school, and six young cadets had leapt to their death rather than surrender it to the invading North Americans.

The animus against foreign intervention now began unifying Mexicans of all stripes, with the exception of the hard-core Conservatives, who stood to regain lands confiscated by the Liberals. This included, of course, the church hierarchy. It was no surprise, therefore, that howls could be heard from the haciendas of Jalisco to the halls of St. Peter's when Maximilian, to prove his liberalism and leave his personal stamp on affairs of state, decided to sustain the reform legislation of Benito Juárez. Did he not understand that he had been brought to Mexico to uphold privilege, not to abolish it? Juárez refused Maximilian's invitation to become prime

minister in the imperial regime. If Maximilian wanted a democracy, Juárez said, let him impose it on the subjects of his brother Francis Joseph. Mexico would go on fighting against the French occupation.

Today, alongside Maximilian's gilded chariot at Chapultepec Castle you can see Juárez' simple black coach. In it he traveled across the deserts of northern Mexico with the legal archives of the nation in tow, waging guerrilla warfare against the French, true to his own words: "If there is only a square inch of national territory on top of a forsaken hilltop, from there I will fight back to reconquer the fatherland." Juárez was the very embodiment of Indian fatality, Roman legality, and Spanish stoicism. He tried to make the dreams of Bolívar and San Martín reality by supporting strong institutions, not strongmen, and civilian government under which no one was above the rule of law. Imagine once again the feelings of this man, an Indian educated in the ideals of French civilization, when he saw that same civilization turning against him and denying Mexico the right to independence. Imagine also his will, with no office but his stagecoach, to defend Mexico to the very last, to establish the principle that no foreign power had the right to determine who would rule a Latin American nation.

The French commander, Achille Bazaine, made the emperor realize that nothing could assure peace except the defeat of Juárez and his ragtag republican army. Maximilian drew up a decree that condemned to death any Mexican found bearing arms. It came to be known as the Black Decree. When Maximilian signed it on October 2, 1865, he signed his own death warrant.

Presiding over a phantom court, Maximilian and Charlotte, now known by her Hispanicized name, Carlota, had nothing to offer and certainly nothing with which to defeat Juárez. Maximilian's independent caprices were laughable. He was *not* independent; instead, he was a puppet of Napoleon III and backed by French bayonets. When the French emperor decided to abandon him in 1867, his fall was inevitable. Other, more pressing matters occupied the mind of the Little Napoleon, as his foe Victor Hugo called him.

The American Civil War was over. Napoleon had supported the South and the South had supported Napoleon. Mexico might have become another stronghold for slavery and feudal plantations, but Lincoln and the North had triumphed, while on France's eastern borders Bismarck had managed to unite Germany under the military aegis of Prussia and was obviously preparing for greater conquests. The Mexican guerrillas, *campesinos* by day, soldiers by night, slippery and quick in their movements, were heirs to Viriatus' tradition of resistance to Rome; they were not about to be crushed by a foreigner. And in France there were growing complaints, attacks in the newspapers and at public meetings protesting the bloodletting in Mexico and mourning the thousands of young Frenchmen returning in coffins. Only one imperial spot shone brightly in Napoleon's eye. He had conquered Southeast Asia, from the Gulf of Tonkin to the Mekong Delta. (A hundred years later, the Juárez of Indochina would be fighting the same war. His name would be Ho Chi Minh.)

As the French forces left Mexico, Carlota rushed back to Paris and scolded Napoleon at the Tuilleries for not keeping his word. It was useless. With only a loyal staff of Mexican officers to defend him, Maximilian was surrounded at Querétaro, and on May 15, 1867, he surrendered his sword to the republican forces. Juárez did not budge in the face of international calls to pardon him. Thousands of Mexicans, victims of the Black Decree, stood in the way of clemency, and on June 19 Maximilian was shot at the Hill of the Bells nearby.

Meanwhile, Carlota had continued her campaign in Europe. While pleading her husband's cause to Pope Pius IX, she became seriously ill and had to spend the night in the Vatican, becoming the first woman officially to do so. Then the terrible truth was confirmed: the young empress had lost her mind. At twenty-seven, she became a recluse at the castle of Bouchout in her native Belgium. From there she wrote letters to her beloved Maximilian. She never found out that he had died. She ate only nuts and drank spring water, convinced that Napoleon was out to poison her. On rare occasions she was seen at grave, funereal functions, shrinking smaller and smaller, each time more distant. When her cousin Kaiser William II invaded Belgium in 1915, guards were posted at the castle to protect "Her Majesty, the empress of Mexico." Finally, in 1927, Carlota died, at age eighty-seven.

Maximilian now rests forever in the crypt of the Hapsburgs in Vienna. The Mexican firing squad blew out one of his eyes and the embalmer could not find a fake blue eye in all of Querétaro, so a black eye was borrowed from a Virgin at a local church and ensconced in the dead emperor's socket. From the depths of the Kapuzinergruft, he now looks at death with one blue Austrian eye and one black Indian eye.

REPUBLICS RESTORED, CULTURES IN WAITING

In 1867 Benito Juárez reentered Mexico City in triumph and restored the liberal republic. Would reformist laws, civilian leadership, democratic rules governing public life, separation of powers, an independent press, and free enterprise now overcome the heavy legacy of Indian autocracy,

Maximilian's execution

Spanish colonial rule, and republican tyranny? Almost at the same time that Juárez came to power in Mexico, and after the fall of Rosas in 1852, two successive civilian presidents in Argentina, Bartolomé Mitre and Domingo F. Sarmiento himself, set their country on a course toward the elimination of local *caudillos* and the settlement of the interior territories through expanded communications, education, and massive immigration.

With Juárez and Sarmiento presidents of the two largest Spanish American nations, it would seem that our dreams of democratic stability and economic prosperity were about to become true. Yet this depended on another all-embracing but slowly emerging factor: the consciousness of cultural life, that slowly shifting bedrock of beliefs, manners, dreams, memories, languages, and passions that truly confirms any society. From Mexico to Argentina, we had much to learn about ourselves before culture and politics truly coincided in a democratic community.

FOURTEEN

The Culture of Independence

Culturally, independent Spanish America turned its back on both its Indian and black heritages, judging them to be barbarous, and was dramatically divided about its Spanish tradition. Many Spanish Americans blamed Spain for all our ills. Had it not deprived its colonies of everything that modern Europe had come to represent, from religious freedom to economic wealth to political democracy? Had it not saddled us with dogma and conformism, with privilege as the norm and charity as the exception, and with the militant church — in other words, with everything that European modernity judged intolerable? And in politics we were left with the absence of democracy, the nullity of the citizen and his rights, the distance between law and practice, between government and the governed.

No wonder that the majority of Spanish American élites also turned their backs on Spain, making their reasons glaringly clear in speech after speech. Sarmiento spoke for many when he said, with great passion and an equally great lack of fairness, that in Spain "there are no authors, no writers, no scientists, no statesmen, no historians, and nothing worthwhile." The Chilean historian José Vitorino Lastarria wrote that between Columbus and Bolívar there had been nothing but "a black winter" in Spanish America. And the Argentine Romantic poet Esteban Echeverría argued that "we are independent, but we are not free; the arms of Spain no longer oppress us, but her traditions hamper us." The social emancipation of Spanish America, he added, called for a repudiation of the Spanish heritage.

Detail from
Dream of
a Sunday
Afternoon in
the Alameda.
Diego Rivera

Such wholesale renunciation of our cultural past naturally left another hole in our independent history, much as the absence of the monarchy had done in political terms. And again the vacuum had to be filled. Many Spanish Americans looked north, toward the United States of

America, which had met with immediate success while we floundered in one protracted failure after another. The liberals were the great admirers of the U.S.A. at the beginning of our long, tortuous, and inevitable relationship. They applauded the vitality, the political institutions, and the modernizing impetus of North American democracy.

But the conservatives opposed the United States for the same reasons. According to them, the worst sins were democracy, capitalism, Protestantism, religious tolerance, and free inquiry. They perceived the United States as a radical, dangerous, revolutionary republic. Above all, conservatives in Spanish America feared the perceived expansionist potential of the young nation. In essence, the philosophy of manifest destiny had already been formulated by Thomas Jefferson and John Quincy Adams. In a letter written in 1821, Adams wrote to Henry Clay, "It is unavoidable that the remainder of the continent shall be ours."

The Mexican War of 1846–1848 and the loss of half of Mexico's national territory to the United States convinced many liberals that the conservatives were correct in their assessment of U.S. territorial ambitions. The cultural question, however, was not easily solved. Where could we turn for inspiration and models if not the United States? The nineteenth century provided a ready-made answer in France, especially in Paris, which Baudelaire called "the capital of the nineteenth century." Parisian influence was felt from The Hague to Algiers and from St. Petersburg to Cairo. But in Mexico City, Bogotá, and Buenos Aires it served a deeper need, filling the cultural vacuum.

The repudiation of Spain came to mean the acceptance of France as the new source of liberty, taste, Romanticism, and all things good. Typically, a Chilean historian, Benjamín Vicuña Mackenna, wrote from the French capital in 1853, "I was in Paris . . . the capital of the world, the heart of humanity . . . the universe in miniature." And the Brazilian aristocrat Eduardo Pardo was quoted as saying with a sigh, "Without a doubt, the world *is* Paris." In the sixteenth century Spanish America had been the Utopia of Europe. Now we returned the compliment and made Europe the Utopia of Spanish America. Guatemala City even called itself "the Paris of Central America." Our secret yearning, of course, was that one day Paris would call itself "the Guatemala City of Europe."

The pity of this admiration for Europe, as the Chilean writer Claudio Veliz points out in his book *The Centralist Tradition of Latin America,* is that it did not extend to the European manner of production but only to the European manner of consumption. The upper classes in Latin America emulated a European sensibility in their expenditure of wealth, style, dress, and architecture, as well as in their taste in literature and in their social, political, and economic ideas. What they neglected to change were the means of production in Latin America.

The opera house became the symbol of an elegant, Europeanized Latin American modernity. From the neoclassical Teatro Juárez in the mining town of Guanajuato in Mexico to the elegant Teatro Colón in Buenos Aires, all was gilt, red velvet, painted backdrops, long intermissions, and striking décolletages. As a matter of fact, the arrival in Bogotá of the first French couturier, a certain Madame Gautron, in the 1840s was long considered a memorable event, as it certified that the Colombian capital had at last become a modern city. A Colombian journalist added that the changing tastes of Bogotá as it went from provincial backwater to cosmopolitan capital could be shown by what the upper classes were drinking, from the 1810s (traditional Indo-Hispanic chocolate) to the 1840s (French coffee) to the 1860s (English tea).

There was, in spite of everything, a lively quality to this "extra-logical imitation," as the French sociologist Gabriel Tarde called it. Even death could be an imitation of Europe in nineteenth-century Latin America. The Recoleta Cemetery in central Buenos Aires is a Potemkin village of the afterlife, a Disneyland of death, where all good Argentine oligarchs are buried and where, it seems, they believed you *could* take it with you. One wonders how many head of cattle, pails of milk, and packs of hides it took to build any one of these extravagant funeral monuments, where angels fly over the bourgeois busts of distinguished merchants and Gabriel's trumpet sounds forever from a worthy general's tomb.

The Recoleta offers us a vision of paradise as a continuation of opulence based on cattle and commerce. But in the meantime, back at the hacienda, Latin America continued to supply sugar, wool, hides, rubber, wheat, and cotton in order to support the lifestyle of economic liberalism, if not the lifestyle of political liberalism. Latin America (I include Brazil) profited from the worldwide expansion of capitalism in the nineteenth century by providing raw materials, but we did not provide ourselves with capital for investment and savings.

The accent of our economic life was put on foreign trade, a necessity determined by a factor quite alien to Latin American initiatives: the accelerated economic growth of Western Europe and the United States. Whereas trade was the basis of our expansion, it derived from European and North American expansion in population, industrialization, commerce, education, urbanization, political institutions, and so on. Latin America was peripheral to all this, although it profited, of course, from

*The Recoleta
Cemetery, Buenos
Aires*

the revolution in modern communications and transportation. The steamship was the principal vehicle of this relationship. In 1876, the first refrigerator ship sailed from the port of Buenos Aires to Europe with a cargo of frozen beef. In the same decade, the first exports of Argentine wheat crossed the ocean. In the phase immediately after independence, Britain managed Latin America's foreign trade; in the latter part of the nineteenth century, the United States came to be the principal partner. However, they employed the same instruments of economic power, namely favorable agreements for their merchants, loans and credits, investment, and the handling of the export economy of minerals, agricultural produce, and natural products required by Anglo-American expansion. A highly privileged local minority served as intermediaries, both for these exports and for the imports of manufactured European and North American goods, which were in demand among the urban population in the interior.

As they expanded into modern trade relationships, Latin American merchants depended on a continuation of the farming and mining structures of colonial times. Large haciendas, intensive exploitation of minerals, and cheap labor forces proliferated. Was this what independence was all about — land- and mine owners profiting handsomely while the majority remained impoverished? By the end of the nineteenth century, life expectancy in most parts of Latin America was below twenty-seven

*Teatro Colón,
Buenos Aires*

years, literacy rates were as low as 2 percent in some regions, and more than half the population lived in the countryside, most of them in conditions of dismal poverty. "The liberal pause," as Claudio Veliz calls this stage of our development, actually consolidated the poverty of colonial times for the majority of our citizens.

In the nineteenth century, we became orphans of our own peripheral capitalism, feverishly exchanging exports for imports to uphold patterns of consumption in the middle and upper classes while again postponing any rational approach to the welfare of the majority. The ruling capitalists of Europe and the United States retained profits and incremented their savings, quickly enhancing productivity. Europe and North America produced their own meat and potatoes. We supplied the desserts: chocolate, coffee, sugar, fruit, tobacco.

A NEW SOCIETY

Liberal reforms, foreign intervention, civil strife, conservative traditions, and foreign trade clashed, shaking up the colonial societies, releasing new forces, and even permitting, along with the confirmation of an upper class of landowners, merchants, and politicians, the slow emergence of a modern middle class. This included lawyers and businessmen, whose services were required by the growing economic relationships between Spanish America and the rest of the world, between city and countryside, and between social classes in the rapidly growing urban conglomerates.

Buenos Aires, which had 44,800 inhabitants in 1810, when the revolution was launched, had a population of 180,000 by 1870, and 1,600,000, largely because of mass European immigration, in 1914, as World War I began. The Chilean port of Valparaíso, hub of the Pacific trade and also of Atlantic trade around the Horn, nearly doubled its population in twenty years, from 52,000 in 1856 to 100,000 in 1876. Mexico City had barely 230,000 citizens after the fall of Maximilian's empire, less than it had after the fall of Moctezuma's empire. When Porfirio Díaz, in his turn, fell in 1911, the city had grown to 350,000. In the sixty years following 1870, Santiago and Caracas multiplied their populations by five, Bogotá by eight, and Montevideo by four.

Journalists, intellectuals, teachers, bureaucrats, and tradesmen, as well as their families, brought activity, discussion, and growth to our cities. These were city folks who saw themselves as a shield against dictatorship and anarchy. Stability was their greatest value. It was in their absence that the liberators of the early nineteenth century had to cling to mere political abstractions. Now two concrete facts of politics and economics were emerging: an urban middle class and a national state. Both searched for an identity throughout the nineteenth century. The middle class found it by having portraits painted. No longer were kings and aristocrats the only subject matter; portraits of doctors, housewives, children, and even postmen became the fashion. In Mexico, the paintings of Juan Cordero, and in Argentina those of Prilidiano Pueyrredón, conveyed the physiognomy of the urban middle class, while Hermenegildo Bustos, a postman in his native Guanajuato, provided an identity for the humbler denizens of the provincial townships. The Spanish American middle class at last had a face. And if these people sometimes idealized themselves, who could begrudge them their newfound sense of identity, their pride, their emergence from obscurity? Did not this social fact suffice to justify the revolutions of independence?

The best example of bourgeois success in Latin America was to be found in Chile, a country defined by its physical remoteness, which obliged its inhabitants to rely on themselves more than people in the metropolitan centers of the Spanish Empire. The Californian and Australian gold rushes opened up great markets for Chile's agricultural products in the Pacific basin, while Europe bought up Chilean copper. The national sense of destiny even pushed Chile into a war with Peru and Bolivia for the saltpeter deposits in the Atacama desert. Bolivia lost its access to the sea, Peru its southern region. Chile, now controlling trade in the Pacific through its free port, Valparaíso, saw great fortunes rise, and along with them political institutions unique on the South American continent.

Eventually, a great price was paid for this expansion. Chile came to rely excessively on two products, copper and nitrates. But as the world price fell or rose, so did Chile's fortunes. The country depended on the world more than the world depended on Chile, and when synthetic nitrate production appeared in Germany, Chile faced ruin. By 1918 the country was bankrupt, forecasting the Great Depression by a decade.

But during the halcyon days of the nineteenth century, Chile's political development achieved a striking balance with its economic progress. Between the political supremacy of Diego Portales in the 1830s and the presidency of José Manuel Balmaceda in the 1880s, Chile developed the most politically structured society in Latin America. Freedoms were reserved for the upper and middle classes; they did not extend to peasants and workers. But within these limits, the nation achieved a political balance based on the principle of diversified élitism. While Mexico and Argentina were crushed under the misgoverning tyrants Santa Anna and Rosas, Chileans could choose between the power of the congress and the

Don Manuel
Desiderio Rojas.
*Hermenegildo
Bustos, 1885*

Maria de los
Remedios
Barajas.
*Hermenegildo
Bustos, 1892*

power of the executive, the secular and ecclesiastical spheres, industrialization and agriculture, private initiative and the public sector. Indeed, Chile became a haven for Argentine exiles under Rosas. It opened its doors to the great teachers Sarmiento and Andrés Bello, and created the best educational system in Latin America. Its thinkers were liberals and anticlericals such as José Victorino Lastarria and Francisco Bilbao; its historians, Benjamín Vicuña Mackenna and Diego Barros Arana, were among the greatest we have ever had.

All of this made of Chile the first relatively modern nation of Latin America. One of the signs of that modernity, complementing the economic realities, was the appearance of a literature of independence — novels and poetry, but also journalism and history. The greatest cultural debates of the nineteenth century took place in Chile, the country with a rising middle class and a growing reading public, the country with institutions that favored the freedoms of the élite. Journalism, at last independent of the surveillance of the Inquisition, was the greatest novelty of all. The two greatest newspapers of the time were both founded in Buenos Aires, within four months of each other: *La Prensa* in 1869 and *La Nación* in 1870.

Latin Americans could, and did, quote the famous words of the French poet and statesman Lamartine: "The press is the principal instrument of civilization in our times." Yet the very definition of civilization was at the core of the cultural debate of the nineteenth century. What was it, this civilized status we aspired to, yearned for, identified with modern life and with well-being itself? By exclusion, we decided that we were not Indian, black, or Spanish. Instead we tried to believe that we were European, preferably French.

The modernizing claims of the Latin American élites were thus self-defeating, because they artificially divided the components of our culture, sacrificing it to a simplistic choice between "civilization and barbarism," as Sarmiento put it. In *Facundo,* he explained that "it is a law of humanity that the ideas . . . of progress shall finally overcome the triumph of the musty traditions, the habits of ignorance or stagnant preoccupations."

CIVILIZATION AND BARBARISM

The true barbarism of this ideology was that it excluded from the notion of civilization all indigenous models of existence. Black, Indian, communitarian, and all property relationships other than those consecrated by liberal economics were left out — most notably, the centuries-old style of life based on shared agricultural produce and properties, such as the *ejido* in Mexico and the *ayllu* in Peru. These alternative cultures ascribed to a different set of values from those of the cities. Tradition, mutual knowledge, a knack for self-government among communities that knew their own people well, an attachment to nature, and a suspicion of abstract laws imposed from above were all denied by the progressive mentality of the nineteenth century. This blatant disregard would come back to haunt Spanish America in the twentieth century, when the example of the alternative society as a Mexican agrarian Arcadia was proposed by the peasant leader Emiliano Zapata.

However, such an alternative culture was seen as a barrier to progress by the liberal élites of the nineteenth century, who professed a so-called scientific ideology. An adaptation of the positivist philosophy of Auguste Comte, it pretended that human history developed in foreseeable, universal stages. A Latin American nation had only to find out what stage it was in to insert itself scientifically into the movement of progress. The motto of this philosophy, "Order and Progress," inspired all the modernizing governments in Latin America. It even ended up smack in the middle of the Brazilian flag.

Positivism allowed the high priests of realpolitik to present themselves wrapped not only in their national flag but in a philosophy that dissipated the mists of a metaphysical past. If one could scientifically forecast the movement of society, one could easily manage change, and subsequently the obstacles to change, the first of which was the Indian population. The Argentine writer Carlos Bunge, in a notorious book speciously called *Our America*, blessed alcoholism, smallpox, and tuberculosis for decimating the Indians and Africans.

This propagandizing against the Indians was a counterpoint to a fervent desire to see white European immigrants come to Latin America. It also perpetuated the image of the Indians as murderers and thieves. "To govern is to populate," wrote the Argentine journalist and educator Juan Bautista Alberdi. But first, evidently, you had to depopulate. In 1878, an army rode out under the command of General Julio Roca with the mission of exterminating the Indians in Argentina's southern territories. Their grazing lands were needed for civilization, that is, for European immigrants. General Roca was eminently successful in his "War of the Desert" and was rewarded, twice, with the presidency of Argentina.

In Chile, the fiercely independent Araucanians, who never gave in to the Spanish conquistadors, were finally subdued by the locomotive and the rifle. In 1880, a military campaign confined them to reservations. In Mexico, the dictator Porfirio Díaz, proclaiming himself to be scientific and inspired by positivism, waged savage campaigns against the Indian population of the northern Mexican states of Sonora, Sinaloa, and Chihuahua. Himself of Zapotec extraction, Díaz wished to give these territories to the landed gentry in Mexico, notably the Limantour family, and to U.S. enterprises such as the Richardson Construction Company of Los Angeles and the Wheeler Land Company of Phoenix. He provoked the rebellion of the Tomochic area in Chihuahua, and in the war against the Yaqui and Mayo peoples, he had the chieftains of the latter tribe put on a warship, chained together, and dumped into the Pacific Ocean. The leaders of the Yaqui rebellion were murdered, and half of the tribe's total male population (30,000 people) were deported and sent on a painful trek all the way to Yucatán. Separated from their women, they were forced to marry Chinese farmhands and forget their families and their heritage.

Where was this barbarism coming from? From the city, from the countryside? One thing was certain, the ideology of progress overrode all objections. The Indians were expendable. And the conquest, obviously, had not ended. Now we, the independent Spanish Americans, were the conquistadors, acting exactly like descendants of Cortés and Pizarro. Only the uniforms had changed.

According to the ideologues of civilization, there was another element of regression and barbarism in the hinterland. Called *charros* in Mexico, *guasos* in Chile, and *gauchos* in Argentina, they generated a language and an imagery that gave voice to a culture apart from that of the cities. They were figures of the countryside — machos, outlaws, bandits on horseback, independent and lonely men in a lonely natural setting, never far from the violence of our social life. Their life stories tell of usurpations of land, rape, somewhere a burning shack, or a *pronunciamiento* by some local *caudillo,* or a foreign intervention or two, so that the *charro* and the gaucho are always hovering on the precipice of becoming the guerrilla fighter, always gazing, blindly perhaps, at the "gates of the abyss" of revolution.

Traditionally, these men told their stories through song, as they had no other record. The *charro*'s song is called the *corrido* and is a derivation of the medieval and Renaissance Spanish romance, an octosyllabic news-poem belonging to a constantly modified and enriched oral tradition. The *charro,* like the gaucho, is the Hector or the Achilles of the rural Latin American epic, asserting a second history in word and in deed, far from the conventional forms of progress and civilization. The gaucho, like the *charro,* sings his story. The *payadores,* the folksingers of the pampas, tell their tales with the power granted them by the absence of any other means of communication. One of the themes of the *payadores* was that the gaucho starts singing in his mother's womb; he is born singing and he dies singing. And what he sings about, of course, are his troubles. Only a song can console him in his pain.

The song of the *payadores* was the newspaper of the pampas. It was the gaucho's only history book, and it was the source of the greatest single work of literature in nineteenth-century Spanish America, the poem *Martín Fierro,* written in 1872 by José Hernández, a city writer who spent some time in the pampas. Hernández wanted to defend the agrarian world against the exploitations and the arrogance of the city. Martín Fierro is not the obstacle to progress; he is the victim of "arrogant little political bosses who abuse his weakness and isolation," Hernández affirmed. (On becoming president of Argentina in 1868, even the humanist Sarmiento expressed his scorn for the gaucho thus: "I do not intend to be thrifty about gaucho blood. Blood is the only human thing about them.")

In the poem, Fierro recalls his life as a free man, then his sufferings at the hands of the military and the corrupt political bosses. After being forcefully drafted into the army, deserting, and being jailed, he returns home. But Ithaca lies in ruins, Penelope has been raped and abducted, and Ulysses has no sea to wander in but the immense, lawless pampa. "I swore," says Martín Fierro, "to be more fierce than a beast." And so his criminal career begins.

Gaucho, Uruguay,
1990

Indeed, the word *gaucho*, like its equivalent across the Andes in Chile, *huaso*, comes from the Araucanian *guacho*, which means fatherless, orphaned, illegitimate. This sense of orphanhood, even of bastardy, conquest's brand on the children of Spain and the Indian world, now reappeared as the secret mark of these lonely, violent figures of our plains and mountains.

TWO TO TANGO

As the cities grew, they began to attract an increasing number of people from the *estancias*, the pampas, the haciendas, and the *llanos*, or plains. In Buenos Aires, this phenomenon occurred earlier than elsewhere, simply because no other Latin American city at the turn of the century grew faster or became such a tremendous magnet for immigration. In 1869 Argentina had a population of barely two million people. Between 1880 and 1905, almost three million immigrants came from Europe. In 1900, fully one third of the population of Buenos Aires was foreign born.

By the end of the nineteenth century, both migratory currents, the gaucho and the European, met in the *orillas flacas,* the "shallow outskirts" of Buenos Aires. "The stars," says Martín Fierro, "are my only map in the pampa." They guide him into the city, where he gets off his horse only to lose himself in a city alley. Lawless, landless, and lonely, the former gauchos were left stranded on the pavements of Buenos Aires. They met the immigrants from Europe in the bars and brothels of the city, in solitude. This was a city of lonely men, men without women. They recognized themselves in the tango, a music of immigrants in a transitional, lonely city.

The tango tells a tale of frustrations, nostalgia, fragilities, insecurities. Jorge Luis Borges has called the tango "the great conversation of

The tango

Buenos Aires." But it is above all a potent sexual event. It takes two to tango: a man and a woman, embracing. And in it they realize both an individual and a shared destiny, and the impossibility of controlling it — hence the composer Santos Discépolo's fitting definition of the tango as "a sad thought that can be danced."

Its sources are as mysterious as its actual presence. But whether it is African or Mediterranean in its origins, there is a verbal contact between its black etymology, *tang*, which means to touch, to come near, and its Latin root, the verb *tangere*, to touch, to approach, to play. All of this certainly has a Castilian resonance: *tañer*, to play, specifically to play a guitar.

Wherever it came from, the tango became a sensation when it went abroad at the turn of the century, traveling from the brothels of Buenos Aires to the Parisian salons. Was it one more of our exported desserts? In any case, it became the rage of Europe and the first dance in which couples embraced. Pope Pius X banned what he called "this savage dance." King Ludwig of Bavaria forbade his officers to dance the tango, and the duchess of Norfolk pronounced it to be contrary to English character and manners. But in 1914, English men and women flocked every evening to the Tango Suppers at the Hotel Savoy in London.

In spite of its international success, the tango always returned to its source, Buenos Aires, and to its primary function of recalling the mystery and the misery of our cities, the difficulty of living as human beings in our urban conglomerations. In the cities as well as in the countryside, a whole culture of mixed, irreverent, and mongrel encounters was rising, manifesting itself in language, in music, in body gestures, in dreams, memories, and desires. Spanish Americans were not simply choosing modernity over tradition but keeping both alive in creative tension.

Which means, of course, that the search for a cultural identity did not exhaust itself in the extremes of cosmopolitanism or chauvinism, promiscuity or isolation, civilization or barbarism, but pointed toward an intelligent, well-governed balance between what we took from the world and what we received from it. The cultural debate of independence passed through all of these extremes, but the fear of being ourselves drove us to be something else, whether French, North American, or English. This reflected our difficulty in placing ourselves in the world or recognizing the world and being recognized by it. We grappled with how to manage our own time and how to live within a context without reducing it to the dangerous misidentifications of past with backwardness, or future with progress.

Through the actual development of a culture at all levels, élitist and popular, middlebrow and even vulgarian, we eventually discovered that to become historical, time must be both past and future, and it can only be so in the present. Certainly our best modern artists understood this. For example, Diego Rivera, the modern Mexican painter, created a mural in the 1940s for the Prado Hotel in Mexico City, facing Alameda Park. In it he described a dream populated by all the historical figures of Mexico from the conquest to the revolution. He presented a dream, but also the profound debate surrounding our identity. Should our culture be native or imported, Indian, Spanish, North American, or French?

It is a false dilemma, answered the Cuban patriot and writer José Martí, who can be seen tipping his hat quite chivalrously to some passing ladies in the mural. Martí, with all of his courteous humility, found the key to this long question of ours. He not only warned of the dangers of importing models of progress for their own sake, he forcefully linked progress to the actual needs of the real people, the resources of the real nation, and the actual social composition of Spanish America. Highlight resources, he demanded, highlight people, needs, culture, traditions, and out of them extract a national model. "The government," he wrote in *Our America*, "must be born from the country . . . the spirit . . . and the form of the government must be that of the country. The government is nothing more than the balance between the natural elements of the country." Once we realized this, we might become really democratic. "If the republic does not open its arms to all, then the republic dies." Based on the strengths of self-knowledge, Martí posited, we might even achieve more international independence: "The people who want to perish, sell to only one people, and those who want to live, sell to more than one. . . . Trade must be balanced, if freedom is to be secured."

Martí's solution continues to be the best one. Through it, a nation can fulfill internal expectations while fully participating in the multipolar, interdependent world that awaits us in the twenty-first century. It is also the most demanding one. "Forget no one," he wrote. "Forget nothing."

This all-inclusive culture was soon to find models in writers such as the Nicaraguan poet Rubén Darío, who was unmistakably both Spanish American and European, and in an extraordinary turn-of-the-century graphic artist from Mexico, José Guadalupe Posada. Both Martí and Posada, like the poet Sor Juana and the sculptor Aleijadinho, wrought their originality out of the great wealth of traditions blessing Latin American existence. For our greatest artists, multicultural diversity, far from being a hindrance, was the source of creativity.

A SKELETON ON A BICYCLE

José Guadalupe Posada chronicled the news in sensational, eye-catching, and even lurid engravings from the window of his printer's shop in Mexico City, where he drew and printed broadsheets, street gazettes, for the people who demanded direct, spine-tingling reportage of what was going on: who had murdered whom, who had given birth to a two-headed baby, who had won the presidential elections, and when a comet was going to fly over their heads. In popular idiom, Posada gave to the urban masses, the voiceless and the untutored, and also to the illiterate immigrants from the countryside, the secular equivalent of ex-votos — the *retablos* and other forms of popular religious expression, usually painted on wood or tin, that can still be found in Mexican churches. In them, the faithful thank the Virgin or the patron saint for favors. The art of Posada also forecast modern-day graffiti, which one finds in North American cities all the way from New York to Los Angeles. Like them, Posada's catchpenny prints gave a voice to the poor.

Posada was the rare kind of artist who is clearly linked to a universal form of culture, the culture of danger, of the bizarre, of extremes, of informality. In this sense he belongs to the Spanish family of Goya and Buñuel, as his is an art that universalizes the eccentric. In Posada, murders abound. The most interesting works show us women of high rank, clad in long black dresses, shooting at each other. He depicted scenes of suicide, murder, and strangulation. A young lady throws herself from the

Dream of a
Sunday
Afternoon in
the Alameda.
Diego Rivera, 1947

*Gang members in
front of graffiti,
Los Angeles, 1989*

highest tower of Mexico City Cathedral. A bullfighter is gored. A tailor is sentenced to death for slitting a woman's throat. And then there is sex — flirting, drinking, dancing. Forty-one homosexuals are discovered cavorting in drag at a private ball. Freaks are born: a child with a face on his ass; a man with legs instead of arms; a pig with a man's face.

Posada rendered other grotesque faces of disaster as dreams and nightmares. These are the disasters that occur within a man's own soul, not in the external world of events. Like Goya's *Caprichos*, Posada's *Demons*, his flying horrors, incubuses and monsters (called Avarice, Luxury, Sloth, and Envy), bite and tug at us; serpents choke us in mortal coils, and ghosts appear at noon to frighten poor Doña Pachita, the corner candle seller.

Ghosts and demons, bats and dragons, all converge into an extraordinary theatrical gravure. In it, the entrance to a fairground attraction, the Theater of Illusion, is a demon's wide-open mouth, fangs and all, waiting to swallow the spectator up as he enters for the last show, the "undiscovered country" guarded by the "fell sergeant, death" (*Hamlet* V.ii.350). Death awaits us behind the fairground, the carnival that overturns social categories and political fictions, the great egalitarian spectacle that dissolves the frontiers between stage and auditorium, player and spectator, viewer and viewed. The "carnivalesque" encounter, the great dissolver of authority since primeval times, led Posada to a vision of death that is fantastically merry and ironical. (His *calaveras*, or death skulls,

A Rich Man Hounded by the Seven Deadly Sins. *Posada, n.d.*

were illustrations for the All Souls and Day of the Dead celebrations.)

Posada's art of the macabre started to climb to its heights when the most modern of vehicles, the bicycle, made its appearance in the phantasmagorical graveyard. In 1890, the bicycle became the great fashion in Mexico City, an event not alien to other proofs of progress: the first electricity plant in 1898; Señor Joaquin de la Cantolla's balloon flight over the city in 1902; Señor Braniff's first airplane flight a few years later. But these "modern" events were offset by the remnants of the past, notably banditry. The Posada etchings recall, along with progress, the dead weight of superstition, ignorance, and highway assault.

In a bold stroke of genius, Posada resolved and united these contradictions in the figure of Death riding a bicycle, meshing the old and the new in the inevitability of death. The bicycle carries off dandies and thugs, congressmen and quacks, shysters and judges, devout old ladies and exploiting Yankees. "Let the gringos beware of the agile cyclists," says one of Posada's prints. Both the peasant and the urban dweller will have to roll down the avenue with death — a fun-loving death, to be sure, puffing a cigar, dancing the Mexican hat dance, and, most comically, made up as a Gay Nineties belle, a sort of macabre Mae West, wrapped in the shawls of Quetzalcoatl, her bald head covered by a sumptuous Parisian hat: "Come down and see me sometime."

Extraordinary in itself, this vision owes as much to tradition as it gives back. In Posada, as in all great artists, creation is a pause that carries

A Fashionable Lady. *Posada, n.d.*

forward a tradition; in one act of genius, it acknowledges and transcends, denies and enriches. Here are the medieval roundelays of the *danse macabre*, which led to the immortal image by Holbein and were then renewed by Posada. Here are Goya's *Caprichos* and Prince Orsini's macabre pleasure garden at Bomarzo, with its tombs opening their jaws to receive the dead. Here also are the traditions of the Aztec *coatepantli*, the wall of skulls recently uncovered at the Templo Mayor in Mexico City, and of the candy skulls eaten by children on the Mexican Day of the Dead. Posada's images are also the precursors of montage techniques. Sergei Eisenstein acknowledged his debt to Posada in the Day of the Dead sequences of his film *Que Viva Mexico!*

Extraordinary in itself, this vision becomes unique when all of the images, especially that of death, flow into a vision of revolution, which means a vision of history as violence and death — a boisterous, animated, grimacing death. The art of Posada not only offers society a mirror in which to see its deformity, it offers us a sleepless vision of history as ruin. Posada also helps us regard our cultural continuity critically. We have paid dearly for the misguided belief that history and happiness can beatifically coincide, but all happiness is relative, because there are no absolutes. History is only historical if it does not deceive us with a promise of absolute success or perfect fulfillment. Life is only livable if it does not shrink from the tragic consciousness, including, as Posada does, the vision of death. In Posada, the cultural contradictions of independence resolve themselves in the grand and perilous meeting of risk and revolution, life and death.

Calavera Don Quixote.
José Guadalupe Posada, c. 1887

Gran Calavera
Eléctrica. *The
cemetery is full of
victims of the
recently introduced
electric trolley.
Posada, 1907*

As the twentieth century dawned, we realized that we had to face
these perils if we were ever to see our true selves, understand the totality
of our past, and envision a future that was not at odds with what we were.
But to reach this, we had to struggle violently through many historical
issues. Violent or reasonable, revolutionary or peaceful, our history now
had to address the most persistent dilemma facing us since Indian and
colonial times, the possession of the land and the rights of the majority.
And nowhere did the people and the land reveal their violent fraternity as
much as in the first great social upheaval of the new century, the Mexican
Revolution.

FIFTEEN

Land and Liberty

The Mexican Revolution was really two revolutions. The first was headed by the popular guerrilla leaders, Pancho Villa in the north and Emiliano Zapata in the south, whose goal was social justice based on local self-rule. The second was led by middle-class professionals, intellectuals, ranchers, and merchants, who envisioned a modern, democratic, progressive Mexico ruled from the center by a strong national government.

Both the agrarian and the middle-class leaders felt that their hopes had been postponed by the prolonged rule of Porfirio Díaz, who governed Mexico with an iron fist between 1877 and 1911. Díaz, a courageous guerrilla fighter himself under Benito Juárez, reached the presidency under the banners of Latin American liberals. For him, "order and progress" did not include democracy or social justice. It meant rapid economic development, favoring an élite and sanctioning undemocratic methods to achieve goals.

At first Díaz courted the middle class. New groups of businessmen, administrators, and ranchers appeared on the scene as he encouraged foreign and national investment in oil, railroads, and land development. (His regime increased trackage in Mexico from 723 miles in 1881 to 9,029 miles by 1900.) But these policies also transformed thousands of traditional peasants and artisans into agricultural and industrial workers, while the hacienda system, invigorated by liberal reform laws, deprived the traditional peasant communities of the last remnants of their hereditary possessions.

Land, water, and forests were absorbed by the haciendas. As more and more peasants lost their lands, they became chattels of the huge estates. One of these, the Terrazas property in Chihuahua, was larger than Belgium and the Netherlands combined, and it took one full day and a night to travel through it by train. Foreign holdings were equally vast.

Porfirio Díaz

By 1910, U.S. property in Mexico amounted to 100 million acres, including much of the most valuable mining, agricultural, and timber land, representing 22 percent of Mexico's land surface. The complexes owned by William Randolph Hearst alone extended to almost eight million acres.

Debt became the principal chain of the *campesino* — debt to the company store, debt passed from generation to generation. By 1910, 98 percent of the arable land in Mexico was owned by the haciendas and 90 percent of Mexico's peasants were landless. The rural masses made up 80 percent of the population, and all but 10 percent were illiterate. But Díaz' development policies also transformed thousands of peasants and artisans into agrarian and industrial workers. Díaz had to establish powerful security forces to see to it that they didn't form unions, that strikes were broken, and that labor remained cheap. Otherwise, neither his local supporters nor the growing foreign interests would profit from or invest in the rapidly expanding Mexican economy.

Discontent and rebellion thus became inevitable among both industrial workers and field hands. Porfirio Díaz had a brutal, biting response for them: "Kill 'em while they're hot!" Within six months, two industrial strikes rocked his administration. In June 1906, workers at the copper mine at Cananea challenged not only the Mexican dictatorship but its foreign allies. Díaz had to call in the Arizona Rangers to suppress the miners' revolt in order to "protect American lives and property." In December, the Circle of Free Workers at the textile mill of Rio Blanco revolted against a situation that included total dependency on the general store, subhuman lodging conditions, the use of identity cards and passbooks, and censorship of reading material. This time Díaz sent in the Federal Army to fire on the workers, load their bodies onto freight cars, take them to Veracruz, and dump them into the sea.

Díaz' scheme, imposed on a basically agrarian society, created a very strong landowning class, a weak bourgeoisie, a crushed peasantry, and a stunted labor movement. In the end, the failure to legitimate the regime created deep alienation toward the leadership. Gradually, even the middle-class enclaves originally favored by Díaz became disaffected. They saw themselves cut off as major profits went to foreign companies, which had great interest in exports from Mexico but little interest in expanding Mexico's internal market. Repression, lack of opportunities, nationalist sentiments (those Arizona ranchers, those Hearst properties), susceptibility to economic crises abroad, claims to the land, and new claims to power finally brought together peasants, workers, the middle class, and the provincial élite in revolution. As often happens, the society had outgrown the state and the state did not know it. But a deeper underlying question for Mexico and all of Latin America concerned the standards by which modernity should be measured in a traditional society. Would economic growth, political freedom, or cultural continuity prevail?

THUNDER OVER MEXICO

In newsreels from the early 1900s, Porfirio Díaz and his entourage look as if they would be more at home in the kaiser's Germany than in the New World. The aging cabinet (most of the ministers were in their seventies and eighties) called themselves *científicos*, or followers of the philosophy of Auguste Comte. According to Comte, progress occurred in three stages, the theological, the metaphysical, and the positivist, in which stage man sheds supernatural or ideal explanations and finally confronts reality. But the reality confronted by the *científicos* was schizophrenic. Half was the reality that they wanted to see, benefiting from progress and modernization. Another, quite different, part was the reality of injustice for the majority of the people.

In September 1910, Díaz received the world's homage as he celebrated one hundred years of Mexican independence. Europe in particular honored the strong ruler who had brought peace, progress, and stability to Mexico. When Díaz gave the final touch to his international image and went on record with a U.S. journalist as declaring that "Mexico was at last prepared for democracy," the people took him at his word.

In 1908, an obscure lawyer and landowner named Francisco Madero, then thirty-five years old, wrote a brief book titled *The Presidential Succession in 1910.* In it, he made a simple call for free elections and an end to Díaz' successive re-elections. In a nation that was 90 percent illiterate, this short book from a short man proved to be the match needed to set fire to the dry, aged forest of the Porfiriato, Díaz' dictatorship. All who could read it, read it, and all who did spread the word.

From the south came a young man who had already headed a delegation of peasants from his native state of Morelos to declare the grievances of the people to President Díaz. As soon as he returned to Morelos, he was punished by being drafted into the Federal Army. In 1909, the villages, still fighting for their rights, elected this same man, Emiliano Zapata, then thirty years old, as their chief. He had become an able horse trainer and muleteer. His powerful, direct, yet dreamy gaze affected all who saw him.

From the north came another man of the people, a former peon on a hacienda, a rebel and sometime cattle rustler named Doroteo Arango, who took on the *nom de guerre* Pancho Villa as he raised an army of cowboys, field workers, and artisans to fight the dictatorship. At the center of this great struggle was the Apostle of Democracy, as he came to be known, the unassuming Francisco Madero, promising no more and no less than full democracy.

Díaz, of course, was not about to accept challenges to his authority. When Madero questioned the aging dictator's decision to run for the presidency once more, he was jailed — an action that made him an instant hero. While he was imprisoned, Díaz re-elected himself. Madero escaped and called for the people to rise in arms; legal measures had been exhausted. Guerrilla bands led by Villa in the north, Zapata in the south, swelled into armies that together defeated the elderly leaders of the old Federal Army. On May 10, 1911, the Federal commander surrendered at Ciudad Juárez, across the border from El Paso, Texas. The revolutionaries now controlled access to arms, supplies, and support in the United States. Porfirio Díaz knew that the game was up. "Madero has unleashed a tiger," he said as he departed to exile and death in Paris. "Let us see if he can control it."

Madero was swept into the presidency on a wave of popular enthusiasm. Cheering crowds greeted him in every town on his journey to the capital. As he entered Mexico City, people thought that they were seeing a new Messiah arrive; a violent earthquake shook the city that day, adding to the sense of portent. Indeed, Madero wanted to give Mexico something almost miraculous, given the challenge of instituting a functioning democracy. He established a free press, gave Congress the right to be independent and critical of the executive, and enabled citizens to form political parties. But he did not address the underlying causes of discontent.

The old bureaucracy remained, the haciendas were untouched, the peasants did not recover their lands, and the army of the dictatorship was there, ready to repress them if they tried. Peasant bands began to invade rural townships. Street battles between trade unions and police occurred. Zapata denounced Madero as a traitor and decided to fight on. As instability grew, so did anxiety in the United States. Rival generals rose to restore the *ancien régime*. Business was fearful, and finally, in February 1913, for ten days — "the ten tragic days" — the streets of Mexico City became a battleground. The tiger was out of control.

Too slow in his reforms to satisfy his friends and too lenient with his enemies, Madero was finally undermined by a conspiracy of the army, the landowners, and the U.S. ambassador, Henry Lane Wilson. At the height of the uprising in Mexico City, Madero's own commander, General Victoriano Huerta, betrayed him, aided and abetted by Ambassador Wilson, who set himself up as a judge of what he called "the immature Mexicans"

Francisco Madero's arrival in Mexico City. José Guadalupe Posada, c. 1911

and "the emotional Latin race." But more than the ineffectual Madero, the Taft administration feared the popular leaders, Villa and Zapata, who were adamant in their demands for wholesale land redistribution and direct self-government for the rural communities.

The gentle Madero was coldly murdered by Huerta. In the words of a North American journalist, "He had posted a deaf and blind sentry at the gateway of his life to cry, 'All's well.' " This brutal event united the country once more. Huerta proved to be a bloody and incompetent tyrant, overly fond of his brandy bottle. He faced the outrage of the nation, as all of the rebel factions united under Venustiano Carranza, a senator under Díaz and now governor of the northern state of Coahuila. Carranza represented the provincial middle and upper classes, who now desired a strong, national, progressive state that would foster the expectations of businessmen, professionals, and small landowners — those who had been excluded from Mexico City's favors during the thirty-year reign of Don Porfirio.

Three military forces joined against Huerta. From the south, Zapata resisted Huerta's scorched-earth policy and retaliated by burning haciendas. In the northern states, Pancho Villa formed a mighty army, La División del Norte, and surrounded himself with *dorados*, "golden boys," winning battle after battle against the Federal Army while seizing haciendas, destroying the landowners and moneylenders, and menacing Carranza, who had been proclaimed "First Chief of the Revolution." After

Villa took Zacatecas, in the mining heart of central Mexico, Carranza counted on the support of the revolution's ablest field commander, Álvaro Obregón, a farmer from Sonora whose divisions included the courageous Yaqui fighters, who were out to avenge themselves against the exterminations ordered by Díaz.

In 1914 Huerta was defeated, and the revolutionary armies were poised to enter Mexico City. But after victory was achieved, the revolution turned against itself. For the Mexican Revolution was indeed two revolutions. Fixed forever in pop iconography was the movement led by Villa and Zapata. A locally based revolt, its purpose was to restore village rights to lands, forests, and waters. It favored a decentralized, self-ruling, communitarian democracy, inspired by shared traditions. Seeing itself as a continuation of the oldest peasant values, it was in many ways a conservative revolution. Revolution number two, blurrier in the icons of the mind, was the national, centralizing, modernizing revolution led by Carranza and finally consolidated in power by two forceful statesmen, Obregón and later his successor, Plutarco Elías Calles, who dominated Mexican politics between 1921 and 1935.

The clash between the two sides of the revolution was to prove even bloodier than the revolution against the old order. Perhaps all revolutions are essentially epic events in which a united people rise against a decaying tyranny. But then they become tragic events, as revolutionary turns against revolutionary, brother against brother.

Carranza was briefly pushed out of Mexico City by Zapata and Villa, who entered the capital together. Villa glowed as he sat on the presidential chair. Zapata, more saturnine, held on to his big sombrero and gazed, unimpressed, at the city below. Their roots were not here, at the top, but deep in the countryside. "The city is full of sidewalks," Zapata told Villa. "And I keep falling off them."

They went back to the countryside, distributing lands, establishing schools, proposing an alternative model for development. Indeed, for one incredible year (1914–1915) Emiliano Zapata and the people of Morelos ruled themselves without central intervention, creating one of the most viable societies ever seen in Latin America. Lands were distributed as communal or individual property, according to the choice of each village; agriculture was restored and even increased. Zapata and his chiefs, of course, were themselves villagers, field hands, and sharecroppers; their authority sprang from the local councils and rested on fidelity to the legal texts they were making forcefully real. On this basis, a politics of confidence rose. In his definitive history of the Zapatista movement, John

Pancho Villa (center) and Emiliano Zapata (holding a large hat) in the Presidential Palace in Mexico City, c. 1916

Womack notes that "significantly, Zapata never organized a state police; law enforcement, such as it was, remained the province of the village councils." Military chiefs were forbidden to interfere in village affairs, and when Zapata had to arbitrate local troubles, he always limited his action to enforcing decisions that the villagers had already reached on their own.

The *campesinos* of Morelos achieved the modest, profound dream for which they had fought so hard. Far from being hopelessly anchored in resignation, they had shown that a rural culture could escape its presumed fate and achieve a humane and functional economic organization on a local basis. They had proven that Mexicans *could* rule themselves democratically. But the very values of the system proved to be its undoing; the Morelos experiment cut against the grain of the national design. In effect, the vision of the national Mexican state presupposed a withering away of provincial peculiarities in favor of a much wider enterprise. Little Morelos had to be sacrificed to greater Mexico, the dynamic, responsible, unscru-

pulous, centralized force that was taking shape around Carranza and his ambitious chieftains, Obregón and Calles.

A national revolution faced a local revolution. The latter was based on accepted common traditions; the former had to elaborate and impose a national plan for progress. Zapatismo could solve problems as they arose; local ethics were clear, concise, and irrevocable; local culture was homogeneous; the people's intimate knowledge of one another favored direct democracy. The national revolution, however, felt it had to concentrate energies in order to transform a heterogeneous society and create a modern infrastructure in a country lacking communications, electric power, and administrative coordination. The Morelos revolution could be internationally irresponsible, but the national revolution had to stand the constant pressure of North American power and the explicit menace, once more, of foreign intervention.

Confused by a revolution on its southern border that it could neither control nor understand, Woodrow Wilson's administration in Washington occupied Veracruz in 1914 and ordered General John ("Black Jack") Pershing to march into Chihuahua against Villa in 1916, but resisted pressure from North American interests affected by the revolution to invade and take over. As World War I ended, the victorious United States of America had a million men under arms and the momentum required to enter Mexico and settle its affairs in favor of U.S. interests. A divided Mexico could have become, like Lebanon in our own times, a festering wound. The revolution had to be settled, the local chieftains eliminated, compromise reached within and without.

The epic had become a tragedy.

THE DEATH OF ZAPATA

The final battle between the two revolutions was at hand. In the field of Celaya, in the year 1915, Carranza's military commander, Álvaro Obregón, had decisively defeated Pancho Villa. The *guerrillero* had always counted on the power of his cavalry to overcome any and all challenges. Obregón knew this, so he posted his artillery at the end of the battlefield, tempting Villa to charge it, and as the cavalry rushed across the plain to overcome the guns, Yaqui troops hiding in foxholes thrust their bayonets up into the bellies of the charging forces. It was in a shower of guts, blood, and smoke that the battle ended. General Obregón lost his right arm in the fighting. It is said that in the massacre he could not find his missing limb, so he flipped a gold coin over the carnage, and sure enough, his arm came flying up to grab the gold. General Obregón, in his honor, told this story about himself.

He also said, "No Mexican general can resist a cannon shot of fifty thousand pesos." Carranza certainly knew this, as he prepared to trap his other serious challenger, the indomitable Zapata. Only Zapata remained, elected by his people to fight on under the banner *"Tierra y Libertad,"* land and liberty. That call to arms, which had governed his life, was about to decide his destiny.

On April 10, 1919, Emiliano Zapata rode into the hacienda at San Juan Chinameca for a meeting with Colonel Jesús Guajardo, who had defected from the government. As he crossed the threshold at two P.M., Guajardo's guard presented arms. Then a bugle sounded and the guard shot two volleys, point-blank, at Zapata. The guerrilla leader would have been forty years old in August.

The colonel, it turned out, was not a defector at all, but a party to a government plan to assassinate Zapata. The uncomfortable, uncompromising Zapata, who lowered neither his flags nor his guard, had insisted on strict compliance with the demand for land and freedom. Instead, Colonel Guajardo was promoted to general and given a reward of 52,000 pesos — the irresistible "cannon shot."

Zapata was loaded onto a mule, taken to Cuautla, and dumped on the pavement. Flashlights were shone in his face and photographs were taken in an effort to destroy his myth. Zapata was dead. But the people of the valley refused to believe it. Zapata could not die. He was far too smart to be killed in an ambush. And hadn't his white horse been spotted waiting for him on top of the mountain? Every single person in this valley of Morelos, from the old veterans of the revolution to schoolchildren, still believe that Zapata is alive. And perhaps they are right. Zapata will live as long as people believe that they have a right to their land and a right to govern themselves according to their deeply held beliefs and cultural values.

A CULTURAL REVOLUTION

By 1920, Carranza himself was dead, mysteriously assassinated as he fled from yet another dissension within the revolution. The newly victorious General Obregón applied the revolutionary constitution in an attempt to embrace the forces of Zapatismo through agrarian reform. He placated Villa with a ranch in northern Mexico (where the guerrilla leader was assassinated in 1923); he resisted North American pressure to postpone implementation of the more radical laws on land ownership and exploitation of the subsoil; above all, he established a comprehensive national education plan under an energetic secretary of education, the writer José Vasconcelos.

When the first teachers were sent out from Mexico City to the old haciendas, many were killed on the spot. Others returned to the capital with their ears or noses cut off by hacienda thugs, but a few managed to defend their rural schoolhouses and teach the alphabet for the first time to thousands of young and old people alike. Vasconcelos also opened up the public buildings of Mexico to mural painters, heralding an artistic renaissance not only in Mexico but throughout Latin America. From the most basic level of teaching a peasant child to read and write to the top level of artistic achievement, had we at last come to terms with the wealth of our traditions and overcome the exclusion of any of its components, ethical or cultural?

The accumulated economic and political problems of Mexico and Latin America have overshadowed the cultural reality for most of the twentieth century. But ultimately it has been the cultural reality that has imposed itself on our politics and economics. The second history of Spanish America, the sometimes buried history, exploded in the struggle of the Mexican Revolution, bringing down the walls of isolation between Mexicans and in effect making the revolution, above all else, a cultural one. A country in which the geographical barriers of mountains, deserts, ravines, and sheer distances had separated one group of people from another since ancient times now came together, as the tremendous cavalcades of Villa's men and women from the north rushed down to meet Zapata's men and women from the south. In their revolutionary embrace, Mexicans finally learned how other Mexicans talked, sang, ate, and drank, dreamed and made love, cried and fought. And if this had happened in Mexico, why could it not happen in Venezuela or Honduras, in Argentina or Colombia — not necessarily through the violence of revolution, but perhaps through a conscious yet passionate approach to the overriding Latin American need to join and identify cultural experience with political and economic projects?

In Mexico, for the first time a Spanish American nation saw itself as it really was, without disguises: brutal at times, at others unbearably tender. We shared a profound sense of personal dignity and a scorn for death. This was most apparent in the sudden revelation of identity that took place when Zapata's troops entered Mexico City in 1914, occupied the palaces of the aristocracy, and saw themselves reflected in the mirror of other people for the first time. Their faces were no longer masks, but the faces of women who had left their villages to follow the men; the scarred, menacing faces of guerrilla fighters having breakfast at the posh Sanborn's Restaurant; the faces of children born between battles, far from their villages. They were all citizens of the revolution and of a new nation, which came to realize that it embodied all that it had been, Indian, Spanish, and mestizo, Catholic and liberal, traditional and modernizing, old and new, patient and rebellious, but finally, deeply abiding.

This nation, revealing all the layers of its rich culture and struggling with all the contradictions that it had inherited, signaled the emergence of a new, fully modern Spanish American society — modern only if it took stock of itself and did not exclude any aspect of its culture. However, this cultural reality was often obscured by the immediate and at times confusing demands of national and international politics. The measure of Spanish American success as modern societies now became the distance

The Soldier's
Farewell.
Posada, c. 1887

between political fragmentation and cultural wholeness. Could we finally come closer to identifying and uniting both our political needs and our cultural values?

As the Mexican Revolution inaugurated the twentieth century for Latin Americans, we could not forecast the answer to this question. We were to live through numerous crises. Sometimes politics and culture would be woefully disparate, and at other times they would seem to come closer together. But joining our political life with our cultural life became our unfinished business as we entered the century of great hopes and universal violence.

PART V

UNFINISHED BUSINESS

SIXTEEN

Latin America

O ne of the figures in the fresco painted by the Mexican artist José Clemente Orozco at Pomona College in Claremont, California, is Prometheus, who, coming all the way from classical antiquity, symbolizes the tragic vision of humanity. Condemned by God for giving the fire of knowledge and freedom to humankind, the hero is chained to a rock, where a vulture eternally pecks at his liver.

In another great mural by Orozco, this one in Baker Library at Dartmouth College, in Hanover, New Hampshire, the myth of Quetzalcoatl, the Plumed Serpent, reflects the Mediterranean myth of Prometheus. In the New World, the creator of humankind, the inventor of agriculture and the arts, is exiled because he becomes human — because he discovers that he has a human face and finds in his heart the pains and joys of humanity.

In yet another magnificent work of art, the cupola of Cabañas Hospital in Guadalajara, Mexico, Orozco resolves both these figures into a single universal image: man on fire, forever doomed to perish in the flames of his own creation and be reborn from them. In Orozco, the two worlds, old and new, European and American, fuse in the heat of the flame, in the rush of the sea, and in the solitude of high mountain air. The elements become human. They are also universally linked in communication, meeting and embracing. The art of Orozco makes perfectly clear that few cultures in the world possess such continuity as those of Indo-Afro-Ibero America. And that is exactly why the lack of a comparable continuity in politics and economics wounds us so deeply.

The continuity of culture does not, of course, demand a political equivalent. The myths of Prometheus and Quetzalcoatl, the paintings of Orozco and Goya, are self-sufficient aesthetic facts. But they also indicate manners of being — of thought, of dress, of eating and loving, of furnish-

Detail from The Legend of Quetzalcoatl. *Diego Rivera*

Overleaf: *Detail of* Flip Over, *Carlos Almaráz*

Prometheus.
*José Clemente
Orozco, 1930*

The Coming of
Quetzalcoatl,
from The Epic
of American
Civilization.
Orozco, 1932–1934

Man in Fire.
Orozco, 1939

ing, singing, fighting, and dreaming. A cultural fact symbolizes and conjugates a whole manner of existing. A painting, a poem, or a film indicates the way we are, what we can do, what we have yet to do.

Culture is borne, after all, by the same people who create politics and economics: the citizens, the members of civil society. Can we, in the coming century, unite the three factors of our existence, initiating political and economic unity in Latin America from the foundation of cultural unity?

We can only answer this question by looking at the concrete problems that besiege us as the quincentennial comes and goes and a new century arrives. Our problems are awaiting solutions. Cultural continuity is both a condition of and a challenge for any lasting social arrangements. Our problems seem to be our unfinished business. But then, are not all of us, the men and women of the Americas, unfinished human beings? Thankfully, we have not said our last word.

UNFINISHED BUSINESS

There is a very tall hotel in Mexico City that has never been finished. Year after year builders add to its height, but one can always look right through its hive of gaping stones. When, if ever, will it receive its hypothetical guests?

This building is perhaps an appropriate symbol of Latin America, growing but unfinished, energetic but full of seemingly unsolvable problems. Three decades of economic growth following World War II, in which production rose by 200 percent, came to an end in 1982 and were followed by a decade of lost development, in which per capita income fell every year to a cumulative loss of 20 percent. Real salaries have regressed to the levels of 1960. The social consequences of the present crisis are there for all to see: food shortages; a decline in housing, education, health, and other public services; crime; a disillusioned middle class; and millions of drifting people of the underclass in city slums. Yet the governments of the region have been forced since 1982 to export scarce capital, to the tune of $45 billion a year, just to service the foreign debt, which totals over $450 billion. Seven percent of Latin America's gross national product is being transferred abroad each year, as is the equivalent of 50 percent of our national earnings. Yet these problems, we must bear in mind, are the result of tremendous changes and enormous growth.

We are approaching the doors of the third millennium and the fifth centennial with a population that has doubled in twenty years, from 200 million in 1970 to 400 million today. By the year 2000 we will have twice the population of the United States. It is a young population, half of it fifteen years old or less. It is a population hungry for jobs, education, and social services. Every single Latin American who will demand a job in the year 2000 has already been born. And for the first time in our history, the majority of our population has been born into urbanized societies. Brazil has become the world's eighth largest economy, and Mexico the world's thirteenth, in terms of gross national product. Half of the 200 million young people in Latin America today were born after Fidel Castro took power in Cuba in 1959. And every child born between now and 2000 will come into the world owing $1,000 to a foreign bank.

As they grow up and look around them, our young people search for answers to these problems and cast a critical eye at our recent history. Why have we not been able to solve our basic problem, which is uniting economic development with social justice under political democracy? And why have we not given politics and economics the continuity that exists in the culture?

The responses to these questions are as varied as the Latin American societies themselves. As we have seen, during the nineteenth century Latin America joined the world economy as a purveyor of raw materials and an importer of manufactured goods and capital. Great fortunes were made this way. It was hoped that the wealth accumulated at the top would sooner or later trickle down to the less fortunate. It did not.

The Great Depression of 1929 hit Latin America harder than it did the metropolitan centers of Europe and North America, prompting the governments to find new economic methods. Mexico nationalized resources, redistributed the land, educated the people, and built an infrastructure. Chile strengthened political pluralism, parliamentary rule, and labor organizations, capitalizing on its extraordinary nineteenth-century experience as a domestic oligarchy with a prosperous middle class. Uruguay parlayed export earnings into the creation of a welfare state, highly urbanized and bureaucratically cushioned. Argentina continued to reap the wealth of its harvest, its cattle, its exports.

World War II pushed us out of the Depression, raising the prices of copper, tin, rubber, meat, wool, and hemp so much that Mayan peasants went into their churches on their knees, praying that the war would never end. Latin America was able to decrease imports, spur national industries, establish the infrastructures to sustain them, and also implement, sometimes, minimal improvements in education and social welfare. Economic growth generated a new middle class, investments, urban expansion. Yet society and its institutions were increasingly at odds. Education was promising people more than the economy was capable of granting them, materially or politically. Indeed, society created demands at a faster rate than it created the political and economic capacity to respond. The result was sometimes authoritarian rule; sometimes it was revolution; sometimes it was a movement toward democracy. But whether through insurgency, repression, mass movements, populism, elections, or revolution, by the 1960s the former Spanish colonies of the New World had been changed beyond recognition.

Basically, the growing middle class and the combative working class demanded that the movement toward greater wealth and greater justice be accelerated. Some nations were more fortunate than others. Although suffering from a long succession of military dictatorships, Venezuela achieved growth through wealth generated by vast natural resources of oil and iron ore. In the 1950s it expelled its last military ruler, and since then it has been able to join economic growth to democratic rule — that is, until the economic crisis of the 1980s divorced this ideal couple. In contrast, Costa Rica made a virtue of necessity, transforming its lack of colonial wealth into a sustained effort to create a modest economy and administer it wisely and democratically.

So if there are no sure or universal formulas, each country must delve into its own historical experience to find its path. Argentina and Mexico, the two largest countries in Spanish America, offer the best study in contrasts, and because of their territorial size, population, and wealth remain extremely representative. Their differences might well shed light on our commonality, from the Rio Grande to Patagonia.

THE HEAD OF GOLIATH

At the turn of the century, Argentina seemed to represent the bright hope of a rich, stable Latin American nation based on liberal principles. After the fall of Rosas, it became the very model of a rapidly modernizing country. Yet for every advantage it enjoyed, an equally great disadvantage seemed to detract from the brightness on the horizon.

The frontiers of "progress" had been extended through wars of conquest against the Indians, but the system of huge landholdings had promptly been extended as well. Old-style *caudillos* such as Facundo Quiroga were eliminated, but new ones promptly sprang up, since the political system of patronage was not reformed. Export-import activities multiplied, but Argentina remained an exporter of raw materials and an importer of manufactured and capital goods, unable to develop its own industrial base. Although it is true that communications were extended, they were mostly in British hands, as were most commercial activities, which gave England a quasi-imperial power over the River Plate. Argentina opened its doors to millions of European immigrants, hoping that they would settle and develop the pampas, but they generally stayed in the cities. They developed useful trades and professions there, but the rural areas continued to sink into anachronistic, semifeudal relationships.

In this way, all the apparent gains of modernization in Argentina were finally diminished by the weakness of the political institutions, the lack of a cultural identity, and excessive dependence on foreign events. Within the nation, the vast distance between the bustling metropolis, Buenos Aires, and the interior, the pampas, created a deep moral and political division, which Ezequiel Martínez Estrada graphically described when he wrote that Buenos Aires is the head of a giant Goliath set on the puny body of David: the Argentine nation.

Strangely, this great country, with its fabulous wealth, the richest farming and grazing land in Latin America, and eventually a homogeneous and literate population, was not able to fulfill its promise. The reason was not only, as in other Latin American republics, that so many problems of the past were not solved. It was primarily that even though the society changed dramatically through immigration, urbanization, education, and economic development, its political institutions remained extremely weak and its cultural identity unresolved. Yet the facade continued for a long time. Was not Buenos Aires in all particulars just as modern and European as the continental cities it resembled — Paris, Madrid, Barcelona? Such a claim was self-defeating, however, because it artificially divided the urban from the rural and sacrificed at least half, if not more, of the culture to an uncritical identification with "civilization," with "Europe."

In 1916, Argentine society, headed by its dynamic middle class, made its most important bid for political power, electing an almost apostolic leader, Hipólito Irigoyen, to the presidency. The revered Irigoyen did not live up to the hopes Argentina held for him. Not only did he prove less efficient, relatively speaking, than the agrarian and commercial oligarchy that had preceded him; he was also more repressive. After the Great Depression hit Argentina, the military staged the first of its successive coups against elected regimes and deposed him.

During World War II, Argentina amassed a huge trade surplus from exports to the war-ravaged economies of Europe. It was the Golden Age revisited. It would seem that, thanks to army rule and booming exports, Argentina would once more become, and would forever be, an oligarch's paradise, presiding like the emphatic tombs of Recoleta Cemetery over a relatively well-off, contented mass of well-fed, literate white workers. But then, as if symbolizing the changes that were occurring, an intruder made her way past the artistocracy to the top of the government.

Her name was Eva Perón, and today she rests in peace in La Recoleta, the cemetery of the oligarchs who humiliated her and whom she detested so much. Her travels to this grave were, to put it mildly, circuitous. Glorified as a saint when she died of cancer at age thirty-three, in 1952, she was the most powerful woman in Argentina and in Latin America. After her death she was embalmed and buried with pomp at the headquarters of the workers' union, the General Confederation of Workers, but when her widower, President Juan Domingo Perón, fell in 1955, her body was stolen, presumably by the military junta, which wished to efface the myth of Peronismo. The junta chose eleven coffins, filled ten of them with stones, put Eva Perón in the eleventh, labeled all of them as the remains of Evita, and sent them all over the world. Eva's coffin went to a cemetery in Milan, from which it was finally recovered when her husband regained power in 1974. He laid her to rest at La Recoleta.

Quite a trip for a small-town girl and second-rate actress. She married both the up-and-coming Perón in 1945 and the Argentine people forever, contributing to the mystique of Peronismo, a form of populism that took the amassed wealth of Argentina's World War II surplus and distributed it, generously but hardly with a productive sense, among the people. This action was coupled with equally generous social laws, but Peronismo did not build a firm infrastructure, foster strong political institutions, or improve productivity and technological prowess. The great potential wealth of Argentina was squandered in demagoguery and self-indulgent measures. While a vast number of invisible Argentineans — the *descamisados*, or shirtless ones — became visible (all too visible, in the eyes of the dominant and domineering trade and cattle aristocracy), their newfound sense of dignity and identity did not make up for the lack of political institutions into which to pour their energy.

This has been the paradox of Argentina. A wealthy nation with a large middle class, certainly the best fed, best dressed, best educated, and most homogeneous nation in Latin America, it has been unable to create political institutions that truly represent it. The weak state can never meet the claims of organized labor, the middle class, the army entrepreneurs, and the foreign creditors, and ends up by surrendering to a few of them.

Perón surrendered to the people, the masses, those who felt forgotten, marginalized, unrecognized, unencouraged, taken for granted in the play of wealth and politics. From this came his long-lasting myth and even

Juan and Eva Perón after Perón's re-election, June 1952

his lasting legislative contributions: woman suffrage; divorce; social security; paid vacations; protection of rural workers, salaries, artisans, even domestic help; labor unions with a democratic base. But his was a statist, bureaucratized leadership with weak political parties and a weak congress. A strong army, from whose ranks Perón came, coupled with competing social classes, was able to rule once the strong leader was gone.

The cycle was thus renewed, fatally, depressingly. The weak civilian government was overthrown by a military coup, chaos was succeeded by tyranny, and tyranny by further chaos. The Recoleta Cemetery is symbolic, as writer Tomas Eloy Martinez put it, of a necrophilic country. Perhaps the most illustrious corpse in the country is Argentina itself.

REVOLUTION AS INSTITUTION

A very different case history took place in what in so many ways constitutes the opposite extreme to Argentina: Mexico, a mestizo country with deep Spanish and Indian roots, no immigration worth mentioning, few export booms, and many problems derived from the traditional weakness of an illiterate, undernourished, and highly reproductive population. Today Mexico has 80 million people, compared with 15 million in 1910. Argentina has 35 million people, only 15 million more than in 1910. And while Argentina has not had a revolution since independence, Mexico had the first and perhaps the most far-reaching of Latin America's twentieth-century uprisings.

As we have seen, the revolutionary regimes in Mexico tried to satisfy the peasants by breaking up the haciendas and liberating them from peonage, giving them land, and permitting them to migrate to the cities and, after President Lázaro Cárdenas nationalized petroleum production in 1938, to the new industrial centers fueled by cheap oil. These changes invigorated the nascent working class, whose organizations came under government protection. All classes, but especially the middle class, were the beneficiaries of extended education, and the entrepreneurial class found that on top of cheap oil, cheap labor, and growing (if captive) internal markets, it could count on government subsidies. A strong policy of public works, initiated by President Calles, linked the country and gave it roads, hospitals, telegraphs, and irrigation.

The price for this development was political, and it was indeed high. Mexico's revolution created a *sui generis* political system whose central players were the president and the Party of the Revolutionary Institutions. Both served the national state, which saved Mexico from internal anarchy and external pressure, making it possible for the country to develop in equilibrium, but at the price of postponing democracy. Cárdenas established the conditions for the Mexican presidency: all power to Caesar, but only during a nonrenewable six-year term. Caesar could not re-elect himself, but he had the right to designate his successor, the new Caesar, and thus to perpetuate the system *ad infinitum*.

So while Argentina created a strong society without strong political institutions, Mexico balanced the weakness of society with a strong government ruled by two powerful institutions, the presidency and the party. However, by strengthening society through economic development and education, the Mexican system made it inevitable that it would be challenged. As long as the trade-off between economic development and political support lasted, Mexico was a model of Latin American stability.

But when crisis plunged the country deep into recession, the children of the revolution demanded a renewal of economic growth, this time with democracy and social justice. Educated in the ideals of revolution, freedom, and democracy, Mexican citizens now wanted those ideals to become a reality in the streets, the factories, and the polling booths.

BIRTH OF THE NATION

The aesthetic responses of the Mexican muralists serve as an illustration of the mental and political makeup of Spanish America during this century. The work of Diego Rivera reflects the theocratic Indian and Hispanic nostalgia for order and symmetry. In his gigantic mural of Mexican history painted on the staircase of Mexico City's National Palace, the Indian panel is completed by a pyramid, on the summit of which sits the emperor, with the sun above him. This is followed by a panel depicting the Catholic church, with a cross on top. The series climaxes with the Communist "church," with a hammer and sickle on top — meaning, of course, that things will turn out all right in the end.

On the contrary, said José Clemente Orozco, who seems to wink and grimace as he depicts a parade of knaves and crooks, corrupt officials, and even a falsely blind justice sashaying by. In his mural at the Ministry of Education, this artist as much as says, "Do not deceive yourselves; things will turn out badly once more unless we open our eyes, and criticize, and warn, and see things as they truly are."

In counterpoint to Rivero and Orozco, David Alfaro Siqueiros, a true disciple of the Italian futurists, was happy to celebrate the sheer energy of Spanish American history. In his mural at the Bellas Artes Palace in Mexico City, Liberty breaks her chains with a joyful yet pained expression, one not very far removed from that experienced during childbirth. Mural after mural conveys this message, and its identifications, clear and loud: the Birth of the Nation.

Latin America first tried to respond to its weak sense of nationhood and stability by creating viable national states. Whatever their differences, Lázaro Cárdenas in Mexico (1934–1940), Getúlio Vargas in Brazil (1930–1945), and Juan Domingo Perón in Argentina (1946–1955) had this purpose in common. What Mexico and Brazil consolidated, Argentina dissipated. Nevertheless, in all three nations education as well as demagoguery, and economic development, no matter how unjustly managed, helped to create modern civil societies — with a strong state in Mexico, a weak one in Argentina, and a metaphorical, metamorphosing, almost surrealistic one in Brazil. In other countries, the weakest in Latin

The Legend of
Quetzalcoatl.
Diego Rivera, 1929

The New
Democracy.
*David Alfaro
Siqueiros,
1944–1945*

America, the urge was to create minimal institutions where none existed at all and a modicum of national independence where geopolitical imperatives seemed to exclude it.

There were the countries of Central America and the Caribbean, and their nemesis was the empire that filled the vacuum left by the final fall of the Spanish Empire in 1898: the United States of America.

DR. JEKYLL AND MR. HYDE

Our perception of the United States has been that of a democracy inside and an empire outside: Dr. Jekyll and Mr. Hyde. We have admired democracy; we have deplored empire. And we have suffered the actions of this country, which has constantly intervened in our lives in the name of manifest destiny, the big stick, dollar diplomacy, and cultural arrogance.

Immediately after its formulation in 1823, the Monroe Doctrine was rejected by Latin America as a unilateral and hypocritical policy. While forbidding a European presence in hemispheric affairs, it certainly did not exclude United States intervention in our affairs. When President James Polk moved against Mexico in 1846 and took half of its national territory, we saw that nothing shielded us from U.S. aggression. Mexico again suffered U.S. intervention in 1914, during the revolution, when President Woodrow Wilson proclaimed, "I will teach Latin Americans to elect good men to office."

But nowhere was U.S. intervention more rampant than in the Caribbean. Puerto Rico, liberated from Spanish rule, went on to become, and remains, a *de facto* colony of the United States. Cuba was given *pro forma* independence but was saddled with the Platt Amendment, which granted the United States rights to interfere in the island's internal affairs. Theodore Roosevelt simply took the province of Panama from the Republic of Colombia, transformed it into a sovereign nation, and then cut it in half with the Panama Canal and the United States–controlled Canal Zone. Roosevelt was simply irritated by "those wretched little republics that cause me so much trouble."

Military interventions and occupations in Haiti, the Dominican Republic, and Honduras were all carried out in the name of stability, democracy, law and order, and protection of U.S. lives and property (notably those of the great agribusiness of that time, the United Fruit Company). But no nation in the region suffered more prolonged humiliation than the Central American republic of Nicaragua, first taken over by the North American freebooter William Walker in 1855 and then almost continuously invaded and occupied by the United States from 1909 through 1934.

In that year the rebel leader Sandino was assassinated, and with the support of the U.S. Marines, his murderer, Anastasio Somoza, was put on the presidential seat at Managua, where he and his family reigned until their defeat by the Sandinista revolution of 1979. During these decades the Somozas got all they wanted from Washington. As Franklin Roosevelt put it, "Somoza is a son of a bitch, but he's *our* son of a bitch."

Yet Roosevelt also represented a sharp turn in traditional U.S. policy toward Latin America. The fulcrum of this policy had been events in the Mexican Revolution. "Mexico is seated on the dock for her crimes against humanity," thundered Frank B. Kellogg, U.S. secretary of state during the Coolidge administration, and President Coolidge himself, generally a taciturn individual, cited Mexico before Congress in 1927 as "the source of Bolshevik subversion in Central America." But Mexican-American relations really fell apart with President Cárdenas' expropriation of oil in 1938. In Washington, President Roosevelt was pressured to break relations, to apply sanctions, and even to invade Mexico. He resisted all of this and instead sat down and negotiated with us.

Roosevelt inaugurated a different era of relations. His "good neighbor policy" translated into respect for the inner workings and local solutions in each of the Latin American countries. He supported the Somozas in Nicaragua, Trujillo in the Dominican Republic, and Batista in Cuba, but he did not oppose the dynamic transformations of the Mexican Revolution under Cárdenas, or the policies of the Popular Front elected in Chile by an alliance between radicals, socialists, and communists, or even the corporate semifascism of Getúlio Vargas' Estado Novo in Brazil. And he accomplished what he ultimately needed: Latin American support during World War II. Pro-German and pro-Japanese sentiments abounded in the region, but thanks to President Roosevelt, the war found us on the side of the Allies.

We also got what we wanted: a set of laws and treaties binding the United States and Latin America to principles of nonintervention, self-determination, and negotiated solution of controversies. Nevertheless, our old Roman law tradition came into acute conflict with the pragmatic common-law Anglo-American tradition, as President Eisenhower's secretary of state, John Foster Dulles, decided that in Latin America, the United States had not friends but interests.

Once the hot war was over, the cold war began, and the achievements of the Roosevelt and Truman administrations were quietly buried. Elected governments in Guatemala and Chile were overthrown with U.S. help and approval because those governments could be construed as possible Soviet beachheads in the hemisphere. Military dictatorships stepped in, torturing and killing in the name of anticommunism. The official terrorism of the successive military regimes in Argentina was best described by the name given to their victims, *los desaparecidos*, the disappeared. What actually disappeared was the nation itself. Proficient at killing their own people, the Argentine generals proved totally inefficient at defeating the British in the Malvinas and subsequently vanished into the sidelines. So, practically, did Argentina, as weak civilian governments once more fought off the military menace. In Chile, the socialist government of Salvador Allende was overthrown in 1973 by a military coup headed by General Augusto Pinochet. In a savage action, Allende partisans were rounded up, gathered in a stadium, and murdered en masse. Others were sent to concentration camps, and still others were exiled and sometimes murdered abroad. Pinochet did all of this in the name of democracy and anticommunism. It is a measure of Chile's strong democratic traditions that it survived this brutal dictatorship and found its way back to democracy in 1990.

These South American military governments were never frontally assaulted by the United States, but in the Caribbean, Washington did actively oppose the revolutionary regime in Cuba. Fidel Castro tried to break his country's bondage to Washington, but he created a new one, to the other superpower, the USSR. U.S. policies, notably the embarrassing Bay of Pigs expedition in 1961 and the continued U.S. embargo on the island, may have failed, but they certainly harassed the Castro regime. They did not, however, suffice to explain the drastic elimination of dissidence and the lack of freedom of expression and economic success in Cuba, nor the Cubans' incapacity to transform the revolution's true achievements — literacy, educational opportunities, the best health-care system in the Third World, the extraordinary development of advanced technology, especially in the medical field — into functioning, objective democratic institutions, beyond the subjective identification with or whimsical subjection to a single charismatic *caudillo*. Lack of diplomatic imagination and generosity on the U.S. side might still lead the two countries to a confrontational bloodbath. The ancient shadow of Numantia hangs over Cuba: a siege, a collective suicide. Latin America must help both sides to negotiate. And Cuban youth inside and outside Cuba must go beyond their fathers' feuds to attempt what José Martí claimed in the dawn of Cuban independence: "If the Republic does not open its arms to all and go forward with all, then the Republic dies."

In Nicaragua, a new, young, and poor revolution managed to remain independent in spite of harassment, blockades, and proxy wars financed by the United States. In one of the deepest pits of our relationship, the

Reagan administration concentrated efforts, money, political will, and even international discredit to suppress the revolution in a country the size of Massachusetts (a country Walter Lippmann once described as "independent as Rhode Island"). Washington defied the United Nations Security Council resolutions and its International Court of Justice and embarked on embarrassing and ill-advised scams — the Iran-contra operation — simply because Nicaragua, a virtual U.S. colony since 1909, had defied it and set out on an independent course. The U.S. creature, the contra army, destroyed schools and crops and maimed children, but it did not stop the dynamics of the Nicaraguan revolution, which were to educate the people; create institutions; release the forces of society, which organized in a broad spectrum from extreme left to extreme right in fifteen political parties; and win Nicaragua's free elections in 1989. In the process, Central America wrested diplomatic initiative from Washington, and kept it, partly because of the peace process led by the Costa Rican president, Oscar Arias, who was honored with the Nobel Peace Prize in 1987.

AFTER THE COLD WAR
When the cold war ended, Latin America found itself in crisis once again. Realizing that both capitalism and socialism, in their Latin American versions, had failed to bring the majority of our people out of their misery, we found our political and economic models crashing down on our heads.

But were they really *our* models? Had we not since independence been imitating the most prestigious foreign models in economics and politics? Were we fatally caught between the Chicago Boys and the Marx Brothers: savage, unrestricted capitalism or inefficient, centralized bureaucratic socialism? Had we not the tradition, the information, the organization, and the intellectual capacities to create our own models of development, truly consonant with what we had been, what we were, and what we wanted to be?

In the midst of this crisis of "the four D's" — debt, drugs, development, and democracy — we realized that we could only answer the questions from within ourselves — that is, from within our cultures. We realized that we had a balkanized, fractured politics, failed economic systems, and vast social inequalities, but we also had a remarkable continuity of culture, which stood on its own two feet in the midst of our generalized crisis.

As the cold war ended, Latin America hoped to free itself from the pressures of the major powers. The principal pretext for U.S. intervention, anticommunism, seemed to evaporate when the former Soviet empire disintegrated. But these events forced us to consider more than ever that we belonged to a world of instant communications and global integration.

We had to put our houses in order. But to do so we had to understand ourselves, our culture, our past, and our traditions as a source of new creation. And we could not understand ourselves without understanding the culture of others, notably the two great reflections and extensions of ourselves, in Spain and in the Hispanic communities of the United States.

Once more, as the tragic history of the twentieth century unfolded, Spanish America looked to Spain and there saw the European shore of the New World. And in the Mediterranean — our sea, Mare Nostrum — an unfinished tower to mirror the one in Mexico City.

SEVENTEEN

Contemporary Spain

ominating the port city of Barcelona and the Mediterranean, the spires of Antonio Gaudí's Expiatory Temple of the Holy Family, La Sagrada Familia, point not only toward heaven but toward earth: a Spanish tendency. They are the extreme of artifice, yet they also resemble stalagmites, or the crags and crevices of lonely mountains. They appear to be as solid as the Gothic cathedrals at Burgos and Compostela, yet they are hollow structures, as light as candles dripping wax.

La Sagrada Familia has been under construction — on and off — for over a century, and during this time it has never ceased to be a source of controversy, of strong passions. Gaudí, whose sinuous, sensual, revolutionary stamp can be seen all over Barcelona — he made it *his* city — was killed by a trolley in 1926, at age seventy-four. When his body was taken to the morgue, no one recognized him, so discreet, unassuming, and indeed unfinished was he. Like the builders of Compostela and the Toltec pyramids, he was an anonymous artisan, the bearer of an unfulfilled promise, the very example of death as the interruption of promise, no matter when it strikes.

And so La Sagrada Familia remained an unfinished statement, a project, a promise, like Spain, like Spanish America. But it is not death which makes our lives unfinished, but life itself. Here in Barcelona, in this port, a hub of commercial activity in the Mediterranean for thousands of years but also a city with deep regional roots, we can recall the cast of characters parading in front of our unburied mirror — Iberian and Celtic hunters, Phoenician and Greek navigators and merchants, Roman legionnaires, barbarian invaders, Muslim armies, El Cid and Columbus, conquistadors off to the New World, Hapsburg princes and Golden Age writers and painters — and reflect that both Spain and Spanish America are the result of a meeting of cultures.

La Sagrada Familia. Antonio Gaudí

Looking out from La Sagrada Familia to the Mediterranean, looking out on a newly proud, progressive, democratic Spain that seems to have intelligently assimilated its past, can we propose progress for *all* the Spanish-speaking peoples? Progress, but with a sense of history, of roots? Can we belong to the global village without ceasing to belong to the local village? Gaudí's unfinished church permits us to ask ourselves not only who we are but what we are becoming. What is our unfinished business, not only in Spain but throughout the Spanish-speaking world?

The old Spanish Empire, the bones of which can be found all over the New World, had no such doubts. It proclaimed itself "royal, corporeal, actual, and eternal." It lasted almost exactly four centuries, from the landing of Columbus in the West Indies in 1492 to its final defeat by the rising young empire, the United States of America, in 1898. Stirred up by William Randolph Hearst's sensationalist *New York Journal,* the United States fought the Spanish American War with the whooped-up patriotism explicit in the cry "Remember the *Maine*! To hell with Spain!" and stripped Spain of Cuba, Puerto Rico, and the Philippines. It was indeed, in the words of Theodore Roosevelt, who fought in it at the head of his Rough Riders, "a splendid little war."

"HERE LIES ONE HALF OF SPAIN"

Nothing was now left of the empire of Charles V and Philip II, where the sun never set. But the sun *had* set, and it provoked a shocked reaction in Spain. The dream of greatness was over. Spain had been fooling itself.

But if this was the illusion, what was the reality of the country? Could Spain look itself straight in the face and see what was buried in the historical mirror? Weakness — a political weakness that had led the country to miss its opportunity, embodied in the liberal constitution of Cádiz of 1812. That legal document embodied the hopes of a generation of modernizing Hispanic citizens in Spain and the Americas. The Cádiz constitution, like so many other laws in Spain's history, was left to wither, assailed by the realities of patrimonial, provincial, grubby practices and interests, while the monarchy, discredited since the times of the Napoleonic invasions, no longer had the energy of the authoritarian Hapsburgs or the paternalistic Bourbons. This rudderless politics often translated into fratricidal strife, leading the nineteenth-century journalist Mariano José de Larra to mourn, "Here lies one half of Spain. The other half killed it."

"Miserable Spain!" exclaimed the poet Antonio Machado. "Yesterday you were an imperial power. Today, shrouded in rags, you despise all

"Remember the Maine!"
From the New York Journal, *February 17, 1898*

that you ignore!" It was a bitter epitaph, and far from unique. Machado's voice was one in a chorus of a generation — the Generation of 1898, the year of the loss of empire — crying out to Spain, "Reform yourself, know yourself, modernize."

Then something occurred that could not have been foreseen in the defeats at Manila Bay and Santiago Harbor. As writers such as Ortega y Gasset, Miguel de Unamuno, and Ramón del Valle Inclán and a bevy of scientists, educators, and artists dragged Spain into Europe and the twentieth century, Europe and the twentieth century plunged into a catastrophe far greater than Spain's loss of empire. The Great War of 1914–1918 destroyed Europe's illusions about human perfectibility, unstoppable progress, and the idyll of stability based on colonialism abroad and liberalism at home. The carnage of the trenches, the loss of a whole generation of young Europeans — 21 million wounded, 10 million dead; in the four-month Battle of the Somme, 420,000 British, 194,000 French, and 440,000 German casualties — made Spain's isolated woes seem rather puny.

Although Spain avoided entanglement in World War I, however, it could not help being affected by two events. First, all the contrasts and dangers of corrupt, war-weary, disillusioned postwar Europe poured into Spain. Second, Spain saw that the world outside was as tragically deformed as it thought itself to be — as deformed as a melting watch in a landscape by Salvador Dali, as shocking as a slit eyeball in the opening scene of Luis Buñuel's film *An Andalusian Dog.* Even the poet of the languorous beauty of Andalusia, Federico García Lorca, saw the world as a barren, sleepless hell: "Out in the world, no one sleeps. No one," he wrote in *The Poet in New York.* And he added, as if answering Calderón de la Barca over the span of centuries: "Life is no dream. Watch out! Watch out! Watch out!"

Inside Spain one had to watch out as well. Lorca's plays and poems are doom-laden; the shadow of death hangs over them. In *The Death of Antoñito el Camborio,* the poet hears "voices of death resounding near the Guadalquivir" but introduces himself as a third person, calling upon his own probable killers: "Oh Federico García / Call up the Guardia Civil!"

If Spain answered its questions in intellectual and even lyrical terms, it failed to do so in political terms. At the top of the system, the king commanded no respect; at its base, local political bosses ruled rural Spain in the midst of unchanging illiteracy, *latifundismo,* and abject peasant poverty. Conservatives and liberals took turns rhetorically governing from Madrid, while Spain's latter-day colonial incursions in Morocco piled disaster on top of defeat. The *dictablanda,* or bland dictatorship, of Miguel Primo de Rivera in the 1920s seemed as mellow as the lovely music of the Spanish form of operetta, the zarzuela, wafting through Madrid's Gran Vía. When King Alfonso XIII dismissed Primo de Rivera in 1930, he only proved his own incompetence, and he abdicated in 1931. The weak monarchy was followed by a weak republic, called by the people "the child republic, the little girl." It brought literacy and dignity to millions of villagers — Lorca himself took his theater group, La Barraca, on tours of the countryside — but Buñuel's terrifying look at the horrors of rural life, ignorant, incestuous, brutal, in *Las Hurdes* (*Land Without Bread*), was forbidden by the republican government.

The republic gave Spain a set of modern laws. It separated church from state, it enacted divorce laws, it brought secular education, and it gave workers the freedom to organize (gigantic strikes and rebellions ensued, especially in Asturias). It galvanized the whole culture, and it also committed many anticlerical excesses, pitting traditionalist groups against the government, which lacked a strong executive and which suffered from Spain's unresolved problems and opposing factions. Feudal estates in the south contended with prosperous northern farms; a rapidly expanding, land-hungry proletariat in the south conflicted with industrialization and financial sophistication in the north. The industries were heavily subsidized, inefficient, and costly, and as one part of Spain dragged the other down, the more sophisticated part dragged itself down. Factional ideology complicated matters enormously: enlightened, pro-European tendencies clashed with regional, isolationist traditions; secular liberalism clashed with revived, aggressive Catholicism; and only a society as authoritarian as Spain's had been could nurture such radical forms of anarchism. The two totalitarian philosophies, fascism and communism, seemed to be waiting in the wings to assert their power over the weaknesses of republican politics and its intellectually brilliant, decent, well-intentioned statesmen, starting with the president, Manuel Azaña.

Lacking backbone, this contradictory, promising, effervescent Spain of the republic was finally subverted from within by a revolt of the armed forces, led by Francisco Franco and his generals, who rose in arms on July 18, 1936. Of Spain's tender parliamentary democracy, Unamuno had said, "Let Spain affirm all of her contradictions, let the extremes play freely. The middle course will be the result." It was not. Unamuno's class at the University of Salamanca was invaded by the brutal Fascist general Millán Astray, who cried, "Death to intelligence!" Unamuno responded with dignity, "You may win, but you shall not convince." A few months later Unamuno was dead, his heart broken by the calamity of civil war. So was García Lorca, one of the first victims of fascist repression; he was coldly assassinated in his native Granada at age thirty-eight.

Very soon the Spanish Civil War became an international conflict. Both sides, Franco and the republicans, got foreign help. The republicans received some Soviet arms and Mexican support and asylum, as well as the sympathy of the international intelligentsia. Several writers — George Orwell, André Malraux, Ernest Hemingway — even came to fight. The International Brigades, including the Lincoln Brigade, from the United States, fought gallantly, giving one of the most moving proofs of international solidarity in the twentieth century.

These men were aware that something ominous was occurring in Spain: a new world war was being rehearsed on the plains and rivers of Castile. Nazi Germany and Fascist Italy lent their full political and military backing to the Franco uprising. On April 26, 1937, Hitler's Stukas pounded the Basque town of Guernica for almost three hours. There were no military objectives; it was an exercise in intimidation of a civilian

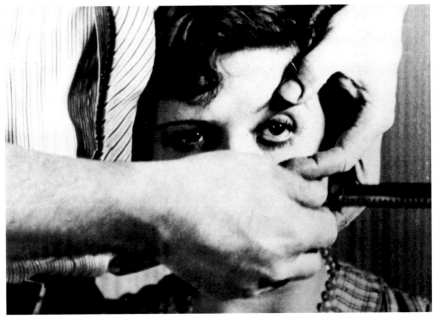

The Persistence
of Memory.
*Salvador Dali,
1931. Oil on
canvas, 9½ x 13
inches. Collection,
Museum of Modern
Art, New York.
Donated
anonymously.*

*From the opening
scene of* An
Andalusian Dog.
Luis Buñuel, 1928

population, a forecast of the London blitz, of the destruction of Coventry. From that time on, the innocent would be among the first victims of war.

But out of the death of Guernica came the rebirth of *Guernica*, the emblematic painting of the twentieth century, by Spain's greatest modern artist, Pablo Picasso. He asks us to look at suffering and death through the ageless Spanish symbols of the arena: the bull and the horse, shattered and disjointed. Spain's painful ability to transform the disasters of history into the triumphs of art is evident in this painting. But now nothing can protect us. We are outside the cave of Altamira. We are outside the chamber of *Las Meninas*. We are in a city street, bombs are falling from the heavens, everything is devastation and misery. Once more, as in the beginning, we are unsheltered. The man-made ruins of history are illuminated by a single technical artifact: the light bulb. A street lamp attempts to change night into day, as the bombs change life into death. Can we reconstruct a world from fragments of art?

Abandoned by the shortsighted cowardice of the European democracies, notably France and England, the republic faced the Fascist armies, supported by Hitler and Mussolini. But it was really two Spains who faced each other, apparently without any possible conciliation: dark and light, shadow and sun, again as in the bullring. Over the Pyrenees, driven into exile, the dying poet Antonio Machado wrote with a sigh, "Oh little Spaniard who comes into the world! May God protect you — for one of the two Spains is bound to freeze your heart!"

After his triumph, Franco built his own grandiose tomb, the Monument to the Fallen, near the Escorial. A vast cavern blasted in the rock, it took over sixteen years to construct. The work was largely carried out by political prisoners. It was the sort of fascistic nightmare that Hitler would have built for himself if he had won World War II.

Franco did not win World War II, but neither did he lose it. He was nimble and wily. Hitler never dragged him into the conflict, and when peace came, Franco parlayed his wartime neutrality into a strategic advantage for the Western alliance. At the entrance to the Mediterranean, he rented airbases to the United States. His anticommunist credentials were impeccable. Although he had greeted Hitler with his arm raised in the Nazi salute, he dropped that habit when he received President Dwight D. Eisenhower in Madrid to confirm his new allegiance.

The facade of Spain under Franco was both monumental and uniform, like the grim Monument to the Fallen. But the country was poor. It needed tourism and trade, investment and credit. And it got them, as a deserving sentinel of the NATO alliance. During those years, the Franco

*Francisco Franco,
c. 1944*

years, Spain achieved economic development, but without political freedom. There was nothing new here: from Korea to Chile, modern dictatorships have followed Franco's example.

RESCUED BY CULTURE

What is truly important, even singular, about Spain is that Franco never managed to take over the totality of Spanish culture. Hitler had managed to kidnap German culture: those who did not agree were exiled or murdered, and no unorthodox works were produced inside Nazi Germany. Spanish culture proved its resilience during the thirty-six years of the Franco regime, once more creating a dangerous margin of heresy, once more mining the unorthodox vein in the Spanish lode. It flourished in exile, certainly, but it never gave up inside. Poetry, the novel, underground journalism, illicit political organizations, and cinema thrived.

And then there was the return of the prodigal: Luis Buñuel's *Viridiana*, a magnificent recovery of the nation's bitter, hopeful, critical, and unorthodox cultural tradition. It was the tradition of Cervantes and the picaresque, Don Juan and San Juan, body and soul, and Buñuel used film as a manner of embracing the marginal, the outcast, the forgotten ones: *Los Olvidados*. The strength of Buñuel's filmmaking was that whether it loved or hated its subject matter, it was profoundly involved with it.

The nation profited from Francoist hibernation to think itself through — to reflect on its past mistakes, deplore its tradition of authoritarianism and repression, but also recall that it had its own democratic tradition. From the freedoms of the medieval townships to the rebellion of the Castilian *comunidades* to the liberal constitution of Cádiz to the failed experiment of the republic, Spain had experience to draw upon. This was the democratic tradition that it set out to consolidate after Franco's death in 1975. A question lingers in the international mind: How could this young and vigorous democracy rise from the decadence of the prolonged Fascist dictatorship? The answer lies in the mediate tradition of Spain's interrupted democratic trends; in the intermediate tradition of its cultural survival throughout the Franco years; and in the new, immediate tradition of political talent shown by all players after 1975.

In that year, there was an evident lack of congruence between Spain's economic development and its political stagnation. The role of Spanish democracy became to balance economic development with fitting political institutions. In this revolution, everyone played his role responsibly. The young king, Juan Carlos, held it all together. He stopped the old putschist military in their tracks, healing the wounds of the past.

A new Spain, young and democratic, has now joined Europe, ending the isolation that began during the Counter-Reformation and that men such as Jovellanos tried to combat in the eighteenth century. But Spain was still absent from Europe through European ignorance of the Spanish cultural contribution to the continent.

Today the Pyrenees have been traversed. Spain has Europe's fastest rate of growth. It offers its citizens the widest spectrum of political choice, which comes only from a mature, self-assured absence of paranoia. The danger is that as it joins the European community, Spain might become too prosperous, too comfortable, too consumerist, insufficiently self-critical — and forgetful of its other face, its Spanish American profile. Spain is in Europe, legitimately so. But it should not forget that it is also in the nations of Spanish America, "the cubs of the Spanish lion," as the Nicaraguan poet Rubén Darío called us.

Can we be without Spain? Can Spain be without us?

The Two Fridas.
Frida Kahlo, 1939

EIGHTEEN

Hispanic U.S.A.

The two-thousand-mile border between Mexico and the U.S.A. is the only visible border between the developed and the developing worlds. It is also the border between Anglo-America and Latin America. But it is an unfinished border, made up of unfinished barriers, ditches, walls, barbed wire fences — the so-called Tortilla Curtain — which are hastily erected by North Americans to keep out the Hispanic immigrant and then abandoned, unfinished.

The frontier is simple to cross where the Rio Grande is shallow or the hills lonely. But it is difficult to arrive on the northern side. In between is a no-man's-land, where the immigrant must brave the vigilant clutches of the U.S. border patrols. But the will of the immigrant workers is strong. Arriving mostly from Mexico, but also from Central America and as far south as Colombia as well as from the Caribbean, they are sometimes pushed north by political misfortune. But predominately, particularly in the case of the Mexicans, they enter the United States for economic reasons.

They congregate in little hotels just south of the border, waiting with their friends and families for the right moment to start across the frontier. The U.S. border patrols work day and night to stop them from coming in. The patrols have every device of modern technology to aid them, but the immigrants have the advantage of numbers, and the pressure of all those millions behind them. They have the desperation of need. These are perhaps the bravest and most determined people in Mexico, for it takes courage and will to break through the timeless circle of poverty and risk everything in the gamble of crossing the northern frontier.

Whole groups are rounded up by the helicopter searchlights of the border patrol. Many are arrested and sent back across the border. But something like half a million a year make it, joining an army of six million undocumented workers who are already there. These are the perfect victims. They are in a foreign land. They do not speak English. They sleep in the open. They carry all their money with them. They fear the authorities. Unscrupulous lawyers and employers hold their lives and freedom in their hands. They are sometimes brutalized, even murdered. But they are not criminals. They are only workers.

They are accused of displacing U.S. workers and of harming the economy and even the nation, threatening the cultural integrity of the United States. But they keep on coming. For one thing, the United States needs five million workers before the century is over, and these people do the jobs that no one else is willing to do anymore: stoop labor in agriculture, to be sure, but also service jobs in transportation, hotels, restoration, hospitals — all of which would come to a stop without the migrants' contribution. Without them, the whole structure of employment in the United States would undergo a drastic change, with salaries coming several notches down and millions of workers and their households suffering as a result.

The immigrants also come because there is a shortage of younger workers entering the U.S. labor market. They fill gaps caused by demographic shifts in the U.S. population. In the conversion from a cold war to a peacetime economy, the United States has shortages not only of unskilled workers but of skilled workers in metallurgy, construction, and crafts. Thanks to the migrants, it remains competitive in these and other sectors. Otherwise, these industries would move overseas, and even more jobs would be lost. Immigrants keep prices low and consumption high, and while they may displace some native workers, they cannot compare with the displacements caused by technology and foreign competition.

Beyond all the economic factors, the immigrant workers represent a broad social and cultural process of paramount importance to the continuity of Spanish American and U.S. culture. Even if Mexico did not have widespread unemployment, workers would come into the United States from somewhere. But they happen to come across a land border, not from across the sea, like their Irish, German, Italian, and Slavic predecessors. The contemporary equivalent of Ellis Island is in the middle of a cactus desert. Steerage is sometimes a tunnel dug between the two Californias, the Mexican state of Baja and the North American state of California.

A CONTINENT OF IMMIGRANTS

The U.S.-Mexico border, some of those who cross it say, is not really a border but a scar. Will it heal? Will it bleed once more? When a Hispanic worker crosses this border, he sometimes asks, "Hasn't this always been our land? Am I not coming back to it? Is it not in some way ours?" He can taste it, hear its language, sing its songs, and pray to its saints. Will this not always be in its bones a Hispanic land?

But first we must remember that ours was once an empty continent. All of us came here from somewhere else, beginning with the nomadic tribes from Asia who became the first Americans. The Spaniards came later, looking for the Seven Cities of Gold, but when they found none in what is today the southwestern United States, they left their language and their religion, and sometimes their blood. The Spanish Empire extended as far north as Oregon and filled the coastal region with the sonorous names of its cities: Los Angeles, Sacramento, San Francisco, Santa Barbara, San Diego, San Luis Obispo, San Bernardino, Monterey, Santa Cruz. When it achieved independence, the Mexican republic inherited these vast, underpopulated territories, but it lost them in 1848 to the expanding North American republic and its ideology of manifest destiny: the U.S.A., from sea to shining sea.

So the Hispanic world did not come to the United States, the United States came to the Hispanic world. It is perhaps an act of poetic justice that now the Hispanic world should return, both to the United States and to part of its ancestral heritage in the Western Hemisphere. The immigrants keep coming, not only to the Southwest but up the eastern seaboard to New York and Boston and west to Chicago and the Midwest, where they meet the long-established Chicanos, the North Americans of Mexican origin, who have been here even longer than the gringos. They all join to make up the 25 million Hispanics in the United States — the vast majority of Mexican origin, but many from Puerto Rico, Cuba, and Central and South America. It is the fastest-growing minority in the U.S.A.

Los Angeles is now the second largest Spanish-speaking city in the world, after Mexico City, before Madrid and Barcelona. You can prosper in southern Florida even if you speak only Spanish, as the population is predominantly Cuban. San Antonio, integrated by Mexicans, has been a bilingual city for 150 years. By the middle of the coming century, almost half the population of the United States will be Spanish-speaking.

This third Hispanic development, that of the United States, is not only an economic and political event; it is above all a cultural event. A whole civilization with a Hispanic pulse has been created in the U.S.A. A literature has been born in this country, one that stresses autobiography — the personal narrative, memories of childhood, the family album — as a way of answering the question, What does it mean to be a Chicano, a Mexican American, a Puerto Rican living in Manhattan, a second-generation Cuban American living in exile in Miami? For example, consider the varied work of Rudolfo Anaya (*Bless Me, Ultima*), Ron Arias (*The Road to Tamazunchale*), Ernesto Galarza (*Barrio Boy*), Alejandro Morales (*The Brick People*), Arturo Islas (*The Rain God*), Tomas Rivera (*Y no se lo tragó la tierra*), and Rolando Hinojosa (*The Valley*); or of the women writers Sandra Cisneros (*Woman Hollering Creek*), Dolores Prida (*Beautiful Señoritas & Other Plays*), and Judith Ortiz Cofer (*The Line of the Sun*); or of the poets Alurista and Alberto Rios. Or consider the definitive statements of Rosario Ferré or Luis Rafael Sánchez, who simply decided to write in Spanish from the island of Puerto Rico.

An art has also been created here; in a violent, even garish way, it joins a tradition going all the way from the caves of Altamira to the graffiti of East Los Angeles. It includes pictures of memory and dynamic paintings of clashes, like the car-crash paintings of Carlos Almaráz, who was part of the group called Los Four, along with Frank Romero, Beto de la Rocha, and Gilbert Luján. The beauty and violence of these artists' work not only contribute to the need for contact between cultures that must refuse complacency or submit to injustice in order to come alive to each other. They also assert an identity that deserves to be respected and that must be given shape if it is not visible, or musical beat if it is inaudible. And if the other culture, the Anglo mainstream, denies Hispanic culture a past, then artists of Latin origin must invent, if necessary, an origin. And they must remember every single link that binds it to them.

For example, can one be a Chicano artist in Los Angeles without upholding the memory of Martín Ramírez? Born in 1885, Ramírez was a migrant railroad worker from Mexico who lost his speech and for this was condemned to live for three decades in a California madhouse, until his death in 1960. He was not mad, he was just speechless. So he became an artist, and drew his muteness for thirty years.

No wonder that the Hispanic culture of the United States must manifest itself as forcefully as in a Luján painting, as dramatically as in a stage production by Luis Valdés, with a prose as powerful as that of Oscar Hijuelos with his mambo kings, or with a beat as life-giving as that of Rubén Blades in his salsa songs of city woes and streetwise humor.

This vast flow of negation and affirmation forces newcomers as well as native Hispanics to ask themselves, "What do we bring? What would we like to retain? What do we want to offer this country?" The answers are determined by the fact that these people reflect a very broad social

Flip Over.
Carlos Almaráz, 1983

Highway 64.
Frank Romero, 1988

group that includes families, individuals, whole communities, and networks, transmitting values, memories, traditions. At one end of the spectrum are 300,000 Hispanic businessmen prospering in the U.S.A., and at the other is a nineteen-year-old Anglo-American shooting two immigrants to death for the simple reason that he "hates Mexicans." If one proudly spouts the statistic that Hispanic-owned businesses generate over $20 billion a year, one can also, far less proudly, report that immigrants are shot at by Anglos with the paint-pellet guns used in mock warfare games. If one records that whole communities in Mexico are supported by the *remesas*, or remittances, of their migrant workers in the United States, and that these *remesas* add up to $4 billion a year and are Mexico's second largest source of foreign income (after oil), then one must also record that many migrant workers are run down by vehicles on black roads near their campsites. And if, finally, one realizes that the majority of Mexican migrants are temporary and eventually return to Mexico, then one must bear in mind the persisting differences between Anglo-America and Ibero-America, as these continue to oppose, influence, and clash with each other.

MEETING THE OTHER

The two cultures coexist, rubbing shoulders and questioning each other. We have too many common problems, which demand cooperation and understanding in a new world context, to clash as much as we do. We recognize each other more and more in challenges such as dealing with drugs, crime, the homeless, and the environment. But as the formerly homogeneous society of the United States faces the immigration of vastly heterogeneous groups, Latin America faces the breakdown of the formerly homogeneous spheres of political, military, and religious power through the movement of the urban dispossessed.

In this movement, which is taking place in all directions, we all give something to one another. The United States brings its own culture — the influence of its films, its music, its books, its ideas, its journalism, its politics, and its language — to each and every country in Latin America. We are not frightened by this, because we feel that our own culture is strong enough, and that in effect, the enchilada can coexist with the hamburger. Cultures only flourish in contact with others; they perish in isolation.

The culture of Spanish America also brings its own gifts. When asked, both new immigrants and long-established Hispanic Americans speak of religion — not only Catholicism, but something more like a deep sense of the sacred, a recognition that the world is holy, which is probably the oldest and deepest certitude of the Amerindian world. This is also a sensuous, tactile religion, a product of the meeting between the Mediterranean civilization and the Indian world of the Americas.

Then there is care and respect for elders, something called *respeto* — respect for experience and continuity, less than awe at change and novelty. This respect is not limited to old age in itself; in a basically oral culture, the old are the ones who remember stories, who have the store of memory. One could almost say that when an old man or an old woman dies in the Hispanic world, a whole library dies with that person.

And of course there is the family — family commitment, fighting to keep the family together, perhaps not avoiding poverty but certainly avoiding a *lonely* poverty. The family is regarded as the hearth, the sustaining warmth. It is almost a political party, the parliament of the social microcosm and the security net in times of trouble. And when have times not been troubled? The ancient stoic philosophy from Roman Iberia is deep indeed in the soul of Hispanics.

What else do Ibero-Americans bring to the U.S.A.? What would they like to retain? It is obvious that they would like to keep their language, the Spanish language. Some urge them to forget it, to integrate by using the dominant language, English. Others argue that they should use Spanish only to learn English and join the mainstream. More and more often, however, people are starting to understand that speaking more than one language does not harm anyone. There are automobile stickers in Texas that read MONOLINGUALISM IS A CURABLE DISEASE. Is monolingualism unifying and bilingualism disruptive? Or is monolingualism sterile and bilingualism fertile? The California state law decreeing that English is the official language of the state proves only one thing: that English is no longer the official language of California.

Multilingualism, then, appears as the harbinger of a multicultural world, of which Los Angeles is the prime example. A modern Byzantium, the City of the Angels receives each day, willy-nilly, the languages, the food, the mores not only of Spanish Americans but of Vietnamese, Koreans, Chinese, Japanese. This is the price — or the gift, depending on how you look at it — of global interdependence and communications.

So the cultural dilemma of the American of Mexican, Cuban, or Puerto Rican descent is suddenly universalized: to integrate or not? To maintain a personality and add to the diversity of North American society, or to fade away into anonymity in the name of the after all nonexistent "melting pot"? Well, perhaps the question is really, once more, to be or not to be? To be with others or to be alone? Isolation means death. Encounter means birth, even rebirth.

Panels depicting Anglo America and Hispanic America, from The Epic of American Civilization. *José Clemente Orozco, 1932–1934*

California, and especially Los Angeles, a gateway to both Asia and Latin America, poses the universal question of the coming century: how do we deal with the Other? North Africans in France, Turks in Germany, Vietnamese in Czechoslovakia, Pakistanis in Britain, black Africans in Italy, Japanese, Koreans, Chinese, and Latin Americans in the United States: instant communications and economic interdependence have transformed what was once an isolated situation into a universal, defining, all-embracing reality of the twenty-first century.

Is anyone better prepared to deal with this central issue of dealing with the Other than we, the Spanish, the Spanish Americans, the Hispanics in the U.S.A.? We are Indian, black, European, but above all mixed, mestizo. We are Iberian and Greek, Roman and Jewish, Arab, Gothic, and Gypsy. Spain and the New World are centers where multiple cultures meet — centers of incorporation, not of exclusion. When we exclude, we betray ourselves. When we include, we find ourselves.

Who are these Hispanic "ourselves"? Perhaps no story better renders the simultaneity of cultures than "The Aleph" by the Argentine author Jorge Luis Borges. In "The Aleph," the narrator finds a perfect instant in time and space where all the places in the world can be seen at the same moment, without confusion, from every angle, in perfect, simul-

taneous existence. What we would see in the Spanish American aleph
would be the Indian sense of sacredness, communality, and the will to
survive; the Mediterranean legacy of law, philosophy, and the Christian,
Jewish, and Arab strains making up a multiracial Spain; and the New
World's challenge to Spain, the syncretic, baroque continuation of the
multicultural and multiracial experience, now including Indian, European, and black African contributions. We would see a struggle for
democracy and for revolution, coming all the way from the medieval
townships and from the ideas of the European Enlightenment, but meeting our true personal and communal experience in Zapata's villages, on
Bolívar's plains, in Tupac Amarú's highlands.

And we would then see the past becoming present in one seamless
creation. The Indian world becomes present in the paintings of Ruffino
Tamayo, who was born in an Indian village in Oaxaca and whose modern
art includes an Indian continuity in the sense of color and the spirit of
celebration, in the cosmic consciousness and in Tamayo's capacity to re-
create on canvas the dream of a form that *can* contain dreams.

A younger painter, Francisco Toledo, also from an Indian village in
Oaxaca, gives the ancient Indian fear and love of nature their most physical and visual proximity to our urban lives, while the Cuban Wifredo

Animals.
Ruffino Tamayo,
1941. Oil on
canvas, 30⅛ x 40
inches. Collection,
Museum of Modern
Art, New York.
Inter-America Fund

Toads and
Bottles.
Francisco Toledo,
1975

The Jungle.
*Wifredo Lam,
1943. Gouache
on paper mounted
on canvas. 7 feet
10¼ inches x 7 feet
6½ inches. Collection,
Museum of Modern
Art, New York.
Inter-America Fund*

Lam permits his African roots to grow in his pictures. The Mexican painter Alberto Gironella bitingly recovers the traditions of Spanish art and commerce: his Velázquez spin-offs are framed by sardine cans.

Culture is the way we laugh, even at ourselves, as in the paintings of the Colombian Fernando Botero. It is the way we remember, as when the Venezuelan Jacobo Borges imagines the endless tunnel of memory. But culture is above all our bodies, our bodies so often sacrificed and denied, our shackled, dreaming, carnal bodies, like the body of the Mexican artist Frida Kahlo. Our bodies are deformed and dreamy creatures in the art of

Retrato Oficial
de la Junta
Militar.
*Fernando Botero,
1971*

Noche de San
Juan I. *José Luis
Cuevas, 1983*

the Mexican José Luis Cuevas. Indeed, like Goya, Cuevas offers the mirror of imagination as the only truth; his figures are the offspring of our nightmares, but also the brothers and sisters of our desires.

The union of Cuevas in the Americas with Goya in Spain also reminds us that when we embrace the Other, we not only meet ourselves, we embrace the marginal images that the modern world, optimistic and progressive as it has been, has shunned and has then paid a price for forgetting. The conventional values of middle-class Western society were brutally shattered in the two world wars and in the totalitarian experience. Spain and Spanish America have never fooled themselves on this account. Goya's "black paintings" are perhaps the most lasting reminder we have of the price of losing the tragic sense of life in exchange for the illusion of progress. Goya asks us again and again to harbor no illusions. We are captive within society. Poverty does not make anyone kinder, only more ruthless. Nature is deaf to our pleas. It cannot save the innocent victim; history, like Saturn, devours its own children.

Goya asks us to avoid complacency. The art of Spain and Spanish America is a constant reminder of the cruelty that we can exercise on our fellow human beings. But like all tragic art, it asks us first to take a hard look at the consequences of our actions, and to respect the passage of time so that we can transform our experience into knowledge. Acting on knowledge, we can have hope that this time we shall prevail.

We will be able to embrace the Other, enlarging our human possibility. People and their cultures perish in isolation, but they are born or reborn in contact with other men and women, with men and women of another culture, another creed, another race. If we do not recognize our humanity in others, we shall not recognize it in ourselves.

Often we have failed to meet this challenge. But we have finally seen ourselves whole in the unburied mirror of identity, only when accompanied — ourselves with others. We can hear the voice of the poet Pablo Neruda exclaiming throughout this vision, "I am here to sing this history."

THE MIRROR UNBURIED

We have the right, five hundred years after Columbus, to celebrate the great wealth, variety, and continuity of our culture. Indeed, as the quincentennial comes and goes, many throughout Latin America will ask themselves, "Why have our artists and writers been so imaginative and our politicians so unimaginative?" Imagination will be needed as a new political agenda takes shape in Latin America, including such problems as drugs, crime, communications, education, and the environment — problems that we share with Europe and North America. But it will also

Witches'
Sabbath.
Goya,
c. 1819–1823

Saturn
Devouring
His Children.
Goya,
c. 1821–1823

be needed as a new agrarian agenda appears, based not on further sacrifice of the villages in favor of the cities and of smokestack industries, but on a basic renewal of democracy from the bottom, through cooperative systems. This agenda proposes a double value that should guide the whole society. Let us feed and educate ourselves first of all; then we might finally become modern technological states with a sound foundation. If the majority of our people continue to be left out of the process, underfed and uneducated, this will not happen.

I have reason for optimism. In crisis, Latin America is changing and moving, but creatively, through evolution and revolution, elections and mass movements, because its people are changing and moving. Professionals, intellectuals, technocrats, students, trade unions, agricultural co-ops, business associations, women's organizations, religious groups, neighborhood committees — the whole spectrum of society — are quickly becoming the protagonists of our history, outflanking the state, the army, the church, even the traditional political parties. As the civil society, the bearer of cultural continuity, acts politically and economically, from the outskirts toward the center and from the bottom up, the age-old, vertical, centralized systems of the Hispanic world will be reversed.

This is the politics of permanent social mobilization, as the Mexican author Carlos Monsiváis calls it. It has manifested itself dramatically in events, such as the Mexico City earthquake of September 1985, when society acted more quickly and efficiently than the government and thereby discovered its own powers. But it also happens every day, silently, when a rural association uses the levers of credit and the organization of production to negotiate with the government or with commercial competitors. It happens when a profession or a group of workers discovers their shared social and cultural values, and through them starts acting cohesively and democratically. It happens when a small flower-grower or a seamstress in a village receives credit, prospers, and repays it punctually. It happens when Indian movements, *campesino* credit unions, collective interest associations, and leagues of communitarian production spring up, as they are doing all over the continent.

We have hope that the initiatives born of crisis at the lower levels will spread. But we also fear that we do not have enough time — that institutions, drowned in debt, inflation, and lost expectations, will be overthrown by the army or by popular riots, and that fascistic organizations or even brutal ideological groups will take over.

The present political institutions, which are truly, although feebly, democratic, urgently need to adapt to social demands, not just to technocratic rationality. Democratic states in Latin America must do what until now only revolutions were expected to do: bring economic development along with democracy and social justice. That we have been unable to do so is the greatest failure of the past five hundred years. The chance to do so is our only hope.

The Monarchs of Spain

SPANISH RULERS (970–1285)

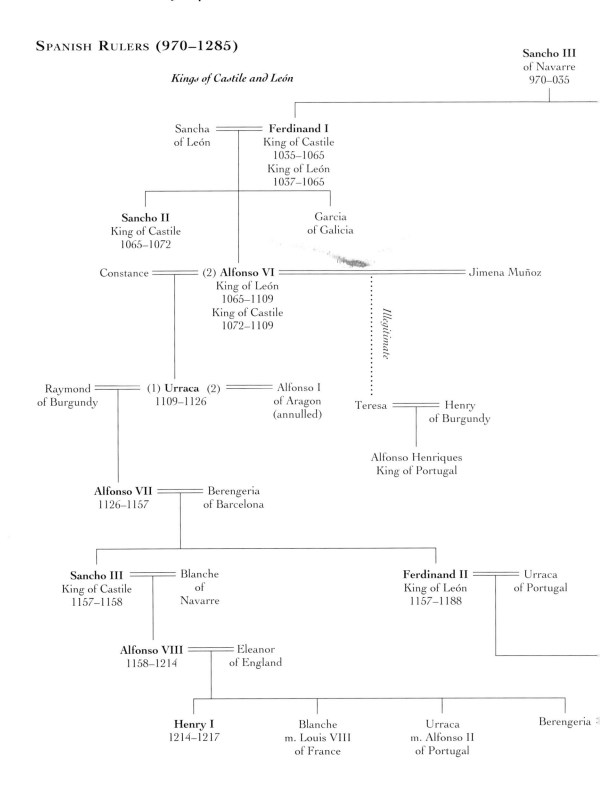

Kings of Castile and León

Sancho III
of Navarre
970–035

Sancha === Ferdinand I
of León   King of Castile
           1035–1065
           King of León
           1037–1065

Sancho II   Garcia
King of Castile   of Galicia
1065–1072

Constance === (2) Alfonso VI ============================ Jimena Muñoz
               King of León
               1065–1109
               King of Castile   *Illegitimate*
               1072–1109

Raymond === (1) Urraca (2) === Alfonso I   Teresa === Henry
of Burgundy   1109–1126   of Aragon   of Burgundy
                              (annulled)

                                                  Alfonso Henriques
                                                  King of Portugal

Alfonso VII === Berengeria
1126–1157   of Barcelona

Sancho III === Blanche   Ferdinand II === Urraca
King of Castile   of   King of León   of Portugal
1157–1158   Navarre   1157–1188

Alfonso VIII === Eleanor
1158–1214   of England

Henry I   Blanche   Urraca   Berengeria
1214–1217   m. Louis VIII   m. Alfonso II
                 of France   of Portugal

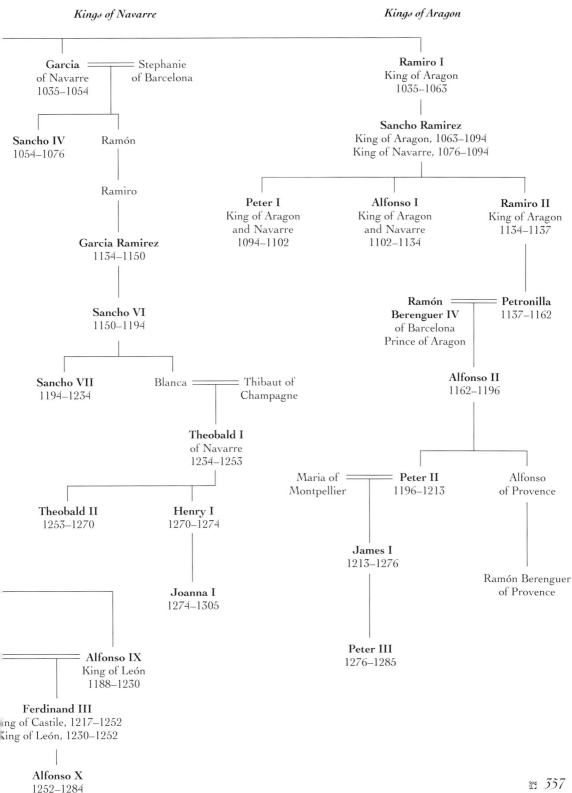

Kings of Navarre *Kings of Aragon*

Garcia ═══ Stephanie
of Navarre   of Barcelona
1035–1054

Ramiro I
King of Aragon
1035–1063

Sancho IV   Ramón
1054–1076

Sancho Ramirez
King of Aragon, 1063–1094
King of Navarre, 1076–1094

Ramiro

Peter I   **Alfonso I**   **Ramiro II**
King of Aragon   King of Aragon   King of Aragon
and Navarre   and Navarre   1134–1137
1094–1102   1102–1134

Garcia Ramirez
1134–1150

Ramón ═══ **Petronilla**
Berenguer IV   1137–1162
of Barcelona
Prince of Aragon

Sancho VI
1150–1194

Alfonso II
1162–1196

Sancho VII   Blanca ═══ Thibaut of
1194–1234   Champagne

Theobald I
of Navarre
1234–1253

Maria of ═══ **Peter II**   Alfonso
Montpellier   1196–1213   of Provence

Theobald II   **Henry I**
1253–1270   1270–1274

James I
1213–1276

Ramón Berenguer
of Provence

Joanna I
1274–1305

Peter III
1276–1285

Alfonso IX
King of León
1188–1230

Ferdinand III
ng of Castile, 1217–1252
King of León, 1230–1252

Alfonso X
1252–1284

THE HOUSE OF CASTILE (1252–1504)

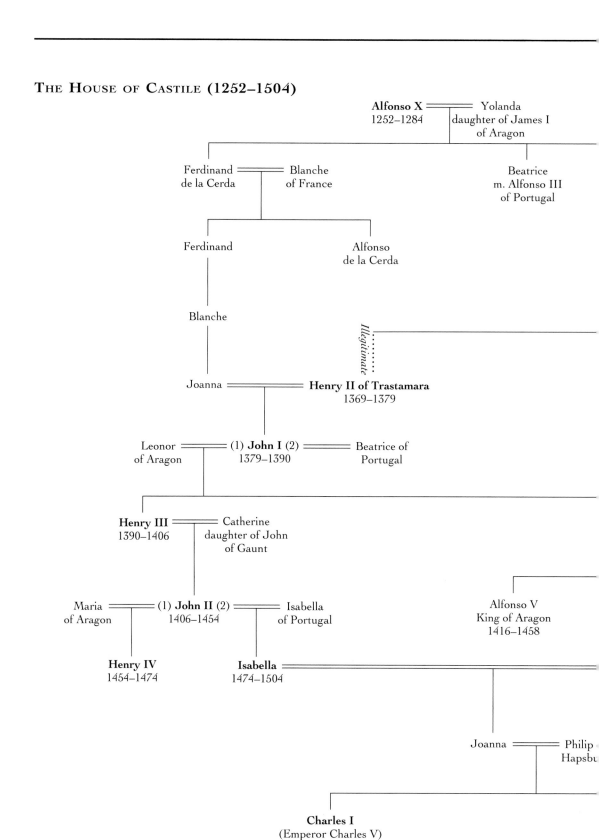

Alfonso X ════ Yolanda
1252–1284 │ daughter of James I
of Aragon

Ferdinand ════ Blanche
de la Cerda │ of France

Beatrice
m. Alfonso III
of Portugal

Ferdinand

Alfonso
de la Cerda

Blanche

Illegitimate

Joanna ════ **Henry II of Trastamara**
1369–1379

Leonor ════ (1) **John I** (2) ════ Beatrice of
of Aragon │ 1379–1390 │ Portugal

Henry III ════ Catherine
1390–1406 │ daughter of John
of Gaunt

Alfonso V
King of Aragon
1416–1458

Maria ════ (1) **John II** (2) ════ Isabella
of Aragon │ 1406–1454 │ of Portugal

Henry IV
1454–1474

Isabella
1474–1504

Joanna ════ Philip
Hapsbu

Charles I
(Emperor Charles V)

Spanish Hapsburgs

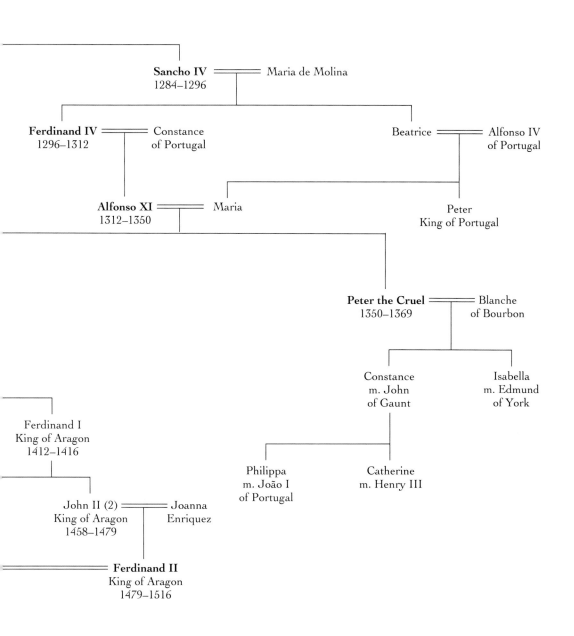

Sancho IV
1284–1296
= Maria de Molina

Ferdinand IV
1296–1312
= Constance
of Portugal

Beatrice = Alfonso IV
of Portugal

Alfonso XI
1312–1350
= Maria

Peter
King of Portugal

Peter the Cruel
1350–1369
= Blanche
of Bourbon

Constance
m. John
of Gaunt

Isabella
m. Edmund
of York

Philippa
m. João I
of Portugal

Catherine
m. Henry III

Ferdinand I
King of Aragon
1412–1416

John II (2)
King of Aragon
1458–1479
= Joanna
Enriquez

Ferdinand II
King of Aragon
1479–1516

Ferdinand I
(Emperor)

Austrian Hapsburgs

THE HOUSE OF ARAGON (1276–1516)

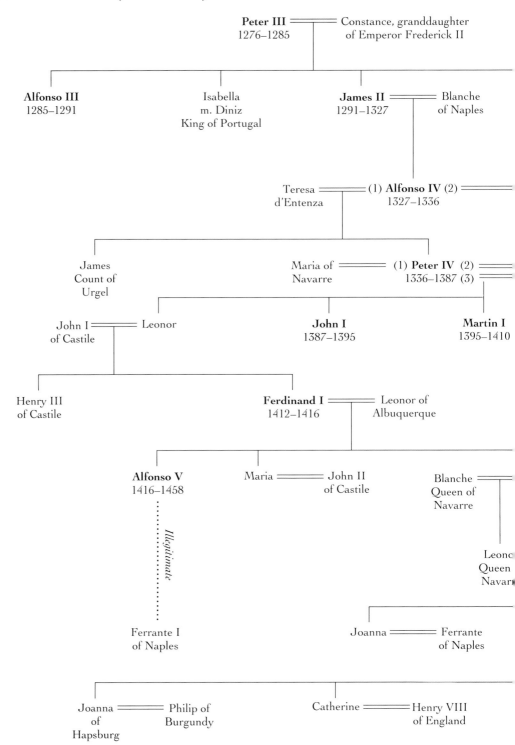

Peter III 1276–1285 ══ Constance, granddaughter of Emperor Frederick II

Alfonso III 1285–1291

Isabella m. Diniz King of Portugal

James II 1291–1327 ══ Blanche of Naples

Teresa d'Entenza ══ (1) Alfonso IV (2) 1327–1336 ══

James Count of Urgel

Maria of Navarre ══ (1) Peter IV (2) 1336–1387 (3) ══

John I of Castile ══ Leonor

John I 1387–1395

Martin I 1395–1410

Henry III of Castile

Ferdinand I 1412–1416 ══ Leonor of Albuquerque

Alfonso V 1416–1458

Maria ══ John II of Castile

Blanche Queen of Navarre ══

Illegitimate

Ferrante I of Naples

Leonc Queen Navari

Joanna ══ Ferrante of Naples

Joanna of Hapsburg ══ Philip of Burgundy

Catherine ══ Henry VIII of England

Federigo III
of Sicily

= Leonor of
Castile

Leonor of Portugal
Leonor of Sicily

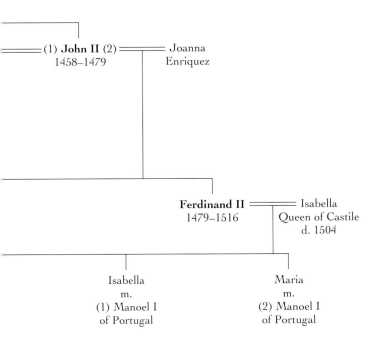

(1) **John II** (2) Joanna
1458–1479 Enriquez

Ferdinand II Isabella
1479–1516 Queen of Castile
d. 1504

Isabella Maria
m. m.
(1) Manoel I (2) Manoel I
of Portugal of Portugal

THE HOUSE OF HAPSBURG (1493–1780)

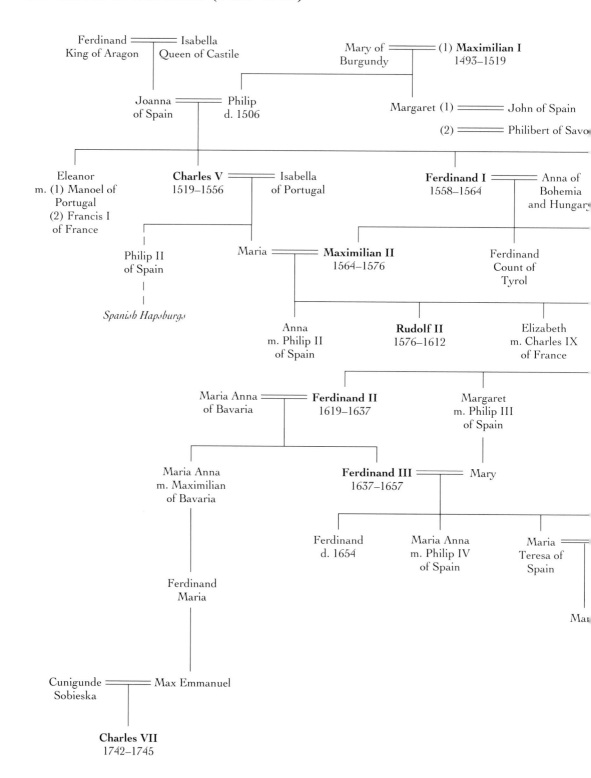

Ferdinand King of Aragon ══ Isabella Queen of Castile

Mary of Burgundy ══ (1) **Maximilian I** 1493–1519

Joanna of Spain ══ Philip d. 1506

Margaret (1) ══ John of Spain
(2) ══ Philibert of Savo[y]

Eleanor m. (1) Manoel of Portugal (2) Francis I of France

Charles V 1519–1556 ══ Isabella of Portugal

Ferdinand I 1558–1564 ══ Anna of Bohemia and Hungar[y]

Philip II of Spain

Maria ══ **Maximilian II** 1564–1576

Ferdinand Count of Tyrol

Spanish Hapsburgs

Anna m. Philip II of Spain

Rudolf II 1576–1612

Elizabeth m. Charles IX of France

Maria Anna of Bavaria ══ **Ferdinand II** 1619–1637

Margaret m. Philip III of Spain

Maria Anna m. Maximilian of Bavaria

Ferdinand III 1637–1657 ══ Mary

Ferdinand d. 1654

Maria Anna m. Philip IV of Spain

Maria Teresa of Spain ══

Ma[r]

Ferdinand Maria

Cunigunde Sobieska ══ Max Emmanuel

Charles VII 1742–1745

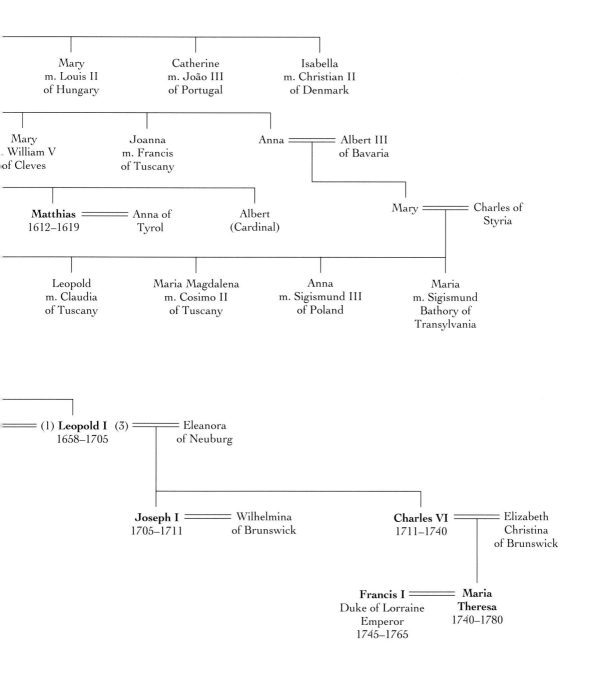

Mary
m. Louis II
of Hungary

Catherine
m. João III
of Portugal

Isabella
m. Christian II
of Denmark

Mary
William V
of Cleves

Joanna
m. Francis
of Tuscany

Anna ══════ Albert III
of Bavaria

Matthias ══════ Anna of
1612–1619   Tyrol

Albert
(Cardinal)

Mary ══════ Charles of
Styria

Leopold
m. Claudia
of Tuscany

Maria Magdalena
m. Cosimo II
of Tuscany

Anna
m. Sigismund III
of Poland

Maria
m. Sigismund
Bathory of
Transylvania

══ (1) **Leopold I** (3) ══════ Eleanora
1658–1705   of Neuburg

Joseph I ══════ Wilhelmina
1705–1711   of Brunswick

Charles VI ══════ Elizabeth
1711–1740   Christina
of Brunswick

Francis I ══════ **Maria**
Duke of Lorraine   **Theresa**
Emperor   1740–1780
1745–1765

THE HOUSE OF HAPSBURG-LORRAINE (1740–1918)

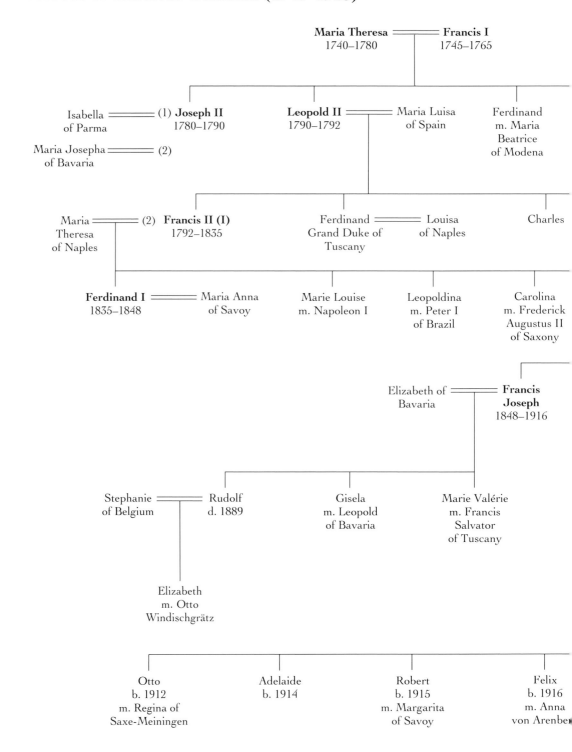

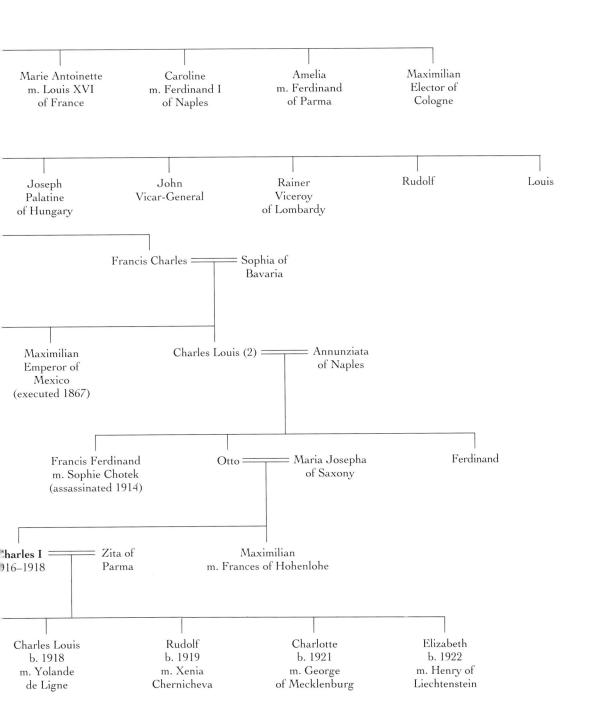

Marie Antoinette
m. Louis XVI
of France

Caroline
m. Ferdinand I
of Naples

Amelia
m. Ferdinand
of Parma

Maximilian
Elector of
Cologne

Joseph
Palatine
of Hungary

John
Vicar-General

Rainer
Viceroy
of Lombardy

Rudolf

Louis

Francis Charles ══════ Sophia of
Bavaria

Maximilian
Emperor of
Mexico
(executed 1867)

Charles Louis (2) ══════ Annunziata
of Naples

Francis Ferdinand
m. Sophie Chotek
(assassinated 1914)

Otto ══════ Maria Josepha
of Saxony

Ferdinand

Charles I
1916–1918 ══════ Zita of
Parma

Maximilian
m. Frances of Hohenlohe

Charles Louis
b. 1918
m. Yolande
de Ligne

Rudolf
b. 1919
m. Xenia
Chernicheva

Charlotte
b. 1921
m. George
of Mecklenburg

Elizabeth
b. 1922
m. Henry of
Liechtenstein

Sources and Readings

Seldom does a writer of fiction have the opportunity to write the biography of his or her culture. The writing and filming of the TV series *The Buried Mirror* gave me just such a chance. Nevertheless, this book is not an outcropping of the series but a biography of my culture, which is really (I understood as I wrote it) a biography of myself. Nothing extraordinary in this: a culture *is* its bearers, those who know it, cherish it, even attempt to enrich it and continue it. But for the purpose of bibliographical reference, I can only say that a book such as this feeds on fifty years of reading. An inclusive list would be interminable. What I offer now is a more judicious but I hope not academic approach to the question — a selection, a reference to works that I did consult or remember while writing the series and the book. What I cannot list are the hearsay, the myths, the family chronicles, the everyday memories, the conversations with friends and teachers that constitute, perhaps, the true bibliography of *The Buried Mirror*.

GENERAL HISTORIES

One of the most useful histories of Spain is Miguel Artola Gallego, *Historia de España* (Madrid: Elliots, 1989).

In five volumes, Leslie Bethell, ed., *The Cambridge History of Latin America* (Cambridge, England: Cambridge University, 1984) provides the most useful current overall view of Latin America. However, my personal favorite source for this region continues to be Bradford Burns, *Latin America* (Englewood Cliffs, N.J.: Prentice-Hall, 1972); it is inclusive, incisive, and cogent on every point. Useful additions to the list are Lewis Hanke, ed., *History of Latin America, Sources and Interpretations* (Boston: Little, Brown, 1967), a particularly rich selection of texts from the conquest to modern times, and Hubert Herring, *A History of Latin America* (New York: Knopf, 1968), which remains a favorite with American students. Along with these, I found support in at least two excellent résumés of culture in general and the arts in particular: Leopoldo Castedo, *A History of Latin American Art and Architecture* (New York, 1969), and Pedro Henríquez Ureña, *Historia de la cultura en la América Hispánica* (Mexico: FCE, 1947).

As a point of interest, there is a five-volume common history of Spain and Spanish America, which stresses the social and economic factors: J. Vicens Vives, ed., *Historia de España y América: social y económica* (Madrid: Vives Bolsillo). For more on the economic factors, see J. Vicens Vives, in collaboration with Jorge Nadal Oller, *Manuel de historia económica de España* (Barcelona: Editorial Vicens-Vives, 1967).

INTERPRETIVE HISTORIES

All cultures produce a variety of self-interpretations, debates on the culture, and even national characterizations. Spain and Spanish America have been richer than most in producing these reflective investigations into the self. Two writers of interpretive history to consider are Américo Castro and Claudio Sánchez Albornoz. The debate between these two historians was long, bitter, and fruitful. Castro argued in favor of the tricultural dynamics of medieval Spanish history, stressing the worth of the Islamic and Jewish contributions; Sánchez Albornoz preferred to celebrate the Christian character of Spain, seeing *la reconquista* as a step forward rather than a loss.

Other twentieth-century interpretations of Spanish history that I find particularly stimulating include Fernando Díaz Plaja, *Otra historia de España* (Madrid: Espasa-Calpe, 1987); Ramón Menéndez Pidal, *Los españoles en la historia* (Madrid: Espasa-Calpe, 1986); and José Ortega y Gasset, *España invertebrada* (Madrid: Espasa-Calpe, 1989).

For Iberian and Roman Spain, I have relied mainly on the texts of Roman and Greek historians; works by such authors as Appianos, Dio Cassius, Sallust, and Strabo provided informed historical accounts. Allen Josephs, *The White Wall of Spain: The Mysteries of Andalusian Culture* (Ames: Iowa State, 1983) is especially useful in its tracing of the remote origins of Andalusia and its culture, while Juan Maluquer de Motes, *Tartessos: la ciudad sin historia* (Barcelona: Ediciones Destino, 1990) gives a good account of Tartessus' misty history. María Zambrano, "La cuestión del estoicismo español," in *Andalucía sueño y realidad* (Granada: Ediciones Annel, 1984), offers what is perhaps the best analysis of Seneca's influence in Spain.

BULLS AND FLAMENCO

Closely associated with the very origins of Spain, these two topics have generated an abundant bibliography. Although I have written on them from the point of view of personal experience, I would like to refer the reader to José M. Cosio, *Los toros: tratado técnico e histórico* (Madrid: Elliots, 1989), a nine-volume set that explores the monumental history of bulls and bullfighting; José M. Caballero Bonald, *Luces y sombras del flamenco* (Barcelona: Editorial Lumen, 1975), a nicely illustrated book with photos by Colita; and Felix Grande, *Memoria del flamenco* (Madrid: Espasa-Calpe, 1987), which focuses on flamenco. Flamenco, however, is also part of the greater history of Spanish music as told by Adolfo Salazar, Spain's greatest musicologist, in *La música en España* (Madrid:

Espasa-Calpe, 1953), a text that traces the country's musical history from Altamira to the Renaissance.

GOTHIC SPAIN

I have centered my chapter on the Visigoths on the cultural figure of Saint Isidore. See Ernest Brehaut, *Encyclopedist of the Dark Ages, Isidore of Seville* (New York: Columbia, 1912). For an especially good study of Saint Isidore, see also Jacques Fontaine, *Isidore de Seville et la culture classique dans L'Espagne wisigothique* (Paris, 1959).

MUSLIM AND JEWISH SPAIN

Perhaps the greatest book of poetry, personal experience, and reminiscence to come from Muslim Spain is Ali ibn Ahmad Ibn-Hazm, *The Ring of the Dove: A Treatise on the Art and Practice of Arab Love,* tr. A. J. Arberry (New York: AMS, repro. of 1953 ed.), a text that exerted great influence over subsequent Spanish writers. Another collection of poems to consider is by Solomon Ibn Gabirol, whom I hold to be the greatest Jewish literary figure of Muslim Spain; see his *Fountain of Life* (New York: Citadel, 1963). For an excellent introduction to Spanish Arab philosophy, see Andrés Martínez Lorca, ed., *Ensayos sobre la filosofía de El Andalus* (Barcelona: Anthropos, 1990). For a different focus, read Ramón Menéndez Pidal, *España, eslabón entre la cristiandad y el islam* (Madrid: Espasa-Calpe, 1968).

In two volumes, the most complete work on Jewish Spain is Yitzhak Baer, *History of the Jews in Christian Spain* (Philadelphia: Jewish Publication Society, 1966). For a slightly more current history, see Julio Caro Baroja, *Los judíos en la España moderna y contemporánea* (Madrid, 1962).

LA RECONQUISTA

The wars of reconquest cover the history of medieval Spain from 711 to 1492. However, this period is part of a European context. Perhaps Marc Bloch, *Feudal Society* (Chicago: University of Chicago, 1964), in two volumes, offers the best single study of feudalism. Luis G. Valdeavellano, *Orígenes de la burguesía en la España medieval* (Madrid: Espasa-Calpe, 1959) expands the bibliography to include repopulation, and José Ángel García de Cortazar and Carmen Díez Herrera, *La formación de la sociedad hispano-cristiana del Cantábrico al Ebro en los siglos VIII a XI* (Santander: Ediciones de Libería Estudio, 1982) adds material on the formation of cities and society. For further information on the birth of political institutions, see Esteban Sarasa, *Las cortes de Aragón en la Edad Media* (Zaragoza: Cuara Editorial, 1979) and José M. Pérez Prendes, *Cortes de Castilla* (Barcelona: Editorial Ariel, 1974). Finally, refer to texts by José Antonio Maravall and Julio González for details concerning the overall gestation of the notion of a Spanish entity; specifically, see Julio González, *Reinado y diplomas de Fernando III* (Córdoba: Monte de Piedad y Caja de Ahorros de Córdoba, 1980). Gabriel Jackson is the author of the best general study of the period, *Medieval Spain* (London: Thames and Hudson, 1972).

As central to the period of *la reconquista* as Saint Isidore was to the Gothic centuries, Ferdinand III's son, Alfonso X (the Wise) of Castile, produced incomparable works of literature; from a history of Spain to a history of the world, from poetry to astronomy, his work encompassed an encyclopedic range. The best current anthologies of Alfonso's work include Antonio Ballestros, ed., *Alfonso el sabio* (Milan: Murcia, 1963); Francisco J. Díaz de Revenga, ed., *Alfonso X el sabio* (Madrid: Taurus, 1985); and Antonio G. Solalinde, ed., *Alfonso el sabio* (Madrid: Espasa-Calpe, 1941).

In addition to reading the famous *Song of the Cid*, tr. Rita Hamilton and Janet Perry (New York: Barnes & Noble, 1975), any researcher of Spanish medieval literature would want to explore these significant historical contributions: Juan Ruiz, *El libro de buen amor*, ed. and tr. Raymond S. Willis (Princeton: Princeton University, 1972), and Fernando de Rojas, *La Celestina*, tr. Lesley Byrd Simpson (Berkeley: University of California, 1955). For commentary on these sources, peruse the pages of Stephen Gilman, *The Spain of Fernando de Rojas: The Intellectual and Social Landscape of "La Celestina"* (Princeton: Princeton University, 1972), a masterpiece of literary and historical criticism, and María Rosa Lida de Malkiel, *Dos obras maestras españolas: "El libro de buen amor" y "La Celestina"* (Buenos Aires: Editorial Universitaria de Buenos Aires, 1971).

INDIAN CIVILIZATIONS

The extensive bibliography makes it possible to choose three categories of writings on this topic: those of the Indians themselves, those of the post-conquest Spanish compilers of the Indian past, and those of contemporary writers. Cultural classification presents another way of approaching these works, by using such categories as Toltecs, Aztecs, and Quechuas, for example. In addition, one could structure one's research by using geographical boundaries as a base, reading about Mexico or Peru. For the sake of a comprehensive overview, I have chosen to combine all of these research strategies.

The Mayas, whose civilization was based in the Yucatán, left two great books of myth, creation, and prophecy. The first, *Heaven Born Mérida and Its Destiny: The Book of Chilam Balam of Chumayel*, is available in a translation by Munro S. Edmonson (Austin: University of Texas, 1986); this bilingual edition offers the reader a chance to examine the Mayan as well as the English version. The second, *Popol Vuh: The Definitive Edition of the Mayan Book of the Dawn of Life and the Glories of Gods and Kings*, tr. Dennis Tedlock (New York: Simon and Schuster, 1986), contains the ancient stories of the Quiché people of Guatemala. A Spanish edition (tr. Albertina E. Saravia; Guatemala: Turismas, 1977) is illustrated with drawings from the Mayan codices.

The Mayas are the subject of a series of increasingly complex studies, as reflected in the following texts: Michael D. Coe, *The Maya*, rev. ed. (London:

Thames and Hudson, 1987); Sylvanus G. Morley and George W. Brainerd, *The Ancient Maya*, 4th ed. (Stanford, Calif.: Stanford University, 1983); John L. Stephens, *Incidents of Travel in Yucatán*, vols. 1 and 2 (New York: Dover, reprint of 1843 ed.); and John E. S. Thompson, *The Rise and Fall of Maya Civilization* (Norman: University of Oklahoma, 1954).

The Toltec-Aztec tradition of central Mexico is the richest in bibliographical sources, beginning with the codices or books of paintings executed by the people themselves. The *Codex Borbonicus* (Graz: Akadem, 1974) resides, in its original format, at the Bibliothèque de l'Assemblée Nationale in Paris, while the original *Codex Borgia* (Graz: Akadem, 1976) can be found at the Vatican Library. The Aztec *Codex Mendoza* (Miller Graphics, 1978) can be viewed at the Bodleian Library at Oxford University, and, finally, the *Codex Tonalamtl Aubin* (Mexico: Librería Anticuaria G.M. Echaniz, 1938) can be found at the Bibliothèque National in Paris.

A good place to begin research based on the Spanish chroniclers of Indian history is Fray Bernardino de Sahagún, *Conquest of New Spain, 1585 Revision: Reproductions of the Boston Public Library Manuscript and the Carlos María de Bustamente 1840 Edition*, ed. S. L. Cline, tr. Howard F. Cline (Salt Lake City: University of Utah, 1989), surely the most extraordinary recapitulation of the ancient Toltec-Aztec past of Mesoamerica, as told to Sahagún by Indian informants in the years following the conquest (when memories were still fresh). Another chronicle, Garcilaso de la Vega, *Comentarios reales* (San Juan: Editorial del Departamento de Instrucción Pública, 1967), written by the son of a Spanish conquistador and an Incan princess, tells the story of the Incas as well as of the conquest. It is the first history text by a mestizo.

Among the other Spanish chronicles written in the immediate post-conquest period and based on either eyewitness accounts or evoked memories, we can include Pedro Cieza de León, *El señorío los Incas* (Madrid: Historia 16, 1985); Diego de Landa, *Relación de las cosas de Yucatán*, ed. Alfred M. Tozzer (Cambridge, Mass: Peabody Museum, 1941); Bernardo de Lizana, *Historia de Yucatán* (Mexico: Museo Nacional, 1893); and Toribio de Benavente Motolina, *Historia de los indios de la Nueva España* (Madrid: Historia 16, 1985).

Finally, one should refer to the work of Miguel León-Portilla, whose writings move from the prophecy of doom found in *Chilam Balam* to the best modern works on the Toltec-Aztec world, a list that includes León-Portilla's own *Cantos y crónicas del México antiguo* (Madrid: Historia 16, 1986), which provides a very close and innovative look at the humanistic side of Aztec life. Another interesting work edited and translated by this author is *Native Mesoamerican Spirituality: Ancient Myths, Discourses, Stories, Doctrines, Hymns, Poems from the Aztec, Yucatec, Quiché-Maya, and Other Sacred Traditions* (New York: Paulist, 1980).

Several notable books splendidly handle the philosophy, art, and literature of the Toltecs and Aztecs. Beginning with Justino Fernández, *Estética del arte mexicano* (Mexico: Universidad Nacional Autónoma de México, Instituto de Investigaciones Estécticas, 1972), a short list includes Ángel M. Garibay, *Histo-*

ria de la literatura Nahuatl (Mexico: Porrua, 1953) and Laurette Sejournée, *Burning Water* (London: Thames and Hudson, 1957).

For more general histories of the Aztecs, one could consult such texts as C. A. Burland, *The Gods of Mexico* (New York: Capricorn, 1967), which is perhaps the most complete study of this particular theme, as well as Alfonso Caso, *The Aztecs: People of the Sun* (Norman: University of Oklahoma, 1958); Nigel Davies, *The Aztecs: A History* (London: Macmillan, 1973); Jacques Soustelle, *L'Univers des Aztèques* (Paris: Hermann, 1979); and George C. Vaillant, *Aztecs of Mexico* (London: Penguin, 1950).

For information on Incan history, I suggest the following texts: Louis Baudin, *A Socialist Empire: The Incas of Peru* (Princeton, N.J.: Princeton University, 1961); Hiram Bingham, *Lost City of the Incas: The Story of Macchu Picchu and Its Rulers* (New York: Athenaeum, 1963); Alden J. Mason, *The Ancient Civilizations of Peru* (London: Penguin, 1950); and Victor Von Hage, *Highways in the Sun* (New York: Duell, Sloan, 1957).

Although the best overall view of Indian civilization remains Friedrich Katz, *The Ancient American Civilizations* (London: Weidenfeld and Nicolson, 1972), informative accounts of ancient Indian art can be found in several texts. Mary Ellen Miller, *The Art of Mesoamerica from Olmec to Aztec* (London: Thames and Hudson, 1987) gives a good general account, as do Salvador Toscano, *Arte precolombino de México y de las Américas* (Mexico: UNAM, 1952) and Paul Westheim, *Prehispanic Mexican Art,* tr. Lancelot C. Sheppard (New York: Putnam, 1972).

DISCOVERY AND CONQUEST

The most notable titles describing the Spanish discoveries and conquests from the late fifteenth century to the eighteenth century begin with *The Diario of Christopher Columbus's First Voyage to America, 1492–1493,* abstracted by Fray Bartolomé de Las Casas, tr. Oliver Dunn and James E. Kelley, Jr. (Norman: University of Oklahoma, 1989) and continue with a Jesuit priest's detailed account of the nature of the Americas: Joseph de Acosta, *The Natural and Moral History of the Indies,* vols. 1 and 2, ed. Clements R. Markham (New York: B. Franklin, 1970). Another text by a Jesuit priest, who describes the nature and peoples of California in the mid-eighteenth century, is Miguel de Barco, *The Natural History of Baja California,* tr. Froylan Tiscareno (Los Angeles: Dawson's Book Shop, 1980). Eyewitness accounts of the Spanish expeditions on the Amazon are included in P. de Almesto, Gasper de Carvajal, and Alonso de Rojas, *La aventura del Amazonas* (Madrid: Historia 16, 1986) and Pedro Cieza de León, *Descubrimiento y conquista del Perú* (Buenos Aires: Jam Kana, 1984).

Bernal Díaz del Castillo, *The Conquest of a New Spain,* tr. J. M. Cohen (London: Folio Society, 1974) gives the unparalleled eyewitness account of a footsoldier on Cortés' expedition, and Ruy Díaz de Guzmán, *La Argentina,* ed. Enrique de Gandia (Madrid: Historia 16, 1986) chronicles the exploration and colonization of the River Plate, using the term *Argentina* for the first time. We also can add Alvar Núñez Cabeza de Vaca, *Cabeza de Vaca's Adventures in the*

Unknown Interior of America, tr. Cyclone Covey (Albuquerque: University of New Mexico, 1983); Francisco Palou, *The Expedition into California of the Venerable Padre Fray Junipero Serra and His Companions in the Year 1769,* tr. Thomas Temple II and Douglas S. Watson (San Francisco: Nueva California, 1934), in which Serra's disciple tells the tale of the missions; Antonio Pigafetta, *First Voyage Around the World* (Manila: Filipiniana Book Guild, 1969), which gives an account of the author's voyage with Magellan; and Jerónimo de Vivar, *Crónica de los reinos de Chile,* ed. Ángel Barral Gómez (Madrid: Historia 16, 1988), a contemporary version of the conquest of Chile by Pedro de Valdivia.

There are a few other volumes I have consulted in reference to the enterprises of conquest and discovery. The three-volume work by the great German historian Georg Friederici, *El carácter del descubrimiento y de la conquista de América* (Mexico: FCE, 1973), describes all of the discoveries and conquests made by Europeans in the Americas, including those by the Spanish, Portuguese, French, Dutch, Germans, and Russians. Antonello Gerbi, *The Dispute of the New World,* ed. and tr. Jeremy Moyle (Pittsburgh: University of Pittsburgh, 1973) furthers the bibliography with the history of a polemic, and Edmundo O'Gorman, *The Invention of America* (Bloomington: University of Indiana, 1958) brilliantly proposes the thesis that America was not discovered but "invented" by the European desire for a new world. Samuel E. Morison, *The European Discovery of America* (New York: Oxford, 1971–74) and Roland Sanders, *Lost Tribes and Promised Land* (Boston: Little, Brown, 1978), an exciting account of how racist attitudes affected the whole process of discovery and colonization, complete the list.

To learn more about the fundamental dispute as to the nature of the conquest and the rights of the Indians, readers should study Bartolomé de Las Casas, *Historia de las Indias* (Hollywood, Fla.: Ediciones del Continente, 1985) and Vasco de Quiroga, *Don Vasco de Quiroga y su "Informacion en Derecho"* (Madrid: Porrua Turanzas, 1974). Other good sources on this topic are Henry Stevens, ed., *New Laws of the Indies for the Good Treatment and Preservation of the Indians* (London: Chiswick, 1893); Francisco Suárez, *Guerra, intervención, paz internacional,* ed. Luciano Perena Vicente (Madrid: Espasa-Calpe, 1956); and Francisco de Vitoria, *Relecciones del estado, de los indios y del derecho de la guerra* (Mexico: Porrua, 1974).

The European reflection on the Americas — discovery, invention, desire, projection of Utopian dreams, warnings of political realism — are best studied through the actual texts of the times. Niccolò Machiavelli, *The Prince,* ed. Quentin Skinner and Russell Price (New York: Cambridge University, 1988); Michel de Montaigne, *Essays,* tr. John M. Cohen (New York: Penguin, 1959); Thomas More, *Utopia,* ed. George M. Logan and Robert M. Adams (New York: Cambridge University, 1989); and William Shakespeare, *The Tempest,* ed. Stephen Orgel (New York: Oxford, 1987) are all excellent editions of the original texts. Two other works to consider are Amerigo Vespucci, "Novus Mundus," in *Vespucci Reprints: Texts and Studies* (Princeton: Princeton University, 1916), the

Utopian vision of America by the man who gave us his name, and Pedro Vaz de Caminha, *A carta de Pedro Vaz de Caminha* (Porto Alegre: L & PM Editores, 1985), a letter to the discoverer of Brazil, Alvarez de Cabral, which is acknowledged as the birth certificate of that country.

Readers may want to delve into material on the general philosophy behind the conquest, found in Silvio Zavala, *Filosofía de la conquista* (Mexico: FCE, 1947). Finally, apart from the eyewitness accounts and memoirs already mentioned, the conquests are described most notably in the following texts:

Albornoz, Miguel. *Hernando de Soto.* New York: Franklin Watts, 1986.

Hanke, Lewis. *The Spanish Struggle for Justice in the Conquest of America.* Boston: Little, Brown, 1965.

Hemming, John. *The Conquest of the Incas.* London: Penguin,1983.

Kirkpatrick, F. A. *The Spanish Conquistadores.* London: Cresset, 1988.

Larreta, Enrique. *Las dos fundaciones de Buenos Aires.* Buenos Aires: Sopena, 1965.

Martínez, José Luis. *Hernán Cortés.* Mexico: FCE, 1990.

Prescott, W. H. *History of the Conquest of Mexico and History of the Conquest of Peru.* New York: Random House, 1979.

THE SPANISH EMPIRE

For the Hapsburg years (1492–1700), the great historian remains John H. Elliot. His work on imperial Spain is an insurpassable rendering of the life and death of the Hapsburg dynasty. Other, more incidental yet essential references to this period are to be found in Paul M. Kennedy, *The Rise and Fall of Great Powers: Economic Change and Military Conflict from 1500 to 2000* (New York: Random House, 1987) and Oswald Spengler, *The Decline of the West,* abridged, ed. Helmut Werner (New York: Modern Library, 1967). Other excellent studies are:

Bertrand, Louis. *Philippe II à l'Escorial.* Paris: L'Artisan du Livre, 1929.

Braudel, Fernand. *The Mediterranean and the Mediterranean World in the Age of Philip II.* Tr. Sian Reynolds. New York: Harper & Row, 1972–73.

Grierson, Edward. *King of Two Worlds: Philip II of Spain.* New York: Putnam, 1974.

Lynch, John. *Spain Under the Hapsburgs.* Oxford: Blackwell, 1981.

Parker, Geoffrey. *Philip II.* Boston: Little, Brown, 1978.

Siguenza, Fray José de. *La fundación del monasterio de El Escorial.* Madrid: Turner, 1988.

The economic events influenced by both the Spanish ascendency and relations between Europe and the New World are described in Rondo E. Cameron, *A Concise Economic History of the World: From Paleolithic Times to the Present* (New York: Oxford, 1989) and John M. Keynes, *A Treatise on Money* (London: Macmillan, 1930). The bibliography must also include a study of one of the great events of Philip II's reign: Garrett Mattingly, *The Defeat of the Spanish Armada* (Boston: Houghton Mifflin, 1959).

For those interested in the Counter-Reformation, a valuable source is A. G. Dickens, *The Counter-Reformation* (New York: Harcourt, Brace & World, 1969). There is no better study of the Spanish Inquisition than Henry Kamen, *Inquisition and Society in Spain in the Sixteenth and Seventeeth Centuries* (London: Weidenfeld and Nicolson, 1985). The revolt of the Castilian communities is brilliantly described by José Antonio Maravall in *Las comunidades de Castilla* (Madrid: Revista de Occidente, 1963).

THE CENTURY OF GOLD

Spanish achievements in literature and the arts must include, first of all, the classic works by Calderón de la Barca, Cervantes, Lope de Vega, Góngora, Tirso de Molina, Quevedo, San Juan de la Cruz, Saint Teresa of Avila, and Juan Luis Vives. In addition, I would like to mention a number of studies that examine these figures and their works. In art, refer to Jonathan Brown, *Velázquez, Painter and Courtier* (New Haven: Yale, 1986). Michel Foucault's *The Order of Things: An Archaeology of the Human Sciences* (London: Tavistock, 1970) contains bold and imaginative interpretations of *Don Quixote* and of Velázquez' *Las Meninas*. One of Spain's most innovative contemporary novelists, Juan Goytisolo, views the figures of La Celestina, Cervantes, Don Juan, and Quevedo in an equally creative light, as our contemporaries; see his *L'Arbre de la littérature* (Paris: Fayard, 1990). Goytisolo's novel *Las virtudes del pájaro solitario* (Barcelona: Seix Barral, 1988) is a brilliant three-tiered projection of San Juan de la Cruz' poems into the Arabic past and our present-day sexuality. Gregorio Marañón, *Don Juan* (Madrid: Espasa-Calpe, 1940) is another useful source.

The legacy of Cervantes can be seen all the way from Laurence Sterne's *Tristram Shandy* and Denis Diderot's *Jack the Fatalist and His Master* to those nineteenth-century heroines who, like Don Quixote, read books and go slightly mad: Catherine Moreland in Jane Austen's *Northanger Abbey* and Emma Bovary in Gustave Flaubert's *Madame Bovary*, for example. The most amusing (and telling) modern spin-off, however, is a short story by Jorge Luis Borges, "Pierre Menard, Author of Don Quixote," in *Ficciones* (New York: Limited Editions Club, 1984). Studies of *Don Quixote* that stress its modernity include works by Fyodor Dostoyevsky, Thomas Mann, José Ortega y Gasset, and Viktor Shlovsky as well as Mikhail Bakhtin, *Rabelais and His World* (Cambridge: MIT, 1968); Milan Kundera, *The Art of the Novel* (New York: Grove, 1988); and Marthe Robert, *Sur le papier* (Paris: Grasset, 1967).

Bartolomé Bennassar, *Un siècle d'or espagnol* (Paris: R. Laffont, 1982); M. Defourneaux, *Daily Life in Spain in the Golden Age*, tr. Newton Branch (Stanford, Calif.: Stanford University, 1971); and Antonio Dominguez Ortiz, *The Golden Age of Spain*, tr. James Casey (London: Weidenfeld and Nicolson, 1971) are three good general sources of information.

A number of sources provide valuable information on Erasmus and his influence in Spain. In contrast to the monumental work on the subject by Marcel Bataillon, José Luis Abellán's *El erasmismo español* (Madrid: Espasa-Calpe, 1976) offers an intimate, Spanish look at this subject. For a broader perspective, John P. Dolan, ed., *The Essential Erasmus* (New York: Mentor, 1964); H. Huizonga, *Erasmus and the Age of the Reformation* (New York: Harper, 1957); and Erika Rummel, ed., *The Erasmus Reader* (Toronto: University of Toronto, 1990) are all significant references. For a look at the works of the two Spanish Erasmians closest to Charles V, see Alfonso de Valdés, *Diálogo de Mercurio y Carón* (Madrid: Espasa-Calpe, 1954) and Juan de Valdés, *Diálogo de la doctrina cristiana* (Mexico: UNAM, 1964).

THE COLONIAL PERIOD

Because of their sweep and their generous embrace of Spain's role in the New World and of the development of Latin America from the colonial experience, two books deserve special attention. The title of the first, David A. Brading, *The First America: The Spanish Monarchy, Creole Patriots and the Liberal State, 1492–1867* (Cambridge, England: Cambridge University, 1991), indicates the broadness of the author's approach; it does not, however, reveal his extreme attention to detail or the interrelationship of ideas in this masterwork from Britain's prime scholar of Mexico. The second book is perhaps the clearest contemporary study of the debate on the legitimacy of conquest; Anthony Pagden, *Spanish Imperialism and the Political Imagination* (New Haven: Yale, 1990) views Spanish America's destiny in terms of the paradox of the Spanish empire's move from universal monarchy to reactionary backwater.

A classic study by Stanley J. and Barbara H. Stein, *The Colonial Heritage of Latin America: Essays on Economic Dependence in Perspective* (New York: Oxford, 1970), describes both the origins and the persistence of colonialism in Latin American life. Information about the organization of land and labor and the emergence of national traits in colonial times can be found in the following:

Chevalier, François. *Land and Society in Colonial Mexico.* Ann Arbor: University of Michigan, 1959.

Gibson, Charles. *Spain in America.* New York: Harper Torchbooks, 1967.

Israel, Jonathan I. *Race, Class, and Politics in Colonial Mexico, 1610–1670.* London: Oxford, 1975.

Liss, Peggy K. *Mexico Under Spain: Society and the Origins of Nationality, 1521–1556.* Chicago: University of Chicago, 1975.

Lockhart, James, and Stuart B. Schwarz. *Early Latin America: A History of Colonial Spanish America and Brazil.* New York: Cambridge University, 1983.

Zavala, Silvio. *La encomienda indiana.* Mexico: Porrua, 1973.

———. *New Viewpoints on the Spanish Colonization of America.* Philadelphia: University of Pennsylvania, 1943.

The black presence is studied in the following works: José Luciano Franco, *La diáspora africana en el Nuevo Mundo* (Havana: Editorial de Ciencias Sociales,

1986); Esteban Montejo, *Biografía de un cimarrón*, ed. Miguel Barnet (Havana: Editorial de Ciencias Sociales, 1986); and Leslie B. Rout, *The African Experience in Spanish America, 1502 to the Present Day* (New York: Cambridge University, 1976).

The prompt creation of a new Hispanic culture in the New World is celebrated by the very men and women who fashioned it. Juana de la Cruz, *A Sor Juana Anthology*, tr. Alan S. Trueblood (Cambridge, Mass.: Harvard University, 1988) is an anthology of works by one of the greatest poets of colonial Spanish America; Alonso de Ercilla, *La araucana* (Santiago de Chile: Editorial Orbe, 1974) is an idealized, epic poem of the Spanish war (in which the author participated) against the Araucanian Indians in Chile. A splendid biography by one of Mexico's most important poets, Octavio Paz's *Sor Juana Inés de la Cruz, or The Traps of Faith*, tr. Margaret Sayers Peden (Cambridge, Mass.: Belknap, 1988) reveals the dimensions of colonial life in New Spain. The complete works of Peru's pre-eminent colonial poet, Juan del Valle y Caviedes — *Obra completa*, ed. Daniel R. Reedy (Caracas: Biblioteca Ayacucho, 1984) — add an excellent satirical source to the list.

Satire leads us to writings that expound on the darker, inquisitorial side of colonial society. Fernando Benitez, *Los demonios en el convento: sexo y religión en la Nueva España* (Mexico: Ediciones Era, 1985), a witty exploration of sexual and intellectual prejudices in colonial Mexico, and Luis Caravajal El Mozo, *The Enlightened*, ed. Seymour Liebman (Miami: Windward, 1967), the memoirs, letters, and testament of a Spanish Jew burned at the stake in Mexico, are just a sampling of works that fall under this heading. Two significant additions are Richard E. Greenleaf, *The Mexican Inquisition in the Sixteenth Century* (Albuquerque: University of New Mexico, 1969) and possibly the most remarkable book of this period, Felipe Guamán Poma de Ayala, *Nueva crónica y buen gobierno*, ed. John V. Murra, Rolena Adorno, and Jorge L. Urioste (Madrid: Historia 16, 1987), a Peruvian Indian's writings and drawings of colonial life sixty years after the conquest.

Several books specifically evoke the quality of life. Both Arzans de Orsua y Vela, *Tales of Potosí*, ed. R. C. Padden (Providence, R.I.: Brown University, 1975) and Irving Leonard, *Baroque Times in Old Mexico* (Ann Arbor: University of Michigan, 1959) are good references. For a broader historical perspective, read José Luis Romero, *Latinoamérica: las ciudades y las ideas* (Mexico: Siglo Veintiuno Editores, 1976), which traces the development of city life in Latin America from the colonial foundations to the twentieth century. One source in particular, David Sweet and Gary B. Nash, *Struggle and Survival in Colonial America* (Berkeley: University of California, 1981), chronicles the extreme difficulty of life in the colonies.

As suggested by Leonard's *Baroque Times*, the art created in this period falls under the designation "baroque" and is shared by Spain and Spanish America. Guillermo Díaz Plaja, *El espíritu del barroco* (Barcelona: Ediciones Críticas, 1983) and P. Kleemen, *Baroque and Rococo in Latin America* (New York: Macmillan, 1951), along with works by Gerard de Cortanze, Juan de Cortreras, and Manuel Toussaint, cover this period nicely.

THE SPANISH ENLIGHTENMENT

Information on the decline of the Hapsburgs and the Bourbon renewal can be found in Antonio Domínguez Ortiz, *Instituciones y sociedad en la España de los Austrias* (Barcelona: Ariel, 1985) and John Langdon Davies, *Carlos, The King Who Would Not Die* (London: Jonathan Cape, 1962). More general information can be found in a number of sources. Two works by Gaspar Melchor de Jovellanos, *Diarios*, ed. Julián Marías (Madrid: Alianza Editorial, 1967) and *Obras completas: edición crítica* (Oviedo: Centro de Estudios del siglo XVIII), are complemented by two good biographies: Fernández Álvarez, *Jovellanos: un hombre de nuestro tiempo* (Madrid: Espasa-Calpe, 1988) and Jávier Varela, *Jovellanos* (Madrid: Alianza Universidad, 1988). Further information on the Spanish Enlightenment can be found in Richard Herr, *The Eighteenth-Century Revolution in Spain* (Princeton: Princeton University, 1958), which is the best book in English on the subject, and Julián Marías, *La España posible en tiempos de Carlos III* (Madrid: Planeta, 1988), in which a distinguished contemporary philosopher describes the polemics surrounding Spain's bid for modernity and European linkage.

Readers could also study this age through works about Goya. One that focuses on Spain is Fernando Díaz-Plaja, *Las Españas de Goya* (Barcelona: Planeta, 1989). Another recent study that relates directly to the Spanish Enlightenment is Alfonso E. Pérez Sánchez and Eleanor A. Sayre, *Goya and the Spirit of Enlightenment* (Boston: Little, Brown, 1989). For a study of this major artist's life and work, see Pierre Gassier and Juliet Wilson, *The Life and Complete Work of Francisco Goya*, ed. François Lachenal (New York: Reynal/Morrow, 1971).

THE LATE COLONIAL PERIOD

A good place to begin a study of this period is with an indispensable travel book abounding in delightfully detailed descriptions of South American life on the eve of independence: Alfonso Carto de la Vandera Concolocorvo, *A Guide for Inexperienced Travelers between Buenos Aires and Lima* (Bloomington: Indiana University, 1965). Other good sources to consider are José Carlos Chiaramonte, *La ilustración en el Río de la Plata* (Buenos Aires: Punto Sur, 1989) and Alexander Von Humboldt, *Political Essay on the Kingdom of New Spain*, tr. John Black (New York: AMS, reprint of 1811 ed.); the latter is a vastly influential scientific study of the wealth of Mexico as the colony ended.

Another informative reference is Peggy K. Liss, *Atlantic Empires: The Network of Trade and Revolution 1713–1826* (Baltimore: Johns Hopkins, 1983). A splendid study of the relationships among trade, politics, and culture on both sides of the Atlantic — and in both Americas, North and South — this sober look at the commercial facts explains the underpinnings of the sometimes rampant ideological stances of the wars of independence. Two other good sources are Giovanni Marchetti, *Cultura indígena e integración nacional: la "Historia Antigua de México" de F. J. Clavijero* (Jalapa: Universidad Veracruzana, 1986) and Magnus Morner, *The Expulsion of the Jesuits from Latin America* (New York: Knopf, 1965). Arthur P. Whitaker, ed., *Latin America and the Enlightenment* (Ithaca, N.Y.: Cornell University, 1958) completes the list.

LATIN AMERICAN INDEPENDENCE

The tendency to view the revolutions of independence through their powerful personalities is both romantic and understandable. Before offering such a personalized reading list, I must highlight the excellence of one book that brings together the personalities, the great themes, and the social currents of the Latin American fight for independence: John Lynch, *The Spanish American Revolutions, 1808–1826* (New York: Norton, 1973). Other texts to consider include the following:

Bolívar, Simón. *Doctrina del Libertador.* Caracas: Ayacucho, 1976. A very complete and well-selected anthology.

Columbres, Manuel Eduardo. *San Martín y Bolívar.* Buenos Aires: Plus Ultra, 1979.

Descola, Jean. *Les libertadors.* Paris: Fayard, 1957.

Lievano Aguirre, Indalecio. *Bolívar.* Buenos Aires: Plus Ultra, 1979.

Medrano, Samuel W. *El libertador José de San Martín.* Madrid: Espasa-Calpe, 1950.

Páez, José Antonio. *Autobiografía del General José Antonio Páez.* Caracas, 1973.

Puiggros, Rodolfo. *De la colonia a la revolución.* Buenos Aires: Ediciones Cepe, 1974.

Real de Azúa, Carlos. *El patriciado uruguayo.* Montevideo: Ediciones de la Banda Oriental, 1981.

The best fictional renderings of this period begin with Alejo Carpentier, *Explosion in a Cathedral* (New York: Farrar, Straus & Giroux, 1989), a novel in which the French Revolution arrives in the Caribbean with two symbols, the decree freeing the slaves and the guillotine. Two other works to consider are Arturo Uslar Pietri, *Las lanzas coloradas y cuentos selectos* (Caracas: Biblioteca Ayacucho, 1979) and Gabriel García Márquez, *The General in His Labyrinth* (New York: Knopf, 1990).

NINETEENTH-CENTURY SPANISH AMERICA

The reference list for this topic is quite extensive, and divides into two broad categories, history and culture.

HISTORY

For a general view of various subjects, consider the following books:

Burgin, Miron. *The Economic Aspects of Argentine Federalism, 1820–1852*. Cambridge, Mass.: Harvard University, 1946.

Burr, Robert N. *By Reason or Force: Chile and the Balancing of Power in South America, 1830–1855*. Berkeley: University of California, 1965.

Calderón de la Barca, Pedro, and E. Frances. *Life in Mexico During a Residence of Two Years in That Country*. New York: AMS, reprint of 1913 ed.

Corti, Egon Cesar. *Maximilian and Charlotte of Mexico*. New York: Knopf, 1928.

Donoso, Ricardo. *Las ideas políticas en Chile*. Buenos Aires: Editorial Universitaria de Buenos Aires, 1975.

Estrada, José Manuel. *Lecciones sobre la república argentina*. Buenos Aires: Librería de Colegio, 1898.

Fuentes Mares, José. *Miramón, el hombre*. Mexico: Joaquín Mortiz, 1974.

Hanighen, Frank C. *Santa Anna: The Napoleon of the West*. New York: Coward McCann, 1934.

Haslip, Joan. *The Crown of Mexico*. New York: Holt, Rinehart & Winston, 1971.

Muñoz, Rafael F. *Santa Anna*. Mexico: Botas, 1945.

Quesada, Ernesto. *La época de Rosas*. Buenos Aires: Instituto de Investigaciones Históricas, 1923.

Roeder, Ralph. *Juárez and His Mexico: A Bibliographical History*. New York: Viking, 1947.

In addition, two extraordinary Mexican works of historiography, Daniel Cosío Villegas, et al., *Historia moderna de México: la república restaurada* (Mexico: El Colegio de México, 1958) and Jesús Reyes Heroles, *El liberalismo mexicano* (Mexico: Fondo de Cultura Económica, 1982), cover this period.

Independence spurred Spanish American historians to take a new look at the past. Vast opuses in several volumes by authors such as Diego Barros Arana, Bartolomé Mitre, and Benjamin Vicuna Mackenna testify to the historical hunger of the period. Perhaps three Mexican historians best personify the very different viewpoints behind this new mentality. Lucas Alamán, *Historia de México desde los primeros movimientos que prepararon su independencia en el año de 1808, hasta la época presente* (Mexico: Instituto Cultural Helénico, 1985) presents the conservative view, praising the conquest and the link with Spain and condemning the United States as a Protestant expansionist power. Lorenzo de Zavala, *Ensayo histórico de las revoluciones de México desde 1808 hasta 1830* (Mexico: SRA, CEHAM, 1981) espouses the liberal view, in favor of progress as identified with the USA. The middle ground is held by José María Mora, *México y sus revoluciones* (Mexico: Instituto Cultural Helénico, 1986), who believes in the *juste milieu*, which translates into an insistence on knowing the facts before acting or speaking, amassing knowledge, and then attempting to be all-inclusive in the process of building nations.

CULTURE

Original histories, such as Mariano Picón Salas, *A Cultural History of Spanish America* (Berkeley: University of California, 1960) and texts by Germán Arcinie-gas and Pedro Henríquez Ureña, are extremely useful for investigating Latin American cultural life. However, the two masterpieces of Spanish American literature in the nineteenth century are a poem and an essay, both from Argentina: José Hernández, *The Gaucho Martín Fierro,* tr. Frank G. Carrino, Alberto J. Carlos, and Norman Mangouni (Delmar: Scholar's Facsimiles and Reprints, 1974) and Domingo F. Sarmiento, *Life in the Argentine Republic in the Days of the Tyrants* (New York: Gordon, 1968). Around these, a cluster of brilliant interpretations form a solid bibliographical resource. Sarmiento's classic is at the center not only of the blossoming of historical studies but of the beginnings of the tradition of national and cultural self-analysis, as expressed in essays and in fiction about the tyrant, whether national or local.

Starting with the works of Andrés Bello, the great Venezuelan humanist who gave Spanish America a solid cultural basis in the early years of independence, we have a number of texts worth examining. Eugenio María de Hostos, *Obras* (Havana: Casa de las Américas, 1976) presents a good choice; its author, a novelist, sociologist, and jurist, was the founder of Puerto Rico's modern allegiance to Hispanic culture. Juan de Montalvo, *Siete tratados: réplica a un sofista seudocatólico* (Madrid: Editorial Nacional, 1977) are essays in the vein of Montaigne, written in a supple, inclusive, American Spanish by Ecuador's foremost nineteenth-century writer. The Peruvian Manuel González Prada, in *Páginas libres/horas de lucha* (Caracas: Ayacucho, 1976), is combative, critical of his country's ills, even radical; he sets the stage for the uncompromising interpretations of Latin American culture of our own time. At the other extreme, José Enrique Rodó celebrates Latin American spirituality by contrasting it with the gross materialism of the United States; this contrast explains the wild success of his book, *Ariel,* tr. Margaret Sayers Peden (Austin: University of Texas, 1988), a rather overblown rhetorical exercise that manages to convey some real insights into the future of urban life in both Americas.

Few truly excellent novels were written in nineteenth-century Spanish America; the overwhelming subjects of political anarchy and dictatorship have received good fictional treatment only in our own time, when the figure of the tyrant has finally been transformed into literature. Among the authors and works I would like to note are Miguel Ángel Asturias, *The President,* tr. Francis Partridge (London: Gollancz, 1967), the first work by a Latin American to present the figure of the president-dictator (in this case based on the Guatemalan tyrant Estrada Cabrera), and the witty Alejo Carpentier, *Reasons of State,* tr. Frances Partridge (New York: Knopf, 1976), based on the Venezuelan despot Guzmán Blanco. This theme reaches its culmination in Gabriel García Márquez' *The*

Autumn of the Patriarch, tr. Gregory Rabassa (New York: Harper & Row, 1975), a work in which the author brings together traits of all dictators, old and new, from Melgarejo in Bolivia and Gómez in Venezuela to Trujillo in the Dominican Republic and Salazar and Franco in Iberia. Two other novels complete the list: Augusto Roa Bastos, *I, the Supreme* (New York: Knopf, 1986), a dazzling re-creation of the Paraguayan dictator Rodríguez de Francia, and Ramón del Valle Inclán, *Tirano banderas* (Madrid: Espasa-Calpe, 1978), the grandparent of the dictator novels.

The poem of *Martín Fierro* raises the whole question of nativist or rather popular culture and its continuity, in contrast to the spurts of "extralogical imitation" of all things European; see Jorge Luis Borges, *El Martín Fierro* (Madrid: Alianza, 1983). Our most lucid writers see the two extremes as mutually defeating and find a creative synthesis of our dual culture, American and European. The excellent Californian historian Bradford Burns, in *The Poverty of Progress: Latin America in the Nineteenth Century* (Berkeley: University of California, 1980), expertly analyzes cultural trends, noting the conflict between the Western model of a cult of progress and the alternative, native models of Latin America. Another book, Rubén Darío's *Páginas escogidas*, ed. Ricardo Gullón (Madrid: Catedra, 1982), is a selection of work by the great Nicaraguan poet, whose art is both Latin American and European. In his own *Páginas escogidas* (Havana: Editorial de Ciencias Sociales, 1974), the Cuban patriot and intellectual José Martí proposed a generous and democratic solution for Latin America: highlight needs, traditions, and resources; emphasize people; include everyone.

The Mexican artist José Guadalupe Posada took popular art into the universal realms of dreams and death; see *Posada, Messenger of Mortality*, ed. Julian Rothenstein (London: Redstone, 1989). Horacio Salas, *El tango* (Buenos Aires: Planeta, 1986) is another book on popular culture that is well worth considering.

Finally, an extraordinary book by Claudio Véliz, *The Centralist Tradition of Latin America* (Princeton, N.J.: Princeton University, 1980), offers the best analysis of nineteenth-century ideology and politics, though it covers Latin America since the conquest, reinforcing what the author considers to be an almost unshakeable centralist tradition.

THE MEXICAN REVOLUTION

The best work on the social components and class aims of the revolution is John Mason Hart, *Revolutionary Mexico: The Coming and Process of the Mexican Revolution* (Berkeley: University of California, 1987); it also offers the most penetrating discussion of relations between the United States and the revolutionary governments. Another work that explores the international dynamics is Friedrich Katz, *The Secret War in Mexico: Europe, the United States, and the Mexican Revolution*, tr. Loren Goldner (Chicago: University of Chicago, 1981). Andrés Molina Enríquez, *Los grandes problemas nacionales* (Mexico: Ediciones Era, 1977), an extremely influential book, describes problems and demands solutions.

Studies that focus on Porfirio Díaz include Francisco Bulnes, *El verdadero*

Díaz y la revolución (Mexico: Ediciones COMA, 1982) and Daniel Cosio Villegas, *Historia moderna de México* (Mexico: Editorial Hermes, 1955), an objective treatment. The classic study of the Díaz regime's ideological foundation is Leopoldo Zea, *Positivism in Mexico*, tr. Josephine H. Schulte (Austin: University of Texas, 1974). Other works include Hector Aguilar Camín, *La frontera nómada: Sonora y la revolución mexicana* (Mexico: Siglo XX Editores, 1977) and John Kenneth Turner, *Barbarous Mexico* (Austin: University of Texas, 1959). The masterpiece on Zapatismo is John Womack's *Zapata and the Mexican Revolution* (New York: Knopf, 1969). Jean Meyer, *La Christiade* (Paris: Payot, 1975) is another classic, dealing with the long-ignored subject of the Catholic rebellion against the revolution. Finally, Anita Brenner, *The Wind that Swept Mexico* (Austin: University of Texas, 1971) strikingly brings together text and photographs of the revolution.

There are numerous personal memoirs by participants in the revolution, as well as a genre unto itself: the novel of the Mexican Revolution. One of the most famous of the latter is Mariano Azuela, *Underdogs* (New York: New American Library, 1963). Later works, such as Juan Rulfo, *Pedro Páramo: A Novel of Mexico* (New York: Grove Weidenfeld, 1990), give detailed impressions of the society and the mindset before the revolution. Suspended somewhere between fiction and reality are the fascinating memoirs of the philosopher and educator José Vasconcelos, *A Mexican Ulysses: An Autobiography*, tr. W. Rex Crawford (New York: Greenwood, 1963). Ultimately, the most visible cultural products of the revolution, mural paintings, are well documented in various books and catalogues.

THE TWENTIETH CENTURY

Spain's 1898 war with the United States and the subsequent loss of empire provoked a deep and healthy reaction. The country decided to take a hard look at itself. This movement was announced by Angel Ganivet in *Idearium español* (Madrid: Espasa-Calpe, 1941) and was continued by the philosophers José Ortega y Gasset and Miguel de Unamuno, the poet Antonio Machado, the playwright Ramón de Valle Inclán, and the novelist Pío Baroja.

The work of the so-called generation of 1927, the generation of the famous poet and playwright Federico García Lorca, was dramatically interrupted by the Spanish Civil War. The war and the events preceding it are described in Gabriel Jackson's *The Spanish Civil War* (Chicago: Quadrangle, 1972) and Hugh Thomas's *The Spanish Civil War* (New York: Harper, 1961). The greatest overall view of twentieth-century Spanish history is Raymond Carr's *Modern Spain* (New York: Oxford, 1980).

Perhaps the most beautiful vision of Spain written by a foreigner is Gerald Brenan's *The Spanish Labyrinth: An Account of the Social and Political Background of the Civil War* (New York: Macmillan, 1943). The war also generated a crop of novels and essays by foreign authors, such as André Malraux, *Days of Hope*, tr. Stuart Gilbert and Alastair MacDonald (London: Routledge & Sons, 1938); George Orwell, *Homage to Catalonia* (London: Secker & Warburg, 1986); and

Ernest Hemingway, *For Whom the Bell Tolls* (New York: Scribner's, 1940). Another author to note is Ian Gibson, whose *Federico García Lorca: A Life* (New York: Pantheon, 1989) is the definitive biography.

For a first-rate history of contemporary Latin America, see Tulio Halperin Donghi, *Histoire contemporaine de l'Amerique Latine*, tr. Anny Amberni (Paris: Payot, 1972). For more specific information on economic and social conditions, discussed from the perspective of the dependency theory, see the classic accounts of Celso Furtado, *Economic Development of Latin America: A Survey from Colonial Times to the Cuban Revolution*, tr. Suzette Macedo (Cambridge, England: Cambridge University, 1970), and Fernando Cardoso and Enzo Faletto, *Dependency and Development in Latin America*, tr. Marjory Mattingly Urguidi (Berkeley: University of California, 1979).

Some of the more interesting books in English on particular Latin American nations are James R. Scobie, *Argentina: A City and a Nation* (New York: Oxford, 1971); Hugh Thomas, *Cuba, or the Pursuit of Freedom* (London: Eyre, 1971); John V. Lombardi, *Venezuela: The Search for Order, the Dream of Progress* (New York: Oxford, 1982); and Brian Loveman, *Chile: The Legacy of Hispanic Capitalism* (New York: Oxford, 1988). Numerous sources on Mexico are available, including Howard F. Cline, *Mexico, Revolution to Evolution, 1940–1960* (New York: Oxford, 1962); Pablo González Casanova, *Democracy in Mexico*, tr. Danielle Salti (New York: Oxford, 1970); Frank Brandenburg, *The Making of Modern Mexico* (Englewood Cliffs, N.J.: Prentice Hall, 1964); and Charles C. Cumberland, *Mexico: The Struggle for Modernity* (London: Oxford, 1968).

On Latin American relations with the United States, I recommend T. O. Allman, *Unmanifest Destiny* (New York: Dial, 1984) and Abraham Lowenthal, *Partners in Conflict* (Baltimore: Johns Hopkins University, 1987). Particularly difficult relationships have been dealt with in greatest depth by Richard Fagen, *Forging Peace: The Challenge of Central America* (Oxford: Blackwell, 1987); Stephen Kinzer and Stephen Schlesinger, *Bitter Fruit: The Untold Story of the American Coup in Guatemala* (New York: Doubleday, 1982); Raymond Bonner, *Weakness and Deceit: U.S. Policy and El Salvador* (New York: Times, 1984); Peter Davis, *Where Is Nicaragua?* (New York: Simon & Schuster, 1987); Robert Pastor and Jorge G. Castañeda, *Limits to Friendship: The United States and Mexico* (New York: Knopf, 1988); and Wayne Smith's account of Cuba-U.S. relations, *The Closest of Enemies* (New York: Norton, 1987). Two outstanding biographies of Latin American leaders by North American writers are Tad Szulc, *Fidel: A Critical Portrait* (New York: Morrow, 1986) and Joseph Page, *Perón* (New York: Random House, 1983).

For information about Hispanic life in the United States, see Edna Acosta-Belen and Barbara Sjorstrom, eds., *The Hispanic Experience in the United States* (New York: Praeger, 1988) and Juan Gomez-Quinones, *Chicano Politics: Reality and Promise 1940–1990* (Albuquerque: University of New Mexico, 1990). The writings of Jorge Bustamente and Wayne Cornelius are essential to an understanding of border and migratory problems.

Twentieth-century events underscore the continued need for further discussions of Latin American identity and self-interpretation. Some exceptionally brilliant essays are José Lezama Lima, *La expresión americana* (Santiago de Chile: Editorial Universitaria, 1969); José Carlos Mariátegui, *Seven Interpretive Essays on Peruvian Reality*, tr. Marjory Urguidi (Austin: University of Texas, 1971); Ezequiel Martinez Estrada, *X-Ray of the Pampa*, tr. Alain Sweitlicki (Austin: University of Texas, 1971); Alfonso Reyes, *Posición de América* (Mexico: Editorial Nueva Imagen, 1982); and Octavio Paz, *The Labyrinth of Solitude*, tr. Lysander Kemp, Yara Milos, and Rachael Philips Belash (New York: Grove, 1985).

The twentieth century has also seen Latin Americans enter the stage of world literature. The works of the poets Pablo Neruda and César Vallejo and of the fiction writers Isabel Allende, Jorge Luis Borges, Alejo Carpentier, Julio Cortázar, José Donoso, Gabriel García Márquez, J. C. Onetti, and Mario Vargas Llosa are a good place to begin.

Illustration Credits

cional de Antropología, Mexico City; page 105 (top), Index; page 105 (bottom), Jake Rajs/Image Bank; page 106, Inge Morath/Magnum; page 112, American Library.

CHAPTER SIX: page 118, The Royal Library, Copenhagen (GKS 2232, 4); pages 122 (top), 142 (bottom), Tony Morrison/South American Pictures; page 122 (bottom), Steve Vidler/Leo De Wys; page 123, Cornell Capa/Magnum; page 131, photo by Christopher Ralling; pages 132, 133, Giraudon/Art Resource; page 135, courtesy of the Trustees of Dartmouth College, Hanover, N.H.; page 142 (top), courtesy of the Hispanic Society of America, New York; page 145, INAH, Museo Nacional de Historia, Castillo de Chapultepec, Mexico City; page 147, American Library.

PART III, pages 148–49: Prado, Madrid

CHAPTER SEVEN: pages 150, 160, 161 (bottom), The Granger Collection; page 152, Prado, Madrid; page 161 (top), by kind permission of the Marquess of Tavistock and the Trustees of the Bedford Estates; page 163, Biblioteca Medicea-Laurenziana, Florence. Photo by permission of Alfa Fotostudio; page 165, Scala/Art Resource NY.

CHAPTER EIGHT: pages 170, 177, by permission of Malone Gill; page 173, Scala/Art Resource NY; page 174, by permission of Annette Gordon; pages 180, 181, 184, 185, Prado, Madrid; page 186, photo by Zoe Dominic.

CHAPTER NINE: page 194, Victor Siladi/Bolivian Photo Agency; page 197, The Granger Collection; page 202, South American Pictures; page 204, INAH, Museo Nacional de Historia, Castillo de Chapultepec, Mexico City; page 206, by permission of the British Library; page 208, Arxiu Mas.

CHAPTER TEN: page 214, Arxiu Mas; page 219, Index; pages 222, 226, 227, Prado, Madrid; page 223, American Library; page 225, Marc Romanelli/Image Bank; page 228 left, courtesy, Museum of Fine Arts, Boston; page 228 right, bequest of W. G. Russell Allen. Courtesy, Museum of Fine Arts, Boston; page 229, gift of Mr. and Mrs. Burton S. Stern, Mr. and Mrs. Bernard Shapiro and the M. and M. Karolik Fund. Courtesy, Museum of Fine Arts, Boston; page 230, gift of Mrs. Russell W. Baker and bequest of William P. Babcock. Courtesy, Museum of Fine Arts, Boston; page 231, Prado, Madrid.

CHAPTER ELEVEN: page 232, The Granger Collection; page 243, Index.

PART IV, pages 246–47: INBA, Museo Mural, Mexico City. Photo by Bob Schalkwijk.

CHAPTER TWELVE: page 248, by permission of Malone Gill; page 250, Military Museum, Caracas. Photo by Christopher Ralling; page 254, The Bettman Archives.

CHAPTER THIRTEEN: pages 260, 269, Culver Pictures; page 265, Columbus Memorial Library; page 271, photo by Christopher Ralling; pages 272, 273, The Bettmann Archive; page 275, UPI/Bettmann.

CHAPTER FOURTEEN: pages 276, 292–93, INBA, Museo Mural. Photo by Bob Schalkwijk; page 280, Robert Frerck/Woodfin Camp; page 281, Gerhard Gscheidle/Image Bank; page 284, INBA, Museo Nacional de Arte. Photo by Bob Schalkwijk; page 288, photo by Christopher Ralling; page 289, Albert Facelly/SIPA; page 293 (bottom), F. Paolini/Sygma; pages 294, 295, 297, The Granger Collection; page 296, William McCallin McKee Fund, The Art Institute of Chicago.

CHAPTER FIFTEEN: pages 298, 303, The Granger Collection; page 305, Culver Pictures; page 309, William McCallin McKee Fund, The Art Institute of Chicago.

PART V, pages 310–11: Courtesy of Jan Turner Gallery

CHAPTER SIXTEEN: pages 312, INBA, National Palace of Mexico, Mexico City. Photo by Bob Schalkwijk; page 314 (top), Pomona College, Claremont, Calif.; page 314 (bottom), courtesy of the Trustees of Dartmouth College, Hanover, N.H.; page 315, photo by Manuel Alvarez Bravo; page 321, UPI/Bettmann; page 324 (top), INBA, National Palace of Mexico, Mexico City; page 324 (bottom), INBA, Museum at the Palace of Bellas Artes, Mexico City. Photo by Cecilia Fuentes.

CHAPTER SEVENTEEN: page 330, Arxiu Mas; page 333, Culver Pictures; page 336 (top), The Museum of Modern Art, New York. © 1992. Demart Pro Arte/ ARS NY; page 336 (bottom), The Museum of Modern Art, Film Stills Archive, New York; page 338, The Granger Collection.

CHAPTER EIGHTEEN: page 340, INBA, Museo de Arte Moderno, Mexico City. Photo by Bob Schalkwijk; page 345 (top), courtesy of Jan Turner Gallery; page 345 (bottom), courtesy of Robert Berman Gallery. Photo by Douglas M. Parker; pages 348, 349, courtesy of the Trustees of Dartmouth College, Hanover, N.H.; page 350 (top), collection, The Museum of Modern Art, New York; page 350 (bottom), private collection. Photo by Bob Schalwijk; page 351, The Museum of Modern Art, New York; page 352 (top), courtesy of Aberbach Fine Art; page 352 (bottom), courtesy of Tasende Gallery, La Jolla, Calif.; page 354, Prado, Madrid.

Acknowledgments

I would like to express my gratitude first to my daughter, Cecilia Fuentes, who punctually and energetically dealt with the mass of paperwork flowing between London, New York, and Mexico City, and to my lifelong friend and agent, Carl Brandt. I would also like to thank a number of people involved with the television series *The Buried Mirror,* among them Peggy Liss, historical adviser, Washington, D.C.; Michael Gill, executive producer, London; Christopher Ralling and Peter Newington, codirectors, London; Jesús de Polanco, Juan Luis Cebrián, Eugenio Galdón, and Miguel Satrústegui, Madrid; Annie Dodds and Annette Gordon of Malone Gill Productions in London; and, last but not least, Terry Hopkins, cinematographer, Cambridge, Massachusetts, and Hugh Newsam, London, for the aesthetic and structural balance they brought to the series. Robert Adams, Marc Pachter, and Alicia Gonzalez of the Smithsonian Institution, Washington, D.C., provided invaluable help, as did Charles Benton of Public Media Inc., Chicago; Ruth Otte, president of the Discovery Channel, Washington, D.C.; and Alan Yentob of the BBC in London. Finally, I would like to thank John Sterling, Betsy Lerner, Liz Duvall, Guest Perry, Karen Holzman, Amy Cohen-Rose, Lisa Sacks, Erika Mansurian, and Denise Fulbrook at Houghton Mifflin, and Alix Colow and Renée Khatami, for their assistance.

Index

Abd ar-Rahman monarchs, 53; Abd ar-Rahman III, 54, 55

Acosta, Father Joseph de, 156, 205, 207

African Americans. *See* Blacks in Latin America

Agatha, Saint, 45, *47*

Age of Gold. *See* Golden Century of Spain

Aguiar y Seijas (archbishop of Mexico), 203, 210–11

Aguirre, Lope de, 128–29

Alba, duchess of, 224–25, *227*

Alcántara (military order), 61

Aleijadinho, 201, 202, 291

Alexander VI (pope), 157–58

Alfonso VI (king of Castile), 61–62

Alfonso IX (king of León), 71

Alfonso X (the Wise) (king of Castile and León), 69, 73, 79

Alfonso XIII (king of Spain), 334

Alhambra, 56–57, *58–59*

Allende, Salvador, 327

Almagro, Diego de, 120–21

Almaráz, Carlos, 344; *Flip Over, 310–11, 345*

Almohads, 55, 76

Almoravids, 55, 76

Altamira, caves at, 17, *18*, 24

Alzate, Antonio de, 237

America, Spanish. *See* Latin America; Spanish America

America, United States of. *See* United States

American Revolution (United States), 240

Anaya, Rudolfo, 344

Anghera, Pedro Mártir d', 125

Animals, from Europe to New World, 206–7, *208*

Anti-Semitism, in Spain, 76. *See also* Jews

Apollonia, Saint, 164, 186

Appianos, 37

Arab Spain, 51–57, 79, 81, 88; Jews in, 53, 76. *See also* Moors

Arana, Diego Barros, 284

Aranda, count of, 216, 217, 259

Arango, Doroteo. *See* Villa, Pancho

Araucanian Indians, 144, 286

Argentina, 318–19; British invasion defeated by, 242; cattle civilization of, 264; and Great Depression, 317; independence movement in, 244, 252, 261–62; independence won by, 255; under Irigoyen, 319; in Malvinas conflict, 327; and military rule, 256, 319, 321; official terrorism in, 327; paradox of, 320; vs. Paraguay, 268; under Perón, 320–21, 323; population growth in, 322; Quiroga in, 263–64; revolution's aftermath in, 261–62; under Rivadavia, 263, 264; under Rosas, 263, 264–67, 283, 284; under Sarmiento, 275; in wars against Indians, 266, 286, 318; during World War II, 319–20

Arias, Oscar, 328

Arias, Ron, 344

Aristotle, and Averroës, 56

Armada, Spanish, 158–59, *161*, 162; and Cervantes, 175

Arms sales, from Europe to Islam, 54

Asbaje, Juana de (Sister Juana), 201–3, *204*, 291

Astray, Millán, 335

Atahualpa, 119, 120

Atlantic exchange, 203, 205–7

Augsburg, Peace of, 155

Augustine, Saint, 143, 240

Authoritarianism: of Hapsburgs, 154; in Latin America, 143, 154; and Spanish democracy, 72; and united monarchy, 88

Auto sacramentales (Calderón), 191

Averroës, 56

Ávila, Spain, 68

Ayala, Guamán Poma de, 118, 132

Ayanque, Simón de, 210

Azaña, Manuel, 335

Aztecs, 96, 99, 109–10; and chocolate, 205; disunity of, 36, 111, 113; sculptures of, 104, 107; Spanish conquest of, 110–17; and Toltecs, 101–2

Bach, Johann Sebastian, 195

Balazote, beast of, 19

Balboa, Vasco Núñez de, 119, 151

Balbuena, Bernardo de, 209

Balmaceda, José Manuel, 283

Barbara, Saint, 199

Barcelona: and expulsion of Jews, 82; and Gaudí, 331; Jewish persecution in, 77; parade of civilizations in, 331

Barcia, Father, 211

Baroque art and poetry, 195; of Latin America, 146, 194, 195–96, 200–203

Barthes, Roland, 210

Bastos, Augusto Roa, 268

Batista, Fulgencio, 326

Baudelaire, Charles, 107, 278

Bay of Pigs expedition, 327

Bazaine, Achille, 273
Beast of Balazote, 19
Bello, Andrés, 284
Benavente, Toribio de, 144
Benítez, Fernando, 210
Berbers, 51
Bertrand, Louis, 163
Bilbao, Francisco, 284
Black Death, 76, 80
Black Decree, 273, 274
Black Legend, 16, 132
Blacks in Latin America: and culture
    of Spanish America, 277, 285;
    freedmen, 198; music of, 199–
    200; number of (1810), 234;
    religion of, 199; servants from
    Spain, 197; settlements of
    former slaves, 198, 239; slaves,
    197–99, 200, 205 (*see also*
    Slavery in Latin America); and
    wars of independence, 252, 257
Blades, Rubén, 344
Bloch, Marc, 69
Boabdil (king of Granada), 88
Bogotá, 209, 279, 282
Bolívar, Simón, 249–52; and
    independence aftermath, 256–
    58, 262; land payment by, 61,
    257, 263; in meeting with San
    Martín, *248*, 256
Bolivia, 268, 283. *See also* Potosí
Bonampak, murals of, *2–3, 90–91,*
    98, *100*
Bonaparte, Joseph, 221, 244
Bonaparte, Napoleon. *See* Napoleon
    Bonaparte
Borges, Jacobo, 351
Borges, Jorge Luis, 9, 289–90; "The
    Aleph," 348–49
Borgia family, 157–58
Botero, Fernando, 351; *Retrato
    Oficial de la Junta Militar, 352*
Bourbon rule over Spain. *See under*
    Spain, history of
Brazil: Afro-Portuguese baroque of,
    201; flag of, 285; vs. Paraguay,
    268; size of economy of, 317;
    slavery in, 198; under Vargas,
    323
Breton, André, 104
Bruno, Giordano, 176
Bry, Theodor de, *78, 87, 152–53*
Buenos Aires, 139, 209, 319; British
    attempt invasion of, 242;
    newspapers founded in, 284;
    population growth in, 282, 288–
    89; Recoleta Cemetery in, 279,
    281, 321; revolution in (1810),
    233; and tango, 289–90; Teatro
    Colón in, 279, *280*

Bull(s), 17, 19; and Iberians, 19;
    and Mediterranean culture, 19,
    34
Bullfight (Villamil painting), *14, 22*
Bullfighter (matador), 20, 22–23;
    Theseus as, 19; and Virgen de
    la Macarena, 31
Bullfighting, 20, 22–24
Bunge, Carlos, 286
Buñuel, Luis, 16, 223; *An Andalusian
    Dog, 334, 336; Las Hurdes (Land
    Without Bread),* 334; *Los
    Olvidados,* 339; and Posada, 292;
    Viridiana, 338–39
Burgos, 69; cathedral of, *69*
Burial of Count Orgaz, The (El
    Greco), 172, *173,* 174
Buried mirror, 10
Bustos, Hermenegildo, 283; *Don
    Manuel Desiderio Rojas, 284;
    Maria de los Remedios Barajas, 284*
Buxo, caves at, 17

Caballeros, 67
Cabildos, 244, 245, 252
Cabrera, Miguel, *Sor Juana Inés de la
    Cruz, 204*
Caciques: and Bolívar, 257; colonial
    administrators as, 136
Cádiz constitution, 251, 332, 339
Calatrava (military order), 61
Calderón, María, 183
Calderón de la Barca, Pedro, 169,
    190–92; and Lorca, 334; and
    Saint Barbara, 199
Calendar, Aztec, 94, 95
Calles, Plutarco Elías, 304, 322
Cameron, Rondo, 156
Caminha, Pedro Vaz de, 125
Cante jondo, 30–31
Cantolla, Joaquin de la, 295
Capitalism, vs. Latin American
    tradition, 72, 328
Caprichos (Goya), 11, 225, 228; and
    Posada, 294, 296
Cárdenas, Lázaro, 322, 323, 326
Carlota (Charlotte) (empress of
    Mexico), 271–74
Carranza, Alonso de, 157
Carranza, Venustiano, 303–4, 307
Cartagena, 140; fortress at, *142*
Cartagena de Indias, 207, 239
Carthage, 34–35
Castelli, Juan José, 261, 262
Castillo, Céspedes del, 138
Castro, Americo, 175
Castro, Fidel, 327
Catalonia, 70
Catholic church: Counter-
    Reformation, 162, 175, 176,

188–90, 195, 339; and El
    Escorial, 162–63, 164; eroticism
    of, 45; Inquisition, 81–82, 162
    (*see also* Inquisition); and
    Isidore of Seville, 45–46, 48–49
    (*see also* Isidore, Saint); Jesuits,
    189–90, 191, 211, 235–37, 267;
    and Jews in Spain, 76–77;
    mass of and bullfighting, 20; in
    Philip II's plans, 159; *reconquista*
    and Spain's role as protector of,
    72; Virgin Mary, 28–29
    IN NEW WORLD, 144–47; and
    Consolidation Bill, 244–45; and
    eroticism, 210–11; Indian
    mistreatment protested by, 125,
    130–32; Indians helped by,
    134–35; land acquired by, 136;
    in Mexico, 270–71, 272; and
    rejection of Spain, 277; and
    Rivera mural, 323; and
    Thomistic political philosophy,
    143. *See also* Christianity
Caudillo(s), 38, 252, 257, 263; and
    Argentina, 264, 275, 318; El
    Cid as, 61; and Cuba, 327;
    Francia as, 267; Páez as, 257,
    263; and wars of independence,
    263
Celestina, La (Rojas), 84
Celtiberians, 34
Celts, 34
Century of Lights: and Goya, 223–
    31; and Jovellanos, 216–23. *See
    also* Enlightenment
Cervantes, Miguel de, 174–76; and
    Age of Gold, 169; and Armada
    preparation, 159; in battle of
    Lepanto, 159; *Don Quixote,* 176–
    79, 192 (*see also Don Quixote de la
    Mancha*); and Jewish ancestors,
    171
Césaire, Aimé, 200
Chacabuco, battle of, 255
Chac Mool figures, 104, *105*
Charles I (king of Spain). *See*
    Charles V
Charles II (the Bewitched) (king of
    Spain), 183, 215; and Calderón,
    191; Coello painting of, 183, *185*
Charles III (king of Spain), 217,
    224, 235–37, 259
Charles IV (king of Spain), 218,
    220, 221, 228, 259; *Family of
    (Goya), 231*
Charles V (Holy Roman Emperor),
    151–53, 272; Cortés' appeal to,
    128; Cortés' letters to, 138, 143;
    election of as emperor, 153,
    166; and El Escorial, 162; and

encomienda system, 127; and hidalgo doctor, 82–83; and Philip II, 163; and slavery, 197; Titian painting of, 151, *152;* and Veracruz, 110

Charros, 286–88

Chichén Itzá, 96, 98; Chac Mool figures at, 104, *105;* great pyramid at, *101*

Chilam Balam, 114

Chile: conquest of, 138; economic development of, 283; and Great Depression, 317; independence movement in (1810), 233; independence won by, 255; Indians subdued in, 286; Pinochet dictatorship in, 327; political development of, 283–84; Popular Front in, 326; U.S. intervention in, 326

Chirinos (royal official), 128

Chocolate; and Bogotá tastes, 279; introduction of to Europe, 205

Christian-Indian syncretism, 146–47, 199

Christianity: appearance of in Spain, 43, 44–45; and clergy in war, 60; and Cortés in Mexico, 113; in Muslim Spain, 53; and Spain's resistance to Islam, 57; virgin martyrs, 44–45, 186. *See also* Catholic church

Christian-Yoruba syncretism, 199

Church of the Good Child Jesus, Congonhas do Campo, 201, *202*

Church of Our Lady of the Pillar, Ouro Preto, 201

Church of San Lorenzo, Potosí, Bolivia, 196; baroque facade of, *194*

Cid, El (Rodrigo Díaz de Vivar), 61–62

Cisneros, Sandra, 344

Cities of Spain: in Arab Spain, 52–53; in *reconquista,* 66–72; revolt of (16th century), 153; Rojas' view of, 84; and unification, 80, 81

Cities of Spanish America, 207, 209–10; Buenos Aires, 139; as fortresses, 158, 239–40; founding of, 140–41; growth of (19th–20th centuries), 282; as legacy of Spain, 69; social tensions in, 209; universities in, 141, 143; uprisings in, 209

Civil rights, 71

Civil society: creation of (Argentina, Mexico, Brazil), 323; and post-independence society, 259; social mobilization through, 355; Spanish America's need for, 257

Civil War, American, 271, 273

Civil War, Spanish, 335, 337; International Brigades, 335

Clavijero, Francisco Xavier, 237

Coatlicue, 27, 102, *103*

Coca leaf, 205

Cochrane, Lord Thomas, 255

Coello, Claudio, *Charles II,* 183, *185*

Cofer, Judith Ortiz, 344

Cold war, 326–27; end of, 328–29

Colonies, Spanish. *See under* Spanish America

Colombia: liberation of, 252; Panama taken from, 325

Columbus, Christopher, 8, 81, 85–87, 128; and Golden Age, 8–9, 125; and New World wealth, 126; quincentennial of voyage of, 9

Committee of Public Safety, in Argentina, 261

Communal property, Indian, 135

Communitarian property, 285

Compostela, Santiago's tomb at, 63–64, 65

Comte, Auguste, 285, 301

Comuneros, 153–54

Condorcanqui, José Gabriel (Tupac Amarú), 120, 212–13, 239, 349

Conference of Panama (1826), 257

Congonhas do Campo, Brazil, Church of the Good Child Jesus in, 201, *202*

Congress of Vienna, 251

Conquistadors, 88, 127, 129–30, 132; and *comuneros'* defeat, 154; in conflict with Crown, 126–30, 131–32, 154, 155; Cortés on, 138; fantasies of, 139–40; final status of, 128–29. *See also* Columbus, Christopher; Cortés, Hernán; Pizarro, Francisco; Spanish conquest in America

Consolidation Bill, 245

Constitution of Cádiz, 251, 332, 339

Coolidge, Calvin, 326

Copernicus, 176

Cordero, Juan, 283

Córdoba (Spain), 38, 52–55, 57; Great Mosque at, 53–54, 57; Jewish persecution in, 77

Coronado, Francisco Vásquez de, 140

Coro rebellion, 198, 239

Corregidores, 71, 136–37, 153

Cortes (assembly), 70–71; Cádiz constitution from, 251

Cortés, Hernán, 88, 110–17, 127–29, 272; and Aztec disunity, 36, 111, 113; and Charles V's policies, 155; on first conquistadors, 138; land payment by, 61, 127; letters of to Charles V, 138, 143; as Quetzalcoatl, 110, 114, 146

Costa Rica, 318

Council of the Indies, 137

Council of Trent, 162

Counter-Reformation, 162, 175, 176, 189–90, 195, 339

Covadonga, battle of, 52

Coyolxauhqui, 102

Creoles, 138, 234; Napoleon as model for, 242; as nation, 235; rebellion by (Mexico), 144; revolution in hands of, 239; in wars of independence, 252

Crete, 19

Croix, marquis de, 236

Cruikshank, George, 179

Crusades, Spain absent from, 60

Cuauhtémoc, 114

Cuba, 325, 326, 327, 332

Cueva, Beltrán de la, 80

Cuevas, José Luis, 353

Cugat, Saint, 44

Cuzco, 121; stones at, *122*

Dali, Salvador, 334; *The Persistence of Memory, 336*

Dama de Baza, 24–25, *26*

Dama de Elche, 25, *27;* headdress of, 27, 44

Darío, Rubén, 291, 339

Dark Night of the Soul, The (San Juan de la Cruz), 187, 188

Daumier, Honoré, 179

David, Jacques-Louis, *Napoleon in His Study, 243*

Death squad, of Rosas, 267

Democracy: absence of (post-independence), 277; as balance between natural elements, 291; and conquistadors, 88, 129–30; and Cuba, 327; and Latin American agenda, 354; and Latin American political culture, 143; Mexico's postponement of, 322; of Morelos revolution, 305; obstacles to (post-independence), 262; origins of in Spain, 70–72; post-Franco Spain as, 339; and revolution of townships, 153–54; and social demands, 355; and Spanish American culture, 349; vs.

Spanish rule in America, 127; as Spanish tradition, 15; of United States, 278, 325

Depression, Great, 317

Descamisados (shirtless ones), and Perón, 320

Descola, Jean, 121, 249

Dias, Bartholomeu, 85

Díaz, Porfirio, 282, 286, *298*, 299–302, 303

Díaz del Castilo, Bernal, 93, 111, 113–14, 206

Diaz Plaja, Fernando, 167

Díaz de Vivar, Rodrigo (El Cid), 61–62

Discépolo, Santos, 290

Dominican Republic, 325, 326

Dominicans, 191

Don Carlos (son of Philip II), 164

Don Giovanni (Mozart), 183, *186*

Don Juan, 183, 339

Don Juan of Asturia, 159

Don Quixote de la Mancha (Cervantes), 176–79, 192; Bolívar's reference to, 252; and dilemma of Spain, 192; Gentleman with the Green Cloak in, 41; Knight of the Mirrors in, 11; Roque Guinart in, 157; Stoicism in, 40. *See also* Cervantes, Miguel de

Doré, Gustave, and *Don Quixote*, *170*, *177*, 179

Dorothea, Saint, 186

Dostoevsky, Fyodor, on *Don Quixote*, 179

Drake, Francis, 158, 159, 205–6

Dream of Philip II, The (El Greco), *165*

Dressed Maja, The (Goya), 224, *227*

Dulles, John Foster, 326

Dürer, Albrecht, 104

Echeverría, Esteban, 277

Eisenhower, Dwight D., 337

Eisenstein, Sergei, 296

El Dorado, 128, 129, 140

El Escorial, 162–63, 164

El Greco, 16; and Age of Gold, 169; *The Burial of Count Orgaz*, 172, *173*, 174; *The Dream of Philip II*, 164, *165*; *The Gentleman with His Hand on His Breast*, 41, *42*

Elizabeth I (queen of England), 158, *161*

Elliot, John, 215–16

El Tajín, ruins at, 10–11

Encomienda system, 127, 131, 132

England. *See* Great Britain and England

Enlightenment, 216; and Argentine independence movement, 253; and Jovellanos, 217, 218; in Peru, 261; and Spanish American culture, 349; and Spanish American revolutionaries, 240

Envy; and El Cid, 61–62; and persecution of Jews, 76

Erasmus, Desiderius, 174–75, 176; on Inquisition index, 175

Espinosa, Manuel, 198

Estancia system, 263, 264

Estrada, Ezequiel Martinez, 319

Eugénie de Montijo (empress of Spain), 271

Eulalia, Saint, 45

Europa, abduction of, 19

Family, in Hispanic culture, 347

Felix, Saint, 44

Ferdinand II (king of Aragon), 80, 82; as Charles V's grandfather, 151; and Columbus, 85; and expulsion of Jews, 81–82; and Pope Alexander VI, 157

Ferdinand III (king of Castile and León), 56, 72–73; inscriptions on tomb of, 73, *74–75*

Ferdinand VII (king of Spain), 221, 230, 244, 251, 259

Ferré, Rosario, 344

Feudalism, 64, 66–67; and conquistadors, 130; vs. Spanish rule in America, 127; and unification, 79–80, 81

Ficino, Marsilio, 84

Flamenco dancing, 30–31

Flanders, and Charles V, 155

France: and Maximilian, 271–74; as model for Spanish America, 278; under Napoleon, 242; vs. Spain, 162, 168, 215, 218; in War with Mexico (1838), 268

Francia, José Gaspar Rodríguez de, 262, 267–68, 269

Francis I (king of France), 155, 158, 166

Francis Joseph (emperor of Austria), 271, 272

Franco, Francisco, 335, 337, *338*

Franklin, Ben, 221

Free trade, 238–39, 264

French Revolution, 219, 239, 240, 241; as model (Sarmiento), 262; social tension resolved by, 71

Frontier, and Spanish feudalism, 66, 67

Fuenteovejuna (Vega), 43

Fugger family, 153, 166

Galarza, Ernesto, 344

Galba (Roman praetor), 38

Gama, Vasco da, 85

Ganivet, Ángel, 155

Garay, Juan de, 139

García Lorca, Federico, 334, 335; on El Escorial, 164; on flamenco dancers, 30

Gauchos, 286–88

Gaudí, Antonio, 330, 331

Gentleman with His Hand on His Breast (El Greco), 41, *42*

Germania, 154

Geryon, 19

Gibraltar, 33, 49

Gibson, Charles, 136

Gironella, Alberto, 351

Godoy, Manuel de, 218, *219*, 220, 221, 231

Goethe, Johann Wolfgang von, 96

Golden Age, and discovery of America, 8–9, 125, 135. *See also* Utopia

Golden Century of Spain, 169, 172; Calderón de la Barca, 190–92; Cervantes, 174–79, 192–93 (*see also* Cervantes, Miguel de); and Counter-Reformation, 188–90; and dilemma of Spain, 192–93; Don Juan, 183; El Greco, 172–74 (*see also* El Greco); San Juan de la Cruz, 187–88; Velázquez, 179–83 (*see also* Velázquez, Diego Rodríguez de Silva y); Zurbarán, 183, 186–87 (*see also* Zurbarán, Francisco de)

Góngora, Luis de, 169

"Good neighbor policy," 326

Gothic invasions, 44, 49

Gothic Spain, 49, 51; and church role, 48; and feudalism, 66; and Jews, 49, 76

Goya, Age of, 20, 215–31

Goya y Lucientes, Francisco José de, 223–31; *All Will Fall*, *228*; *Los Caprichos*, 11, 225, 228, 294, 296; *Don Manuel de Godoy*, *219*, 231; *The Dressed Maja*, 224, *227*; *The Executions of the Third of May, 1808*, *222*; as extreme, 16; *The Family of Charles IV*, *231*; *The Festival of San Isidro*, 226; *Hunting for Teeth*, *228*; Jovellanos portrait, *214*, 216, 220–21; *The Matador Pedro Romero*, 24, *25*; *The Naked Maja*, 224–25, *227*; and Posada, 292; *Saturn Devouring His Children*, *354*; *Self-Portrait*, *223*; *The Sleep of Reason Begets Monsters*, 225–

26, 228, *229; What Courage!*, *250; Witches' Sabbath,* 354; *Woman Under a Parasol, 226*

Graffiti: in Los Angeles, 293; and Posada, 292

Granada (city), 52; Alhambra of, 56–57, *58–59*

Granada (Arab monarchy), 56, 70; defeat of by Ferdinand and Isabella, 79, 81

Great Britain and England: and Argentine commerce, 319; and Armada, 158–59, 161, 162; as commercial competitor, 242; in Malvinas conflict, 327; vs. Spain, 162; Spanish America attacked by, 158; tango in, 290; as trading partner, 281

Great Depression, 317

Great Mosque at Córdoba, 53–54, 57

Great War of 1914–1918, 333–34

Greek philosophy: and Averroës, 56; and Islamic Córdoba, 53

Greeks, as settlers, 34, 35

Guadalajara, Mexico, 140, 313

Guadalupe, Virgin of, 145–46

Guajardo, Jesus, 307

Guanajuato, Mexico, Teatro Juárez in, 279

Guaraní Indians, 211

Guatemala, U.S. in, 326

Guernica, bombing of, 335, 337

Guernica (Picasso), *12–13*, 19, *21*, 337

Guerrero, Vicente, 263

Guerrilla warfare: by Iberians, 36; against Maximilian, 273–74; and resistance to Islam, 57; and Spanish-American insurgents, 231

Guisando, bulls of, 19, *20*

Hacienda, 135–36, 281; Indians' flight to, 156; in Mexico, 299–300, 302, 308

Hadrian (Roman emperor), Spain as birthplace of, 43

Haiti, 198, 325

Hannibal, 35

Hapsburg rule over Spain. *See under* Spain, history of

Havana, Cuba, 140, 217, 239

Hawkins, John, 158

Hearst, William Randolph: Mexican property of, 300; and Spanish-American War, 332

Hemming, John, 120

Henriquez, Camilo, 245

Henry II (king of Castile), 80

Henry IV (king of Castile), 80

Henry the Navigator (prince of Portugal), 85

Hercules, 19, 34

Hernández, José, 287

Hidalgo, 41, 67; and bureaucracy, 83; and conquistadors, 130; in urban Spanish America, 209

Hidalgo y Costilla, Miguel, 233, 245

Hijuelos, Oscar, 344

Hinojosa, Rolando, 344

Ho Chi Minh, 274

Hogarth, William, and *Don Quixote,* 179

Holbein the Younger, 175, 296

Hölderlin, Friedrich, on nature and humans, 96

Holy Alliance, 251

Honduras: Cortés' expedition to, 127–28; U.S. in, 325

Huáscar, 119

Huayna Capac, 119–20

Huerta, Victoriano, 302

Hugo, Victor, on Napoleon III, 273

Huitzilopochtli, 99, *101,* 102

Humboldt, Baron Alexander Von, 237–38, 240

Iberians, 19, 34; Rome against, 35–38

Icaza, Francisco de, 57

Ignatius of Loyola, 189–90

Inca empire, 121–24; Spanish conquest of, 36, 119–21

Indians, 116, 124; Argentine wars against, 266, 286, 318; and church, 144–47, 199; and culture of Spanish America, 277, 285; decimation of as reason for slavery, 197, 205; desire to exterminate, 285–86; education for, 143; and Golden Age or Utopia, 8, 125, 126, 134–35; Inca civilization, 121–24; in Jesuit Utopia, 211, 267; Mesoamerican civilizations, 93–110; migration of to America, 93; numbers of, 126, 234; property relationships among, 135, 285; Spaniards' treatment of, 8, 125–26, 127, 130–36, 143, 156, 286; Spanish conquest of, 110–17, 119–21; Tupac Amarú rebellion by, 120, 212–13, 239; and wars of independence, 253, 255, 257, 261. *See also specific peoples*

Inquisition, 81–82; books forbidden by, 175; and Jews, 162, 171; and journalism, 284; Jovellanos against, 220; and Moors, 162,

164; Napoleon abolishes, 221; under Philip II, 162; revolutionary literature condemned by, 241

International law (*jus gentium*), Father Vitoria on, 134

Iran-contra operation, 328

Irigoyen, Hipólito, 319

Isabella (queen of Castile), 8, 80, 82; as Charles V's grandmother, 151; and Columbus, 85; and expulsion of Jews, 81–82; and Pope Alexander VI, 157

Isidore, Saint (bishop of Seville), 45–46, 48–49, 57; Alfonso X as continuing work of, 73; and Jews' rejection, 76; and Roman law, 48, 66, 79; and Santiago Matamoros, 63; and separation of religious from political, 60

Islam, 51; and *jihad,* 60. *See also* Moors; Ottoman Empire

Islas, Arturo, 344

Jackson, Andrew, 269

Jackson, Gabriel, 82

Jaina, sculpture figures of, 107, *108–9*

James, Saint (Santiago), 62–63

James I (king of England), 205

Jebel-al-Tarik, 51

Jefferson, Thomas, 240, 257, 278

Jesuits, 189–90, 191; expulsion of, 190, 235–37; national histories written by, 237; in Paraguay, 211, 267

Jews in Spain; under Alfonso X, 73; Christian persecution of, 49 76–77, 162, 171; colonizing forbidden to, 138; as converts to Christianity, 77, 162; delegation of, 83; expulsion of, 81–83, 88; Ferdinand III's appeal for, 73; in Muslim Spain, 53, 76; remaining in Spain, 171; and Spanish language, 73, 76; in triculturalism, 88

Jihad (holy war), 60

Joanna the Mad (queen of Spain), 151, 215

John II (king of Castile), 80

Jovellanos y Ramírez, Gaspar Melchor de, 216–23; Goya portrait of, *214,* 216, 220–21; isolation opposed by, 339; and *The Sleep of Reason Begets Monsters,* 225, 226

Juana, Sister. *See* Sor Juana Inés de la Cruz.

Juan Carlos (king of Spain), 339
Juárez, Benito, 270–71, 274–75; Díaz under, 299; and Maximilian, 272–74
Juárez, Catalina, 128, 144
Judaism. *See* Jews in Spain
Jugurtha (Numidian prince), 37
Julian, Count (governor of Ceuta), 51
Junta General, 154
Justin, on Viriatus, 38
Juvenal, on flamenco dancers, 30

Kahlo, Frida, 351; *The Two Fridas*, 340
Keaton, Buster, and *Life Is a Dream*, 191
Kellogg, Frank B., 326
Kleist, Heinrich von, and *Life Is a Dream*, 191
Knight of the Mirrors (*Don Quixote*), 11
Kondori, José, 194, 196

Lam, Wifredo, 349, 351; *The Jungle*, 351
Lamartine, Alphonse de, 284
La Paz, 209
Larra, Mariano José de, 332
Las Casas, Bartolomé de, 130–32, 145; statue of, *131*
Las Navas de Tolosa, battle of, 52, 70
Lastarria, José Vitorino, 277, 284
Latin America: and armies of *la reconquista*, 61; current crisis in, 9, 328; life expectancy in (end of 19th century), 281–82; literacy rates in (end of 19th century), 281–82; political agenda for, 353–54; population growth of, 316–17; social mobilization in, 355; WWII growth of, 317–18
CULTURE OF, 9–10; and problem of orphans/bastards, 144; unity in, 141, 316; and U.S. culture, 346
ECONOMICS OF: Chilean development, 283; consumption vs. production, 278–79; current problems in, 316; foreign debt, 316, 317; foreign trade, 238–39, 264, 279, 281–82; and Great Depression, 317; and *hacienda* system, 136, 281; liberal economics vs. indigenous relationships, 285; plantation economy, 197; in WW II and

after, 317–18 (*see also* Middle class) *See also* Spanish America; *individual countries*
Law, Roman. *See* Roman law
Laws of the Indies, 41, 131, 132, 136; and viceroys vs. conquistadors, 120
Leander, 46, 48
Legend of the five suns, 94
León (city), 69
León-Castile, 70
León-Portilla, Miguel, 116
Leopold I (king of Belgium), 271, 272
Leovigild (Gothic king), 46
Lepanto, battle of, 158–59, 160
Lerma, duke of, 166–67
Liberal economics, vs. indigenous property relations, 285
Liberals and liberalism: in Bolívar's conception, 257; and Díaz, 299; Don Juan as, 183; of Jesuits, 191; of Juárez, 270–71, 273, 274; and Maximilian, 271, 272; and Napoleon's invasion of Spain, 221; of 19th century ("liberal pause"), 282; post-independence programs of, 262, 263; and United States, 278. *See also* Enlightenment
Life Is a Dream (*La vida es sueño*) (Calderón de la Barca), 190–91; and Saint Barbara, 199
Lima, 141, 209, 210
Limantour family, 286
Lincoln, Abraham, and Mexican-American War, 269
Lincoln Brigade, 335
Liniers, Santiago, 242
Lippmann, Walter, 328
Lisboa, Antônio Francisco (Aleijadinho), 201, 202
Liss, Peggy, 203
López de Hoyos, Juan, 174
Lorca. *See* García Lorca, Federico
Los Angeles, 343
Louis XIV (king of France), 157, 168; cocoa introduced by, 205; and Philip V, 215
Lucan, 40
Lucilius, 37
Lucy, Saint, 44. *See also* Saint Lucy
Ludwig III (king of Bavaria), and tango, 290
Lugones, Leopoldo, 139
Luján, Gilbert, 344
"Lukumi" culture, 199
Luna, Alvaro de, 80
Lynch, John, 245, 255

McCarthyism, and Charles IV's persecutions, 218
Machado, Antonio, 332, 337
Machiavelli, Niccolò, 129, 175
Machu Picchu, 121, 122
Mackenna, Benjamin Vicuña, 278, 284
Madero, Francisco, 301–3
Madrid, 224; fountain of Cibeles in, 225
Maeztu, Ramiro de, 84, 192
Maimonides, 56
Malaca (Málaga), 34
Malinche, La, 111, *112*, 113, 117, 128, 144
Malvinas conflict, 327
Manco Inca Yupanqui, 120
Manila, England captures, 217
Mansur, Abu Al-, 72
Maracaibo, 207
Maravall, José Antonio, 67
Margaret, Saint, 186
María Luisa of Parma (La Parmesana), 218, 221
Marina, Saint, 186
Márquez, Gabriel García, 9, 258
Martel, Charles, 52
Martí, José, 291, 327
Martial, 30, 40
Martinez, Tomas Eloy, 321
Martín Fierro (Hernández), 287, 289
Marx, Karl, 238
Mary I (queen of Scotland), 158
Matador. *See* Bullfighter
Matador Pedro Romero, The (Goya), 24, *25*
Mathematics, and Muslims, 53
Maximilian (archduke of Austria), 271–74; execution of, 274, *275*
Mayan civilization, 96, 98; Bible of (*Popol Vuh*), 93; and Chichén Itzá, 96, 98, 101, 104, 105; *Chilam Balam* of, 114
Mazarin, Jules (cardinal), 167
Medina Azahara, palace at, 55
Medina-Sidonia, duke of, 159
Mediterranean Sea, 33, 85
Mendoza, Pedro de, 139
Menéndez y Pelayo, Marcelino, 48
Meninas, Las (Velázquez), 11, *148–49*, 179, *180*, 181–82
Mérida, theater at, 38, *39*
Mérimée, Prosper, 200
Mesoamerica, 94
Mesoamerican Indian civilizations, 95–96; architecture of, 96–98; art of, 104–7, 108; in Bonampak murals, 98, 100; and Coatlicue/Coyolxauhqui, 102–

4; and gods, 94–95, 96; and
Quetzalcoatl, 93, 99; and
sacrifice, 93–94; and time, 98–
99
PEOPLES: Aztecs, 99, 101–2, 109–
10 (*see also* Aztecs); Mayans,
93, 96, 98, 114; Olmecs, 10, 96,
104, 106, 107; Toltecs, 96, 99,
101–2; Zapotecs, 96
Mestizos, 138, 196, 234, 249; culture
of, 200, 348; fathers of, 144; La
Malinche's child as first, 117;
and national identity, 237;
rebellion by (Mexico), 144; and
social tensions, 209
Mexican-American War (1846–
1848), 269, 278
Mexican Revolution, 297, 299–307;
as cultural revolution, 307–9;
and Díaz government, 299–
301; Díaz overthrown, 301–2;
Madero as president, 302–3;
overthrow of Huerta, 303–4;
two sides of, 299, 304, 306; and
United States, 302–3, 306, 307,
326; Villa defeated, 306; Zapata
killed, 307; Zapatista
movement, 304–6, 349
"Mexico," origin of, 99
Mexico, 322–23; and Great
Depression, 317; Hispanics in
U.S. from, 343, 346; Indian
population decimated in, 126,
286; and Maximilian, 271–74;
Mexican-American War, 269,
278; national identity formed in,
237; population growth in, 322;
revolution in (1810), 233; size
of economy of, 317; territories
of lost to U.S., 269, 343
RULERS OF: Guerrero, 263; Santa
Anna, 263, 268–70, 283;
Juárez, 270–71, 274–75; Díaz,
299–301, 303; Madero, 301–3;
Carranza, 303–4, 307;
Obregón, 304, 306–7; Calles,
304, 322; Cárdenas, 323
Mexico City, 127; attempt to expel
women from, 211; Balbuena's
description of, 209–10;
earthquake in (1985), 355; as
highland city, 209; long life of,
99; population growth in, 282;
university in, 141
Middle class: in Argentina, 319; in
Chile, 284, 317; conquistadors
as, 129; and Díaz, 299;
emergence of, 282–83; vs.
hidalgos of Spanish America,

209; in Mexico, 300, 322;
portraits of, 283; from WWII
economic growth, 317
Minotaur, 19, 23
Mirror, 10–11; buried, 10; of
Quetzalcoatl, 109; unburied,
353
Miscegenation, 144
Mitre, Bartolomé, 275
Moctezuma, 110, 111, 113, 114, *115*,
116; and chocolate, 205
Modernity: of Chile, 284; and Don
Quixote, 177; and Mexican
Revolution, 301; tradition in
tension with, 290. *See also*
Enlightenment
Molina, Juan Ignacio, 237
Monarchy (kings): and cities, 70,
71, 127; Ferdinand and
Isabella's strengthening of, 80–
81; vs. feudalism, 70, 79–80;
and government of Spanish
America, 127, 137; and
reconquista, 70, 71–72
Monastic life, 48
Monroe Doctrine, 325
Monsivais, Carlos, 355
Montaigne, Michel, 125
Monte Albán, 96, 97, 98
Montesinos, Antonio de, 125, 130
Montesquieu, 240
Montevideo, 282
Monument to the Fallen, 337
Moore, Henry, 104; *Reclining Figure,
105*
Moors in Spain, 51–60; expulsion
of, 164; and Ferdinand III, 72–
73; Inquisition against, 162,
164; and *reconquista,* 60–62, 79
(*see also Reconquista, La*); revolt
of, 156; in triculturalism, 88
Morales, Alejandro, 344
More, Thomas, 124, 134
Morelos revolution, 304–6
Moreno, Mariano, 244
Moriscos. See Moors in Spain
Morocco, incursions in, 334
Mosque at Córdoba, 53–54, 57
Mother figures, 24–29
Motolinia (Toribio de Benavente),
144
Mozárabes, 52, 76, 79
Mozart, Wolfgang Amadeus, *Don
Giovanni,* 183, *186,* 187
Mudéjares, 52, 79
Muladíes, 52
Mulattos, 234, 249; and wars of
independence, 257
Multilingualism, 347

Murillo, Bartolomé, 169
Muslim invasion of Spain, 35, 51–
52, 60. *See also* Moors

Naked Maja, The (Goya), 224–25, *227*
Napoleon Bonaparte, 242, 243; and
Bolívar, 250; Spain invaded by,
221–22, 240, 242, 244–45
Napoleon III (emperor of France),
271, 273, 274
Nationalism in Latin America,
rightist origins of, 268
Navarre, 70
Nazca lines, 123
Nebrija, Antonio de, 81
Neruda, Pablo, 353; on Indian art,
107; on Tupac Amarú, 213
Netherlands: as Charles V's
inheritance, 151; English aid to,
158; revolt of, 156
Newton, Sir Isaac, 176
New World: animals introduced
into, 206–7, *208;* and "Atlantic
exchange," 203; Columbus in,
8, 85, 86, 87; commodities
introduced to Europe from,
205–6; division of by pope,
157; Inca Empire, 121–24;
Mesoamerican Indians, 93–110
(*see also* Mesomerican Indian
civilizations); original
population of, 93; plants and
animals introduced into, 207;
Spain's arrival in, 15, 87–89;
and Utopia, 8–9, 124–25, 126,
134, 195
Nicaragua, U.S. intervention
against, 325–26, 327–28
Niño de Guevara, Cardinal
Fernando, 175
Novel, birth of (*Don Quixote*), 176
Numantia, siege of, 36–38, 327

Obregón, Álvaro, 304, 306–7
O'Gorman, Edmundo, 125
Ogún, 199
O'Higgins, Bernardo, 255
Olmecs, 10, 96; sculpture of, 104,
106, 107
Olson, Mancur, 238
Opera houses, 279, 280
Oquendo, Mateo Rosas de, 210
Ordás, Diego de, 128
Orozco, José Clemente, 313, 323;
*Benito Juárez, 271; The Epic of
American Civilization, 155,* 314,
348–49; Man in Fire, 315;
Prometheus, 314
Ortega y Gasset, José, 333; on Holy

Week in Seville, 29; on Velázquez, 182

Osborne brandy, and bull, 19, *20*

Osuna, bulls at, 17

Ottoman Empire, 85, 155, 158–59

Our Lady of Regla, 199

Pacific Ocean, Balboa's discovery of, 119

Padilla, María, 80

Páez, José Antonio, 252, 257, 263

Pagden, Anthony, 166

Paine, Thomas, 240

Palenque, 96–97

Palmares settlement, Brazil, 198

Panama, Roosevelt's creation of, 325

Panama Canal, 325

Paoli, Giovanni (Juan Pablos), 141

Paraguay, 268; Francia's dictatorship in, 262, 267–68, 269; Jesuit-Indian community in, 211, 267

Pardo, Eduardo, 278

Pardocracia, 239

Pardos, 198, 257

Parliamentary institutions, Spain's development of, 70–72. *See also* Cortes; Democracy

Parmesana, La (María Luisa), 218, 221

Party of the Revolutionary Institutions, Mexico, 322

Pasha, Ali, 159

Payadores, 287

Pelayo, 52; and El Cid, 61

Peonage, 135–36

"Peoples of the Book," 53, 73

Perón, Eva, 320, 321

Perón, Juan Domingo, 320–21, 323

Pershing, John ("Black Jack"), 306

Peru: drawing of scene in, *118*; horses introduced to, *208*; Inca civilization in, 121–24; independence aftermath in, 255, 261, 262; Nazca lines in, *123*; Spanish conquest of, 119–21; in war with Chile, 283

Peter, Saint, Ogún as, 199

Peter the Cruel (king of Castile), 80

Philip I (the Fair) (king of Spain), 151

Philip II (king of Spain), 155–56, 158–64; El Greco's *Dream of*, *165*; and Saint Teresa of Ávila, 189; study abroad forbidden by, 175

Philip III (king of Spain), 136, 164

Philip IV (king of Spain), 168, 182, 183, 191

Philip V (king of Spain), 215

Philippines, 332; English capture of Manila, 217

Phoenicians, 34

Picasso, Pablo: and *Don Quixote*, 179; *Guernica*, *12–13*, 19, *21*, 337

Pietri, Arturo Uslar, 249

Pillars of Hercules, 19

Pinochet, Augusto, 327

Pirandello, Luigi, and *Life Is a Dream*, 191

Pius IX (pope), 274

Pius X (pope), 290

Pizarro, Francisco, 88, 119, 120, 155

Pizarro, Gonzalo, 119, 121, 128

Pizarro, Hernando, 119, 121

Pizarro, Juan, 119

Plantation economy, 197. *See also* Hacienda

Plants: from Europe to New World, 207; from New World to Europe, 205–6

Platt Amendment, 325

Plutarch, 36

Poitiers, battle of, 52

Political Essay on New Spain (Humboldt), 240

Polk, James, 325

Polybius, 37

Ponce de León, Juan, 140, 207

Popol Vuh, 93

Portales, Diego, 283

Portugal, 70; and Brazil, 87; exploration by, 85

Posada, José Guadalupe, 291, 292, 294–96; *Calavera Don Quixote*, *296*; *A Fashionable Lady*, *295*; *Gran Calavera Eléctrica*, *297*; *A Rich Man Hounded by the Seven Deadly Sins*, *294*; *The Soldier's Farewell*, *309*

Positivist philosophy (Comte), 285, 301

Post, Frans, 197

Potosí, Bolivia: Church of San Lorenzo in, 194, 196; revolution spread to, 253; silver mine of, 139, 140, *142*, 156

Prado Museum, 224

Prida, Dolores, 344

Primo de Rivera, Miguel, 334

Prince, The (Machiavelli), 129

Priscillianus, 44, 45

Prometheus, 99, 313, *314*

Property rights, traditional, 135, 285

Protestant Reformation, 195

Protestants: Charles V against, 155; Inquisition against, 162; vs. Spain, 162; Spain's financing of, 157

Puehyrredón, Juan Martín de, 254

Puente Viesgo, caves at, *18*

Puerto Rico, 325, 332

Pueyrredón, Prilidiano, 283

Pyramid of the Niches, 10

Quechuas, 144, 261

Quesada, Gonzalo Jiménez de, 128

Quetzal bird, 207

Quetzalcoatl, 11, *92*, 93, 99, 101, 109–10; Cortés as, 110, 114, 146; in Orozco paintings, *135*, 313, *314*; in Rivera painting, *324*; and Viracocha, 120

Quevedo, Francisco de, 169, 175

Quilombos, 198

Quintilian, 40

Quiroga, Juan Facundo, 263–64, 265

Quiroga, Vasco de, 134–35, 145, 318

Rake of Seville (Tirso de Molina), 183

Raleigh, Sir Walter, 205

Ramírez, Martín, 344

Ramsay, Allan, *Jean-Jacques Rousseau*, 252

Recoleta Cemetery, Buenos Aires, 279, *281*, 321

Reconquista, La, 60–62; battle of Las Navas de Tolosa, 52; and cities, 66–72; end of, 79; and Ferdinand III, 72; and feudalism, 64, 66–67; and kingdoms, 70, 71–72; and New World conquest, 88, 129; and parliamentary institutions, 70–72; and Saint James, 62–64; as war among Christian kingdoms, 62

Renaissance, 79; and city pattern, 140–41; and Don Quixote, 178; and European expansion, 84; and Utopia, 124, 125, 126, 195

Repartimientos, 131

Revillagigedo (Mexican viceroy), 238

Revolutionary War (U.S.), 240

Richardson Construction Company, Los Angeles, 286

Richelieu, Cardinal, 167

Rilke, Rainer Maria, 30

Rios, Alberto, 344

Rios, Alurista, 344

Ríos, Pedro de los, 138

Rivadavia, Bernardino, 263, 264

Rivera, Diego, 16, 268, 323; *Dream of a Sunday Afternoon in the Alameda*, 246–47, 291, *292–93*; *The Legend of Quetzalcoatl*, *324*

Rivera, Tomás, 344

Robespierre, Maximilien, 262
Roca, Julio, 286
Rocha, Beto de la, 344
Rocroi, battle at, 167, 168
Roderick (Visigoth king), 51
Rodríguez, María Teresa, 249–50
Rojas, Fernando de, 84
Roman law, 41; and cities of
    Spanish America, 141; and
    Isidore of Seville, 48, 66, 79; of
    Juárez, 273; and kingdom vs.
    feudalism, 79, 81; Muslim
    assimilation of, 53; and Spanish
    character, 57
Román y Zamora, 121
Rome (ancient): and Carthage, 35;
    and Spain, 35–41, 43–44
Romero, Francisco, 141
Romero, Frank, 344; *Highway 64, 345*
Romero, Pedro, 24, 25
Romulus Augustulus, 44
Roosevelt, Franklin, 326
Roosevelt, Theodore, 325, 332
Rosas, Juan Manuel de, 262, 263,
    264–67, 283, 284
Rousseau, Jean-Jacques, *252*, 240–
    41, 261, 262
Ruiz, Juan, 84

Sacrifice: in bullfighting, 20; of bull
    to Hercules, 19; and Indian
    society, 93–94; in Indians' view
    of Christ, 146
Sáenz, Manuelita, 258
Sagrada Familia, La (Gaudí
    cathedral), *330*, 331–32
Saint Agatha (Zurbarán), *47*
Saint Lucy (Zurbarán), *52*, 186
Saint-Quentin, battle at, 162
Salamanca, university in, 73
Salanueva, Father, 270
Salmantica (Salamanca), 38
San Antonio, Texas, 343
Sanchez, Luis Rafael, 344
Sandino, Augusto César, 326
San Juan de la Cruz, 187–88, 189,
    190, 211, 339
San Juan de Puerto Rico, 207;
    fortress of, 239
San Lorenzo de los Negros, 198
San Martín, José de, 253–55; and
    independence aftermath, 256;
    on "lower orders," 259; in
    meeting with Bolívar, *248*, 256
San Salvador, 87
Santa Anna, López de, 263, 268–70,
    283
Santander, Francisco de Paula, 259
Santería, 199
Santiago (military order), 61

Santiago Cathedral (Spain), 63–64,
    65; road to, 63, 67
Santiago Matamoros, 62–63
Santiago del Nuevo Extremo, 138–
    39
Santo Domingo, university in, 141
Santuola, María de, 17, 19
Sarmiento, Domingo F., *260*, 261–
    62, 275; and Chile, 284; on
    gauchos, 287; on progress, 285;
    and Quiroga, 264; on Rosas,
    266; on Rosas' death squad,
    267; on Spanish culture, 277
Sartre, Jean-Paul, 89
Saura, Antonio, and *Don Quixote*,
    179
School of Translators at Toledo, 53
Scipio, Publius Cornelius, 37
Segovia, Roman aqueduct at, 38, *39*
Seneca, 40, 89, 221
Señora de los Reyes, 28
Sephardim, 76
Sepúlveda, Juan Ginés de, 125, 134
Seven Cities of Cibola, 140
Seven Cities of Gold, 343
Seven Years War, 217
Seville, 55–56; building of, 52; and
    expulsion of Jews, 82; gold and
    silver into, 156; Holy Week in,
    28–29, 31; Jewish persecution
    in, 77; *plaza de toros* at, 23; plaza
    of La Maestranza in, 24; siege
    of, 72
Seville, Isidore of. *See* Isidore, Saint
Sex: and bullfighting, 22; in Spanish
    American baroque society, 210–
    11; and Spanish Catholicism, 45
Shakespeare, William: and
    Cervantes, 176; *The Tempest*,
    125
Sigüenza y Góngora, Carlos de, 210
Siqueiros, David Alfaro, 323; *The
    New Democracy, 324*
Sister Juana. *See* Sor Juana Inés de
    la Cruz
Slavery in Latin America, 197–98;
    Bolívar's proclamation of
    freedom from, 252; and
    decimation of Indians, 197, 205;
    encomienda as, 127; languages
    spoken, 198–99; Peru
    abolishes, 255; slave rebellions,
    198, 200; on sugar plantations,
    205
Slave trade, 197; by Hawkins, 158;
    suffering in, 200
Sleep of Reason Begets Monsters, The
    (Goya), 225–26, 228, *229*
Sobremonte, marquis of, 242
Socialism: Inca, 124; vs. Latin

American tradition, 72, 328
Society of Jesus. *See* Jesuits
Somoza, Anastasio, 326
Song of El Cid, 61
Sor Juana Inés de la Cruz (Sister
    Juana), 201–3, *204*, 291
Spain: and Americas, 15–16; and
    Catholicism, 72 (*see also*
    Catholic Church); Christianity
    appears in, 43, 44–49;
    contemporary challenges to,
    332, 339; and Mediterranean,
    33; vs. native American
    civilization, 35; prehistoric
    caves of, 17–19; various
    stereotypes of, 16
  CULTURE OF: dilemmas in, 88; and
    Franco era, 338–39; and
    geographic position, 33; Golden
    Century, 169, 172–92; Goya,
    223–31 (*see also* Goya y
    Lucientes, Francisco José); as
    incorporation, 196; orthodoxy
    required, 76; *otium* over
    negotium, 166; regional
    particularism, 35–36; Spanish
    Americans repudiate, 277;
    Stoicism, 40, 57; triculturalism,
    73–79, 88; unpunctuality, 167
  OPPOSITES IN, 15–17, 88; and
    Bourbons, 215; in Charles V,
    155; in Civil War, 337; and
    conquistadors, 88; Iberian vs.
    Mediterranean culture, 33–34;
    ideal vs. real, 192; and
    Napoleon or Napoleonic
    invasion, 221, 242, 251; during
    Republic, 335. *See also*
    Enlightenment
Spain, history of: conquered and
    conquering in, 34; duration of
    empire of, 332; invaders and
    settlers in, 17
  ANCIENT PERIOD: interior
    (Celtiberian) civilization, 33–
    34, 35–36, 57, 60;
    Mediterranean civilization, 34;
    and Rome-Carthage conflict,
    34–35; Rome's conquest, 35–
    38; Rome's occupation, 38–41,
    43–44
  MIDDLE AGES: barbarian
    invasions, 43–44; barbarian
    (Goth) kingships, 49, 51;
    Islamic occupation, 51–57;
    reconquista, 60–72 (*see also*
    Reconquista, La)
    1492, 81; Columbus' voyage, 81,
    85–87; Granada recaptured, 79,
    81; Jews expelled, 81–82, 88;

unity achieved, 38, 79–81
DISCOVERY AND CONQUEST:
conquistadors, 87–88, 126–30;
and Portuguese exploration, 85;
and Renaissance optimism, 83–
84 (*see also* Spanish conquest in
America)
HAPSBURG EMPIRE: achievements
of, 167–68; Armada, 158–59,
161, 162; Charles II's death,
215; under Charles V, 151–55,
157; corruption in, 166–67; and
dilemma of Spain, 192–93;
economic decline, 136, 156–57,
164, 166; and European
cultural fashion, 168–69;
France defeats, 167, 168;
military force, 168; under Philip
II, 155–56, 157, 158–64; under
Philip III, 164; precious metals
from America, 156, 166, 171;
revolution of cities, 153–55;.
social order, 172; and Spanish
America, 129, 137, 234; thieves
and beggars, 164, 171; United
States compared to, 166, 167–68
UNDER BOURBONS: Age of
Reason, 213; Charles III, 217,
235–37, 259; Charles IV, 218,
220, 221, 259; Consolidation
Bill, 244–45; and
Enlightenment, 216, 217;
Ferdinand VII, 221, 230, 259;
French Revolution brings
reaction, 218–19; Jesuits
expelled, 211, 235–37;
Napoleonic invasion, 221–22,
231, 244–45, 251; and Spanish
America, 235, 238, 244–45, 251
19TH AND 20TH CENTURIES:
Spanish-American War and
aftermath, 332–33; WWI and
after, 333–35; republic (1931–
1936), 334–35; Civil War, 335,
337; under Franco, 337–38
Spanish America: blacks in, 197–
201, 234, 239, 252, 257 (*see also*
Blacks in Latin America;
Slavery in Latin America); and
distribution of wealth, 127; and
division of New World, 157–
58; and foreign trade, 279, 281–
82; and Indians, 116, 124, 125–
26, 127, 130–36, 143–47, 156,
285–86 (*see also* Indians);
populations of (1810), 234; and
Roman law, 41; and sexuality,
210–11; and Spain, 15–16;
Spanish-American War, 332,
333; Tupac Amarú's rebellion

in, 212–13; and United States,
325–29 (*see also* United States);
and Virgin Mary, 28
CULTURE OF, 290–91, 348–53;
baroque, 195–96, 200–203;
black influences in, 199–200;
and consumption vs.
production, 278–79; continuity
in, 313, 316, 328; France or
Europe as model, 278, 285; and
gauchos (*charros*), 286–88; and
Hispanics in U.S., 346–47;
ideology of progress, 285–86; as
incorporation over exclusion,
196; and Jesuits, 236; and
Mexican Revolution, 308–9;
and middle class, 282–84; and
opera houses, 279, 280; and the
Other, 353; past repudiated,
277, 285; Posada, 292, 294–96,
297; religious syncretism, 146–
47, 199; tango, 289–90;
Thomistic political philosophy,
141, 143; triculturalism, 124,
249; and U.S., 277–78
COLONIAL PERIOD: church, 144–
47 (*see also* Catholic church, IN
NEW WORLD); cities, 140–41,
207, 209–10; and conquistadors
vs. Crown, 126–30, 131–32,
154, 155; education, 143;
English attacks on, 158; and
Golden Century, 193; and
Hapsburg administration, 129,
137, 234; immigrants in, 138–
39; legal vs. real in, 136–38;
silver mining, 140, 142, 156;
universities, 141, 143
INDEPENDENCE MOVEMENTS,
233–34; and Bourbon reforms,
235–36, 238, 244–45;
economic/political tensions,
238–39; and Enlightenment
philosophers, 240–41; and
French Revolution, 241; and
Jesuits' expulsion, 235–37; and
Napoleon's invasion of Spain,
242, 244–45, 251; and national
identity, 237; and North
American Revolution, 240
WARS OF INDEPENDENCE: in
Argentina, 252–53; Bolívar's
beginning declarations, 250–51,
251–52; Bolívar's campaigns,
252; campaigns of San Martín,
253–55; and commonwealth
proposal, 259; and postwar
societies, 256–59, 262–68. *See
also* Latin America; *individual
countries*

Spanish-American War, 332, 333
Spanish Civil War, 335, 337
Spanish conquest in America, 16;
Balboa's discovery of Pacific,
151; Columbus' voyages, 8, 81,
85, 86, 87, 125, 128; Cortés'
conquest of Mexico, 110–17;
and counterconquest, 124; and
dilemmas of Spanish character,
87–88; fantasy and energy in,
139–40; founding of Buenos
Aires, 139; and loss of Indian
civilization, 124; and the Other,
42, 89; Pizarro's conquest of
Peru, 119–21; Spanish
Americans' reprise of, 286;
treatment of Indians, 125–26,
127, 130–36, 143, 156, 197, 286
*Spanish Imperialism and the Political
Imagination* (Pagden), 166
Spanish language: and American
hemisphere, 117; Arab origins
of, 52, 168; beginning of, 43;
first grammar of, 81; and
Hispanics in U.S., 347; Jews'
promotion of, 73, 76
Spengler, Oswald, 168–69
Squillace, marquis de, 217
Squillace riots, 217, 235–36
State, vs. citizens, 41–42. *See also*
Authoritarianism; Civil society;
Democracy; Monarchy
Stein, Barbara, 126
Stein, Stanley, 126
Stoicism, 40, 57, 347; in Jovellanos
portrait by Goya, 220, 221; of
Juárez, 273. *See also* Seneca
Strabo, 36
Strindberg, August, and *Life Is a
Dream*, 191
Suárez, Inés, 138–39

Tabasco, Olmec head at, 104, *106*
Tablado flamenco, 30–31
Talleyrand, on Bourbons, 230
Tamayo, Ruffino, 349; *Animals, 350*
Tango, 289–90
Tannenbaum, Frank, 200
Tarascan Indians, 134
Tarde, Gabriel, 279
Tarik (Muslim commander), 51
Téllez, Gabriel, 183
Tempest, The (Shakespeare), 125
Temple of the Sun at Teotihuacán,
98–99
Tenoch, 99
Tenochitlán, 99, 102, 113, 114, *115*,
127
Teotihuacán, 96; Temple of the Sun
at, 98–99

Teresa of Ávila, Saint, 171, 187, 189, 190, 192
Tertullian, 28
Tezcatlipoca, 11, 109
Theodosius (Roman emperor), Spain as birthplace of, 43
Theseus, 19
Thomas, Hugh, 114
Thomas Aquinas, Saint, 76, 141, 143, 236, 240
Thoreau, Henry David, 269
Tirso de Molina (Gabriel Téllez), *Rake of Seville*, 183
Titian, Charles V paintings by, 151, *152*, 155
Tito Bustillo, caves at, 17
Tlatelolco, college at, 143
Tlaxcala, 113
Tlazolteotl, 27
Toledo, Francisco, 349; *Toads and Bottles, 350*
Toltecs, 96, 99, 101–2
Tonantzin, 145, 199
Tonantzintla, chapel at, 146–47
Tornadizos, 52
Torquemada, 82, 171
Totonacs, 10
Towns. *See* Cities of Spain; Cities of Spanish America
Trafalgar, battle of, 245
Tragic destiny, in *cante jondo*, 30
Trajan (Roman emperor), Spain as birthplace of, 43
Treaty of Tordesillas, 158
Trogus, 35
Trujillo, Rafael, 326
Tudó, Pepita, 220
Tupac Amarú, 120, 212–13, 239, 349

Uceda, duke of, 166–67
Umayyad dynasty, and Spain, 53, 54
Unamuno, Miguel de, 17, 333, 335
United Fruit Company, 325
United States, 325–29; Civil War in, 271, 273; and Conference of Panama (1826), 257; Hapsburg Spain compared to, 166, 167–68; McCarthyism, 218; post-independence attitudes toward, 277–78; and Spanish-American War, 332, 333; territorial ambitions of, 257, 278; as trading partner, 281
  HISPANICS IN; Anglos in conflict with, 346; art and literature of, 343–44, 345; and border crossings, 341–43; cultural contributions of, 346–47; and

integration issue, 347; jobs performed by, 342; numbers of, 343
  AND MEXICO; in Mexican-American War, 269, 278; and Mexican Revolution, 302–3, 306, 307, 326; and oil expropriation, 326; property owned, 300
Unity: achievement of by European nations, 72; achievement of by Spain, 38, 79–81; as Latin American goal, 316; and Latin American political culture, 141; and medieval outlook, 64
Ureña, Pedro Henríquez, 130
Uruguay, 267, 317
Utopia: New World as, 8–9, 124–25, 126, 134, 195; in Paraguayan Indian community, 211
Utopia (More), 124, 134

Valdes, Alfonso de, 174
Valdés, Luis, 344
Valdivia, Pedro de, 88, 138–39
Valle Inclán, Ramón del, 24, 333
Valparaíso, 207, 282, 283
Vandals, 44
Vargas, Getúlio, 323, 326
Vasari, Giorgio, 160
Vasoncelos, José, 307–8
Vega, Lope de, 169; *Fuenteovejuna,* 43
Velázquez, Diego Rodríguez de Silva y, 16; and Age of Gold, 169; *Don Sebastian de Morra, 184; The Jester, 184; Las Meninas* (mirror painting), 11, *148–49,* 179, *180,* 181–82
Veliz, Claudio, 278, 282
Venezuela: black rebellions in, 198, 239; economic growth of, 318; liberation of, 252; post-independence reaction in, 263
Veracruz, Mexico: El Tajín ruins in, 10; fortress of, 239–40; founding of, 110, 140
Vespucci, Amerigo, 125
Víbora, Gonzalo de, 205
Vietnam War, and Juárez vs. Maximilian, 274
Villa, Pancho, 299, 301–2, 303–4, *305,* 306, 307
Villalar, battle at, 154, 155
Villamil, Eugenio Lucas, *Bullfight, 14, 22*
Viracocha, 120
Virgen de la Macarena, 24, 28, 31
Virgen del Rocío, 28

Virgen de Triana, 28
Virgin of Coromoto, 146
Virgin of Guadalupe, 145–46, 199
Virgin of La Caridad del Cobre, 146
Virgin Mary, 28–29; and flamenco dancer, 31
Viriatus, 36, 38, 61, 273–74
Viscardo y Guzmán, Juan Pablo, 237
Visigothic crown, *46*
Visigoths, 43, 44, 49, 51, 60; and Jews, 49, 76
Vitoria, Francisco de, 134
Vives, Juan Luis, 175
Voltaire, 240, 241, 261

Waleska, Marie, 266
Walewski, Count Alexandre, 266
Walker, William, 325
"War of the Desert," 286
Warlords, 265, 267
War of the Pastries, 268
War of the Spanish Succession, 215
War between the States, 271, 273
Wheeler Land Company, Phoenix, Arizona, 286
William II (German kaiser), and Carlota, 274
Wilson, Edmund, 269
Wilson, Henry Lane, 302–3
Wilson, Woodrow, 325
Womack, John, 304–5
Women: in Buenos Aires expedition, 139; and church of baroque Latin America, 210–11; as colonists, 138–39
World War I, 333–34
World War II, 317, 326, 337

Xangó, 199
Xerez, Francisco de, 119
Xirau, Ramón, 10

Yanga (black rebel leader), 198
Yaqui rebellion, 286
Yeats, W. B., 15
Yemayá, 199

Zambo, 234
Zamora, 69
Zapata, Emiliano, 299, 301, 302, 303, 304–5, 307; and alternative culture, 285; and rights granted by Crown, 135
Zapotec peoples, 96
Zumárraga, Juan de, 145
Zurbarán, Francisco de, 44, 169, 183, 186–87; *Saint Agatha, 47; Saint Lucy, 32,* 186